Boundaries of Utopia – Imagining Communism from Plato to Stalin

The idea that socialism could be established in a single country was adopted as an official doctrine by the Soviet Union in 1925, Stalin and Bukharin being the main formulators of the policy. Before this there had been much debate as to whether the only way to secure socialism would be as a result of socialist revolution on a much broader scale, across all Europe or wider still. This book traces the development of ideas about communist utopia from Plato onwards, paying particular attention to debates about universalist ideology versus the possibility for 'socialism in one country'. The book argues that although the prevailing view is that 'socialism in one country' was a sharp break from a long tradition that tended to view socialism as only possible if universal, in fact the territorially confined socialist project had long roots, including in the writings of Marx and Engels.

Erik van Ree is an Assistant Professor at the Institute of European Studies at the University of Amsterdam, the Netherlands.

Routledge Contemporary Russia and Eastern Europe Series

1 **Liberal Nationalism in Central Europe**
Stefan Auer

2 **Civil-Military Relations in Russia and Eastern Europe**
David J. Betz

3 **The Extreme Nationalist Threat in Russia**
The growing influence of Western Rightist ideas
Thomas Parland

4 **Economic Development in Tatarstan**
Global markets and a Russian region
Leo McCann

5 **Adapting to Russia's New Labour Market**
Gender and employment strategy
Edited by Sarah Ashwin

6 **Building Democracy and Civil Society East of the Elbe**
Essays in honour of Edmund Mokrzycki
Edited by Sven Eliaeson

7 **The Telengits of Southern Siberia**
Landscape, religion and knowledge in motion
Agnieszka Halemba

8 **The Development of Capitalism in Russia**
Simon Clarke

9 **Russian Television Today**
Primetime drama and comedy
David MacFadyen

10 **The Rebuilding of Greater Russia**
Putin's foreign policy towards the CIS countries
Bertil Nygren

11 **A Russian Factory Enters the Market Economy**
Claudio Morrison

12 **Democracy Building and Civil Society in Post-Soviet Armenia**
Armine Ishkanian

13 **NATO-Russia Relations in the Twenty-First Century**
Aurel Braun

14 Russian Military Reform
A failed exercise in defence
decision making
Carolina Vendil Pallin

15 The Multilateral Dimension in
Russian Foreign Policy
*Edited by Elana Wilson Rowe
and Stina Torjesen*

16 Russian Nationalism and the
National Reassertion of Russia
Edited by Marlène Laruelle

17 The Caucasus – An Introduction
Frederik Coene

18 Radical Islam in the
Former Soviet Union
Edited by Galina M. Yemelianova

19 Russia's European Agenda and
the Baltic States
Janina Šleivytė

20 Regional Development in
Central and Eastern Europe
Development processes and
policy challenges
*Edited by Grzegorz Gorzelak,
John Bachtler and
Maciej Smętkowski*

21 Russia and Europe
Reaching agreements,
digging trenches
*Kjell Engelbrekt and
Bertil Nygren*

22 Russia's Skinheads
Exploring and rethinking
subcultural lives
*Hilary Pilkington,
Elena Omel'chenko and
Al'bina Garifzianova*

23 The Colour Revolutions in the
Former Soviet Republics
Successes and failures
*Edited by Donnacha Ó Beacháin
and Abel Polese*

24 Russian Mass Media and
Changing Values
*Edited by Arja Rosenholm,
Kaarle Nordenstreng and
Elena Trubina*

25 The Heritage of Soviet
Oriental Studies
*edited by Michael Kemper and
Stephan Conermann*

26 Religion and Language in
Post-Soviet Russia
Brian P. Bennett

27 Jewish Women Writers in the
Soviet Union
Rina Lapidus

28 Chinese Migrants in
Russia, Central Asia and
Eastern Europe
*Edited by Felix B. Chang and
Sunnie T. Rucker-Chang*

29 Poland's EU Accession
Sergiusz Trzeciak

30 The Russian Armed Forces
in Transition
Economic, geopolitical and
institutional uncertainties
*Edited by Roger N. McDermott,
Bertil Nygren and
Carolina Vendil Pallin*

31 The Religious Factor in Russia's
Foreign Policy
Alicja Curanović

32 **Postcommunist Film – Russia, Eastern Europe and World Culture**
Moving images of postcommunism
Edited by Lars Kristensen

33 **Russian Multinationals**
From regional supremacy to global lead
Andrei Panibratov

34 **Russian Anthropology After the Collapse of Communism**
Edited by Albert Baiburin, Catriona Kelly and Nikolai Vakhtin

35 **The Post-Soviet Russian Orthodox Church**
Politics, culture and Greater Russia
Katja Richters

36 **Lenin's Terror**
The ideological origins of early Soviet State violence
James Ryan

37 **Life in Post-Communist Eastern Europe after EU Membership**
Edited by Donnacha Ó Beacháin, Vera Sheridan and Sabina Stan

38 **EU – Border Security**
Challenges, (mis)perceptions, and responses
Serghei Golunov

39 **Power and Legitimacy – Challenges from Russia**
Edited by Per-Arne Bodin, Stefan Hedlund and Elena Namli

40 **Managing Ethnic Diversity in Russia**
Edited by Oleh Protsyk and Benedikt Harzl

41 **Believing in Russia – Religious Policy After Communism**
Geraldine Fagan

42 **The Changing Russian University**
From state to market
Tatiana Maximova-Mentzoni

43 **The Transition to National Armies in the Former Soviet Republics, 1988–2005**
Jesse Paul Lehrke

44 **The Fall of the Iron Curtain and the Culture of Europe**
Peter I. Barta

45 **Russia After 2012**
From Putin to Medvedev to Putin – continuity, change, or revolution?
Edited by J.L. Black and Michael Johns

46 **Business in Post-Communist Russia**
Privatisation and the limits of transformation
Mikhail Glazunov

47 **Rural Inequality in Divided Russia**
Stephen K. Wegren

48 **Business Leaders and New Varieties of Capitalism in Post-Communist Europe**
Edited by Katharina Bluhm, Bernd Martens and Vera Trappmann

49 **Russian Energy and Security up to 2030**
 Edited by Susanne Oxenstierna and Veli-Pekka Tynkkynen

50 **The Informal Post-Socialist Economy**
 Embedded practices and livelihoods
 Edited by Jeremy Morris and Abel Polese

51 **Russia and East Asia**
 Informal and gradual integration
 Edited by Tsuneo Akaha and Anna Vassilieva

52 **The Making of Modern Georgia, 1918–2012**
 The first Georgian Republic and its successors
 Edited by Stephen F. Jones

53 **Digital Russia**
 The language, culture and politics of new media communication
 Edited by Michael S. Gorham, Ingunn Lunde and Martin Paulsen

54 **Eastern Christianity and Politics in the Twenty-First Century**
 Edited by Lucian N. Leustean

55 **Punk in Russia**
 Cultural mutation from the "useless" to the "moronic"
 Ivan Gololobov, Hilary Pilkington and Yngvar B. Steinholt

56 **Chechnya at War and Beyond**
 Edited by Anne Le Huérou, Aude Merlin, Amandine Regamey and Elisabeth Sieca-Kozlowski

57 **The Russian Presidency of Dmitry Medvedev, 2008–2012**
 The next step forward or merely a time out?
 J. L. Black

58 **Fashion and the Consumer Revolution in Contemporary Russia**
 Olga Gurova

59 **Religion, Nation and Democracy in the South Caucasus**
 Edited by Alexander Agadjanian, Ansgar Jödicke and Evert van der Zweerde

60 **Eurasian Integration – The View from Within**
 Edited by Piotr Dutkiewicz and Richard Sakwa

61 **Art and Protest in Putin's Russia**
 Lena Jonson

62 **The Challenges for Russia's Politicized Economic System**
 Edited by Susanne Oxenstierna

63 **Boundaries of Utopia – Imagining Communism from Plato to Stalin**
 Erik van Ree

64 **Democracy in Poland**
 Representation, participation, competition and accountability since 1989
 Anna Gwiazda

65 **Democracy, Civic Culture and Small Business in Russia's Regions**
 Social processes in comparative historical perspective
 Molly O'Neal

Boundaries of Utopia – Imagining Communism from Plato to Stalin

Erik van Ree

LONDON AND NEW YORK

First published 2015
by Routledge
2 Park Square, Milton Park, Abingdon, Oxon OX14 4RN

and by Routledge
711 Third Avenue, New York, NY 10017

Routledge is an imprint of the Taylor & Francis Group, an informa business

© 2015 Erik van Ree

The right of Erik van Ree to be identified as author of this work has been asserted by him in accordance with the Copyright, Designs and Patent Act 1988.

All rights reserved. No part of this book may be reprinted or reproduced or utilised in any form or by any electronic, mechanical, or other means, now known or hereafter invented, including photocopying and recording, or in any information storage or retrieval system, without permission in writing from the publishers.

Trademark notice: Product or corporate names may be trademarks or registered trademarks, and are used only for identification and explanation without intent to infringe.

British Library Cataloguing in Publication Data
A catalogue record for this book is available from the British Library

Library of Congress Cataloging in Publication Data
Ree, Erik van.
  Boundaries of utopia : imagining communism from Plato to Stalin / Erik van Ree.
     pages cm. – (Routledge contemporary Russia and Eastern Europe series ; 63)
  Includes bibliographical references and index.
  1. Communism–History. 2. Communism–Soviet Union–History. 3. Stalin, Joseph, 1879-1953. I. Title.
  HX40.R37867 2015
  335.43–dc23
                    2014048780

ISBN: 978-0-415-70372-7 (hbk)
ISBN: 978-0-203-76250-9 (ebk)

Typeset in Times New Roman
by Taylor & Francis Books

Printed and bound by CPI Group (UK) Ltd, Croydon, CR0 4YY

Contents

Preface	xi
Introduction	1

PART I
Early Communism   **15**

1 Communism as New Jerusalem	17
2 Communism as utopia	28
3 Communism as armed fortress	37

PART II
Marx and Engels   **51**

4 Communism as Triple Alliance	53
5 Permanent revolution	62
6 Marxist patriotism	75

PART III
The socialist movement   **83**

7 Socialism as trading company	85
8 Socialism as vast state	91
9 Russian socialism takes a back seat	104
10 Marxism in industrialised Germany	115

| 11 | Socialism as autarky | 123 |
| 12 | Socialism as war economy | 134 |

PART IV
Revolution **151**

13	Socialisation of the national economy	153
14	Socialism in one country	163
15	The Great Debate	176
	Conclusion	188

| *References* | 197 |
| *Index* | 230 |

Preface

This book has been very long in the making. Writing it has cost me perhaps two years, but the theme of socialism in one country, which is at the heart of the work, had my attention for many more. The first article I wrote about the subject was published in 1998.

Boundaries of Utopia might be read as a prequel to my 2002 book *The Political Thought of Joseph Stalin*, in which I focused on the Soviet dictator's revolutionary patriotism. One of the points the present book makes is that the patriotic sentiment carried much weight in the socialist movement all along. Stalin was merely taking things a step further.

The patriotic element in socialism has long fascinated me. Socialism is commonly perceived as radically opposed to chauvinism and ethnocentrism. We all know, of course, that socialists did not always take internationalism all that seriously. It was quite common for them to appeal to the fatherland. National realities were too powerful to ignore. But it is not uncommon to find it being asserted that the internationalist ideal only began to be diluted at some point in time, for example by the social democrats in August 1914, or by Stalin when he announced in February 1931 that he would see to it that Russia would never be beaten again. Academics studying Stalinist chauvinism and xenophobia tend to frame these phenomena in terms of a process of degeneration of an essentially broad-minded, cosmopolitan, Marxist ideal. It is a feeling of uneasiness with this type of analysis that drove me to write this book.

Framing the problem of socialist patriotism in terms of a process of subversion has a powerful, intuitive attractiveness about it. It appeals to a widespread, often unconscious way in which we appreciate ideological systems in general. We tend to think – to feel might be the better word here – that the founders of such systems (be they Jesus Christ, Mohammed or Karl Marx) were great souls and that it is only the people that come after them, their followers, that convert their supposedly humanitarian messages into blood and iron. But what if some of the problems began with Jesus, Mohammed and Marx?

I have always felt that excellent studies of Stalinism go wrong the moment their authors assert that Stalin was adding all kinds of nasty qualities to

Marxism that the original did not have. This did not sit well with what I thought I knew about Marxism and other early socialisms. I can only hope that my analysis will come across as convincing.

It may come as a surprise to him, but I must first of all thank Arfon Rees for the idea of this book. At a presentation I gave about socialism in one country a few years ago, Arfon reminded me that communist utopians such as Thomas More tended to locate their ideal societies on islands, thus effectively reducing utopia to a state within certain boundaries: 'socialism in one country'! This train of thought led me to the working hypothesis that confined, 'insulated' communism was always the rule rather than the exception – from the early utopians to Stalin.

I must admit that it was an immense relief to be able to write this book, which uses published writings of socialists and communists as the main source, without exhausting trips to Moscow archives. It was a real luxury to have everything available in the library of the University of Amsterdam, five floors from my office, and in the International Institute of Social History (IISH), 500 metres from my home. I want to thank the staff of the library of the Faculty of Humanities and of the IISH for their excellent and friendly service through the years.

David Brandenberger, Robert Gellately, Artemy Kalinovsky, Michael Kemper, Ronald Suny, Ian Thatcher and Michael Wintle read the original book proposal and made many sober and helpful comments. Thank you. I would also like to thank Stephen White for his role in making this book possible. I want to thank Lars Lih, Christopher Read, Hans Schoots and Joris Versteeg for fruitful discussions over the years. The book has a very wide (some would say too wide) scope. I have ventured into areas where I am not at home. I couldn't have done this without the help of experts in these fields. The following people read and commented on one or more chapters: Andrew Bradstock, Kevin Callahan, Terrell Carver, Thomas von der Dunk, Thomas Fudge, Ernst Hanisch, Annie Jourdan, Lars Lih, Philip Pomper, Albert Rijksbaron, Jürgen Rojahn, Quentin Skinner, James Stayer, F. Peter Wagner and James White. Your comments have been very much appreciated. If my observations on Plato, the Anabaptists or Gerrard Winstanley are out of focus I am the only one to blame. My special thanks go to my friends David Brandenberger and Ian Thatcher who read the manuscript cover to cover, who were very critical as ever, and who forced me to rethink the outline and argument of the book. I hope the result is up to your standards. I have been endlessly pestering my Amsterdam colleagues about the title, which I just couldn't get right. The following people were my main victims: Nanci Adler, Sarah Crombach, Alex Drace-Francis, Dina Fainberg, Marc Jansen, Ben de Jong, Michael Kemper, Christian Noack, Menno Spiering and Michael Wintle. Thank you for not getting fed up with me (or not showing it). Finally, I am always afraid that I have forgotten somebody who needs to be thanked. If I have, please forgive me!

Some of the work used here was published in journal articles. I thank the editors/publishers for permitting me to reprint material from the following articles: 'Socialism in One Country: A Reassessment', in *Studies in East European Thought*, 1998, vol. 50, no. 2: 77–117; 'Nationalist Elements in the Work of Marx and Engels: A Critical Survey', in *MEGA-Studien*, 2000, no. 1: 25–49; 'Lenin's Conception of Socialism in One Country, 1915–17', in *Revolutionary Russia*, 2010, vol. 23, no. 2: 159–81; '"Socialism in One Country" before Stalin: German Origins', in *Journal of Political Ideologies*, 2010, vol. 15, no. 2: 143–59; 'German Marxism and the Decline of the Permanent Revolution, 1870–1909', in *History of European Ideas*, 2012, vol. 38, no. 4: 570–89; 'Georgii Plekhanov and the *Communist Manifesto*: The Proletarian Revolution Revisited', in *Revolutionary Russia*, 2013, vol. 26, no. 1: 32–51; 'Marxism as Permanent Revolution', in *History of Political Thought*, 2013, vol. 34, no. 3: 540–63.

I dedicate this book to my father, Frank van Ree (1927–2013), who sadly did not live to see it published.

Erik van Ree

Introduction

When the Bolsheviks seized power in the Russian capital of Petrograd in November 1917, they expected the workers' revolution to spread to other parts of Europe. They had especially high hopes for Germany, but their expectations failed to materialise. The failure of the communist revolution in January 1919 severely tested the nerves of Vladimir Il'ich Lenin and his comrades. The murder of the celebrated communist leaders Rosa Luxemburg and Karl Liebknecht hit them especially hard. To add to the disaster, the Hungarian Soviet Republic survived no longer than a couple of months, until the Romanian army put Béla Kun's regime out of its misery. In 1920 Lenin took the initiative into his own hands, when he sent the Red Army into Poland, in response to a Polish invasion of Soviet Russia. The Bolshevik leader hoped to establish a proletarian–socialist government in Warsaw so as to create a corridor to provide the German communists with military assistance. But in another bitter disappointment the Red Army was defeated before Warsaw. The so-called German October of 1923 formed the crown on this series of failures. The revolution fizzled out after some street fighting in Hamburg.

In the aftermath of the Great War many parts of Central and Eastern Europe were shaken by violent social unrest. But, not counting distant Mongolia, the communists did not manage to seize state power and to hold on to it in any other country. Soviet Russia remained alone. This was a dramatic turn of events for Lenin, who feared the proletarian state would be crushed if socialism failed to spread to other nations.

After Lenin's death the Bolshevik leadership decided to adapt party doctrine to the new geopolitical realities. They concluded that the Russian Revolution was less dependent on the world revolution than they had assumed back in 1917. In April 1925 the Russian Communist Party (Bolsheviks) convened its Fourteenth Conference. It was at this occasion that the party officially adopted the doctrine of 'socialism in one country'.

The resolution adopted at the conference held that the construction of a socialist society did not depend on the world revolution. It was possible to construct a 'complete' socialist society in a single country surrounded by hostile capitalist states, and this even in 'backward' Russia. Yet, the resolution did not bid farewell to the world revolution. It was admitted that the successful establishment of socialism in one country could never signify the '*final*' victory of socialism. After all, however perfect its inner order might become, an isolated socialist state could never experience real security. One could never be sure that socialism in this one country would not be overthrown by foreign intervention. For victory to become final in the sense of irreversible, revolution in a number of other key capitalist states remained a requirement.[1]

Socialism in one country has always, and rightly so, been considered one of the hallmarks of Stalinism. The doctrine reflected one of the main underlying motives of General-Secretary of the Communist Party, Iosif Vissarionovich Stalin: the drive to go it alone. It was Stalin's ambition to set up an economically and militarily powerful socialist state that would be as independent from external circumstances as possible. The world revolution was never abandoned, but Moscow's attention to it was considerably reduced. In the course of the years, socialism in one country spilled over into a robust Soviet patriotism and a Russo-centric cult of the Soviet state.[2]

On a closer look, we can distinguish three, largely overlapping motives in Stalinist socialism. First of all, socialism in one country: the establishment of a socialist economy in one particular country was not made conditional upon the spread of the revolution to other countries. It was assumed that even without the world revolution one country could have a fully functioning socialist economy. Second, the Stalinists nurtured a siege mentality. They regarded socialism as an isolated, embattled community in a hostile capitalist environment. And, third, as patriots, they took pride in the fact that it was their own country that was pioneering the new order.

This compound of Stalinist ideas and sentiments is usually regarded as sharply breaking with the internationalist tradition of the socialist movement. On the contrary, the present book argues that these Stalinist patterns are better read as confirmation and sanctification, albeit in a course, brutal form, of patterns that always had marked the socialist ideology. This is the way socialists had been imagining communism all along. It had been the rule rather than the exception to imagine the new order as an isolated and embattled community, quite often even as a single country, and more often than not socialists cast their own country in the honourable role of pioneer. As we will see, though they ruled out socialism in a single country, even staunch internationalists like Marx and Engels had been imagining the new society in insular and patriotic terms.

Socialism in one country before Stalin?

The assumption that single-country socialism represented a radical new departure on Stalin's part, a sharp break with a socialist tradition that was profoundly and essentially internationalist is quite widespread. To be sure, some eminent scholars have pointed out that socialism in one country was not Stalin's invention. In his biography of Nikolai Bukharin, Stalin's ally during much of the 1920s and his victim in the 1930s, Stephen Cohen suggests that it was he, not Stalin, who in the early 1920s began to consider the possibility that isolated Russia could create a socialist society. Cohen furthermore argues that Stalin and Bukharin were justified in claiming that Lenin's final writings of 1922–3 had been pointing in that direction.[3] Richard Day takes us back a little further in time, when he refers to War Commissar Leon Trotsky, of all people, as the first important Bolshevik to have developed a conception of socialism in one country during the years of the Civil War.[4] Perhaps the first to have made the point is Christopher Hill, who suggested already in 1965, in an almost self-evident way, that, from 1917 onwards, Lenin worked under the assumption that, if necessary, Russia could construct socialism on its own.[5] But all this takes us back no more than a few years.

My interest in the subject was aroused when I was writing my book about Stalin's political thought. I was struck by Trotsky's polemical observation that the real father of the idea of socialism in one country was the Bavarian social democrat, Georg von Vollmar, author of the 1878 *The Isolated Socialist State*.[6] Undoubtedly, Trotsky enjoyed disclosing this, for Vollmar had been on the right wing of the German socialist party for most of his active life. It was highly embarrassing for Stalin that his celebrated idea had this kind of precursor. The existing literature contains incidental references to other German socialists that might have commented favourably on socialism in one country.[7]

I was also struck by what I learned about Karl Kautsky, the German social democrat who was widely regarded as the 'pope of orthodox Marxism' after Friedrich Engels's death in 1895. Kautsky predicted that international trade would be strongly reduced under socialism, and that socialist nations would have autarkic economies. He wrote this in his book about the social democratic programme adopted at the 1891 Erfurt party congress.[8] The book was one of the most influential social democratic tractates of the time.

What also continued to bother me was Lenin's straightforward observation made in August 1915 that 'socialism in one country' was possible, and that this meant for the victorious proletariat to organise 'socialist production at home'.[9] There is a powerful tendency in the scholarly literature not to take this literally, because Lenin just couldn't have intended this to be taken as such. To me this seemed a bit odd, and I wondered whether it did not say more about preconceptions about Lenin than about the man himself.

All this was enough to cast doubt on the established idea that Stalin's adoption of socialism in one country represented a sharp break with the existing socialist tradition. It seemed worth the effort to trace back the idea of single-country socialism and to find out how influential it had really been before Stalin.

Socialist patriotism

That it would not have been unusual for nineteenth-century socialists to imagine socialism locked up within one state runs up against the objection that the two foremost theoreticians of nineteenth-century socialism, Marx and Engels, ruled out this scenario for the era of the world market. They predicated the new society upon the contributions of a number of countries.

But this is less straightforward than it seems. To begin with, Marx and Engels were not the only voices in socialism. Marxist influences in nineteenth- and early twentieth-century French and British socialism were limited. In Germany, Marxism became the most influential ideology in the social demo- cratic party, but it never achieved anything like monopoly status. Even among Russian social democrats, the Marxist monopoly was never complete, and among the populists and socialists–revolutionaries Marxism was only one of a number of systems of thought competing for influence.

Also, the arguments against single-country socialism employed by Marx and Engels were never as scientifically self-evident as they thought they were. Nineteenth-century socialists trusted that socialism would be a vastly more efficient productive system than capitalism. Given that assumption, there was no obvious reason why an isolated socialist economy could not outcompete its competitors on the world market. And even though an isolated socialist state would in all likelihood be subjected to economic blockades, it would depend on the size of the country and on the financial and natural resources at its disposal, whether it might be able to withdraw into a form of autarky or might wither and collapse, as Marx and Engels expected. And why would it be preordained that a powerful socialist country with a powerful army would suffer defeat against a capitalist coalition? There is no reason to assume that Marx and Engels's position would have been accepted by other socialists as a matter of course.

That said, it still sounds counterintuitive that many socialists would have accepted the possibility of socialism in one country. Wouldn't the spirit of socialist internationalism have prevented this?

The current interpretation of Stalinism as a radically new departure is embedded in a historical myth of great dramatic power. Essentially, it is a myth of betrayal. As the story goes, the socialist movement was originally infused with idealistic internationalism. The famous appeal of the 1848 *Communist Manifesto: 'Proletarians of all countries, unite!'* captures the essence of the spirit.[10] The very name of the International Workingmen's Association, estab- lished by Karl Marx and others in 1864, breathed internationalism. After the unfortunate demise of this organisation in the 1870s, a Socialist International was restored in 1889. The frequent congresses of this organisation highlighted the sincere attempts of the socialists to find a common platform in the struggle against capitalism and war. However, the story continues, in August 1914 patriotism abruptly gained the upper hand in the socialist movement. When the Great War broke out, most member parties of the International surrendered their laudable idealism and turned round to support the war efforts of their own governments. This represented the first great betrayal. Lenin is the single most influential person to have made us see 1914 in these terms. The Russian social democrats were among the few to uphold the old idealism, but, as the story reaches its dramatic climax, only a decade on they too – they were now calling themselves communists – cast the principle of international solidarity overboard. In what for Trotsky represented the second great betrayal, Stalin established state patriotism under the façade of socialism in one country.

So much for the myth. The problem is that the serious scholarly literature never presented what occurred in August 1914 as either a great betrayal or as an abrupt transition from internationalism to patriotism. Socialism was never a pristine internationalist movement.

Proletarian internationalism reflected the position of nineteenth-century industrial workers with very few political and economic rights. This served effectively to lock them out of the nation. Left out in the cold among their own national communities, radical workers would naturally look to their companions in distress in other countries for support and solidarity. Furthermore, the socialists understood that, for all the cut-throat competition on the international market, economic globalisation also served to bring the bourgeois classes together. The entrepreneurs of the world knew how to defend their common interests against the working people. The workers had no other choice, the socialists believed, than to respond with close international cooperation of their own.

Even so, socialist patriotism represented a powerful reality. There were many reasons for this, the first of which is to be found in the emotional sphere. With Igor Primoratz, we can define patriotism as 'love of country, identification with it, and special concern for its well-being and that of compatriots'.[11] Patriotism as an emotion, 'natural or instinctive patriotism', can be distinguished from those varieties in which a particular philosophy or ideal underpins it.[12] But the very definition of 'love of country' suggests that an emotion lies at its basis. There is no good reason why socialists would be immune to this emotion. Socialists too may love their country, regardless even of whether or not it hosts a socialist economy. As long as the love of other peoples for their country would be accepted as equally legitimate, there would be no necessary conflict with socialist internationalism.

From the political angle, the state simply was the main existing framework, and the socialists could ignore this reality only at their peril. As revolutionaries, they were keen on mobilising a following, which would consist mostly of compatriots. To ignore patriotic sentiments would have condemned the socialists to irrelevance.

Sociologically, the strengthening of the patriotic urge in the European socialist parties can be tied to an underlying process of working-class integration. In the course of the second half of the nineteenth century the workers were provided with ever more security and rights. This would have increased their sense of having a stake in the country, and, as they became socially more integrated, the workers became correspondingly more open to patriotic concerns.[13]

Arguably, the very fact that socialists were revolutionaries defined them as patriots. By the act of revolution, revolutionaries seize power and seize their own country. Revolution turns the people lining up behind the revolutionaries, those devoid of political and economic rights, into citizens of the state. Even the most internationalist of socialists understood this mechanism. Marx and Engels recognised that, 'in form', the struggle of the proletariat against the bourgeoisie at first remains 'national', in so far as each proletariat must overthrow its own bourgeoisie. In another celebrated passage of the *Communist Manifesto*, they declared that the workers 'have no fatherland', only to continue in a clear echo of the spirit of the French Revolution:

> Since the proletariat must first of all acquire political supremacy, must become the national class [*sich zur nationalen Klasse erheben*], must constitute itself the nation, it remains national itself, though not at all in the bourgeois sense of the word.[14]

In short, the revolution would provide the workers with the fatherland they did not have. In his first Elberfeld speech in February 1845 Engels confirmed that the workers of a communist state would have a '*real* fatherland' to defend and that they would act with the kind of enthusiasm and courage the French revolutionary armies had displayed from 1792 to 1799.[15] The idea that the workers would acquire a fatherland through revolution was accepted by SPD luminaries Kautsky, August Bebel as well as Eduard Bernstein.[16]

The inspiring example of the French Revolution was another important historical factor keeping socialism under the spell of revolutionary patriotism. The spectacle of a powerful revolutionary state throwing its armies against the rest of Europe continued to inspire socialists. Also, through much of the nineteenth century, the national question remained on the agenda. The socialists were only too willing to contribute to the patriotic movements of Poland, Hungary, Italy and Germany, to mention only the most celebrated causes championed by the revolutionary left. Somewhat paradoxically, it was precisely the extra dose of patriotism that provided socialists with the needed emotional momentum to allow their followers to identify with an internationalist ideology that might otherwise have been experienced as too sterile.[17]

It is acknowledged in the literature that socialist patriotism had been an important reality in the decades before the Great War broke out. Tellingly, for example, even though the socialist parties went out of their way to avert international war, they never relinquished their right to national defence to counter aggression. Even the most outspoken Marxist leaders such as Bebel proudly presented themselves as patriots.[18] In his last years, Engels was particularly insistent that, in case Russia attacked Germany, the country's 'national existence' would have to be defended in the spirit of the French revolutionary wars of 1793.[19]

Werner Conze and Dieter Groh conceptualise the predominant mood among the German social democrats in the decades prior to the war in terms of a 'double loyalty' to the international working class and to the fatherland.[20] Kevin Callahan introduced the term 'inter-nationalism' to characterise the parties of the Socialist International. Callahan acknowledges the reality of proletarian internationalism, but in his interpretation this idea was meant to refer to close cooperation between independent nations, to each of which the socialists of those nations felt themselves to be patriotically indebted.[21]

All this helps us to understand why socialism in one country long antedated Stalin. The academic literature has an elegant sociological explanation for the Bolsheviks' acceptance of single-country socialism during the 1920s: they adapted Marxism to the geopolitical context in which they were forced to operate. Soviet Russia *was*, after all, an isolated state. In formulating socialism in one country, Stalin simply adapted the idea to the realities of the day. Context was all. So far so good, but if other socialist parties had been subject to a process of national integration, wouldn't those parties have allowed their imagination of socialism to be stamped by their own national contexts as well? And if the patriotic sentiment had in fact been all too common, wouldn't socialists of other nations have felt just as thrilled as the Bolsheviks by the idea that their own nation might play a pioneering role in the new world order? How plausible is it, on the face of it, to assume that socialism in one country began with Stalin?

Imagining communism

As will be shown in this book, many nineteenth- and early twentieth-century socialists had been assuming that, as a first step, the new society could and most likely would be constructed within the confines of a single country. Socialism in one country was no radical new departure on Stalin's part, but the reinvention of an existing idea in a new context.

This conclusion gains in historical depth if we include older utopian schemes of common ownership from the era before the socialist workers' movement in our exploration. Plato envisioned his ideal state, ruled by a 'communist' elite voluntarily refraining from owning private property, on the scale of a city. Thomas More did not fantasise about a communist world but about a single communist island. The seventeenth-century Digger, Gerrard Winstanley, expected England to become the first communist commonwealth in the world, and eighteenth-century French communist utopians never doubted that France would blaze the trail. Seen over the long historical run, 'socialism in one country' represented the rule rather than the exception.

Things changed, of course, when modern socialism emerged and Marx and Engels's views began to gain ever wider currency. Undeniably, these two men firmly ruled out the single-country scenario. What is more, it became the official standpoint of the German and Russian social democratic parties that socialism required the input of a number of advanced countries.

Yet, the first socialist community continued to be imagined as an 'island'. Marx and Engels expected the new order first to come into existence in a 'little corner' of the world, as Marx wrote to his friend in October 1858.[22] The two friends worked under the assumption that revolution was a contagious process, touching one country after another. Even so, only a very small number of countries possessed the requisite conditions for proletarian government. The socialist mode of production would first be established on the territory of an alliance of countries, most likely Great Britain, France and Germany, that would have to survive in a world dominated by hostile forces. This scenario was only marginally more universalist than what Vollmar and others were proposing: in both cases, socialism was imagined as a community within borders that did not need the global scope to survive.[23]

The alternative scenario of radical dependence on the world revolution ruled out socialism within borders. The creation of a socialist society in any one place would always be dependent on the progression of the revolution to other places. If no new revolutions occurred, the victorious workers of the trailblazing community would not be able to consolidate their rule and establish socialism. Remarkably, it is very hard to find socialists who took this radical position. The most significant case I found was Russian social democrats, for example Trotsky, who during the Great War suggested that socialism was incompatible, *as matter of principle*, with state borders, and that a socialist economy required the scale of all of Europe to be viable. But even that can, of course, be regarded as a non-territorialised scenario only from a Eurocentric perspective.

That Thomas More located his utopia literally on an island was a literary genre that came and went. But, metaphorically, the socialists continued to sing to his tune. Almost all socialists, including Marx and Engels, expected the socialist society to come into the world as an island surrounded by a capitalist sea, an oasis in the capitalist world desert.

Generally speaking, the whole idea of refashioning a country on a principle antagonistic to that ruling in all the rest of the world is bound to focus citizens on the preservation and cultivation of their own community. And it will be hard for them to regard other countries, representing a hostile principle, as anything other than a threat.

More concretely, the ideal of common ownership is highly conducive to the insular imagination of socialism. If it is about bringing people together, then, in a universalising dynamic, the crowning achievement would be to extend common ownership worldwide. But turning citizens into co-owners would also open up another dynamic working in the opposite direction. There would be created a strong and exclusive bond between citizens and an orientation onto each other that formerly was not there. Under private ownership, the individual entertains distant but essentially similar economic relations with compatriots and foreigners: there is no sharing with either category. This cosmopolitan orientation would, however, abruptly be destroyed once a community would introduce common ownership. This would create a wholly new distinction between compatriots, with whom one shares one's property, and foreigners, with whom, as before, one does not, and with whom, therefore, one would not experience the strong communitarian bond. Common ownership fosters a collective inward-looking orientation, a drawing together, and a sense of separateness that tends to overrule universalist commitments.

The ideal of common ownership always had strong communitarian connotations. Socialists were fantasising about a powerfully integrated, 'intimate' commonwealth of dedicated citizens held together by a sharing scheme. Dependent on times and conditions, they would fantasise either about a city-state, a nation state, an empire or about an alliance of countries – but in the beginning there would always be this commonwealth. That the system in due course would have to spread to the rest of the world went without saying, but that was a consideration of the second order. The world revolution came last not first.

It cannot be denied that socialism was a universalist ideology. For Marx and Engels, the socialist *Dreibund* was a mere step on the ladder of world communism. That even remained the case for Stalin, for whom socialism in one country was a mere phase, and who even in his darkest anti-cosmopolitan days would have rejected the idea that socialism suited only one chosen people. But the socialist imagination did allow the establishment of the new society on the territory of one or a few countries. The stagnation of the world revolution would *not* doom it to collapse. The socialist ideology can best be regarded as a form of 'confined universalism', a universalist ideology that *initially* could, and most likely would, remain locked within territorial boundaries.[24]

We will furthermore see in the course of this book that it was very common for proponents of common ownership to dream of *their own* country as the pioneer of socialism. The nineteenth-century Italian patriot Giuseppe Mazzini introduced a term that is particularly useful here. Mazzini speculated that the republican order would be pioneered by one particular vanguard nation, which he called the 'initiator-people'.[25] Mazzini's term fits the socialist movement very well. Socialists following the single-country scenario with only few exceptions assumed that their own people would be the initiators. Strikingly, even Marx and Engels conformed to this patriotic pattern: they never doubted that their own fatherland would be among the trailblazers. To be sure, Germany couldn't do it alone, but it would be among the select group of most favoured nations breaking the path.

Why was socialism wedded to these insular and patriotic patterns? It is not as if More's island utopia, or any other work of communist fantasy, made such an impression on socialists that they couldn't let go of it. Strictly speaking, we are not even dealing here with a tradition. There was no chain of references from one socialist to another, underpinning the idea that the new society would first emerge in a little corner of the world. Stalin was not interested in establishing a pedigree for socialism in one country. Apart from references to Lenin, there is no indication that he was inspired by Vollmar, Kautsky or by anybody else. Rather than copying prescriptions, Stalin was acting on circumstance: the Bolsheviks accepted socialism in one country for the pragmatic reason that they were alone and had to make the best of a critical situation. The contextual interpretation of the Soviet ideology as an adaptation to geopolitical realities is convincing.

The recurrent pattern speaks to the enduring nature of certain contextual factors. First of all, for centuries patriotism put a powerful mark on the minds of socialists and communists. The wide spread and attraction of the patriotic sentiment would have made it difficult for them not to get thrilled by the idea that that own country might lead the way. For all their internationalist idealism, the bottom line is that they *wanted* their own country to be first.

Also, living in a world order consisting of separate states, the socialists were bound to imagine communism in terms of states and countries. Even the imagination works with what it finds. The idea that the revolution would have the power of an avalanche breaking down state borders, rolling on, and only subsiding when the world would be completely covered, sounded just too fantastic. Realistically, in the world as it was, the revolution could hardly proceed in any other way than state by state. And given that socialists would come to power in one or a few states first, it only made political sense to assume that this would be a sufficient framework to create the new society. This is the simple thinking that guided communists from Winstanley to Marx to Stalin.

Scope of the research

This study deals with the socialist imagination. It explores the way utopian communists and socialists imagined how the new order based on common ownership would come into the world, before it was actually established in the Soviet Union. The study confines itself to Europe. I have been able to study original materials from Britain, France, Germany, Austria and Russia, but my limited linguistic skills did not allow me to explore other important contributions, for example those of the Italians and the Poles. The time scope of the study is ambitious, however, with a beginning in classical antiquity and an ending with the Great Debate in the Soviet Communist Party in the 1920s.

Unfortunately, the wide scope over time generates certain terminological problems that defy completely satisfactory solution. The study will focus on socialists who committed themselves to the ideal of common ownership and who can be defined as communists. Socialists who advocated social justice but accepted private ownership of the means of production have largely been ignored.[26] The anarchist tradition falls outside of our scope as well.

Before the terms socialism and communism came in use the ideal of common ownership was most often referred to as 'community of goods'.[27] The proponents of community of goods began to call themselves communists only in 1840. In that year revolutionary secret societies in France adopted the term. Étienne Cabet, Théodore Dézamy and Jean-Jacques Pillot were among the first to use it.[28] Referring to those adherents of community of goods that were active prior to 1840 as communists is therefore an anachronism. To compound the problem, even though they continued to advocate wholesale expropriation of the means of production, during the second half of the century the Marxists began to call themselves social democrats. Altogether, there is no single, obviously best way to refer to the aficionados of community of goods. I have opted for a loose use of the terms socialist and communist, as seemed best.

An additional terminological problem arises from Marx's division of the communist society into two stages. The first, lower stage was characterised by socialisation of the means of production and the disappearance of money, markets and the state. At this stage, products would however still be distributed according to individual labour achievements. The second stage, when people will receive according to need, would emerge only after bourgeois psychology, scarcity and the major social divisions of labour have been overcome.[29] Confusingly, Lenin referred to first-stage communism as the *socialist* society. He also differed from Marx in assuming that the state would survive into this first, socialist stage.[30] In speaking loosely of 'socialist' and 'communist' society, we will, then, all the time be sinning in the eyes of Marxist and Leninist purists. That too is unfortunate but unavoidable if this book is to remain readable at all.[31]

Notes

1 'Tezisy o zadachakh Kominterna i RKP(b) v sviazi s rasshirennym plenumom IKKI, priniatye XIV konferentsiei RKP(b)', *Kommunisticheskaia partiia* [*KPSS*], vol. 2, 1953: 48–9.
2 See Brandenberger, 2002.
3 Cohen, 1974: 147–8, 186–8.
4 Day, 1973. Recently, Christopher Read (2013: 171–4) argued that Lenin had 'a prototype of "socialism in one country" in mind from early 1918, in the sense of a socialist economy in a single country'.
5 Hill 1965: Chapter 7.
6 See Fel'shtinskii, 1990, vol. 3: 101; Trotsky, n.y.b: 283–4. Trotsky's observations about Vollmar have been picked up in the scholarly literature: Jansen, 1958: 16, 21–3; Goodman, 1960: 4; Deutscher, 1963: 34; Fetscher, 1967: 33, 644, 647; Steinberg, 1979: 22, 31; Knei-Paz, 1979: 339n.
7 On Ferdinand Lassalle, see Baron, 1923: 110; Ramm, 1953: Chapter 4, 180–93. On Eugen Dühring, see Albrecht, 1927: 228–9, 239–40. On Karl Rodbertus, see Dietzel, 1888: 94; on Friedrich Engels, see Soell, 1972: 137. On Eduard Bernstein, see Schröder, 1978: 170–1; Fletcher, 1983: 84; Fletcher, 1984: 162–3.
8 Kautsky, 1919: 115–16, 118f.
9 See 'O lozunge soedinennykh shtatov Evropy', Lenin, *Polnoe sobranie sochinenii* [*PSS*], 1969: vol. 26: 352–5.
10 'Manifest der Kommunistischen Partei', Marx and Engels, *Werke* [*MEW*], 1977: vol. 4: 493.
11 Primoratz, 2013.
12 See Kautz, 1995: Chapter 6 (quotation p. 140).
13 For a comparative analysis of working-class integration in a number of European countries, including Germany, in the period 1871–1914, see van der Linden, 1988.

14 *MEW*, vol. 4: 473, 479. For a discussion of this Manifesto passage, see also Nation, 1989: 7–10.
15 *MEW*, vol. 2: 543
16 See for example Kautsky, 1905d: 345–7; Bebel at 1907 Essen Party Congress (Schröder, 1910: 331); Bernstein, 1909: 614–15.
17 See David Brandenberger (2002 and 2011) for a similar argument on the function of Soviet patriotism in the USSR under Stalin. See also Alon Confino's (1997: 3–23, 211–15) analysis of the process of German national identity formation in the period 1871 to 1918: familiar local and regional identities and memories were preserved in the national memory, and it is that which allowed citizens to identify with the new, overarching and impersonal nation.
18 For German social democratic patriotism, see for example Armstrong, 1942; Maehl, 1952; Braunthal, 1961: 17–21, 50; Roth, 1963; Conze and Groh, 1966; Niemeyer, 1966; Groh, 1973; Lidtke, 1985; Groh and Brandt, 1992; Smaldone, 2014: 148. See also Wette, 1971. For an analysis of Bebel's socialist patriotism, see Jung, 1986. For the 'contradictory mélange of cosmopolitanism, patriotism, and militarism' in socialism, see also Nation, 1989: 6–7. For the compatibility of patriotism with communism, see Mevius, 2011: 2. Martin Mevius observes that the opposite thesis is a myth, which is defended by academics on all kinds of fora, yet is seldom comprehensively argued in the academic literature. According to Mevius it is a characteristic of such myths that they are ubiquitous yet mostly 'not presented in a systematic way'.
19 See for example 'Der Sozialismus in Deutschland' (written October 1891), *MEW*, vol. 22: 252–6.
20 Conze and Groh, 1966: 101, 105, 114.
21 Callahan, 2000; Callahan, 2010: xviii, 15, 18–19, 299.
22 8 October 1858 letter, *MEW*, vol. 29: 360.
23 Frank Manuel (1966: 79–80) and Northrop Frye (1966: 28–9) have suggested that Marxism broke the insular pattern of utopian communism: with the world market and new technological developments, a socialist utopia *within* a pre-socialist world supposedly became unthinkable. But the conception of the socialist alliance shows that they were wrong.
24 I adopt this term from a study of the kings of fragmented medieval India. The king, the *chakravartin*, represented the universal ideal of world rule, but in fact ruled over a small territory: Kulke and Rothermund, 2010: xvii, 101.
25 See Salvemini, 1956: 37.
26 See for definitions of socialism and communism, for example Kolakowski, 1981, vol. 1: 182–3, 187; Taylor, 1982: 9–11, 14; Oizerman, 2001: 64–5. See also Leopold, 2007: 220.
27 Gütergemeinschaft, communauté des biens, obshchnost' imushchestva.
28 Bestor, 1948: 261, 279–81. See also Desroches, 1955: 29. Maurice Dommanget (1965: 318) traces its use in France back to around 1834. James Billington (1980: 79–81, 243, 246, 582) and Jacques Grandjonc (1989: 13, 16, 19, 21, 27ff.) have shown that the word communism was in fact invented earlier. It was first used in print by Restif de la Bretonne in 1785. The occasion was Restif's review of a book by Joseph-Alexandre-Victor Hupay de Fueva. Restif was quoting a 1782 letter of Hupay de Fueva, who called himself a communist. However, the term was not used again, by others than Restif, with perhaps a single exception, until 1840. David Coward (1991: 607, 631) mentions Restif's use of the term 'communisme' in his 1776 *L'école des pères*. For Restif's frequent use of the term 'communisme' in *Monsieur Nicolas*, see Restif de la Bretonne, 1959: vol. 6: 40, 242–57, 309–86. The term socialism in the modern sense originated in England in the 1820s in the circle of Robert Owen (Bestor, 1948: 277–8; Billington, 1980: 245; Claeys, 1986: 83;

Grandjonc, 1989: 96–8; Claeys, 2000: 209). For the origin of the terms communism and socialism, see also Angenot, 1993: 104–8.
29 See 'Kritik des Gothaer Programms' (1875), *MEW*, vol. 19: 19–21.
30 See 'Gosudarstvo i revoliutsiia' (1917), *PSS*, vol. 33: 90–102.
31 For Marx and Engels and the ideologists of the Second International on the communist society, see Angenot, 1993.

Part I
Early Communism

1 Communism as New Jerusalem

Jean-Jacques Rousseau and Karl Marx were not altogether wrong when they surmised that once upon a time humanity lived under much more egalitarian conditions than those prevailing in their own days. The earliest human societies were prejudiced against the accumulation of private property and private wealth.[1] The idea that community of goods remains the best form of human society probably was never entirely absent. It appeals to a widespread sense that a just and civilised society ought to prioritise not the individual but the community. Community of property suggests itself as consistent counterpoint to egoism. Also, in times of mass poverty the rich are easily held responsible for the plight of the poor. Communism offers itself as the answer to exploitation and as the way to restore the well-being of the downtrodden masses. However, the attractions of communism are not sufficient to provide it with the permanent attention of a wide audience. It is only under certain conditions that communist reformism gains substantial influence and a real following.[2]

Plato and the Pythagoreans

In Europe, the communist idea can be traced back to classical antiquity. It was a common enough assumption to be found in the works of Greek as well as Latin authors, that at the dawn of history people had been living under conditions of equality. Diodorus Siculus, Virgil, Ovid, Seneca and others believed that property was originally held in common, and that private ownership was a late and unfortunate development.[3] These ancient authors were however writing mythologised history rather than projecting utopias into the future. The state of community of goods was not considered a condition to be restored.

Plato was one of the few thinkers of antiquity to have formulated communism as an ambition for the reform of the state. Yet, even in his *Republic*, this ambition was tempered. Plato restricted the communist lifestyle to the ruling elite. In the ideal republic only the so-called Guardians 'shall have no private property beyond the barest essentials'. The Guardians were army officers living a collective and disciplined life. They would be responsible for safeguarding the state. To allow them land and businesses of their own, Plato feared, would make them forget their military duties.[4] The logic behind Plato's proposal was that an elite deprived of private property makes for virtuous administrators. They have no private interests that they could be tempted to prioritise over the interests of the state.[5]

To the degree that he expected his communist proposals to become reality at all, Plato never doubted that the framework of one state would suffice. His republic exemplifies the degree to which utopianism tends to be contextually defined by existing state structures. The philosopher warned that the ideal state must not be allowed to grow beyond the limits where 'unity' among the populace would be endangered.[6] It was only natural for Plato to imagine his utopian republic on the scale of a city-state, the community he, as a Greek living around the year 400 BC, was most familiar with. According to Lewis Mumford, the commonwealth Plato envisaged was 'a definite parcel of land whose limits he could probably see from any convenient hilltop'. Ideally, it was a 'city which was surrounded by enough land to supply the greater part of the food needed by the inhabitants'. It should not much exceed 5,000 people.[7]

Plato's utopian republic was not only modelled on the city-state in a general sense, its communist spirit was obviously inspired by the austere militarism of one particular city-state, Sparta. This city was widely admired in antiquity for its stability and for its determination not to succumb to the temptations of luxury.[8] Another example that may have inspired Plato when he composed the outlines of his republic was the city-state of Tarentum in Greater Hellas, southern Italy, which in Plato's days probably was ruled by the brotherhood of the Pythagoreans, though that remains somewhat speculative.

The philosopher Pythagoras, born on the island of Samos, lived in the sixth century bc. Not much is known about him with any degree of certainty, but it is likely that he established a small brotherhood whose members voluntarily refrained from owning property. According to ancient historians, at some point Pythagoras emigrated to the south Italian city-state of Croton. Croton's fortunes were at low ebb, and it was this that provided the Pythagoreans with the opportunity they needed. They had something to offer that was in demand – good advice on how to turn the city's fortunes around. In a pattern that was common enough at the time, the philosopher Pythagoras was asked to take up a position as adviser of the city. It seems that the city's conditions improved under the rule of the brotherhood, but in the end the Pythagoreans were deposed. When Plato sailed to southern Italy around 389 BC, he found Pythagoreans, led by one Archytas, in charge of the city-state of Tarentum. Most likely, Pythagorean rule in that city helped Plato formulate his ideal of the philosopher-king and of the city ruled by a communist elite.[9]

Pythagorean rule in Croton and Tarentum are the first examples known from European history for a communistically organised and philosophically inspired elite to have wielded real power. To be sure, there is no definite evidence that the Pythagorean brotherhood ruled either of these cities, or that it even existed for that matter, but the ancient stories most likely reflected some kind of reality. Quite appropriately, the scale of this antique proto-communism was that of one city-state, the political order that dominated the Greek world.

Monasticism and itinerant preachers

The Fathers of the Christian church assimilated the myth that humanity originally lived under conditions of communist equality into their belief system.[10] Like the pagan thinkers who first propounded this myth, the Christians treated the egalitarian order as a past irretrievably lost, not as something to be re-established.

However, there were some passages in the Bible to suggest that the church could not ignore the principle of community of goods. According to the Acts of the Apostles, the early Christian community had been a communist congregation: 'And all who believed were together and had all things in common; and they sold their possessions and goods and distributed them to all, as any had need.'[11] This principle came to be reflected in the life of the Christian monasteries, whose inhabitants made a vow of poverty.[12] The communist spirit was furthermore kept alive in the heretical movements that arose in Western Europe, mainly in southern France and northern and central Italy, in the twelfth century. In the words of one scholar, in that century the belief that apostolic life consisted pre-eminently in wandering preaching in poverty 'gained ground ... at the expense of the older, traditionally monastic view, practising community of goods'.[13] Heretical movements such as the Cathars and the Waldensians followed this trend. The itinerant preachers who formed the leaders of these movements hoped to resurrect the apostolic church by living in voluntary poverty. For the most part they abstained from owning private property.[14]

It should be recognised, though, that, as in Plato and the Pythagoreans, community of goods remained an elite lifestyle. The monks, nuns and wandering preachers were living according to a perfect rule that was not deemed suitable or achievable for the general populace. The ambition to reform the whole of society along communist lines is a modern phenomenon.

The Táborites

To see communism being introduced beyond the boundaries of monastic and ecclesiastical communities, we must turn to the Holy Roman Empire at the time of the Reformation. It is here, albeit only on a number of sporadic occasions, that radical Christian movements established regimes of community of goods in areas under their control. With its fragmented power structure, the Empire provided particularly favourable conditions for religious dissidents to strike root and to develop their own autonomies either on a regional or urban scale. Not seldom, princes or local nobility provided protection to communities dissenting from Roman Catholic orthodoxy. The main ones to profit from this pattern were the Lutherans, but here and there communistically inclined religious dissenters were able temporarily to take advantage of the fragmentation of imperial power as well.

The fourteenth and fifteenth centuries in Western and Central European history have been described in terms of a 'late medieval crisis'.[15] The steady growth of market and money economies from the twelfth century onwards had worked itself out unevenly on the peasant and artisan classes. Overall, in the fifteenth century the position of the peasants deteriorated. Many of them shifted from agriculture to an uncertain existence in other employments. The lower strata of the population experienced increasing insecurity. Peasants rebelled, and the nobles engaged in endless civil wars. In the Holy Roman Empire, princely families fought each other for the imperial throne.[16]

Medieval Western Europe was a highly fragmented society. Even so, on an imaginary level, this part of the world had been unified by the papacy and the empire. Both of these institutions laid a claim to universality. In the fourteenth and fifteenth centuries, however, the sense of unity was being shattered. Even at the very summit, society seemed to be cracking up. To quote one scholar, 'By 1410, when there were three emperors, three popes, and two kings of France, the leaders of Catholic Christendom were in despair.'[17]

The troubled times created an environment in which heresies flourished. According to Malcolm Lambert, the Great Schism threatened the legitimacy of the church and generated a widespread desire for church reform. When the prestige of the church reached low ebb, anticlericalism gained currency. Peasant rebellions and the discontent among the new classes of artisans in the towns contributed to new forms of popular religion. Movements led by charismatic preachers increased their followings.[18] Apocalypticism, the belief that history was approaching its end point, became widespread. Such speculations were not necessarily revolutionary. Mostly, they were not directed against the established church and social order.[19] In a number of cases, however, apocalypticism assumed the form of radical millennialism, to be defined as the active aspiration after the establishment of God's thousand-year kingdom on earth.[20]

Millennialism had biblical foundations. The Bible announces the coming of a divine kingdom at the end of time. The Book of Daniel predicts that one worldwide empire after another will fall, until finally 'the God of heaven will set up a kingdom which shall never be destroyed'. The divine kingdom is compared to a stone that becomes 'a great mountain' that fills 'the whole earth'.[21] Central to the establishment of 'a new heaven and a new earth' is 'the holy city, new Jerusalem, coming down out of the heaven from God', and from which God will rule his empire: 'By its light shall the nations walk'.[22]

It is from the world of the millennialist heresies that Christian communism arose.[23] On the ideological level, the myth of the divine worldwide kingdom ruled from one city was quite usable. The 'heretics' would baptise the city where they had acquired predominant power the New Jerusalem, and imagined that their rule would spread from there to the rest of the world by force of arms. In the terminology of this book, the city was the initiator-state, where the system of common ownership was established, anticipating its worldwide dissemination.

Apocalypticism turned revolutionary with the Hussite movement in Bohemia.[24] The first occasion for community of goods to be tried out on the scale of a city was in Bohemian Tábor, where the radical wing of the Hussites seized power. The experiment lasted only for about a year. Hussitism arose in the early fifteenth century in Bohemia, which made up part of the Holy Roman Empire. The Kingdom of Bohemia was a prime example of late-medieval crisis conditions. Early capitalism had contributed to the wealth of the area, but from the late fourteenth century onwards conditions of the peasants deteriorated. Many of them moved to the towns, which, again, negatively affected the conditions of the urban poor. Also, there were signs of disintegration at the upper levels of society. The king was unable to establish effective control over the nobles, who were gradually extending their powers.[25]

In 1415 the Czech priest and reformer Jan Hus was burned at the stake as a heretic. The Bohemian nobles, who were Roman Catholic in their majority but had a minority of Hussites, collectively protested against the outrage. The nobles did not actively join the resistance, but Hussites among them provided protection to the preachers of their faith on their lands, especially in the south and east of the country.[26] The Hussite revolution broke out in 1419. Wide strata of the population participated in the movement – from gentry to town burghers and from urban poor to peasants.[27] Astonishingly, the Hussite armies, commanded until his death in 1424 by the blind Jan Žižka, successfully defended themselves against the Catholic crusader armies sent into the field by heir to the Bohemian throne and (from 1433) Holy Roman Emperor, Sigismund. In 1436 the warring parties finally came to an agreement. Sigismund was accepted as king but the Hussites would be left in peace.[28]

Leadership in the revolution fell to the towns. For the purpose of defence, the Hussites organised themselves into three leagues of towns centred on Prague, Tábor (in the south) and Oreb (in the east).[29] When the Hussites had been banned from their churches in 1419, radical preachers had called upon their followers to celebrate the divine service in the open, on the hills of southern Bohemia. Tens of thousands answered their call. The most popular hill was baptised Tábor.[30] Howard Kaminsky pinpoints the time when the Táborite message turned millennialist in the winter of 1419–20. In the words of a report written by a moderate Hussite in the 1420s, the priests had told their flock congregated on the hills that the 'new coming of Christ' was imminent. At the day of God's wrath, everybody 'on the whole world' would be killed, save for the faithful, who were to move to the 'five cities of refuge'. Another document quoted by Kaminsky says: 'In that time those places cannot be in a village or elsewhere on account of the strong and dreadful Antichrist, but in fortified cities'. Not surprisingly, the five fortified cities were Hussite strongholds.[31]

During that winter the Táborites gained, lost and regained several cities. In the cities they controlled, the priests ordained that, in the words of a contemporary report, 'all the brethren should pool absolutely everything, and for this purpose the priests set up one or two chests which the community almost filled up for them.' According to Kaminsky, the chests served to distribute the limited resources available to 'an abnormally large number of people'. The practice reflected the apostolic spirit, which now however was applied to whole urban communities. In the end, the Táborites converged on the 'abandoned fortress of Hradiště', situated on a projecting rock near the confluence of two rivers. This fortress was again baptised Tábor.[32] The priest Martin Húska was Tábor's main leader in the early communist days.[33]

According to a Táborite document, the Hussites would be like 'an army sent by God through the whole world'. The avengers would have to 'visit afflictions on the nations'. According to another document, written by a moderate Hussite, the self-appointed 'elect of God' expected to 'rule in the world for a thousand years with Christ' upon completion of the military campaign of eradication.[34] The Táborite brethren, 'God's angels', would occupy every place that the soles of their feet would tread. They were to destroy and burn 'all towns, villages and hamlets', including 'Prague, that great Babylon'.[35]

It was at Tábor that the experiment with community chests gained its widest scope. In the language of the Táborites, in their city 'nothing is mine and nothing thine, but all is common ... and no one shall have anything of his own'.[36] Barrels and tubs were set up for the people to fill, to be used mainly for the needs of the army.[37] All taxes, rents and dues were declared invalid and all debts were remitted.[38] Although Táborite communism was not strictly a class issue, for obvious reasons it was especially popular among the town poor.[39] Very soon, however, the experiment came to an end. In October 1420 the Tábor authorities reimposed feudal taxes on the peasants.[40] Most likely, the community chests evolved into a system of taxation for maintaining the church.[41]

In their own imagination, the communist Táborites had seen themselves taking the world by storm, in advance of Christ's second coming. Theirs was a millennialist phantasy of a kingdom of the elect ruling with Christ over the whole world. In practice, however, the communist project remained confined to a very small territory. Significantly, when in the winter of 1419–20 the Táborites mentioned the 'five cities of refuge', they were referring to the prophet Isaiah, who had located five cities speaking the language of Canaan within Egypt.[42] In this way, the Táborites were expressing their sense of being trapped in isolated urban strongholds in a hostile country. At one point they even became confined to one city, Tábor. The first communist experiment certainly known to the world played itself out in an encircled fortress, where much of the population was engaged in soldiering and improving fortifications.

The Anabaptists

During the sixteenth century new order began to replace chaos. Gradually, the new national monarchies of England, France and Spain consolidated themselves. The kings profited from cooperation with the prosperous merchants and towns. The Holy Roman Empire remained fragmented, but the princely states managed to reinforce their position as pseudo-sovereign territorial entities at the cost of the papacy as well as of the emperor.[43] It was princely states that provided the new heresy of Lutheranism with its main territorial base within the Empire. Many of the princes adopted Luther only after the latter had turned against the violent popular uprisings of 1524-6, the so-called German Peasants' War, which undermined the stability of the state order.[44]

That Luther condemned the rebellious peasants caused serious concern among a group of preachers who hoped to maintain the spirit of the Radical Reformation, which in their view Luther had belonged to but was now in the process of betraying. Among them were Thomas Müntzer and Melchior Hoffman. A number of these radical preachers offered their services to the rebellious peasants.[45] Müntzer managed to establish brief control over the Thuringian city of Allstedt in 1524. In March 1525 the newly appointed city council of Mühlhausen, also in Thüringen, fell under his dominant influence. Müntzer used the city as a base for his unsuccessful intervention in the Peasants' War, leading to his death in May of that year.[46]

In his 1850 *The German Peasants' War*, Engels put Müntzer in the spotlights as an early communist.[47] It is however questionable whether he deserves this honour. Overall, the scholarly literature tends to minimise Müntzer's communist credentials.[48]

By far the most significant tendency among the Radical Reformation to adopt a communist perspective was Anabaptism. James Stayer sees Anabaptist community of goods as a continuation of the radicalism of the commoners in the Peasants' War.[49] Anabaptism arose in Switzerland during the 1520s, to spread quickly to southern Germany and Tyrol. In the latter part of the decade, persecution drove many followers to Moravia. On two occasions, in 1535 and 1547, the Moravian communities suffered from repression, but they survived. The Anabaptists followed the Acts of the Apostles and advocated community of goods from early on. However, in Switzerland and Germany they had mostly been unable to live according to their ideals. In Moravia, however, the nobles were prepared to protect the flourishing Anabaptist communities, which they considered, in Stayer's words, 'a means of yielding windfall profits'.[50]

The 'Hutterites', after Jakob Hutter from Tyrol, survived the 1535 persecution better than other Moravian Anabaptists, and it was their lifestyle that became the dominant model from about 1536. Hutterites produced collectively and shared the produce among them. Their handicrafts were excellent, and by the late sixteenth century the flourishing communities together counted a minimum of 20,000 people.[51]

The Hutterites were not of the millennialist cast of mind.[52] But other Anabaptists were. Melchior Hoffman, who converted to this faith after the Peasants' War, predicted that the kingdom of God was near, and that the city of Strasbourg, one of the centres of Anabaptism, would become the New Jerusalem. When the end did not come as he predicted, and Hoffman was arrested in 1533, his followers transferred their hopes to the city of Münster, situated more to the north.[53]

Münster had been able to commit itself to the Reformation against the will of its overlord, the prince-bishop in 1533, through the protection of the Lutheran landgrave of Hesse. Power in the city had been taken over from the old elite by wealthy notables from the guilds.[54] In February 1534 Hoffman's successors managed to gain control of the city council, upon which the bishop began a siege. A large number of Anabaptists from Westphalia and the Low Countries moved to Münster. Jan Matthijs, a baker from the Dutch city of Haarlem, and his successor, the tailor Jan Beukelszoon of Leiden, who made himself Davidic king, adhered to the apostolic principles and proclaimed community of goods. The expropriation of all money allowed the city to take care of new arrivals that came in poverty. However, the city's notables preserved enough of their influence to subvert the experiment. In practice, houses and land were not redistributed. In Stayer's words, community of goods soon 'became little more than wartime rationing'. In June 1535 the bishop's army retook the city.[55]

Even though communism remained at a very primitive stage and was soon undone, Münster again displayed the pattern of one city establishing community of goods on its own. Just like with the Táborites, the fortified city played a crucial role in the millennialist expectations of the Münster Anabaptists. They highlighted their city's viability from a military as well as from an economic angle. In a February 1534 sermon, Jan Matthijs assured his followers that Münster, 'this new Jerusalem', had nothing to fear because it had a majority of Anabaptists and because it was 'a fortified city that is richly endowed with all things'.[56] In March of that year the Anabaptists were called to Münster, 'the new Jerusalem, city of saints', to escape from God's punishment. Sympathisers were only asked to bring their weapons. 'There is enough of everything [*Gut genug*] for the saints.'[57]

Again like the Táborites, the Münsterites were ambitious enough to believe that their own city would serve as the base from which the kingdom of God would spread over the world. Their temporary confinement to a city did not detract from the universalism of their ideals. An undated document related a nightly vision of 'three cities', clearly visible over the Münster skies – Münster itself, Strasbourg and the Dutch city of Deventer. God had elected these cities for his 'holy people'. There, his word would strike root first, only to travel from there 'across the whole world'.[58] In the understanding of Jan of Leiden, the 'apostolic church' established at Münster represented an example for the rest of the world to follow. 'The example is now ready to be followed throughout the world, just as it was started here, in this holy city.'[59] Jan claimed to have received the revelation 'that he would be king over the New Israel and over the whole world'.[60]

The millennialist illusion was convincing enough to reassure the Anabaptists of the small, isolated and beleaguered city of Münster that, before long, they would rule the whole world. The system would be spread through force of arms as well as on the strength of its example, two mechanisms that we will have occasion to meet much more often. Unfortunately for the warriors of God, it was not to be. The Münster experiment with 'socialism in one city' came to an even more ignominious end than its Tábor predecessor.

Notes

1 See for example Flannery and Marcus, 2012; Fukuyama, 2012: Chapter 3.
2 I find David Graeber's understanding of communism particularly helpful. Graeber regards it as one of the three basic 'moral principles on which economic relations can be founded, all of which occur in any human society', the other two being hierarchy and exchange. Communism is when people share and cooperate without respecting property boundaries. Simply put, it is the opposite of going Dutch. Taken in this basic sense, the communist moral principle is an everyday reality to which we take recourse all the time. It is displayed when two people wash the dishes together. Partners in marriage with an arrangement of shared ownership live under communism. Traditional peasant communities that have preserved the 'commons' represent another important case in point (Graeber, 2012: 94–102). From this angle, communism as a utopian political project can be interpreted as taking a pre-existing and very ordinary human principle out of its everyday context and imposing it on the whole of society.
3 See Cohn, 1961: 195–8, 201; Johnson, 1990: 259.
4 Plato, 1983: 184–5.
5 See Lane, 2014: 165–6.
6 Plato, 1983: 190.
7 Mumford, 1959: 29, 32–3, 39; see also Ferguson, 1975: 9; Desmond Lee's introduction to Plato, 1983: 26.
8 Munford, 1959: 83–4; Desmond Lee's introduction to Plato, 1983: 24; Ferguson, 1975: 29.
9 Ferguson, 1975: 40–8, 62–4; Ferguson, 2011: 4–5, 43–6, 99–100, 115–20, 136.
10 See Cohn, 1961: 196–8, 201–5.
11 Oxford Annotated Bible [OAB], 1965: Acts 2:44–5; Acts 4:32–5; 5:1–6.
12 See Saxby (1987: Chapters 5 and 6) for medieval Christian monasticism and community of goods.
13 Lambert, 1998: 32; Audisio, 1999: 13.
14 Leff, 1967: vol. 1: 2–3, 389; vol. 2: 446–57, 483–4, 576–82; Lambert, 2010: 52–97; Johnson, 1990: 249–50.
15 Wallace, 2004: 260. For a critical discussion of this concept, see Kaminsky, 2000.
16 This paragraph discussing fourteenth- and fifteenth-century developments is based on Wallace, 2004: Chapter 1; Merriman, 2004: 8–12, 18.
17 Davies, 1997: 394–5.

26 *Communism as New Jerusalem*

18 Lambert, 2010: 239–46.
19 McGinn, 1979: 28–36; Emmerson and McGinn, 1992; Stayer, 2010–14.
20 For classical studies of this phenomenon, see Cohn, 1961; List, 1973; List, 2010. See also Stayer, 2010–14.
21 OAB: Daniel 2:35, 44.
22 Ibid.: Revelation 21:1–2, 24.
23 According to Cohn (1961: 208–9), millennialists advocating community of goods first emerged around 1380. Cohn mentions John Ball, who was active during the English Peasants' Revolt (ibid.: 209–11, 215ff.); the Free Spirit (ibid. 149–94, 208); the radical wing of the Hussites (ibid.: 220–37); the 'Revolutionary of the Upper Rhine' (ibid. 114–22); and Thomas Müntzer and radical Anabaptists (ibid.: 251–306).
24 For Hussitism, see Lambert, 2010: 306–70.
25 Fudge, 1998b: 5–11, 19, 21–3, 28–9; see also Fudge, 1998a: 28, 45.
26 For an analysis of the complex, ambivalent position taken by the nobles, see Klassen, 1978; Fudge, 1998a: 45.
27 Macek, 1958: 34–7, 45–50; Klassen, 1978: 2–3; Fudge, 1998b: 173–4.
28 For Žižka, see Heymann, 1955. For the crusade, see Fudge, 2002.
29 Fudge, 1998b: 99–100, 123.
30 Kaminsky, 1967: 278–88.
31 Ibid.: 311–13, 317–18, 324. For an excerpt of the first report, see McGinn, 1979: 264–5.
32 Kaminsky, 1967: 329–36. For a brief overview of the developments leading up to the occupation of Tábor in early 1420, see also Macek, 1958: 34–7; McGinn, 1979: 260–2.
33 Macek, 1958: 38; Kaminsky, 1967: 343.
34 Kaminsky, 1967: 340, 345–8. For an excerpt from the last text, see McGinn, 1979: 265–6. See also Fudge, 1998b: 150, 155.
35 For this text, here called 'From the Taborite chiliast articles of 1420', see Macek, 1958: 130–3.
36 Ibid.: 132.
37 Ibid.: 39; Fudge, 1998a: 33.
38 Fudge, 1998b: 169.
39 Kaminsky, 1967: 397–8; Fudge, 1998a: 30. See also Macek, 1958: 37.
40 Fudge, 1998a: 34, 37–40. For the end of the communist experiment in 1420–1, see also Macek, 1958: 51–4, 95; Werner, 1960: 346–7; Cohn, 1961: 230–5.
41 Kaminsky, 1967: 389–90.
42 Ibid.: 313, 317.
43 Merriman, 2004: 3–5, 18, 27, 90–2, 110; Wallace, 2004: 71.
44 See Blickle, 1995: 173–8; Hamm, 1995: 206–7; Merriman, 2004: 101–2. See also Wallace, 2004: 86.
45 Stayer, 1995: 249–54.
46 For Müntzer's life and career, see Smirin, 1952; Friesen, 1965; Elliger, 1975; Scott, 1989. See also Schwarz, 1977; Bensing, 1978.
47 'Der deutsche Bauernkrieg', *MEW*, vol. 7: 327–413.
48 See Smirin, 1952: 298–9, 303; Elliger, 1975: 696; Scott, 1989: 170–2. Müntzer condemned exploitation and oppression of the common people, but he was also trying hard to obtain princely protection. Neither in Allstedt nor in Mühlhausen did he engage in social reform. See Elliger, 1975: 688–9; Scott, 1989: 83, 87, 146–7. There are only a few traces of communism in his writings. Müntzer expressed the ideal most clearly in his May 1525 confession: 'All things are to be held in common and distribution should be to each according to his need, as occasion arises' (Matheson, 1988: 437). See also Smirin, 1952: 297–8, 300–1. That Müntzer's clearest testimony of communism was forced out of him under torture does not speak for its seriousness.

49 Stayer, 1994: 3–16.
50 See Stayer, 1995: 254–63, 265–6, 276 (quotation p. 276). For the development of Anabaptism, see also von Dülmen, 1977: 176–8, 182–3, 185, 200, 209–12; Packull, 1995: 54, 65–9.
51 Stayer, 1995: 265–7, 275. See also von Dülmen, 1977: 219–21.
52 von Dülmen, 1977: 219–21.
53 On Hoffman and Strasbourg, see Deppermann, 1979.
54 von Dülmen, 1974: 10; von Dülmen, 1977: 364; Stayer, 1994: 124ff.; Stayer, 1995: 268.
55 Stayer, 1995: 268–70; see also von Dülmen, 1974: 14–15, 18–19, 23–4; Cohn, 1961: 283–95.
56 'Der Prophet Jan Matthys verlangt die Tötung der Gottlosen (Katholiker wie Lutheraner)' (25 February 1534), in von Dülmen's (1974: 71) collection of documents from Anabaptist Münster.
57 'Aufruf der Täufer, nach Münster zu kommen' (ibid.: 78–9).
58 'Visionen über Münster' (ibid.: 91).
59 'Jan van Leiden predigt' (undated) (ibid.: 122–3).
60 'Jan van Leiden wird König' (undated) (ibid.: 147). See also the 'Königsproklamation' (undated) (ibid.: 148–9).

2 Communism as utopia

The late medieval and early modern experiments in community of goods owed much to the fervour of the Reformation. Others to show interest in the communist principle were Renaissance humanists. Thomas More's famous work, the first great modern utopia, was published in 1516. Humanism restored the connection with classical antiquity, especially in the central role that it assigned to community-oriented virtue. This part of our story will take us to the new national monarchy of England, but first we will make a brief visit to late-medieval northern Italy, where humanism as a political philosophy was originally formulated.

Renaissance humanism

In the late Middle Ages, northern Italy remained part of the Holy Roman Empire. The emperors, however, failed to establish effective control over the city-states that dominated the area.[1] The humanist political philosophy was most famously represented by Florentine officials Leonardo Bruni and Nicolò Machiavelli, who were looking back nostalgically to the Roman Republic. The republicanists advocated citizen participation and the citizen militia, and found the solution for the problem of endemic civil discord in the city in the classical concept of virtue: citizens were supposed to subject their private interests and passions to the common good.[2] The republicanists served their cities in the capacity of government counsellors. The idea was to make the humanist ideal of the virtuous classical education available to the state. Men like Bruni and Machiavelli were not on principle averse to princely rule, though. In their view, *all* city-states were in need of virtuous government.[3]

By the beginning of the sixteenth century, England too had what Quentin Skinner calls 'a new and self-confident humanist culture'.[4] More's book *Utopia*, about an imaginary communist island in a non-communist world, was one of its great products. According to David Loades, late-medieval England had been the most centralised and unified monarchy in Europe.[5] After mounting the throne in 1485, Henry VII, the founder of the Tudor dynasty, brought an end to the existence of private armies controlled by the great lords, and generally reinforced the power of the monarch.[6] At the same time, the Tudor monarchy uniquely rested on a very broad ruling class of nobles, gentry and non-aristocratic officers working for the king in a 'network of offices and preferments'. Relatively speaking, this monarchy rested on consent and participation.[7] Humanism could find a fertile soil in this monarchy that importantly depended on counsel by officers of the state.[8]

The lawyer More was elected to Parliament in 1504. In 1510 he became undersheriff of the City of London. In 1518 he was appointed Privy Councillor to Henry VIII. Skinner argues that More understood community of goods in terms of the humanist preoccupation with virtue and justice, and that, for More, communism represented the best way to deal effectively with civil discord. More re-established the link with the Platonic tradition. If indeed, as in Plato, virtuous government presupposes the subjection of private interests to the commonwealth, then truly virtuous government would mean to abolish private property as the root cause of all social discord. Or so More would have been thinking.[9]

For utopian authors who stood in the humanist tradition the ideal of the city-state remained extremely powerful, referring as it did both to the antique polis and to the living Italian example. However, More could not very well adopt the city-state in unadulterated form. Instead, he adapted it to a scale an English audience would appreciate. George Logan characterises More's Utopia as a 'federation of fifty-four city-states', together making up a territory the size of England, i.e. of a 'Renaissance nation-state'.[10]

More's utopian state interacted uneasily with other states and nations. One of the available options for the Utopians was to engage in relations of equality and cooperation with the rest of the world, in what twentieth-century communists called 'peaceful coexistence'. The Utopians entertained diplomatic relations with other countries, eagerly adopted foreign ideas, welcomed foreign tourists, and engaged in foreign trade.[11] But they also displayed a powerful isolationist ethos, highlighted by king Utopos's order to cut a channel through the isthmus connecting what was originally a peninsula with the mainland.[12] Again, the Utopians could also be expansionists. They saw no glory in war, but to avoid overpopulation they colonised new areas on the mainland. In case the natives were not prepared to 'do what they're told' they would be expelled from the area marked out for annexation.[13] Foreshadowing twentieth-century revolutionary war by communist states, the Utopians 'liberated most of the countries round them from dictatorships long ago'. They also assisted allied countries in repelling invaders.[14]

Logan conceptualises Utopia's foreign relations in terms of the 'boundary problem'.[15] In this interpretation, More followed Erasmian humanism and the ideals of the Christian–Stoic world-state. But the confinement of Utopia to a single state reduced these ideals to the territory within the boundaries of that one state. Inevitably, relations with the outside world were determined by national interest. That is why, Logan concludes, Utopia's foreign policies acquired these imperialist features.[16]

More's island exemplifies the dilemmas of single-country communism. It would be in the nature of an island of virtue to aim for peaceful relations with its neighbours. But, at the same time, the islanders are bound to feel threatened by their neighbours: almost inevitably, they will suspect that they are the object of the jealousy and hostility of the less virtuous powers encircling them. With its communitarian and universalist predispositions communism has *two* survival strategies at its disposal: the insular, inward-looking community may withdraw into itself, isolate itself, and put its cards on its own consolidation; or, alternatively, it may attempt to break out of its confinement and to realise its universalist ambitions through expansion and revolutionary war. We will see these two alternative survival strategies featuring in the communist imagination all the time.

City of the Sun

The Italian Dominican friar, Tommaso Campanella's *City of the Sun* was the other major communist utopia of the era. The work was first published in 1602.[17] Campanella was born in the south Italian region of Calabria, which was part of the Kingdom of Naples. He entered the Dominican order in 1582. Campanella was a convinced, lifelong adherent of Roman Catholicism. His thought was marked by the atmosphere of the Counter-Reformation. He was also an eccentric in views and behaviour. Campanella was arrested for his leading role in the failed Calabrian uprising of 1599. It was as a prisoner that he wrote *City of the Sun*.[18]

In the latter part of the sixteenth century, Habsburg Spain had become the predominant power in Italy. The Kingdom of Naples was one of the parts of the peninsula that the Spanish king directly controlled. The Spanish empire also included vast territories in the New World.[19] According to Campanella's biographer, John Headley, at the beginning of the seventeenth century much of West and Central Europe, including the Holy Roman Empire, seemed to be disintegrating into 'an assemblage of territorial sovereign states', which belied any universalist claims. But the rapid growth of the Spanish empire and the remarkable recovery of the Counter-Reformation papacy combined to a 'Habsburg-papal recrudescence of universal dominion'.[20] For obvious reasons, Spanish and papal universalism made a particularly strong impression on the Italians, as well as personally on Campanella, a subject of the Kingdom of Naples.

Campanella's utopianism diverged, in Headley's words, 'toward a return to a medieval catholic theocracy of Spanish-papal amalgam'.[21] His high ideal was for the Spanish empire, which he identified with Daniel's divine kingdom, to encompass the whole earth. The king was to be directed by the pope, and world evangelisation was to be the empire's mission.[22]

There was a deep ambivalence to Campanella's political views, though. Oddly for a man setting his hopes on the Spanish king and the pope, he was also highly appreciative of the principles of republican liberty and self-government. Campanella particularly admired the Republic of Venice.[23] Both his republicanism and his regional patriotism revealed themselves during the Calabrian rebellion. By the end of the century Calabria, the area where the Pythagoreans may once have been conducting their experiments in communist city administration, was suffering from an economic downturn in the Kingdom of Naples that particularly struck the common people. In 1599 a number of friars and local church dignitaries planned an uprising, which plan was however prematurely given away. After his arrest Campanella confessed that he had been expecting the millennium and the realisation of a 'heavenly city' to be established in his own land of birth: the *City of the Sun* was the outline for a millennial republic that Campanella had hoped to establish in Calabria.[24]

Campanella, who was familiar with More and the Anabaptist experiments, decked out his city with a regime of community of goods. He deplored the fact that the ideals of the early apostolic church had come to be confined to the monastery, and hoped to return those ideals to the world.[25]

In concretely outlining his new society, Campanella held fast to the Italian tradition of the city-state. In the words of one scholar, *City of the Sun*, yet another utopia located on an island, represented 'an idealisation of the Italian city-state', as opposed to 'the typical English utopia which is national in character'.[26]

Campanella praised the Solarians for surpassing even the Roman Republic in patriotic virtue: 'they have so much love for their country that it is a thing to marvel at, being much greater than the Romans are said to have had, so free are they from all self-interest'.[27] Campanella's utopian society displayed the same paradoxical combination of an inward-looking, defensive orientation and confident universalist expansionism that we found in More. War was never far away. The city's formidable walls were guarded day and night, and all inhabitants received military instruction.[28] The point was that the inhabitants of the four other kingdoms on the island 'would like to live as the people of the City of the Sun'. No wonder, then, that their kings frequently attacked the exemplary city. The Solarians were prepared to learn from other countries, but they made sure to subject all visiting foreigners to surveillance, so as to prevent them from corrupting the city. But – and this is again very reminiscent of More – the City would do more than merely defend itself: 'if some city oppressed by tyranny appeals to them as liberators' it would seize the initiative. Liberated cities would accept military occupation and 'immediately place all property in common ownership'. The Solarians' technological superiority made them confident that 'the world will eventually have to decide to live as they do'.[29]

The Diggers

The last patriotic-communist hero of this chapter, Gerrard Winstanley, returns us to England. Winstanley imagined the communist utopia in terms of the nation-state. The city-state, which had preserved a rudimentary presence in More's phantasies, disappeared from view. The English national monarchy had significantly reinforced its position since the sixteenth century. In 1534 Henry VIII broke with Rome to make the Church of England an independent national organism under royal supremacy. The English church embraced the predestinarian viewpoint best known from the French church reformer Jean Calvin, but remained an inclusive and episcopal organisation. In the 1630s archbishop William Laud proposed a number of reforms that unleashed violent emotions and created a radical momentum for strict, Puritan Calvinists.[30] By 1642 tensions between parliament and King Charles I, who ruled without much respect for parliament, had increased to the point of spilling over into Civil War.[31]

In the course of the conflict, the position of the parliamentary party radicalised ever further. The end of the monarchy came when Oliver Cromwell's victorious New Model Army staged a coup d'état in December 1648. The king was executed on 30 January 1649, and on 19 May of that year the purged Rump Parliament declared England a republican Commonwealth. The Civil War ended only in 1651, when parliamentary forces defeated Charles II.

Cromwell's was not the most radical position within the parliamentary party. In May 1649 he crushed a number of mutinies organised by the so-called Levellers, democratic republicans who occupied influential positions in London and in the Army.[32] It was in the period of maximum Leveller influence that Winstanley began his campaign. Winstanley called himself a 'true' Leveller, thus indicating that the Leveller position would have to be radicalised further to complement political equality with measures against private ownership.[33]

Gerrard Winstanley announced his conversion to the system of community of goods a few days before Charles's execution. He informed his readership in *The New Law of Righteousness* that he had heard in a trance that all must work together and eat bread together, and that everybody must look upon himself as equal to everybody else. Winstanley concluded that the earth must be made a 'common treasury'. He added that he would take action and begin to manure and work upon the 'common Lands', once the Lord had informed him of which particular commons would be the most suitable to begin the experiment on.[34] On 1 April 1649 Winstanley and a few friends began 'digging' on St George's Hill in Surrey. Law suits and frequent harassments prevented the communist colony from surviving for more than a few months. The Diggers moved to nearby Cobham Heath, but this new colony was dispersed in April 1650. Other Digger colonies sprang up in other parts, but none of them proved viable.[35]

Winstanley was a London merchant tailor who had gone bankrupt around 1643. He had then moved to Surrey, but in his new business as a grazier he had not been successful either. Poor harvests and the conditions of civil war had a deleterious effect on his financial position.[36] Winstanley, in other words, became personally entangled in the difficulties that were experienced by many common people during the Civil War. England was visited by famines, most dramatically in the winter of 1648-9. Prices and taxes rose steeply. Tenants were evicted from their lands, and many of the poor were condemned to the drifting life of vagabonds and beggars. The policies of enclosure of common waste lands by landowners and businessmen made it difficult or even impossible for the poor to take refuge on these lands.[37]

In the eyes of the prophet of the Diggers, the establishment of the earth as a common treasury would represent a return to the world as it had been before the Fall.[38] Winstanley also frequently referred to the Acts of the Apostles.[39] He furthermore adhered to a heterodox interpretation of the millennium as signifying the potential divinity of all people.[40] George Shulman analyses Winstanley's communism as a radicalisation of the Puritan concept of virtue. The Puritans abandoned all pride and submitted to God, but they interpreted their own worldly successes as signs of God's grace. Winstanley, Shulman argues, interpreted the Puritan attachment to property and worldly power as a rudiment of pride, and he expected the truly virtuous person to submerge him or herself in the community.[41]

The Puritans rejoiced in England's military, political and economic achievements and in the national independence of its church. It became common opinion among leaders such as Cromwell and John Milton that God had elected the English to play the leading role in his work of Protestant Reformation. A ready-made model of the elect nation was available in the Old Testament.[42] For the Puritans, England became the New Israel.[43] The Puritans could however never develop their reading of England as elect nation into a consistent nationalism. Protestantism after all remained a universalist creed.[44]

When Winstanley announced the liberation of Israel from Egyptian bondage in *The New Law of Righteousness*, he was not referring to England. Instead, he hoped for the godly people of all nations, the common people, to be set free through the abolition of the principle of mine and thine.[45] In Winstanley's later writings the universalist identification of Israel with the oppressed of the world remained intact, but a patriotic note slipped in. In *The True Levellers' Standard Advanced*, Winstanley and his fellow Diggers observed that it was the 'enslaving conquest' of the country by the Normans in 1066 that had brought the common people of England under a yoke that was to be compared to the 'Babylonish yoke laid upon Israel of old'. The liberation of the 'poor enslaved English Israelites' was, then, cast as liberation from foreign oppression.[46] In the eyes of the Diggers, the English monarchs continued to represent the Norman Yoke. Communism would re-establish the ancient freedoms that England had lost under centuries of foreign rule.[47]

It did not take Winstanley long to begin to play out to the patriotic card more fully. In their appeal to the House of Commons issued in July 1649, he and his friends announced that their proposal to hand over the commons to the common people would turn England into the 'first of nations' and 'the most flourishing and strongest land in the world'.[48] In his *A New-Year's Gift for the Parliament and Army*, Winstanley responded as follows to the accusation that he wanted to drive England into isolation:

> And what other lands do, England is not to take pattern ... now England is the first of nations that is upon the point of reforming: and if England must be the tenth part of the city Babylon that falls off from the Beast first, and would have that honour, he must cheerfully ... cast out kingly covetous property ... and so be the leader of that happy restoration to all the nations of the world. And if England refuse, some other nation may be chosen before him, and England then shall lose his crown.[49]

In his most famous and last work, his 1652 The *Law of Freedom in a Platform*, Winstanley addressed himself directly to Cromwell. He explained that England as a nation could only profit from taking the road of the commons. This would provide her with predominant military power, for in a true commonwealth the people will gladly defend their government from all threats.[50] '*While Israel was under this commonwealth's government, they were a terror to all oppressing kings in all nations of the world; and so will England be, if the righteous law become our governor.*'[51] England would also profit from the economic superiority of the new system, which would, again, convince other nations to follow her example:

> In that nation where this commonwealth's government shall be first established, there shall be abundance of peace and plenty, and all nations of the earth shall come flocking thither to see his beauty, and to learn the ways thereof; and the law shall go forth from that Sion, and that Word of the Lord from that Jerusalem, which shall govern the whole earth.[52]

Winstanley further explained that, pending the spread of the commonwealth system to the rest of the world, there would be no avoiding foreign trade with countries remaining under the system of monarchy and of commercialism, but the state should have the monopoly on foreign trade.[53]

Winstanley absorbed the Puritan notion of the English as elect nation, only to provide it with his own spin. This was probably the first time for it to be argued that communism would be worthwhile not only for justice's sake but also to make one's country the predominant military and economic world power. Winstanley also suggested that universal revolution would not end with England: other nations would want to follow the example of the initiator-state. Winstanley suspected that the obvious superiority of the communist system in terms of power and prosperity would convince other nations that they could not stay behind. Revolution by example is another way in which an isolated communism might break out of its confinement. Notwithstanding his Christian preoccupations, Winstanley provided the first case of 'socialism in one country', *avant la lettre*, in a recognisably modern form.

Communism as utopia 35

Notes

1 See Baron, 1966: xxv–xxvi, 8–13, 357–9; Skinner, 1978: 3–6, 23–5, 69–70, 113–15; Hankins, 1995: 317–22; Pocock, 2010: 145–6.
2 For Italian republicanism, see Baron, 1966; Pocock, 1975: Part 2; Skinner, 1978; Pocock, 2010: 146–8.
3 See Baron, 1966; Skinner, 1978: 6–7, 23–7, 35–41, 71–3, 84–8, 116–30; Hankins, 1995: 325–30.
4 Skinner, 1978: 198. For a brief discussion of English humanism, see Guy, 1988: 15–21.
5 Loades, 1997: 1.
6 Palmer and Colton, 1992: 67, 69.
7 Loades, 1997: 4–8.
8 See Pocock, 1975: 334–41; Skinner, 1978: 193–201, 213–48.
9 Skinner, 1978: 255–62. On *Utopia* as a programme of humanist education, see also Kenyon, 1989: 108. Utopian community of goods also reflected the ideals of the early apostolic church and Roman Catholic monasticism. The Roman Catholic More lived in a Carthusian monastery for some time. See Davis, 1981: 59; Kenyon, 1989: 72–6. On More's reconnecting with Greek thought, see Nelson, 2004: Chapter 1.
10 Logan, 1983: 245. On More's utopian state as country and city, see also Davis, 1981: 52; Eliav-Feldon, 1982: 12.
11 More, 1984: 67–8, 85, 87, 101, 112.
12 Ibid.: 69–70, 73.
13 Ibid.: 79–80.
14 Ibid.: 107–9, 112–13.
15 Logan, 1983: 244–6.
16 See ibid.: 204–46. Compare Pocock, 1975: 3, 185; Davis, 1981: 54, 57. For a discussion of More's imperialism and colonialism, see also Bruce, 2012.
17 I decided not to discuss the Lutheran scholar, Johann Andreae's *Christianoplis*, published in 1619. Community of goods was implied here rather than explicitly stated. The whole of the city's production was organised according to a common plan, as a 'single workshop' (Andreae, 1977: 32–4, 36, 41–2). On Andreae, see von Dülmen, 1978; Brecht, 2008.
18 For Campanella's life and thought, see Headley, 1997.
19 See Cochrane, 1988: 165–8; Hanlon, 2000: 33–4, 62–4, 74–5.
20 Headley, 1997: 198–201.
21 Ibid.: 31.
22 Ibid.: 33–4, 211–13, 225, 282. For Campanella's millennialism, see also pp. xix–xxii, 3, 33–7, 39, 316.
23 Headley, 1997: 31, 45, 271–4.
24 Ibid.: 3, 9–13, 32–45, 312, 314 (quotation p. 39). See also Cochrane, 1988: 170–1; Hanlon, 2000: 67–70; Pohl, 2010: 58.
25 Headley, 1997: 304–8, 311, 314.
26 A. L. Morton's introduction to Campanella, 1981: 3, 5.
27 Ibid.: 21.
28 Ibid.: 15–16, 18, 22, 25, 36, 41.
29 Ibid.: 37, 40, 42–5.
30 On these church issues, see Lake, 1995; Sharpe, 1995; Tyacke, 1995; White, 1995.
31 For the origins of the English Civil War, see Russell, 1995; Gaunt, 2000: part 2; Hill, 2000; Morrill, Manning and Underdown, 2000.
32 On the Levellers, see Sharp, 1999: introduction; Bradstock, 2011: Chapter 2.
33 On Winstanley and the Levellers, see Sabine, 1941: 4, 12–13, 52; Wolfe, 1967: 2–4; Hill, 1972: 91, 97; J. C. Davis, 2000: 283–5, 287. Winstanley's communism might

36 *Communism as utopia*

be interpreted as a collectivist radicalisation of the Levellers' conception of 'self-ownership'. For self-ownership, see Richard Overton's 17 July 1647 'An appeale from the degenerate representative body' (Wolfe, 1967: 162). For the concept of self-ownership, see Cohen, 1995.

34 Sabine, 1941: 190–1, 194.
35 For the Diggers, see Bradstock, 2011: Chapter 3. For the Digger colonies, see Sabine, 1941: 2, 11, 14–21; Hill, 1972: 88–91, 95, 99–103; Davis, 1981: 173–4; Hill, 1983: 31; Taylor, 2000: 37–8.
36 Alsop, 2000: 22–3, 27–8.
37 Hill, 1972: 17, 32–44, 86–7; see also Aylmer, 2000: 9–10; David Underdown in Morrill, Manning and Underdown, 2000: 27–8.
38 See Hill, 1978: 33.
39 See for example, *New Law*, in Sabine, 1941: 84, 191.
40 See Hill, 1978.
41 Shulman, 1989. For a study of the Puritan mind, see Walzer, 1965. For Winstanley's ideology, see also Davis, 1981: Chapter 7; Hill, 1983: introduction; Bradstock, 1997; Petegorsky, 1999; Gurney, 2012.
42 God had 'chosen' the people of Israel 'to be a people for his own possession' (*OAB*, Deuteronomium 14:2). God had furthermore defined Israel as his 'kingdom of priests and a holy nation' (Exodus 19:6). He had promised them a particular land with well-defined boundaries. See for example Genesis 15:18–21; Exodus 23:31.
43 See Haller, 1963; Lamont, 1969; Pocock, 1975: 337, 341–7, 396; Christianson, 1978; Guy, 1988: 353–4; Grabes, 2001.
44 Claydon and McBride, 1998: 9–15; Kumar, 2003: 103–14.
45 See for example Sabine, 1941: 84, 149–50, 153, 191, 195–6, 199, 215.
46 20 April 1649 (Hill, 1983: 86–7).
47 Winstanley could have derived the notion of the Norman Yoke from the Levellers. See Sabine, 1941: 56–7; Hill, 1958: Chapter 3; Kenyon, 1989: 131–45; Jowitt, 2000. For later occasions when Winstanley referred to the Norman Yoke see for example: *A Declaration from the Poor Oppressed People of England* (1 June) (Hill, 1983: 106); *An Appeal to the House of Commons Desiring their Answer* (11 July) (ibid.: 109–24); *A Watch-word to the City of London, and the Army* (26 August) (ibid.: 125–51).
48 Hill, 1983: 111.
49 1 January 1650 (Hill, 1983: 198). See also the conclusion that 'I must wait to see the spirit do his own work in the hearts of others, and whether England shall be the first land, or some other, wherein truth shall sit down in triumph' (ibid.: 208).
50 Ibid.: 356–7.
51 Ibid.: 292.
52 Ibid.: 313, see also 302, 311.
53 Ibid.: 311, 366, 369, 384. For Winstanley and national defence, see also Nation, 1989: 6–7.

3 Communism as armed fortress

Communist utopianism acquired new characteristics in the intellectual environment of the Enlightenment. Before the eighteenth century, those attracted to community of goods tended to ground the system in a Christian worldview. The new communists, most importantly in France, discovered an underpinning for their system in the philosophy of natural law. They tended to identify the virtuous society with the principle of equality.

There are a number of reasons why the egalitarian principle became popular in France. Sociologically, egalitarianism was fed by processes such as the rationalisation of administration, commercialisation of the economy, the spread of literacy and reading, and the new norms of sociability introduced in the salons.[1] Internationally, France had been fighting a series of wars with Britain over a hundred years, from 1688 to 1783, with, overall, unfavourable outcomes. The constitutionalist political system of the country that had been able to outgun France despite its much smaller population became an object of fascination for the French Enlightened public.[2] Politically, successive French kings from Louis XIV onwards failed to eliminate rival centres of power that obstructed the consolidation of their divine-right national monarchy.[3] To defend their traditional rights and liberties against the Bourbon kings, the French noble estate referred to the egalitarian heritage of an 'ancient constitution' that the conquering Frankish warriors supposedly had established in the old days, only to be perverted by later kings.[4]

Equality was not well served by the myth of the ancient Frankish constitution. The aristocratic and feudal ethos was, after all, in reality anything but egalitarian. The philosophy of natural law, mainly formulated in Britain, Germany and the Netherlands, offered better underpinnings for egalitarianism: the abstract and therefore equal individual took centre stage in that philosophy. It was also surmised that people had been free and equal in the original state of nature; perhaps, community of goods had been that original state.[5]

Natural law put a powerful mark on the thought of French Enlightenment luminaries such as the baron de Montesquieu, Voltaire and Rousseau. The *philosophes* never developed a coherent political programme, but to the degree that there was any consensus among them, the *Encyclopédie*, which came out under the editorship of Denis Diderot and Jean le Rond d'Alembert between 1751 and 1772, reflected commonly held views. Tellingly, the entry for natural equality identified that principle with 'natural law (*droit naturel*)'. It was argued, though, that the 'absolute equality' of the original 'state of nature' could not be restored and that equality before the law was the best one could hope for.[6] This brings us to the communist utopians, for whom this platform was too narrow, and who saw themselves as the real egalitarians.

Armed fortress

France saw a veritable explosion of communist utopian writing from the late seventeenth century onwards. The thought that nature has made us all equal was foundational in the major works of the new communism to be discussed presently.[7] The suggestion that natural equality could still be observed in the raw among primitive, savage people breathed new life into the classical myth of the egalitarian golden age.[8]

Egalitarianism carried the important implication that the communist ideal was a universalist one and suited all of humanity, which is what French communists surely believed. Even so, the scale on which they were describing community of goods was that of the single state.[9] The communist state imagined by the French utopians strongly emphasised the isolationist survival strategy. Communism would withdraw into itself in splendid isolation. The state would be secured not by offensive revolutionary war but by a superior military valour that would make its defences impregnable. As an autarkic state, communism would have little to gain from economic and cultural cooperation with the rest of the world.

One important reason why the communist state would have to shun foreign contacts as much as possible was to avoid contamination with foreign commercialism. But the more fundamental motive seems to have been that the communist state simply did not need anything other nations might have to offer. Given the size, large population and rich resources of France, it was natural enough for French utopian communists to endow their fantasised communist nation with a self-sufficient, autarkic economy. The second key asset providing their utopia with defensive staying power was the superior virtue of the communist citizenry. The citizens would have a rugged indifference to material goods that made the sober lifestyle that comes with autarky bearable. Heroic virtue would make their armies invincible. What the communist nation in this French reading resembled most of all was an armed fortress protected by courageous soldiers and with sufficient provisions to prevent the population from being starved into submission.[10]

François Fénelon's Boeticans represent the most extreme case of communist isolationism. This nation was so uninterested in what the rest of the world had to offer that they allowed foreign traders to acquire the goods they desired without offering anything in return. They didn't even mind foreigners appropriating their excess lands. Expansion abroad was never even considered. Surrounded as they were by mountains and the sea the Boeticans felt safe. Even so, one reason why they didn't send out their young men to acquire an education abroad was the fear of corruption of their virtuous state.[11] Denis Vairasse's communist Sevarambians nurtured the same sense of self-sufficiency. 'Their Government being such that they have no need of a Commerce with other Nations.'[12] Another reason to ban or restrict trade with other civilised nations was in order to avoid the danger of restoration of private property.[13] The Sevarambians refrained from conquests, unless they would be forced by population pressure or if they came under attack, for which reason they maintained a huge army.[14]

In the mysterious Morelly's *The Code of Nature* (1775), a communist nation could comprise anything from a single city to an agglomeration of provinces.[15] With Morelly, even separate provinces would have to aim for autarky. He insisted that, to the degree that foreign economic contacts were unavoidable, the state must make sure that 'commerce will not introduce even a trace of property [*la moindre propriété*] into the Republic'.[16] Morelly entrusted foreign trade to a selected 'group of Citizens' representing 'the whole Fatherland'.[17] With Dom Deschamps, communist autarky was part of a wider process of global homogenisation. As community of goods would gradually spread across the globe, all nations would acquire the same self-sufficient economies and the same language and habits. Eventually, Deschamps suggested, people would lose interest in other parts of the world. Travel would fade away.[18]

Gabriel Bonnot de Mably was born in Grenoble in 1709, and attended a Jesuit seminary.[19] Mably provided powerful arguments for communism in his *Doubts Proposed to the Economic Philosophers* (1768) and in *On Legislation* (1776), but at the same time strangely denied that the system could in fact be introduced.[20] According to Johnson Kent Wright, Mably was as a classical republican at heart.[21]

Mably emphasised the superior qualities of the virtuous citizen as the basis of communist self-reliance. He frequently referred to the example of Sparta.[22] Like Campanella and Winstanley before him, Mably saw republican and patriotic virtue as a source of economic strength. He argued that the citizenry of a communist nation would work for glory and respect, which were, he believed, more effective economic stimuli than private interest.[23] But economic effectiveness was not his main point.[24] Mainly, the virtuous citizen would be indifferent to material wealth and to luxuries to be had from abroad, which, again, would allow him to commit himself to the state and to the business of warfare: there would be 'as many heroes as there are citizens'. According to Mably, 'a poor army composed of happy citizens is invincible'. Even a 'rich nation's army' surpassing it three times in numbers would be soundly beaten.

> The citizens of my Republic will compare their situation with that of the enemies that want to subjugate them; proud of their equality, jealous of

their liberty, they will see that they have everything to lose ... and their despair will add new strength to all their virtues.

Mably finally added that lack of interest in worldly goods would also help the communist nation to obtain military assistance from other nations to counter foreign threats: prospective allies would be won over by promising them the spoils of the enemies, which the virtuous state despised in the first place. Mably concluded optimistically that 'a good Government and wise Laws form the securest bastion [*rempart*] of a state against its enemies'.[25]

The French Revolution

With the French Revolution, egalitarianism turned from ideal to reality. In practice, the ideal could not avoid being severely compromised. The revolution began on the occasion of the resistance of the law courts, the *parlements*, against royal attempts to subject the nobility to taxation. By rebelling against Louis XVI, the noble estate triggered a process of radicalisation that proved their own undoing. In May 1789 the Estates-General convened for the first time since 1614. This was the occasion for the representatives of the Third Estate to force the transformation of the Estates-General into a National Assembly. After the storming of the Bastille on 14 July the king seemed to accept his reduction to constitutional monarch.[26] The representatives of the Third Estate were mostly wealthy citizens who had reinvested money earned from commerce in land and public offices. It was this '*rentier* class of lawyers and office-holders' that now acquired predominant power.[27] In August 1789 the abolition of feudalism, privileges and venality was announced. The Declaration of the Rights of Man and the Citizen proclaimed natural freedom and equality.[28]

In August 1792 France became a republic. In what amounted to a second revolution, power shifted to the Brissotins (after their leader Jacques Brissot) and the Jacobins, who relied on the popular element of the *sans-culottes*, described by George Rudé as 'the small shopkeepers, workshop masters and wage-earners' of Paris.[29] The process of escalation and radicalisation ended in the 1793-4 Terror under Maximilien de Robespierre and Louis Saint-Just, who now also turned against the sans-culottes faction of the *Enragés* led by Jacques Roux. After the two main Jacobin leaders had been guillotined in July 1794, the new Directory further curbed the rebellious activities of the sans-culottes.[30]

In May 1796 the authorities quashed a conspiracy to seize power by a group of so-called Equals. Its main leader, François-Noël ('Gracchus') Babeuf, was executed in 1797. The failure of the conspiracy can partly be attributed to the lack of response from the side of the sans-culottes. Babeuf had arrived in Paris in 1793. He became involved in Jacobin circles, but his sympathies lay mainly with the sans-culottes. Babeuf was particularly keen on seeing the 1793 democratic Constitution, which had been immediately suspended upon its acceptance, brought into effect. After July 1794, Babeuf clashed with the Thermidorians over their policy to reign in the sans-culottes.[31]

Babeuf considered himself a radical, egalitarian republican.[32] He laid out his communist ideals in a 28 July 1795 letter to a friend, and in the 'Manifesto of the plebeians', published on 30 November of that year.[33] In his system of *'perfect equality'*,[34] producers would hand over their produce to public storehouses, from which the products would be redistributed on equal terms.[35] Babeuf referred to Rousseau, Mably and Morelly, but Robert Rose argues that his experiences as secretary of the Paris Food Administration as well as his acquaintance with the Jacobin policies of price control, requisitioning and rationing were more important in turning Babeuf to communism than 'the literary influence of Enlightenment utopianism'.[36]

Be that as it may, the continuity of Babeuf's thinking with the earlier utopianism is striking. Babeuf too imagined egalitarian France as a self-sufficient, autarkic state that could do without foreign trade. He furthermore nurtured the same virtuous indignation over imports of 'foreign superfluities' that would reintroduce the taste for luxuries and the 'mercantile spirit'.[37] Like Mably, Babeuf referred to the heroes of classical antiquity, mainly from Sparta and republican Rome, to fulminate against commercialism, luxury and voluptuousness.[38]

When Babeuf entrusted his communist reflections to paper, the French Revolution was internationally on the march. Initially, revolutionary France had no expansionist goals. The new government had renounced wars for conquest. But in October 1791 the Brissotins called for a 'crusade for universal liberty' against Europe's monarchs. The Jacobins did not go along with these ambitions, but in April 1792 France declared war on Austria. A November 1792 edict offered 'fraternity and help' to 'all peoples who wish to recover their liberty'.[39] France set itself two goals. Areas falling within its 'natural frontiers' were to be annexed; beyond these frontiers, 'sister republics' would be established where possible. When Britain entered the war, French expansion was checked. When Belgium was lost in March 1793, Jacobin leader Danton proposed that France free other peoples not by force of arms but by example, 'by her shining spirit and energy'.[40] We met the conception of revolution by example earlier, with Winstanley and embryonically even with Jan van Leiden, and we will have occasion to meet the myth of the exemplary state more often. Notwithstanding the successful mass mobilisation of August 1793, France remained on the defensive during the period of Jacobin predominance, which lasted until July 1794. When the advance was resumed, Belgium was annexed in 1795. Sister republics were established in Holland, Italy and Switzerland.[41]

The French Revolution had an ambiguous effect on communist thinking. On one hand, the military–heroic interpretation of the revolutionary process received a powerful boost. The proof was in that a revolutionary state could hold its own on the battlefield even against a coalition of enemy-states. But

Babeuf did not adopt the aggressive romantics of liberatory warfare. It was enough for him that the communist revolution, which he compared to the conquest of the land of Canaan by the Israelites, could protect itself: 'We will proclaim the true code of nature under the protection of our hundred thousand lances and our guns.'[42] In Babeuf's imagination, communist France remained an armed fortress rather than an army on the march.

In the spirit of Danton, Babeuf expected communist France to play the role of initiator of world revolution not through revolutionary war but through her example. This offered the prospect of communist expansion without abandoning the restrained foreign policies that were characteristic of French communism. In his July 1795 letter Babeuf explained that it would be impossible to liberate France in one blow. Power would have to be seized first in a small part of the country, which he referred to as 'Our Vendée'. The liberated area would then serve as a 'centre [*foyer*]' from which the new system would spread across the country, *through imitation*. Later, when all of France was liberated, visitors from the rest of Europe would be welcomed to 'enjoy the spectacle of our happiness', so as to infuse them with the 'desire to imitate us'.[43]

Babeuf's co-conspirator Sylvain Maréchal too saw France as initiator-state and example worthy of emulation. He called in his 1796 'Manifesto of the Equals' for the establishment of a '*Republic of Equals*', based on '*community of goods*', only to proclaim: '*People of France*! The purest of all earthly glories has been reserved for you – yes, 'tis you who are first destined to present the world with this touching spectacle.'[44]

The French were also glorified as the future initiator-people by another communist that cannot remain unmentioned, Nicolas-Edme Restif de la Bretonne. Restif was born in the Burgundian village of Sacy in 1734 and became a printer by profession.[45] He acquired some fame with a communist utopia.[46] His *Mr. Nicholas*, with a systematic exposé of the communist principle, appeared in 1794–7.[47]

Restif's communism was eccentric in its extreme chauvinism. He cared only for the French national interest and admitted that the welfare of other nations did not concern him.[48] In an echo of the century-long rivalry between his fatherland and Britain, Restif hoped that communism would finally allow France to emerge as victor.

Restif appreciated communism as the secure path to French superiority on the international market: under communism workers could be forced to accept wage reductions, so that 'the price of our industry will turn out below that of all neighbouring Nations, and especially of the English. You'll soon see our commerce revive.'[49] Restif concluded that, 'Until such time as the neighbouring Nations will have imitated us, we will be the superior power.' There was no escaping, though, that other nations would become aware of 'the Happiness of the French' and would express the desire to 'voluntarily join us'. But Restif preferred the new communist nations to be annexed by France – if necessary by force. He was particularly looking forward to the annexation of 'this vile nation', England.[50]

Neo-Babouvism

After the defeat of Napoleon, the Bourbons returned at the helm of France in 1814. Absolutism was restored. It was an overriding concern of the Great Powers (Britain, Austria, Prussia and Russia) to prevent revolutions from upsetting the new balance.[51] However, Restoration Europe was frequently shaken by revolutions, made by motley companies of constitutional monarchists and republicans. The latter remained the most radical opponents of the absolutist status quo.

In the late 1830s a communist workers' movement emerged in France. These communists no longer relied on the former sans-culottes, now an anachronism, but the broad outlines of their doctrine remained remarkably similar to what Babeuf had proclaimed in the 1790s. The neo-Babouvists still thought of themselves as radical republicans. In the case of some individual leaders, for example Louis-Auguste Blanqui, it is difficult to pinpoint when or even if radical republicanism morphed into communism.[52]

Another republican leader, Filippo Buonarotti, did however never leave any doubts about his communist proclivities. Buonarotti, born in Pisa, had been put on trial with Babeuf in 1797. He had escaped with his life, to be released in 1806.[53] In 1828 Buonarotti published an account of the 1796 Conspiracy of Equals that represented the starting point of neo-Babouvism as a doctrine.

Buonarotti referred to Plato, Lycurgus, More and Mably in support of his ideal of community of goods.[54] He trusted that communism was feasible even in 'a small state or tribe', and therefore most certainly 'in a great association like the Republic of France'.[55] He claimed, with Babeuf, that the citizenry of the revolutionary state would be uninterested in acquiring foreign luxuries.[56] France would become a self-sufficient, autarkic economy. Buonarotti admitted that a state limited to 'the scanty territory of a commune or district' would be forced to engage in foreign trade and might become subject to corruption, but in 'an immense Republic, composed of several millions of men' this unwelcome development could be avoided: districts could help each other out. This would have the additional advantage of creating a mutual feeling of devotion that would protect the country from invaders.[57] Buonarotti trusted that egalitarian France would be 'defended with the courage of a lion by an immense population', and that it would find more soldiers and resources 'than can, in the present order of things, be furnished by all the financiers of Europe'.[58] Finally, Buonarotti also agreed with Babeuf that the expansion of communism beyond France would not be effected by force of arms but through the 'brilliant example of a powerful institution founded upon equality and liberty'.[59]

In July 1830, King Charles X was overthrown, when he attempted to limit the already very narrow suffrage. After three days of fighting on the barricades, his place was taken by the Duke of Orléans, who would rule as Louis Philippe. After the fall of the Bourbons, Buonarotti returned to Paris.[60] In the words of Pamela Pilbeam, he became, the 'guru' of the Paris republican organisations and his book the 'little red book' of the younger generation of revolutionaries.[61] Several republican organisations emerged in Paris during the 1830s. They were dominated by Buonarotti's associates and by Blanqui and his friends. Buonarotti himself died in 1837, but the last and most famous of the republican groups, the Blanquist *Society of Seasons*, staged a failed uprising in Paris in May 1839, which landed Blanqui in prison.[62]

Artisans made up an important segment of the republican societies. The work of these societies received a boost from the uprising of the Lyon silk workers, who in November 1831 temporarily seized power in the city. Another uprising of Lyon artisans was crushed in 1834.[63]

In the wake of the failed uprising by the Society of Seasons a process of reorientation was set in motion, resulting in the emergence of a number of communist workers' groups in Paris and Lyon, mainly consisting of artisans and workers in the cottage industries. Also, a new generation of leaders mounted the stage to proclaim the communist doctrine, most prominently Jean-Jacques Pillot, Theodore Dézamy, Richard Lahautière and Albert Laponneraye. The so-called Belleville Banquet, organised in July 1840 by Dézamy and Pillot, may be considered the official launch of modern communism.[64]

Like Buonarotti before them, Pillot and Dézamy remained close to Babeuf's principles. Pillot explained in his 1840 *The History of the Equal*s that communist France would have to interdict all communications with the monarchies surrounding it. He trusted that France's huge territory, inexhaustible economic resources and well-defensible natural frontiers would secure the country. Most importantly, France need not fear an invasion because 'slaves would never be able to pit themselves against free men'.[65] In his 1842 *Code of the Community*, Dézamy predicted that one day the whole world would be united into a 'universal fatherland, complete *communion*'.[66] In the meantime, communist virtue guaranteed superior strength. France need not fear 'that a communist government would initially be isolated and defenceless'.

> These apprehensions can often have some validity, but never against communism. No system is more capable than ours of rallying quickly, instinctively, energetically all generous passions; it is an ... invincible shield against injustices and all tyrannies.

Dézamy accused Robespierre of having left the available resources of popular 'enthusiasm' and 'heroism' untapped. He had failed to understand that 'community [*la communauté*]' was 'the most powerful and most sublime weapon to bring down the enemies'. Dézamy concluded that even 'the whole world' could begin nothing against a state that had realised the 'earthly paradise'.[67]

Neo-Babouvism did not remain an exclusively French phenomenon. An important occasion was the establishment of the League of the Just in Paris in 1836 by German emigrants Karl Schapper and Wilhelm Weitling, a travelling journeyman tailor.[68] The bulk of the membership of this and other German republican organisations were intellectuals and travelling journeymen.[69] The League of the Just soon turned to communism and fell under the influence of neo-Babouvism.[70]

In 1838 Weitling's *Mankind, As It Is and As It Should Be* was published, and was enthusiastically received by the membership. After the 1839 fiasco of the Society of Seasons, the French authorities forced many of the Germans out of the country. Schapper moved to London and Weitling to Switzerland. But this did nothing to diminish the status of *Mankind*, which remained the main programmatic document of German communism until late 1842.[71] Heinrich Heine called it 'the catechism of the German communists'.[72]

Weitling predicted the demise of nations and the unification of the whole of humanity, but only in due course. He described a communist state that would have the 'decisive [*überwiegende*] advantage in war'. Weitling suggested that communism could even survive within the confines of a small German princely state:

> a small area, with only 3 or 4 million inhabitants, would be a match for all European enemies of the people combined, and be victorious; for with every step the enemy advances, its courage and its efforts will double, and with every step the enemy retreats it liberates its brothers and augments the means for its struggle.[73]

In December 1842 Weitling's *Guarantees of Harmomy and Freedom* was published. This remained the League's most authoritative statement of principle until the late 1840s.[74] Weitling repeated that, one day, the world would be one. But he did not reject patriotism out of hand: the workers had no property, and therefore no real fatherland either; the revolution would give them a fatherland worth dying for.[75]

Weitling did not trust that a relatively small communist state could be economically self-supporting, though. In case 'neighbouring peoples not living in community' would refuse to help the communist state out with food products, war might have to be declared on them.[76] Like his French comrades, Weitling was confident about the outcome of such a conflict. The citizenry would be fuelled up by the heroic 'enthusiasm of equality', and under the new system a 'country with ten million inhabitants could raise an armed force of two million. Everything is possible in the community [*in der Gemeinschaft*], even waging war without money!'[77] The communist state could stand alone.

Notes

1 See Smith, 2005: 6.
2 See Anchor, 1967: 27; Gay, 1969: 24–5; Palmer and Colton, 1992: 268; Wright, 1997: 126–9.
3 For the conflicts between king and nobility, see Anchor, 1967: 13–15, 20–4; Palmer and Colton, 1992: 183–9, 265–6, 362–5; Wisner, 1997: 2–3, 39, 44, 67–70; Fitzpatrick, 2004: 134–55; Anderson, 1989: 176–81.

4 For the *thèse nobiliaire* and its appeal to egalitarianism, see Anchor, 1967: 14–15, 21–3; Hampson, 1987: 177–8; Wright, 1997: 25–7, 126–32; Tomaselli, 2006; Smith, 2005.
5 For the natural law tradition and egalitarianism in France, see Crocker, 1963: esp. 3–12; Manuel, 1965: introduction, esp. 5–8; Hampson, 1987: 38–9, 99–103, 111; Girsberger, 1973: 14–20, 51–64, 78–83, 236–41; Palmer and Colton, 1992: 308–11; Haakonssen, 1996: 5–6, 26–8, 31–2, 38; Fitzpatrick, 2004: introduction to sixth part of the book, esp. 423–4; McGowen, 2004: 508–9; Smith, 2005: 6; Tomaselli, 2006: 19–25, 28–9, 34–6; Roche, 2006: 189–94.
6 The entry is reproduced in whole in Delaporte, 1987: 6–7.
7 See for example d'Allais, 1738: 171–2, 177; Archbishop, 1798: 133–4, 138; Meslier, 1971: 17–18, 61–2; Mr. M [Morelly], 1753: 36–7, 55–79; Morelly, 1950: 1950: 165–9, 179; Mably, 1789: 10–11, 15, 18–19; Mably, 1776: 47, 49, 51, 58, 68, 74, 96–8; Restif de la Bretonne, 1977: 98, 108, 225–6, 251. Deschamps prioritises reason over the 'law of nature'. See Thomas and Venturi, 1963: 85–6, 104–5, 120–1, 126–7, 169, 187.
8 See for example Vairasse on the original communism of his native people (d'Allais, 1738: 174). With Fénelon, the Boeticans had preserved 'the pleasures of the golden age' (Archbishop, 1798: 131). Meslier (1971: 18) refers to Seneca on natural equality.
9 The only exception seemed to be Jean Meslier, but only seemingly so. The unknown village priest Meslier, born in 1664, best candidate for first communist atheist in history, led an unremarkable life (Deprun, Desné and Soboul, 1970: 12). Meslier's explosive testament was discovered only after his death in 1729 (*Mémoire des pensées et des sentiments de Jean Meslier*: Meslier, 1970, 1971, 1972). For Meslier, see Dommanget, 1965: 13–99; Rihs, 1970: 103–46; Desné, 1970; Girsberger, 1973: 122–30. On a close look Meslier too predicts the communist transition nation by nation. He insists (1972: 146–7) that the communist revolution can only succeed if 'all peoples' rise simultaneously. However, according to Dommanget (1965: 326–7), in Meslier's times the term 'peoples [*peuples*]' designated the 'various populations of our provinces'. Meslier was referring to French regional populations. Meslier (1972: 149) takes the way the Dutch and the Swiss liberated themselves as examples of how the oppressed must unite against the tyrants.
10 There are obvious similarities between the communist utopias and Jean-Jacques Rousseau's draft constitution for Corsica (1765), envisioning an insulated state safe from invasion, economic self-sufficiency, a frugal spirit and equal sharing (Wokler, 2001: 82–3, 94–5).
11 Archbishop, 1798: 135–8. Fénelon described the communist Boeticans in *Les aventures de Télémaque* (1699). As archbishop of Cambrai and ideologist of the noble estate, he surely never hoped to see France actually brought under community of goods. On Fénelon, see Rihs, 1970: 24–8; Girsberger, 1973: 190–5. See also Schuurman, 2012: 182–3.
12 d'Allais, 1738: 248: *History of the Sevarambians* appeared in English in 1675, and paints the conditions of a distant land populated by an autocratically ruled, primitive people. For Vairasse, see Girsberger, 1973: 111–22.
13 d'Allais, 1738: 189–91.
14 Ibid.: 190, 193, 243–4, 247–9.
15 See Morelly, 1950: 287, 304–5, 308. The true identity of Morelly has never been established. See Gilbert Chinard's introduction in Morelly, 1950: 7–147; Coe, 1961; Rihs, 1970: 147–205; Girsberger, 1973: 130–57; Wagner, 1978: 15–64. Morelly also wrote a utopia, the 1753 *Basiliade* (Mr. M [Morelly], 1753).
16 Morelly, 1950: 290–2. For Morelly on regional and national autarky, see also Coe, 1961: 221–3, 244–6, 250, 292. For provincial autarky, see also Meslier, 1971: 90.
17 Mr M [Morelly], 1753: 108f. In Coe's interpretation (1961: 210–41), the *Basiliade* described a politically and economically autarkic isolated society.

Communism as armed fortress 47

18 Thomas and Venturi, 1963: 173–4, 184–7. Dom Deschamps lived in a small Benedictine monastery in Montreuil-Bellay for most of his life. His communist work, later collected under the name *Le Vrai Système*, was probably written between 1770 and 1774. See introduction in Thomas and Venturi, 1963; Rihs, 1970: 206–37.
19 Wright, 1997: 23–4, 36. For Mably's biography, see also Girsberger, 1973: 158–78; biographical section in Bödeker and Friedemann, 2000: 11–16.
20 On the impossibility of introducing communism, see for example Mably, 1789: 12; Mably, 1776: 101ff.
21 Wright, 1997. See on Mably also Rihs, 1970: 71–85; Girsberger, 1973: 158–78; Bödeker and Friedemann, 2000: 20–4.
22 Mably, 1789: 5–8; Mably, 1776: 96. See also Rihs, 1970: 78–9; Girsberger, 1973: 166, 171–2, 175–6; Wright, 1997.
23 Mably, 1789: 9 (see also pp. 28, 87–91). Morelly too insisted that 'community of all goods ... can move people more effectively than the miserable motives of private interests' (Mr. M [Morelly], 1753: 73–4).
24 See Mably, 1789: 12–3, 91.
25 Ibid.: 96–101 (see also p. 14). For republican virtue in eighteenth-century France, see Linton, 2013: Chapter 1.
26 For the events leading up to the revolution and its early stages, see Fitzsimmons, 2013: 75–82. For general accounts of the revolution, see Furet, 1981; Schama, 1989; Rudé, 1994; Israel, 2014.
27 Campbell, 2013: 7–9; see also Rudé, 1994: 230–1.
28 According to Rudé (1994: 59–60), the Declaration reflected the natural law school of philosophy. For the 'principles of 1789', see also Fitzsimmons, 2013: 83–6.
29 Rudé, 1994: 72. For the urban crowds in the revolution, see Sutherland, 2013; Andress, 2013: 297–9; Woloch, 2013: 445–7.
30 See Mason, 2013; Andress, 2013: 301–3.
31 For Babeuf prior to 1795: Rose, 1978: Chapters 1–12. On Babeuf and the Thermidorians, see Mason, 2013: 317. For the conspiracy and its suppression, see Rose, 1978: Chapters 15–17.
32 Wright (1997: 210–11; also 7) calls Babeuf 'clearly a lineal descendant of the classical republican tradition'. See also Sonenscher, 2006.
33 For the letter, see Dommanget, 1935: 207–21; for the manifesto (ibid.: 250–64). Rose (1978: 230–2) mentions two programmatic texts not written by Babeuf (*Analyse de la doctrine de Babeuf*, 9 April 1796; *Réponse à ... M.V.*, 18 Avril 1796) from the period of the conspiracy (March–May 1796).
34 Dommanget, 1935: 251.
35 Ibid.: 215.
36 Rose, 1978: 197–8, 321, 332–5.
37 Dommanget, 1935: 216–7. Elsewhere in the letter he leaves a loophole for foreign trade, under strict political control: 211–2.
38 Dommanget, 1935: 207–10. For references to the heroes of antiquity, see also 252, 254–5.
39 Rapport, 2013: 386.
40 Cited in Lawday, 2009: 196–7.
41 See for French revolutionary foreign policies, Rudé, 1994: 10–11, 76–9, 83, Chapter 6; Lawday, 2009: 156, 174–5, 194–7; Rapport, 2013: 386–7.
42 Dommanget, 1935: 257, 264.
43 Ibid.: 217, 219–20.
44 Bronterre, 1836: 315–16.
45 Poster, 1971: 3–4. For Restif's communism, see ibid.; Girsberger, 1973: 178–88; Jacques Lacarrière's foreword to *La Découverte australe* (Restif de la Bretonne, 1977: 9–25); Billington, 1980: 79–83; Coward, 1991.

48 Communism as armed fortress

46 *La Découverte australe* appeared in 1781 (Restif de la Bretonne, 1977). Restif's imaginary kingdom had the size of Great Britain and entertained cordial commercial relations with another communist island kingdom in the vicinity resembling France (ibid.: 86–7, 90, 98, 108, 207, 226, 246). Restif also designed small-scale utopias for single villages and cities, modelled on Sacy, antique city-states and 'the self-contained peasant families of Auvergne' (Poster, 1971: 68–70). See also Coward, 1991: 342–55, 630–3, 650.
47 Restif de la Bretonne, 1959. The philosophical section of the work with the communist principles appeared in 1796. See Restif de la Bretonne, 1959: vol. 1: xv.
48 See ibid.: vol. 6: 351–3.
49 Ibid.: 103. For Restif on the efficiency of the communal over the private motive, see ibid.: 47, 353–4, 384.
50 Ibid.: 98, 129, 395–6.
51 For the transformation of European politics, see Schroeder, 1994: part II.
52 See Spitzer, 1957: Chapter 5, 112–21; Loubère, 1959.
53 Hearder, 1990: 177–8. For Buonarotti's early activities, see also Billington, 1980: 87–91.
54 Bronterre, 1836: 8, 10.
55 Ibid.: 371–2.
56 Ibid.: 170–9, 226.
57 Ibid.: 155–8, 187 (see also p. 423).
58 Ibid.: 371–2.
59 Ibid.: 190–1 (see also pp. 151–2).
60 Hearder, 1990: 177–8.
61 Pilbeam, 2000b: 51–2.
62 For the republican *sociétés* and the 1839 coup, see Spitzer, 1957: 3, 5–7, 122–9; Ramm, 1968: xv–xvi; Höppner and Seidel-Höppner, 1975: vol. 1: 211–47; Billington, 1980: 179–81; Pilbeam, 2000a: 30–3; Pilbeam, 2000b: 51; Löwy, 2003: 68–9.
63 Spitzer, 1957: 166; Höppner and Seidel-Höppner, 1975: vol. 1: 194–209, 221–47; Magraw, 1992: 55–70, 114; Pilbeam, 2000b: 53–4.
64 For these organisations, leaders and journals, and for the banquet: Johnson, 1974: 63–66; Höppner and Seidel-Höppner, 1975: vol. 1: 229–84, 337–473; Billington, 1980: 246ff.; Löwy, 2003: 64–73.
65 Pillot, 1840: 49–60. Pillot's 1840 *Ni châteux ni chaumières, out état de la question sociale en 1840* discusses the future France under community of goods, but does not explicitly treat the question of its survival in a hostile environment. For the text, see Höppner and Seidel-Höppner, 1975: vol. 2: 436–64.
66 Dézamy, 1842: 237 (see also pp. 31, 156ff., 236f., 265, 268–9).
67 Ibid.: 285, 287, 291–2. Neither Laponneraye's 1838 *Catéchisme démocratique* (Höppner and Seidel-Höppner, 1975: vol. 2: 280–91) nor Lahautière's (1839) *Petit catéchisme de la réforme sociale* (ibid.: 251–68) discuss the question of communism in one country.
68 For German republican organisations, see Seidel-Höppner, 1961: 16, 18–20, 26ff.; Schieder, 1963: 14, 19–35, 44–5, 49–54, 156–9; Schraepler, 1972: 40–52; Hansch-midt, 1977: 28–33; Billington, 1980: 183–5; Hearder, 1990: 181–9; Bouvier, 1992: 102; Sarti, 2000: 79–86; Löwy, 2003: 73–4. For the history of the League of the Just, see Hundt, 1993: Chapters 1–5.
69 Schieder, 1963: 82, 84; Schraepler, 1972: 2, 9–30, 40–99; Bouvier, 1982: 42–54.
70 For this characterisation, see Bouvier, 1982: 48; Taylor, 1982: 197, 199; Löwy, 2003: 74. See also Seidel-Höppner, 1961: 169, 172; Schieder, 1963: 270–1.
71 Seidel-Höppner, 1961: 26–8, 33–8; Schieder, 1963: 10, 12, 241–3, 254ff.; Schraepler, 1972: 52–64; Bouvier, 1982: 45–6, 48–9.

72 Cited in Noyes, 1966: 40.
73 Weitling, 1895: 24, 45–6.
74 See Förder and Hundt, 1970: 65.
75 Weitling, 1908: 80, 84–9.
76 Ibid.: 230–3, 236–7.
77 Ibid.: 205–6. For Weitling's revolution in one country, see Hundt, 1993: 165.

Part II
Marx and Engels

4 Communism as Triple Alliance

In June 1847 the League of the Just rebaptised itself League of Communists. That year Karl Marx and Friedrich Engels joined the League.[1] This event signalled the end of Weitling's ideological supremacy. Marx and Engels broke with what proponents of community of goods had been thinking for centuries. The ways in which radical Hussites, Anabaptists, humanist utopians, the Diggers, French Enlightenment utopians and Babouvists had imagined the first communist society varied substantially, from strongly inward-looking and communitarian to more universalist and expansionist designs. But none of these early 'communists' had doubted that the new order could be established on the territory of a single state. This was now to change. With Marx and Engels communist thinking re-established itself on a new footing.

In his *Principles of Communism*, written in October–November 1847, Engels asked: '*Is it possible for this revolution to take place in only one, single country?*' Engels answered with a blunt '*No*'. Marx's friend explained that the world market had made nations dependent on each other, and that, furthermore, industry had levelled out social development in 'all civilised countries' to such a degree that 'bourgeoisie and proletariat have become the two decisive classes of society in all these countries'. The 'communist revolution' would therefore be 'no purely national one, it will be a revolution taking place simultaneously in all civilised countries, i.e. at any rate in England, America, France and Germany'. Engels added that the revolution in these countries would have a profound effect on the rest of the world, where developments would be accelerated: 'It is a universal revolution and will therefore, accordingly, have a universal range.'[2]

In the view of both Marx and Engels, the communist revolution required the joint efforts of the most developed nations. The Communist Manifesto, appearing in early 1848, defined 'combined [*Vereinigte*] action, at any rate of the civilised countries', as one of the preconditions of the liberation of the working class.[3] They never changed their minds on this. Almost at the end of his life, Engels wrote to Marx's son-in-law, Paul Lafargue, in words that he could as well have used half a century earlier:

> neither the French nor the Germans nor the English will play the glorious part of overthrowing capitalism all by themselves; France may, *perhaps*,

give the sign, but the battle will be decided in Germany ... all the same, neither France nor Germany will be able to guarantee final victory as long as England stays in the hands of the bourgeoisie. The liberation of the proletariat can only be an international action.[4]

The observations made by Marx and Engels in 1847–8 are the more remarkable if we realise that the League's main ideologist, Weitling, was on record that community of goods could even survive in a small country besieged by all of the rest of the world. What would have made Marx and Engels break with traditional communist thinking?

Moses Hess

Marx and Engels were born in Prussia, in what in 1822 became its *Rheinprovinz*; the former in Trier in 1818, the latter in Westphalian Barmen in 1820. Marx studied law and philosophy but became a journalist. As a radical liberal he joined the so-called Young Hegelians. In 1842 he became editor of the *Rheinische Zeitung* in Cologne, the next year co-editor with Arnold Ruge of the *Deutsch-Französische Jahrbücher* in Paris. We can date Marx's conversion to communism to the years 1843–4. In early 1845 he settled in Brussels. Engels, who was more of an autodidact, was taken out of school at 16, but even so attended classes at Berlin University. In 1844 he met Marx in Paris. In the summer of the next year he too moved to Brussels, where the two men would stay until early 1848.[5]

Marx and Engels were not really the first to inject into the communist movement the idea that community of goods would stand or fall with its simultaneous introduction in a number of countries. This honour goes to the Jewish philosopher and communist Moses Hess.[6] Hess's *The European Triarchy* appeared in 1841. Hess predicted a wholly new kind of emancipatory revolution in England that would quickly trigger similar revolutions in France and Germany. The three countries would then have to join up in a 'European triple alliance [*Dreibund*]'. Hess believed that none of the three states would be able to survive on its own against the counter-revolutionary powers, but together they would be 'invincible'. The league would form Europe's defence against expansionist Slav Russia.[7]

Hess played an important part in the young Marx and Engels's journalistic and other writing endeavours as well as in their conversion to communism.[8] In Brussels their mutual relations grew cold, but Hess too joined the League of Communists.[9] Engels's views on the impossibility of communism in one country were closely aligned to Hess's. In a 14 October 1847 article in the *Deutsche-Brüsseler Zeitung*, appearing precisely at the time when Engels was writing his *Principles*, Hess wrote that the preconditions of a 'revolution of the proletariat' existed only in England. However, 'the social conditions of the whole civilised world' were so closely intertwined 'that the revolution in one country (and especially in a country like England with a commerce and industry enveloping the world) must result in a revolution in all other countries'. Hess expected the example of the British workers nationalising their industries irresistibly to inspire the workers of the other civilised nations to seize power as well.[10]

It was Hess who injected the proposal of a triple alliance of the main 'civilised countries' of Europe into the communist movement, but he was not the proposal's inventor. The idea of French–German cooperation was popular among radical liberal activists, many of whom as political refugees were continuously on the move between French, German, British and other European cities.[11] European unity was also popular among the socialists, those who dreamed of an egalitarian and just society without however questioning private property.[12] Hess referred in his *European Triarchy* to the socialist Henri de Saint-Simon to support his ideas of French–German cooperation.[13] In his 1814 *On the Reorganisation of European Society*, Saint-Simon had proposed that France and Germany adopt the English constitution. The three nations should join up in a parliamentary confederacy, as a first step to European unity.[14] In his 1821 *On the Industrial System*, Saint-Simon proposed a 'great European combination' based on parliamentarism and industrialism. He insisted that 'the complete establishment of the industrial regime would be impossible in any nation taken separately, if all peoples of Western Europe do not simultaneously engage themselves in it'.[15] Saint-Simon's and Hess's internationalism contributed to a fundamental transformation of neo-Babouvist communism. The transformation received its most powerful expression with Marx and Engels, whose conclusions reflected Hessian and Saint-Simonian influences as well as being the fruit of their own thinking.

Universal revolution

In discussing Marx and Engels, one is always in danger of treating them as if they were one mind trapped in two bodies. Most of their works were in fact written separately. But in my view there was little if any light between the way each of the two men envisioned the national and international preconditions and strategies of proletarian revolution, which is what we are concerned with here.[16]

That Marx and Engels came from the land of the Rhine, an area of historical rivalry and interaction between France and Germany, may have helped them to accept that the success of the communist revolution depended on cooperation between these two countries. But, above all, the new internationalist scenario drew inspiration from the example of capitalism. That industrial capitalism quickly spread from one country to another convinced them that communism would spread in a similar contagious process. The *Communist Manifesto* best reflects how Marx and Engels experienced what they saw happening around them: 'The bourgeoisie has rearranged production and consumption of all countries in a cosmopolitan pattern [*kosmopolitisch gestaltet*], through its exploitation of the world market.' The low prices of the modern industry of one nation served as the 'heavy artillery' to force other nations to 'assimilate the mode of production of the bourgeoisie'. As a result, the 'old local and national self-sufficiency' turned into 'all-round mutual dependence of nations'.[17]

The scholarly literature has abandoned the idea that the factory system and the new technologies (steam engines, railroads, modern textile and iron industries) simply swept away everything else. That was not even the case in Britain, let alone in France and Germany. In the latter two countries, capitalist industrialisation was only at a very early stage at the time of writing of the *Communist Manifesto*. Nonetheless, Britain's domination of the world market did generate an international dynamic of industrialisation. Undeniably, the industrialisation of France and Germany was helped on the way by the import of technologies, knowledge and skilled personnel from Britain, as well as by participation in the international division of labour. Early industrialisation involved Britain, France and Germany in an integrated process. This coloured Marx and Engels's understanding of how the communist order would be established.[18]

Engels's work in the German-British family company gave him first-hand experience with international trade and commerce. He was excited about the new, cosmopolitan world of speed and technology. The first occasion for him and his friend to expand on the revolutionary effects of the world market had been in *The German Ideology*, written in Brussels in 1845–6. They argued that the 'universal development of productive forces' and 'global commerce [*Weltverkehr*]' made the nations dependent on each other in two ways. First, globalised commerce allowed human needs to be satisfied at much higher levels than before. This is what made 'local communism' so unattractive to Marx and Engels. The autarkic communism that the French utopians had been imagining would deprive the population of the cultured abundance communism was supposed to provide, by cutting the country off from the international economy. Second, an autarkic regime could not survive the 'extension of commerce'. Communism therefore required an 'act of the dominant peoples, "all at once" and simultaneously'.[19] In sum, isolated proletarian states simply would have to break out of their isolation to survive.[20]

The idea of internationalisation of revolution not only reflected the effects of industrialisation and economic globalisation, but also the actual course of European revolutions. After 1792, French revolutionary armies had spread the revolution far and wide. The French revolution of February 1848 likewise spilled over to other countries. The establishment of the Second Republic triggered revolutionary uprisings throughout the German League and the Habsburg Empire. People rebelled against absolutist rule in Berlin, Vienna, Budapest, Milan and Venice, as well as in many other cities and regions.

Marx and Engels's works offer two scenarios of the internationalisation of communist revolution, in close connection with the idea of the all importance of the world market. In the first scenario, the initiator-revolution quickly triggers others in a chain reaction, a scenario Hal Draper dubbed '*contagious revolution*'.[21] In the alternative scenario, resting on a 'Kausalnexus war-revolution', the proletarian state would propagate communism through warfare.[22]

Marx was especially hopeful that a proletarian uprising in France would trigger revolution in Germany.[23] In his January 1849 'The revolutionary movement', he wrote:

> Without England, a revolution in the national-economic conditions ... on the whole of the European continent is a tempest in a teapot. Industrial and commercial relations within nations ... are conditioned by their relationship to the world market ... every French social revolution necessarily breaks down in the face of ... Great Britain's industrial and commercial world domination.

Marx expected the social revolution to begin in France, but the French would have to carry their revolution over into *'world war'* against Britain, thus sweeping the British revolutionary party to power. Otherwise, revolutionary France would be doomed.[24] In his 1850 *The Class Struggles in France 1848 to 1850*, Marx repeated once again that a French proletarian revolution was impossible within 'national walls', because the 'French relations of production are conditioned by the foreign trade of France'. Revolutionary world war against Britain, 'the despot of the world market', was the only way out. The social revolution could only succeed by conquering the 'European terrain'.[25] Revolutionary France and Germany were not only to wage war against the economic superpower Britain, but also against Russia, the country Marx and Engels saw as the bastion of reaction. No revolution could be finally victorious unless Russian absolutism was toppled.[26]

Triple Alliance

All the same, Marx and Engels's imagination of the first breakthrough to communism in the world remained a territorialised one. For all their internationalism and universalism, they were far from assuming that the communist mode of production would be established more or less simultaneously throughout Europe, let alone throughout the world.[27] The extreme differences in levels of economic development ruled out such a thing. At first, the new order would remain confined to the territory of a few 'civilised' nations.

It was difficult to decide what area of control would suffice for communism to withstand the pressures of the world market and to stand up to armed intervention. Marx and Engels were not really sure what the minimum of required countries was. As we saw, on some occasions they included America in this select company.[28] Mostly, however, they were focusing on the European dynamic of Britain, France and Germany.[29]

Both men remained concerned whether even the great civilised nations would have the power to maintain themselves. In the 8 October 1858 letter to Engels referred to earlier, Marx suggested that the first communist nations might be overturned by outside forces: 'Will [the revolution] not be necessarily crushed in this little corner, since on a much larger terrain the movement of bourgeois society is still in the ascendant?'[30] Engels showed similar concern. In a 12 September 1882 letter to Kautsky he suggested optimistically that a socialist Europe and North America would accumulate such power that 'the semi-civilised countries might automatically be taken in tow'. However, he could not rule out the need of 'defensive wars of various kinds'.[31]

Marx and Engels were famously averse to expand on the concrete political and economic structures of communism. They obviously wanted communist Britain, France and Germany to engage in some kind of cooperation, but they did not have a complete vision of that cooperation.[32]

Fortunately, though, Engels's works provide important clues. In November 1847, Engels indicated that the proletariat in power would have to 'centralise not only every country taken separately but even all civilised countries taken together'.[33] However, in his 'The role of violence in history', written in 1887–8, he wrote that independent 'large nation-states' formed the 'indispensable precondition for the creation of harmonious international cooperation of the peoples, without which the rule of the proletariat cannot exist'.[34] Then again, in a 20 June 1893 letter to Laura Lafargue, in which he discussed proletarian 'patriotism', Engels asserted that the building blocks of 'international union [*Vereinigung*]' would be nations with a guaranteed 'existence, autonomy and independence *in internal affairs*'.[35] These points made over the course of many years suggest that Engels envisioned a combination of independent proletarian nation-states voluntarily agreeing to centralise some of foreign-policy functions.

It bears repeating that Hess had referred to a communist Dreibund. According to Thilo Ramm, Saint-Simon's 'triple alliance', a parliamentary confederacy of three nations, remained Marx and Engels's model.[36] On 25 December 1890 Engels confirmed that Saint-Simon was the father of the idea that 'the league [*Bund*] of the three great Western nations – France, England and Germany – is the first international condition of the political and social liberation of the whole of Europe.' Engels hoped that 'the proletarians of the three nations' would establish such a league, which would again serve as the 'nucleus of the European league'.[37] In an interview with *L'Éclair*, published on 1 April 1892, Engels once again referred to Saint-Simon's project as the 'true "Triple Alliance"'.[38]

The term *Bund*, used by Engels to characterise the alliance of future proletarian states, is essential here. In nineteenth-century Germany, the term *Bund* (alliance, league, confederacy) was used to refer to a cooperative of independent states voluntarily relinquishing some of their sovereignty in order to operate as a unity in foreign affairs.[39] The *Deutsche Bund* (1815–66) was perhaps the main existing example. The historical *Dreibund* concerned a defensive alliance signed in 1882 by Germany, the Habsburg Empire and Italy. Engels – and we have no reason to assume that Marx would have thought otherwise – was imagining an alliance of three independent communist states, maintaining some sort of confederal tie to secure their position vis-à-vis the capitalist world – the island of communism newly imagined.

Notes

1. See Hundt, 1993: 277ff. Hundt (1993) is the most complete history of the League.
2. 'Grundsätze des Kommunismus', *MEW*, vol. 4: 374–5.
3. Ibid.: 479.
4. 27 June 1893 letter (*MEW*, vol. 39: 89).
5. For Marx's biography, see McLellan, 1973; Schieder, 1991; Manuel, 1995; Wheen, 2001; Sperber, 2013. For Engels, see McLellan, 1977; Carver, 1989; Hunley, 1991; Hunt, 2009.
6. For Hess's life and work, see Silberner, 1966; Lademacher, 1977; Na'aman, 1982; Avineri, 1985.
7. Hess, 1961: 83–4, 97, 102–9, 120, 149–50 (quotations pp. 106–7). On the communist element in the 1837 *Die heilige Geschichte der Menschheit. Von einem Jünger Spinoza's* and in the *Europäische Triarchie*, see Silberner, 1966: 44, 49, 82; Avineri, 1985: 13, 36–40. In his 1843 'Kritik der Schrift *Qu'est-ce que la propriété?*', Hess (1961: 258) attributed the failure of the French Revolution to the preservation of private property and to the failure of the revolution to spread to rest of the 'civilised world'.
8. See introduction to Hess, 1961: xxix; Silberner, 1966: 87, 122; Manuel, 1995: 55–6, 187–8; Sperber, 2013: Chapters 3, 4.
9. Manuel, 1995: 188.
10. 'Die Folgen einer Revolution des Proletariats' (Hess, 1961: 430–3). See also the 1846 'Kommunistisches Bekenntnis in Fragen und Antworten' (ibid.: 365); 'Rother Katechismus für das Deutsche Volk', written in 1849–50 (ibid.: 453, 456).
11. The Young Hegelian Ruge, for example, advocated an 'intellectual alliance' between France and Germany. See Hanschmidt, 1977: 33–4; see also Schraepler, 1972: 134–5.
12. The Fourierist, Victor Considérant, advocated a league of nations carried mainly by France and Germany (Hanschmidt, 1977: 33–4). In his 1848 *A General View of Positivism*, the sociologist Auguste Comte (1865: 85–91) proposed the establishment of a 'Positivist Republic' consisting of a number of west European nations, with France taking the lead.
13. Hess, 1961: 148. The idea of a French–German '*holy league*' was already in evidence in Hess's (1961: 65–6, 69) 1837 *Heilige Geschichte*. Avineri (1985: 24; see also: 54–6) notes that at that time Hess had not yet properly acquainted himself with Saint-Simon's writings. Hess 'obviously picked up some notions ... from the general *Zeitgeist*'.
14. de Saint-Simon, 1966: vol. 1, part 1: 150–248.
15. Ibid.: vol. 3, parts 5, 6 and 7 (pp. 15–95) (quotations, part 6: 23–4). See also Polinger, 1943. Saint Simon could again look back to similar projects of European or world unification advocated during the 1790s by Thomas Paine (1985: 146–7, 208–9), Anacharsis Cloots (1979), Nicolas de Condorcet (1988), and Immanuel Kant (1795). All of them were indebted to the abbé de Saint-Pierre, whose work on perpetual peace appeared in 1713. See Mastnak, 1998.
16. The debate about differences and identity of views between Marx and Engels focuses on the question of whether Engels's naturalistic–scientistic philosophical system constituted a new departure compared to Marx's humanistic orientation, and is therefore not immediately relevant for the matter discussed in this chapter. For the case for a rift between Marx and Engels, see Lichtheim, 1961; Avineri, 1968; Levine, 1975; McLellan, 1977; McLellan, 1979: Chapter 1; Kolakowski,

1981: vol. 1: 376–408; Carver, 1983; Carver, 1989; Walicki, 1995: 111–207. For the essential sameness of Marx and Engels's thinking, see Hunt, 1974; Draper, 1978: 23–6; Gouldner, 1980: 250–86; Hunley, 1991.
17 *MEW*, vol. 4: 466.
18 For early industrialisation in Britain, France and Germany, see Landes, 1969: Chapters 2, 3; Kemp, 1969: Chapters 1–4; Goodman and Honeyman, 1988: Chapter 11; Sylla and Toniolo, 1991; Tilly, 1991; Crouzet, 2001; Tipton, 2003; Fontana, 2006; Eigner, 2011.
19 'Die deutsche Ideologie', *MEW*, vol. 3: 34–5 (see also pp. 60, 72).
20 Hartmut Soel lists a number of occasions when Engels fantasised about a proletarian Germany defending itself against its capitalist neighbours: first Elberfeld speech (February 1845), *MEW*, vol. 2: 542–3, 548; 12 September 1882 letter to Kautsky, vol. 35: 357–8; 13 October 1891 letter to Bebel, vol. 38: 176. Soell (1972: 137, see also p. 112) concludes that Engels may have allowed the possibility ('if only momentary') of a single proletarian state securing its 'territorial base and defensible frontiers'. That may be the case, but Engels would not have expected that an isolated proletarian Germany could long survive, let alone build a socialist economy on its own.
21 Draper, 1978: 242.
22 Soell, 1972: 153, 179–84.
23 See for example 'Zur Kritik der hegelschen Rechtsphilosophie' (Marx, 1844), *MEW*, vol. 1: 391.
24 *MEW*, vol. 6: 149–50.
25 Ibid.: vol. 7: 19, 34, 79. For the revolutionary 'world war', see also 'Lohnarbeit und Kapital' (Marx, 1849), vol. 6: 397–8; 'Die standrechtliche Beseitigung der "Neuen Rheinische Zeitung"' (Marx, May 1849), vol. 6: 506.
26 See for example 'Bedingungen und Aussichten eines Krieges der Heiligen Allianz gegen ein revolutionäres Frankreich im Jahre 1852' (Engels, April 1851), ibid.: vol. 7: 468; 'Worum es in der Türkei in Wirklichkeit geht' (Engels, April 1853), vol. 9: 17; 'Rede auf dem Polenmeeting in London am 22. Januar 1867' (Marx), vol. 16: 204; Marx's 28 February 1867 speech at the 'Stiftungsfest des Deutschen Bildungsvereins für Arbeiter' in London, vol. 16: 524; 'Eine polnische Proklamation' (Engels, June 1874), vol. 18: 526; 'Vorbemerkung zur der Brochure "Soziales aus Russland"' (Engels, May 1875), vol. 18: 585; 'Marx und die 'Neue Rheinische Zeitung', 1848–49' (Engels, March 1884), vol. 21: 22.
27 According to Hans Mommsen (1979: 43–4, 65–6) Marx and Engels's term 'universal revolution' was a misnomer in so far as the proletarian revolution would acquire global dimensions only in the long run. According to Soell (1972: 111–12, 115f.), this is why Marx and Engels avoided the more ambitious term 'world revolution'. For the universal revolution, see also Draper, 1978: 203, 241–6; Davis, 1967: 20–3; Wette, 1971; Gilbert, 1981: 36, 149, 156–7, 162–3, 184, 189, 215; Hundt, 1987: 31–64; Szporluk, 1988: Parts 1 and 3; Anonymous, 2003: 600–4, 618–34, 656–7.
28 The *Communist Manifesto* mentioned America as one of the four most advanced states, but did not list it in so many words among the initiator-states (*MEW*, vol. 4: 472).
29 See for example also 'Fortschritte der Sozialreform auf dem Kontinent' (Engels, November 1843) (*MEW*, vol. 1: 480–1); Marx's March 1845 draft on Friedrich List's *Das Nationale System der Politischen Oekonomie* (Marx and Engels, *Collected Works* [CW] 1975: vol. 4: 281). Engels quite often pointed to the decisive role of these three nations in general. See for example 'Die Lage Englands' (August 1844), *MEW*, vol. 1: 552; 'Das Fest der Nationen in London' (1846), vol. 2: 614–16; 17 August 1891 letter to Laura Lafargue, vol. 38: 147; 31 March 1893 letter to Julie Bebel, vol. 39: 60.

30 Ibid.: 360.
31 Ibid.: vol. 35: 357–8. Also, the Slavs had to be patient and let the 'West-European proletariat' liberate themselves first. Their own liberation would then follow easily enough: 22 February 1882, Engels to Bernstein (ibid.: 279–83).
32 Bouman (1933) observes that Marx and Engels never discussed economic relations between future communist and capitalist states.
33 'Der Schweizer Bürgerkrieg' (*MEW*, vol. 4: 397). In June 1848, Marx's *Neue Rheinische Zeitung* advocated a unitary German republic within a '*European federation*': 'Programme der radikal-demokratischen Partei und der Linken zu Frankfurt' (*MEW*, vol. 5: 42).
34 Ibid.: vol. 21: 407.
35 Ibid.: vol. 39: 87 (emphasis added). Compare: 'Was hat die Arbeiterklasse mit Polen zu tun?' (Engels 31 March 1866), vol. 16: 156; 1892 foreword to Polish edition of *Communist Manifesto*, vol. 4: 588.
36 Ramm, 1957: 84, 116. See also Soell, 1972: 116f.
37 'An den Nationalrat der französichen Arbeiterpartei' (*MEW*, vol. 22: 87).
38 Ibid.: 536–7.
39 See Koselleck, 1972.

5 Permanent revolution

The project of the communist Triple Alliance suffered from a serious problem: Marx and Engels's historical conception suggested that neither Germany nor even France possessed the level of development required to join the club. In Marx and Engels's historical vision, communist relations of production depended on a degree of industrialisation that was lacking in both of these countries.

It is again in the *German Ideology* that the fathers of modern communism systematically laid out the industrialisation argument for the first time. They explained that the outbreak of the proletarian revolution could not be expected before the 'mass of humanity' had lost all property. Only that would make their situation unbearable. The proletarianisation of the majority of the population again presupposed a spectacular 'development of the productive forces'. This development, the argument continued, furthermore served as precondition of the communist society. For without the abundance produced by modern industry, communism simply meant generalisation of poverty, and 'with destitution, the struggle for necessities and all the old shit would necessarily be reproduced'. Marx and Engels suggested that where scarcity reigns the communist society would lack stability and would soon revert to capitalism.[1] They returned to the theme of communism's dependence on mature industrialism in a number of important writings.[2]

This constituted another significant break with neo-Babouvism. Earlier advocates of community of goods had almost completely disregarded the question of the material preconditions of the new society. It wouldn't have occurred to those who nurtured an ideal of republican citizenship resting on the rejection of luxury and abundance and on stoic neglect of material interest, to make the success of their ideal community dependent precisely on the availability of technologies capable of fitting out the community with material abundance.

Marx and Engels adapted communism to the new age of industrialisation. Here they were again in line with contemporary *socialist* thinking. According to Frank Manuel, Marx wholeheartedly rejected the ideal of ascetic egalitarianism. Instead, he was inspired by the ideal of 'progressive self-actualization of the species man'. He and Engels felt more at home with the Saint-Simonian ideals of technological progress and Charles Fourier's generous acceptance of the diversity of human needs and desires than with the austere Babouvism.[3]

The problem was, however, that, during the mid-nineteenth century, the workers' movement in France as well as in Germany still consisted mostly of skilled artisans, itinerant craftsmen, labourers in the cottage industries and seasonal workers. Mostly, those undergoing a process of proletarianisation had yet to become industrial workers. For the time being, the latter remained a small minority.[4]

France and Germany were among the very few nations to have begun the process of industrialisation at all, which is what allowed Marx and Engels to classify them as 'civilised nations', in the same category as Britain. But the process was only just beginning. France and Germany *were not yet* highly industrialised capitalist nations. In 1850 the German industrial working class made up less than 3.5 per cent of the economically active population.[5] Even around 1870 that figure did not yet exceed 10 per cent either in France or in Germany.[6] Roughly half of the active population in both countries were still employed in agriculture.[7] Peasants were still the largest single occupational segment of the population. The industrial share of the national income did not yet exceed one-third in France and one-quarter in Germany.[8]

Even as late as 1870 Marx and Engels were observing that only Britain possessed the material conditions for the transition to communism.[9] In 1851 Engels specifically indicated that the abolition of all class contradictions required 'at least a doubling of the means of production now existing in Germany and France'.[10] On their own terms, then, the preconditions for the communist transition existed in neither of the two main 'civilised' countries of continental Europe on which they set their hopes. So much for the Triple Alliance!

Permanent revolution

Marx and Engels, however, could not imagine the great transformation process of humanity without a trailblazing role for their own fatherland. It was simply unacceptable for them to exclude Germany from the category of countries that would initiate the worldwide communist breakthrough. To exclude the country of the revolution, France, from that category would have been even more absurd. Politically, as well as psychologically, Marx and Engels were bound to fine-tune their theories so as to allow proletarian revolutions in Germany and France after all. That is what they did.[11]

The *Communist Manifesto* announced an imminent 'bourgeois revolution' in Germany, which was to result in the overthrow of the remaining forces of feudalism and absolutism. Remarkably, it was also announced that the event would serve as the 'immediate prologue of a proletarian revolution'.[12] In other words, Marx and Engels, predicted proletarian revolution in 'backward' Germany for the near future.

The first, bourgeois revolution would aim for the unification of Germany and the establishment of a democratic republic, issues that were of overriding concern for the politically engaged public of the time. In March 1848 the League of Communists formulated seventeen demands, the first of which was: 'All of Germany is declared to be a united indivisible republic.'[13] Unfortunately, during the Springtime of the Peoples of 1848–9 the bourgeoisie did not play the role Marx and Engels expected of it. Struck by the cowardly performance of this class, they shifted their hopes onto the 'petty bourgeois democrats' to seize power. They indicated furthermore in their March 1850 address to the League of Communists that the democratic revolution would have to escalate quickly into a proletarian revolution, in order 'to make the revolution permanent'. The process was to continue until the proletariat had conquered power in 'all ruling countries of the whole world'.[14] Importantly, Engels later suggested that the strategy proposed by him and Marx in 1848, i.e. in the *Communist Manifesto*, had been an instance of permanent revolution as well.[15]

The term 'permanent revolution' does not often occur in Marx and Engels's works.[16] But the process was quite central to their thinking. They were imagining a revolution in two stages: a national–democratic revolution would be rapidly succeeded by a workers' revolution, in an uninterrupted process of escalation. On some occasions during the years 1843–50, Marx and Engels suggested that the workers would take responsibility for the democratic revolution.[17] Overwhelmingly, however, they expected the first revolution to be carried out by bourgeois forces. What is more, to my knowledge Marx and Engels never used the term permanent revolution to refer to a workers' revolution consecutively resolving democratic and socialist tasks.[18]

In itself, permanent revolution had nothing to do with the question of socio-economic backwardness. The crucial point that Marx and Engels were making was rather a political one: the workers could not engage in their struggle for power as long as democracy and national independence were lacking. This democratic–proletarian revolutionary sequence applied in a highly developed capitalist country like Great Britain no less than in backward Germany.[19] Tellingly, in the 1880s and 1890s, when the latter country was turning into a developed industrial power, Engels continued to insist on the relevance of the bourgeois–radical stage and the permanent revolution.[20] Having said that, the notion of permanent revolution was particularly helpful in solving the problem of proletarian revolution in not fully industrialised countries.

The idea of permanent revolution provided Marx and Engels with a trigger for the proletariat that would work even in 'backward' countries like Germany, where class polarisation had not yet run its full course: the democratic revolution would precipitate the working class into decisive action. Engels's works of the late 1840s are the most illuminating in laying out the logic behind the permanent-revolutionary scenario. He explained that the seizure of political power by the bourgeoisie would mark the moment when that class would cease to be revolutionary and turn 'stationary'. The working class would then assume the initiative and become the party of movement.[21]

Engels had a precise understanding of why the seizure of power by the bourgeoisie would precipitate the workers into revolutionary action: the bourgeois revolution would prepare the ground for the proletariat. It would, as it were, sweep the lane. Engels's expression of preference was the *'gefegtes Feld'*. The workers needed political democracy as well as the broad arena of the nation-state to be able to fight effectively. In Engels's eyes, the independent democratic republic would serve as a launching pad for the proletarian revolution, because its establishment would remove all other remaining concerns of the workers: the removal of foreign interference, as well as of the old aristocrats and landowners, would leave only one exploiting class, the bourgeoisie, in the field. Only with the bourgeoisie in possession of political power, Engels believed, the workers would be able to see clearly who their real enemies were, and only then the two classes would be directly facing each other.[22] The German bourgeoisie would rule for 'at most a few years', before being deposed by the workers.[23]

On the face of it, it was not unreasonable for Marx and Engels to assume that the historical moment for the proletariat would arrive very soon after the bourgeoisie seized power. In their view, there was a mechanism at work here guaranteeing that, once the bourgeoisie would have accumulated sufficient strength to act, the workers would likewise have acquired that capacity. Engels observed in his *Principles of Communism* that the industrial bourgeoisie could not reinforce its own economic position without augmenting the numerical strength of its mortal enemy, the proletariat, to the same degree.[24] This formula returned continually in his and Marx's works.[25]

Historically too, it was only natural for Marx and Engels to imagine the proletarian revolution as the immediate aftermath of the democratic revolution. The latter category of upheavals formed a recurrent phenomenon in nineteenth-century continental Europe. In what Eric Hobsbawm called the 'Age of Revolution' (1789–1848), Europe had been struck by wave after wave of revolution, in France, Naples, Spain, Greece, Belgium, Poland, Germany and the Habsburg Empire. These movements were aiming for democratisation and national unification and independence.[26] Marx and Engels would have realised that democratisation as well as the unresolved national questions in Italy, Hungary, Poland and their own fatherland had a far greater potential to move large masses than the social question. Their strategy was based on the hope that the minorities of workers of continental Western Europe could surf the waves of the national–democratic rebellions, and manoeuvre themselves into power in the heat of those struggles, which is essentially what the idea of permanent revolution was all about. The pattern of escalation and radicalisation displayed in the French Revolution would have convinced them that such a thing was possible.[27]

Worker–peasant alliance

The triggering effect of the democratic revolution did not solve the problem that the proletariat remained a tiny minority in 'backward' countries like Germany, though. The *Communist Manifesto* defined the proletarian revolution as a 'movement of the immense majority'.[28] However, it is extremely difficult to find either Marx or Engels defining a workers' majority as a *requirement* of the revolution in so many words. As we saw, they suggested so much in the *German Ideology*, but I did not find any other occasion for them to repeat this thought, which would, of course, have made nonsense of their hopes of proletarian revolution in France and Germany for decades to come.[29]

That Marx and Engels defined proletarian majorities as a requirement for the revolution is, really, a myth. The point that they were making all the time was that capitalist competition was bound to end in proletarianisation of the majority of the population, and that this process was, again, bound to end in proletarian revolution.[30] But they never claimed that the revolution was impossible before this process of class polarisation had run its course. One searches in vain in the works of Marx and Engels for a clear answer to the question of how large a segment of the population the proletariat must comprise for a successful revolution. On several occasions Marx suggested that a substantial minority of industrial workers would do.[31] He was clearly under the impression that, given its strategic role in production, the proletariat could be considered the decisive class in society long before it turned into a majority.

Marx and Engels did realise, though, that successful revolutions required the backing of a majority in society, so as to avoid degenerating into a sectarian coup. To solve the problem of the missing workers' majority they looked in the most obvious direction: the peasantry. Engels observed in 1870 that, as a minority in Germany, the class of permanent wage workers needed the poor peasants and agricultural day labourers as 'allies' in its struggle for power.[32] According to Marx, the peasants provided the '*proletarian revolution*' with '*the choir without which its solo performance becomes its death song in all peasant nations*'.[33] In 1856 he made the 'Proletarian revolution' in Germany dependent on another peasant war.[34] Marx argued that proletarian governments could be established even in countries with a majority of peasants, which was the situation 'in all states on the West-European continent'.[35]

This seems to be at odds with Marx and Engels's well-known opinion of the peasants as representatives of the idiocy of village life and as a class doomed to extinction by the process of capitalist competition. In their view, individual peasant proprietors had no intrinsic interest in socialism. But Marx and Engels's aversion to the peasants was never total. In 1875 the former famously rejected the idea that the petty-bourgeois classes formed 'one reactionary mass'. The party, Marx argued, had a duty to win over the 'artisans, small industrialists etc. and *peasants*'.[36]

The reason why the small peasants could be won over for the proletariat was precisely because they lived under the permanent threat of being ruined on the capitalist market. This might convince them that a socialist workers' government would be in their best interest after all. Marx and Engels expounded this thought in their writings from 1850 to the end of their lives.[37]

Socio-economic conditions

Again, alliance with the peasantry did not solve the problem of Germany's socio-economic backwardness. Marx and Engels's numerous analyses of the German conditions of the years 1843 to 1853 are strikingly ambivalent. On one hand, they decried the retardation of German industry and trade, and the concomitant weakness of the German bourgeois and proletarian classes. On the other, however, they concluded that the triumph of free enterprise over the guild principle was turning Germany into a bourgeois society, and that the bourgeois forces were preparing to clear away the remaining 'feudal' obstacles to capitalist development.[38]

What they were referring to is clear enough. By the mid-nineteenth century the German states, and especially Prussia, had made great progress. The so-called Stein–Hardenberg Reforms, which Prussia introduced in response to the catastrophic military defeats against Napoleon in 1806, had placed this state on a new legal footing. Serfdom was abolished in 1807. Prussian citizens became free to acquire property, choose their own professions, and live at places of their own choice. In 1810 *Gewerbefreiheit* was introduced: free enterprise and free competition. The guilds lost their monopolistic privileges and their rights to interfere in economic life. The 1834 *Zollverein* turned the German states into a single free-trade zone.[39]

Modern industries were only beginning to emerge in Germany, but the country was in the process of liberating itself from 'feudal' rules and restrictions and of becoming a commercialised, free-competition economy. This is another way of saying that the country was in the process of turning capitalist. Evidently, Marx and Engels assumed that, despite the extremely modest achievements in industrialisation, the emerging German market economy was sufficiently robust to infuse bourgeois forces (petty-bourgeois radicals if not the bourgeoisie itself) with the strength and resolve to make their attempt to seize power, and which might again trigger the proletarians into action.

The solution Marx and Engels hit upon for the missing preconditions of the communist transition was that the elimination of poverty and the founding of the required productive infrastructure could as well be effected *after* the proletarian revolution. In early-capitalist, semi-industrialised countries like Germany, the new proletarian government would have to make a major effort at industrialisation to prepare the country for the transition to the new economic order.[40] This programmatic suggestion completed the conception of the permanent revolution. What it all adds up to is that a country did not have to be *industrialised* to become ripe for the proletarian revolution. Proletarian revolution was the formula for *industrialising* countries, a category into which Germany surely did fall.

It bears mentioning that the fact that Marx and Engels predicated the communist transition in Germany upon assistance by France and Great Britain does not diminish the significance of their acceptance of a communist perspective for that backward country. That an isolated Germany would fail was in their view not because of the backward state of its economy, but because *no* country could go it alone. In their perception, even highly developed Britain would be unable to make the breakthrough to communism without the French and German input.

The question of the exhausted potential

Marx seriously compounded the theoretical problems for himself by asserting that a new social order could only be established once the old one had fully exhausted its developmental potential. Close reading of the relevant passage suggests that he did not want his dictum to be taken quite so literally.[41] Nonetheless, we can hardly assume that in 1848 he and his friend believed that capitalism had lost its potential for development and expansion in Germany, where industrialisation had only just begun.

But we have it from the horse's mouth that they did! In 1895 Engels wrote that back in 1848 he and his friend had considered the time was ripe for the workers to seize power in Germany and France. 'History has proved us wrong', Engels sadly admitted. *'It has made it clear that the state of economic development on the continent at that time was not, by a long shot, ripe for the elimination of capitalist production.'*[42] In other words, they had indeed been working under the assumption that capitalism was ripe for elimination. Engels explained their disastrous mistake as follows: at the time, they had failed to recognise that capitalist France and Germany still had a 'great potential for expansion [*sehr ausdehnungsfähiger Grundlage*]'. It was the impressive economic progress after 1848 that had proved them wrong.[43]

In other words, in 1848 Engels and Marx believed that, regardless of the country's industrial backwardness, German capitalism had already exhausted its developmental potential. The reason why they could have drawn this odd conclusion was because the capitalist system had become subject to periodic crises of overproduction. It was the waste and destruction of capital that came with these crises that Marx and Engels took as a sure sign that the capitalist system had lost its potential for sustained expansion already by the early nineteenth century.[44]

The question of premature revolution

It has been suggested that Marx and Engels sobered up and abandoned the idea of an early German workers' revolution in the course of the year 1850.[45] That is correct, but only as far as it goes. The two friends lost confidence in an early proletarian uprising in their fatherland, but they never concluded that the matter would have to be delayed until the process of capitalist industrialisation had worked itself out.

In the early 1850s Marx and Engels famously warned against rash, premature revolutionary plans, but such warnings had nothing to do with the lack of capitalist industrialisation in Germany. The disappointing performance of the German proletariat during the Springtime of the Peoples convinced them that this class was sorely lacking in revolutionary experience. In his famous 15 September 1850 speech at the Central Committee of the League of Communists, Marx established bluntly that the German workers' development was 'rudimentary', and that they needed to be told: 'you will have to go through 15, 20, 50 years of civil wars and national struggles not only to bring about a change in society but also to change yourselves, and prepare yourselves for the exercise of political power'.[46] Clearly, Marx was not referring here to insufficient levels of capitalist industrialisation. Economic development is after all not brought about by civil wars and national struggles.

In another warning against premature revolution, quoted ad nauseam, Engels discussed the failures of socialist minister Louis Blanc in the 1848 French revolutionary government. He concluded that the French proletariat had been 'too weak to count on a rapid passage through the bourgeois period and on an early conquest of power'. But, again, this did not refer to insufficient levels of capitalist development in France. Engels compared Blanc's failure with Thomas Müntzer's, whose position, he added, had been 'much more precarious' than Blanc's, the difference being that in Müntzer's days 'not only the movement of his time but also the age were not ripe'.[47] This observation is extremely significant: Engels was confirming here that, even though the 1848 proletarian movement had been immature, the age, i.e. *capitalism*, had been ripe for the workers' revolution.

It did not take Marx and Engels long once more to begin suggesting that the German bourgeois revolution would place the communist revolution on the agenda.[48] In 1853 both men advised the workers to entrust the democratic revolution to the bourgeois classes, subsequently to establish themselves as opposition party.[49] Once again, though, there was no hinting that the democratic revolution would end in a protracted period of capitalist development.[50]

Aside from the 1871 intermezzo of the Paris Commune, after the early 1850s Marx and Engels experienced no further revolutionary days. Correspondingly, their pronouncements on revolutionary strategy became much more sporadic. Even so, on several occasions during the 1850s and 1860s they expressed the hope of early proletarian, socialist revolutions in Germany and France, countries that by that time were very far from being fully industrialised.[51]

It has been suggested that, in his 1867 foreword to *Capital*, Marx finally acknowledged that Germany would have to follow the British capitalist pattern of industrialisation all the way, without any hope of an early proletarian revolution.[52] Marx indeed mentioned 'natural laws of capitalist development' operating with an 'iron necessity': 'The industrially more developed country only shows the less developed one a view of its own future.' However, Marx's discussion here was not about capitalism and proletarian revolution. He was asking himself whether or not the iron laws of capitalism doomed capitalist Germany *precisely* to repeat the example of capitalist Britain. He did not think so:

> One nation must and can learn from the other. Even when a society has begun to discover the natural laws of its movement ... it can neither skip natural stages of development nor decree them out of existence. But it can shorten and extenuate the labour pains.

Marx pointed out that, outside the industrial sphere, Germany suffered 'not only from the development of capitalist production, but also from the lack of this development'. The country also suffered from an absence of protective labour laws. But Marx hoped Germany could make up for such arrears and overcome such abuses more rapidly than the British had in their days, precisely by learning from the British experience.[53] There are really no indications that Marx ever retracted his conclusion that the workers of semi-industrialised Germany could overthrow capitalism.

Notes

1. *MEW*, vol. 3: 34–5 (see also p. 312).
2. See for example 'Das Elend der Philosophie' (Marx, 1846–7) (ibid.: vol. 4: 181); preface of 'Zur Kritik der politischen Ökonomie' (Marx, 1859), vol. 13: 9; first volume of 'Das Kapital' (Marx, 1867), vol. 23: 789–91; 'Herrn Eugen Dühring's Umwälzung der Wissenschaft [Anti-Dühring]' (Engels, written September 1876 to June 1878), vol. 20: 136–40, 249–65; 'Ludwig Feuerbach und der Ausgang der klassischen deutschen Philosophie' (Engels, written early 1886), vol. 21: 300.
3. Manuel, 1995: Chapter 8 (quotation p. 174). For the question of the influence of 'utopian socialism' (Saint-Simon, Fourier, Owen) on Marx and Engels, see Geoghegan, 1987; Löwy, 2003: 64; Hobsbawm, 2011: 22–7. The isolated communist island state described by the pacifistic communist Étienne Cabet in his 1839 utopian novel *Icaria* had a technology and industry surpassing that of England. Luxuries and pleasure were not avoided. See Cabet, 2003. For Cabet, see Robert Sutton's introduction (ibid.: vii–xlix); Johnson, 1974; Taylor, 1982: 163–82.
4. See Schraepler, 1972: 9–27; Moss, 1976: 2–41; Bouvier, 1982: 42–54; Hanagan, 1989: 1–46, 208–10; Magraw, 1992: 51–72, 91–112, 140–63.
5. Out of an economically active German population of 15.8 million people in 1850, 24 per cent worked in the secondary sector, i.e. approximately 3.8 million people. An estimated 1.75 million people were engaged in *Handwerk*, and 1.5 million in *Verlag*, adding up to 3.25 million artisans. This would leave 550,000 industrial workers (Henning, 1996: 351, 877, 885).
6. In 1860–5 there were an estimated 1.2 million industrial workers in France (Beaud, 1981: 135, 187–8). According to information provided by Roger Price (1981: 168–9), the active population of France stood at 15.1 million in 1866. The figure was 10 per cent in 1875 for Germany (Henning, 1996: 351, 678).
7. France: 49 per cent in 1870–1; Germany: 50 per cent in 1870 (Maddison, 1991: 248; Maddison, 1995: 39).
8. For 1872–82 France (30 per cent) and 1860–9 Germany (24 per cent), see Kuznets, 1967: 88–9.

Permanent revolution 71

9 See for example 'England' (Engels, January 1852) (*MEW*, vol. 8: 210–11); 'Brief an das Arbeiterparlament' (Marx, March 1854), vol. 10: 125–6; 'Der Generalrat an den Föderalrat der romanischen Schweiz' (Marx, January 1870), vol. 16: 386–7; 'Konfidentielle Mitteilung' (Marx, March 1870), vol. 16: 414–15; Marx to Sigfrid Meyer and August Vogt, 9 April 1870 (vol. 32: 669). See also Larsson, 1970: 30.
10 'Bedingungen und Aussichten', *MEW*, vol. 7: 480–1. See also Larsson, 1970: 30–1; Draper, 1978: 238.
11 For the interpretation that Marx absolutely ruled out communism in countries of early industrialisation, see for example Leonhard, 1962: 106–9; Tucker, 1969: 100–4; Leonhard, 1970: 46; McLellan, 1979: 1–3; Cohen, 1982: 203, 206–7; Pipes, 1990: 345–8; Steenson, 1991: 3–4, 20; Pipes, 1994: 501–2; Eagleton, 2011: Chapter 2. Others assumed that Marx (as well as Engels) might have been of two minds: see Alvin Gouldner's (1980) thesis of 'two Marxisms'. See also Priestland, 2007: introduction. Reidar Larsson (1970: 9–11) concluded bluntly that between 1846 and 1852 Marx and Engels 'devoted themselves almost wholly to drawing up theories precisely for 'backward' societies: their native Germany and to some extent France'.
12 *MEW*, vol. 4: 493.
13 'Forderungen der Kommunistischen Partei in Deutschland' (Marx/Engels) (ibid.: vol. 5: 3). See also Hundt, 1993: 443ff.
14 *MEW*, vol. 7: 246–8.
15 'Marx und die "Neue Rheinische Zeitung"' (ibid.: vol. 21: 21–2).
16 'Zur Judenfrage' (Marx, written August–December 1843) (ibid.: vol. 1: 357); 'Die heilige Familie' (Marx/Engels, written September–November 1844), vol. 2: 130; 'Der magyarische Kampf' (Engels, January 1849), vol. 6: 166; 'Die Klassenkämpfe in Frankreich, 1848 bis 1850' (Marx, written 1850), vol. 7: 89; March 1850 address (ibid.: 248, 254); statement of the 'Weltgesellschaft der revolutionären Kommunisten' (Marx/Engels, April 1850), vol. 7: 553; 'Marx und die "Neue Rheinische Zeitung"' (vol. 21: 21–2).
17 See for example introduction to 'Zur Kritik der hegelschen Rechtsphilosophie' (Marx; written late 1843/January 1844), vol. 1: 380–91; 'Zustand in Paris' (Marx or Engels/January 1849), vol. 6: 211. For a discussion of the three varieties of democratic revolution (bourgeois, petty bourgeois, proletarian), see Larsson, 1970: 31–49, 58–60, 125–7; Hunt, 1974: Chapters 6–7; Draper, 1978: 27, 169–288, 317, 358–452; Gilbert, 1981: Chapters 2, 4, 7–12; Hundt, 1987; Hundt, 1993: section II; Hobsbawm, 2011: 63–9.
18 Löwy (1981: Chapter 1) and Day and Gaido (2009: introduction) suggest that, with Marx and Engels, permanent revolution did refer to such a democratic-socialist workers' revolution. Löwy (1981: 3) discovers 'different threads of theory – "stagist" and "permanentist"' in Marx and Engels. In my opinion this is confusing: the permanent revolution represents a particular form of stagism.
19 See for example 'Revue' (Marx and Engels, 1850) (*MEW*, vol. 7: 446).
20 See for example 22 September 1882 letter to Bernstein (ibid.: vol. 35: 366); 27 August 1883 letter to Bernstein (vol. 36: 54–5); 6 June 1884 to August Bebel (ibid.: 159–60); 11 December 1884 to Bebel (ibid.: 252); 25 October 1885 to Bebel (ibid.: 379); 'Zur Geschichte des Bundes de Kommunisten' (October 1885), vol. 21: 220; 'Die künftige italienische Revolution und die Sozialistische Partei' (January 1894), vol. 22: 439–42.
21 'Deutsche Zustände' (1846) (ibid.: vol. 2: 580). See also 'Die preussische Verfassung' (March 1847), vol. 4: 35; 'Grundsätze' (ibid.: 379). Also: 'Die moralisierende Kritik und die kritisierende Moral' (Marx, October 1847) (ibid.: 352).
22 See 'Grussadresse der deutschen demokratischen Kommunisten zu Brüssel an Herrn Feargus O'Connor' (Engels, with Marx, 1846) (ibid.: 24); 'Der Status quo in Deutschland' (1847) (ibid.: 42–4); 'Schutzzoll oder Freihandels-System' (June

1847) (ibid.: 60–1); 'Preussische Verfassung' (ibid.: 35); 'Revolution und Konterrevolution in Deutschland' (written by Engels in 1851–2, but published under Marx's name), vol. 8: 8–11, 42; 12 April 1853 Engels to Weydemeyer (vol. 28: 579–80). References to national independence as precondition for the proletarian revolution are to be found in the last two references. See for that point also Engels to Marx 25 July 1866 (vol. 31: 240–1); Marx to Engels 27 July 1866 (ibid.: 243); Engels to Kautsky 7 February 1882 (vol. 35: 269).
23 'Die Bewegungen von 1847' (January 1848) (ibid.: vol. 4: 500, 502).
24 Ibid.: 368.
25 See for example 'Manifest' (ibid.: 468); 'Revolution und Konterrevolution' (vol. 8: 8–11); 'Die preussische Militärfrage und die deutsche Arbeiterpartei' (Engels, 1865), vol. 16: 66–71. See also 'Marx und die "Neue Rheinische Zeitung"' (vol. 21: 17–20). In 1870 Engels added to this that, in every country there comes a 'turning point' when the bourgeoisie notices that its 'proletarian double' is even *outpacing* it. From that moment on the bourgeoisie no longer even wants to seize power. In Germany, the year 1848 had marked that moment: preface to 'Der deutsche Bauernkrieg' (written summer 1850), vol. 7: 534–5. See also Draper, 1978: 227–8.
26 Hobsbawm, 1975: Chapter 6.
27 For Marx on this pattern, see 'Der achtzehnte Brumaire des Louis Bonaparte' (written December 1851–March 1852) (*MEW*, vol. 8: 135).
28 Ibid.: vol. 4: 472.
29 Even in the *German Ideology* they stated that it was not impossible for minority proletariats to make revolution: 'Deutsche Ideologie' (ibid.: vol. 3: 73).
30 See for example: 'Umrisse zu einer Kritik der Nationalökonomie' (Engels, 1843–4) (ibid.: vol. 1: 522–3); 'Die Lage der arbeitenden Klasse in England. Nach eigner Anschauung und authentischer Quellen' (Engels, 1845), vol. 2: 232–3; first Elberfeld speech (ibid.: 536–7); 'Kommunismus in Deutschland' (Engels, May 1845) (ibid.: 517); 'Manifest' (vol. 4: 463); see for example: the first volume of 'Das Kapital' (vol. 23: 789–91); 'Anti-Dühring' (vol. 20: 136–40, 249–65); 'Ludwig Feuerbach' (vol. 21: 300).
31 In 1860 Marx identified 'the first precondition of a proletarian revolution' as the presence of 'an *industrial proletariat* on a national scale [*Stufenleiter*]': 'Herr Vogt' (*MEW*, vol. 14: 450). In his 1874 and 1875 comments on Mikhail Bakunin's *Statehood and Anarchy*, Marx observed that a proletarian revolution was only possible in countries, where the industrial workers occupied 'at least an important position among the popular mass' (vol. 18: 632–3). Gilbert (1981: 219) bluntly observes that Marx 'never argued that the triumph of socialism in any particular country required that the proletariat be a majority (as opposed to a sizable portion) of the population'. See also Hobsbawm, 2011: 62.
32 Preface to his study of the German Peasants' War (*MEW*, vol. 7: 535–7).
33 First edition of 'Achtzehnte Brumaire' (1852) (ibid.: vol. 8: 204).
34 Marx to Engels, 16 April 1856 (ibid.: vol. 29: 47).
35 Comments on *Statehood and Anarchy* (ibid.: vol. 18: 632–3).
36 'Kritik des Gothaer Programms' (ibid.: vol. 19: 23).
37 See for example 'Klassenkämpfe in Frankreich' (ibid.: vol. 7: 21, 84, 87–8); 'Achtzehnte Brumaire' (vol. 8: 201–2); Marx to Engels, 16 April 1856 (vol. 29: 47); First draft of 'Der Bürgerkrieg in Frankreich' (Marx, 1871), vol. 17: 549, 551–3; 'Bürgerkrieg in Frankreich' (1871) (ibid.: 341–4); 'Die Bauernfrage in Frankreich und Deutschland' (Engels, 1894–95), vol. 22: 486, 498–500. For an analysis of the agrarian question in the German and international social democracy, see Lehmann, 1970. In the 1880s Engels suggested that the conditions for proletarian revolution were even better in semi-industrialised countries than in the most developed ones: the socialist orientation of the British workers was weak because they profited from the imperialist hegemony of their own country. See for example

Permanent revolution 73

12 September 1882 letter to Kautsky (vol. 35: 357); 30 August 1883 letter to Bebel (vol. 36: 58). There had emerged an 'aristocracy' within the British working class: 'England 1845 und 1885' (written February 1885) (vol. 21: 194–7).

38 See for example introduction to 'Zur Kritik der hegelschen Rechtsphilosophie' (ibid.: vol. 1: 380–91); 'Umrisse' (ibid.: 522–3); first Elberfeld speech (vol. 2: 536–7); Marx's 1845 List critique (*CW*, 1975, vol. 4: 265–6, 274, 281–3); Engels to Marx December 1846 (*MEW*, vol. 27: 71); 'Status quo' (vol. 4: 42–6, 49–51, 56); 'Moralisierende Kritik' (ibid.: 341–2); 'Drei neue Konstitutionen' (Engels, February 1848) (ibid.: 517–18); 'Die Bourgeoisie und die Kontrerevolution' (Marx, December 1848), vol. 6: 104–11; 'Der Prozess gegen den Rheinischen Kreisausschuss der Demokraten' (Marx, February 1849) (ibid.: 244, 252–3); 'Die deutsche Reichsverfassungskampagne' (Engels, 1850), vol. 7: 117; 'Lage der arbeitenden Klasse' (vol. 2: 232–3, 242, 250, 306); 'Revolution und Konterrevolution' (vol. 8: 8–11); 12 April 1853 Engels to Weydemeyer (vol. 28: 579–80).

39 For German legal and socio-economic development in the first half of the nineteenth century, see Kemp, 1969: Chapter 4; Tilly, 1991; Crouzet, 2001: 121–6; Tipton, 2003a.

40 See for example 'Grundsätze' (*MEW*, vol. 4: 372–5); 'Manifest' (ibid.: 481). See also some later texts: 'Zur Wohnungsfrage' (Engels, 1873), vol. 18: 220–1, 243; Marx's 1875 comments on the Gotha programma (vol. 19: 21); 'Karl Marx' (Engels, June 1877) (ibid.: 104). According to Larsson (1970: 30–1), all this prefigured the Bolshevik industrialisation drive. See also Draper, 1978: 238. Engels suggested in an 8 November 1884 letter to Kautsky (*MEW*, vol. 36: 230–1) that the revolutionary perspectives in Germany were *better* than in Britain precisely because the country's capitalism had not yet fully crystallised.

41 In 1859 Marx famously explained that an 'epoch of revolution' begins when the relations of production turn into a fetter on the productive forces. 'No social formation is ever destroyed before all the productive forces for which it is sufficient have been developed' (preface to 'Zur Kritik der politische Ökonomie', *MEW*, vol. 13: 9). But he added that the material preconditions of the new system need merely be 'in the process of formation'. See also Gilbert, 1981: 6. In Engels's writings we find similar nuances. See for example: 'Anti-Dühring' (*MEW*, vol. 20: 138–9, 249). For another exposé on the conflict between productive forces and relations of production, see also 'Deutsche Ideologie' (vol. 3: 69, 73).

42 1895 introduction to 'Klassenkämpfe in Frankreich' (ibid.: vol. 22: 515, emphasis added).

43 Ibid.

44 See for example Engels's first Elberfeld speech (ibid.: vol. 2: 537–8); Marx to P. V. Annenkov, 28 December 1846 (vol. 27: 455); 'Grundsätze' (vol. 4: 369–70); 'Manifest' (ibid.: 467–8); 'Lohnarbeit und Kapital' (vol. 6: 423); 'Anti-Dühring' (vol. 20: 257–8); 'Karl Marx' (vol. 19: 104); 1891 edition of Engels's 'Die Entwicklung des Sozialismus von der Utopie zur Wissenschaft' (written in 1880) (ibid.: 227); 'Ludwig Feuerbach' (vol. 21: 300); 'Die Trade-Unions' (Engels, May 1881), vol. 19: 256. See for this question also Hundt, 1993: 393–4.

45 See for example Plamenatz, 1954: 133–5, 217; Lichtheim, 1961: 122–9; Avineri, 1968: 196–201; Plamenatz, 1992: 278–93. See also Szporluk, 1988: part 1, esp. p. 31; also pp. 169–92. For a critique of Lichtheim's position that Marx's 1850 writings represented a temporary aberration, see Löwy, 2003: 150.

46 See 'Enthüllungen über den Kommunisten-Prozess zu Köln' (Marx, 1853) (*MEW*, vol. 8: 412).

47 'Deutsche Bauernkrieg' (ibid.: vol. 7: 400–1, 412).

48 'Revolution und Konterrevolution' (ibid.: vol. 8: 8–11). In his 'Der Kommunisten-Prozess zu Köln' (December 1852), Engels confirmed that the seizure of power of the petty bourgeois democrats would trigger the proletarian revolution (ibid.: 399).

74 *Permanent revolution*

49 See 'Enthüllungen' (ibid.: 461); Engels to Wydemeyer, 12 April 1853 (vol. 28: 579–80).
50 See for this interpretation also Hunt, 1974: 244, 254–5.
51 See for example: 'Die wirklichen Ursachen der verhältnismässigen Inaktivität der französischen Proletarier im vergangenen Dezember' (Engels, February 1852) (*MEW*, vol. 8: 228); 'Die Aussichten in Frankreich und England' (Marx, April 1855), vol. 11: 182; Marx to Engels, 8 October 1858 (vol. 29: 360); Marx's 28 February 1867 speech to German workers in London (vol. 16: 524); Engels to Marx 5 November 1867 (vol. 31: 378). See also Hobsbawm, 2011: 65–6, 76–9. For the view that from late 1850 onwards Marx and Engels began to lose faith in proletarian revolution in countries without developed capitalism, see Hundt, 1993: 646.
52 See for example Szporluk, 1988: 176.
53 *MEW*, vol. 23: 12, 15–16. For a nuanced interpretation of this passage, see also Davidson, 2012: 179–80.

6 Marxist patriotism

In this chapter, we will discover that Marx and Engels not only wanted Germany to turn to communism *despite* its backwardness, but also *because of it*: as German patriots they hoped that the introduction of communism would help their country to overcome its backward condition.

Many earlier communists had recommended communism for the good it would do the fatherland. Communists from Campanella to Weitling had been arguing that community of goods would spawn fantastic military prowess. Winstanley and Restif even promised predominant world power to the first country to embrace the new order. This kind of thinking was not entirely alien to Marx and Engels. In early 1850, for example, they asserted that the only chance for the 'European civilised countries' to secure their industrial 'superiority' over the rest of the world lay in a 'social revolution' that would open the way for the development of new productive forces.[1] But this reflected a west European rather than a narrow German orientation. Marx and Engels never recommended communism to make Germany master of the world.

With Marx and Engels the focus of communist patriotism shifted from military prowess and world power to national development. Marxist communism promised liberation to all of humanity. In that sense there was nothing German about it: the German interest would have to remain subordinated to the interests of the international working class at all times. Even so, Marxism was never a pure internationalist utopia. The other, patriotic motive just can't be missed. Marx and Engels were deeply troubled by their country's backwardness. They were obsessed with the question of how to put an end to this embarrassing state of affairs. They thought capitalism had run out of steam and was no longer of any help. That is where communism, the wave of the future, came in: the superior order that promised Germany healthy national development and restoration to honour and prestige.

Resurrection of Germany

Marx and Engels's early writings reflect this patriotic motive most forcefully. In a letter he wrote to his friend Arnold Ruge in March 1843, on his way to the Netherlands, Marx confessed to feeling 'shame for our country [*Nationalscham*]':

'Even the most insignificant Dutchman is a citizen [*ein Staatsbürger*] compared to the greatest German.' Germany's *false* patriotism was unbearable to Marx. And to those who told him that shame doesn't make a revolution, he answered:

> Shame is already a revolution ... Shame is a kind of anger turned inwards. And if a whole nation really experienced a sense of shame, it would be like a lion, crouching ready to spring.[2]

This early work suggests that the young Marx's desire for revolution in Germany in part arose out of disgust for the deplorable situation in which his country, a provincial backwater compared to Britain, found itself, and for which he, *as a German*, felt deeply embarrassed.

Marx's introduction of his critique of Hegel's philosophy of right, written late in 1843 and in January 1844, elaborates on this theme. It was in this text that Marx announced his discovery of the proletariat as the carrier of the revolution. He observed that Germany was far behind the 'modern peoples'. Once again, the backwardness of his fatherland, the 'German mess [*Zustände*]', aroused enormous '*indignation*' in him.[3] Marx asserted that only a 'radical German revolution' aiming for 'general human emancipation' could lift the country from its misery.[4] He trusted only the proletariat to bring about 'the emancipation of the *German* into a *human being*' and the 'liberation of Germany'. The '*day of Germany's resurrection*' would be triggered by the 'crowing of the Gallic cock', i.e. by revolution in Paris.[5]

The importance of this text for understanding Marx's road to communism can hardly be overestimated. To be sure, far from being specifically tied to Germany, communism represented humankind's collective project. But the communist revolution would *also* serve to put an end to the state of shameful degradation of Marx's fatherland and to bring about its resurrection.[6]

In his March 1845 draft of an article of Friedrich List's book *The National System of Political Economy*, Marx once again poured scorn on empty, dirty, shallow bourgeois Germany. He argued that Germany's backwardness could never be overcome through a capitalist economy behind protective walls. Only through the abolition of capitalism (which Marx calls either 'industry' or 'competition' in this article) things could improve for Germany. Once again Marx identified with Germany, whose depressed and backward state he hoped communism would put an end to:

> England dominates us because industry dominates us. We can free ourselves from England abroad only if we free ourselves from industry at home. We shall be able to put an end to England's domination in the sphere of competition only if we overcome competition within our borders.[7]

Once again, Marx assigned a double meaning to communism. It would serve to liberate humanity as a whole and liberate Germany from British economic domination.[8]

Engels was no less hurt than his friend about the 'despicableness, dull tedium and filthiness of the German society'. He too despised the 'fragmentation [*Zerlumpung*] of Germany in thirty-eight local and provincial states', which made the country powerless.[9] In February 1848, Engels wrote that Germany was a country where people could only sleep and babble: the 'mockery of all Europe'. But the day would come when not the bourgeoisie but the workers would rise up and 'put an end to the whole dirty, confused official German economy and restore German honour through a radical revolution'.[10] And this is how Engels commented on the February 1848 revolutionary events in Paris:

> Hopefully Germany will follow. Now or never she will lift herself up from her humiliation. When the Germans possess any energy, any pride, any courage, within four weeks we too can cry out: '*Long live the German republic!*'[11]

All this is not to deny that communist internationalism remained Marx and Engels overriding drive. But neither can it be denied that they identified with their fatherland, that their feeling of hurt was quite intense, and that one of the reasons for setting their hopes on communism lay in its alleged function in restoring Germany to life.

Great nations

Marx and Engels were never German patriots in a narrow, exclusive sense. In their eyes, other nations too were deserving of modern development and of being restored to greatness: the communist mode of production possessed a superiority that was bound to reinvigorate any country that embraced it. In his comments on the 1871 Paris Commune, which he and Engels regarded as a proletarian dictatorship, Marx displayed the same patriotic orientation that he had earlier displayed in relation to his own fatherland – but this time France was its object. The Communal revolution, Marx wrote, served to save France and to allow its national 'rebirth'.[12]

On this occasion Marx classically formulated the dual function of communism, characterising the Commune as the 'brave champion of the liberation of labour and in the full sense of the word international' *and* as the 'true representative of all healthy elements of French society, hence veritably the national government'.[13]

Yet, not all nations aspiring to development and greatness could count on Marx and Engels's sympathies. They believed that some nations did not possess the potential of development, which made it a waste of time and even harmful to support their ambitions. Engels was particularly adamant that only 'great' not small nations deserved their own independent states.[14] If the modern economy depended on a large population and a compact territory, then there was no conceivable role for the many tiny nationalities scattered

78 *Marxist patriotism*

over Europe.[15] Whereas the Germans, Poles, Italians and Hungarians deserved to have states of their own, the various South Slav peoples did not. These latter peoples would have to allow themselves to be assimilated in the great nations.[16]

Marx paid less attention to this matter, but that he allowed one of Engels's main articles arguing this point to be published under his own name suggests that he agreed.[17] The two men were indebted to Hegel's distinction between 'historical' nations, the vehicles of civilisation and progress, and the 'history-less' nations that merely hindered humanity's forward march.[18] This was not only a matter of demographic and economic potential. Marx and Engels's works are rife with references to national character. The guiding idea seems to have been that some nations were endowed with a *Lebenskraft*, life force or vitality, that others lacked.[19] Marx and Engels were chauvinists of the great nations. These were the nations they called 'civilised', and which expressed their assessment that they had the potential of developing the modern productive forces and of helping humankind on the way to the bright future.

Communism and the nation

All this, however, begs the question of why the development and resurrection of the fatherland – German, French or any other – would have had any significance for devoted communists in the first place. What would be the point? Wouldn't nations, the great no less than the small, merge and disappear under communism anyhow?

Marx and Engels initially indeed assumed the stance that the proletarian class was opposed to the national principle as such, and that global communism signified full assimilation of nations [*Nationen*] and nationalities [*Nationalitäten*] into a single world community.[20] But the latest instance that I found for either of them to express this view was in *The German Ideology* in 1846.

Marx and Engels seem to have sensed that they were in danger of overshooting the mark. The Communist Manifesto was already much less ambitious, in predicting only the disappearance of the 'mutual isolation of nations and the contradictions between peoples [*nationalen Absonderungen und Gegensätze der Völker*]', as well as of the 'hostile stance of the nations'.[21] The revolution would even help the proletariat to constitute itself as the nation. Engels mentioned the ideal of the 'fraternisation of nations', a principle he derived from the French Revolution and which surely did not entail the erasure of national identity.[22] As we saw in a previous chapter, Engels imagined a confederation of independent proletarian nation-states.[23]

According to Engels, it was the historical merit of the bourgeoisie to have centralised the fragmented feudal world into modern nations. Healthy development of the productive forces required national centralisation. Concentration of the means of production in the hands of the nation (nationalisation) would allow the proletariat to take this process one step further. In Engels's view, the proletariat needed the nation as a civilising institution and as indispensable instrument to speed up economic development.[24] Marx agreed that the principle of 'unity of the nation' served as a 'powerful factor of social production' among 'great peoples'. The proletarian state should strengthen rather than discard it.[25]

Marx and Engels were no theorists living in an ivory tower. Far from operating in a vacuum, they were part of an existing milieu of the revolutionary left. In the mid-nineteenth century the default mode of the internationalist left was to fight for the restoration of politically subjected and fragmented nations. What Peter Alter calls 'Risorgimento Nationalism' was inherited from the French Revolution. Nationalists of the Mazzini type 'justified their nationalism in terms of their mission to propagate the universal human ideals of liberty, equality and fraternity throughout Europe'. Their goal was a 'world order founded upon the plurality of free nations'.[26] Marx and Engels's view of a communist world of nations was adapted to this type of Risorgimento nationalism, which was so popular among the European radical left. The reason why they wanted communism to breathe new life into the great, historic nations is, then, that they regarded these nations as indispensable building blocks of the new world.

Notes

1 'Revue', *MEW*, vol. 7: 221.
2 Ibid.: vol. 1: 337.
3 Ibid.: 379–81.
4 Ibid.: 386, 388.
5 Ibid.: 388–91.
6 Robbie Shiliam (2006) argues that it was Marx's awareness of Germany's backwardness that led him to the discovery of the proletariat in the first place, as the class that would help Germany break out of its backwardness.
7 *CW*, vol. 4: 283.
8 In his discussion of the introduction to the critique of Hegel's philosophy of right and of the List critique, Szporluk (1988: Chapters 2 and 3) argues that Marx 'did not believe in a specifically *German* solution of the German problem' (p. 23). Szporluk refers to Marx's rejection of a national capitalist road for Germany and to his identification of communism with general human emancipation. However, the fact that Marx regarded communism as a worldwide, not exclusively German, solution does not alter the fact that it *also* represented a specific solution for Germany. Communism would lift that country from its backwardness and restore the balance with Britain.
9 'Status quo', *MEW*, vol. 4: 50.
10 'Drei neue Konstitutionen' (ibid.: 517–18). Compare: 'Kritische Randglossen zu dem Artikel "Der König von Preussen und die Sozialreform. Von einem Preussen"' (Marx, 10 August 1844) (ibid.: vol. 1: 405).
11 'Revolution in Paris' (27 February 1848) (ibid.: vol. 4: 530).
12 'Bürgerkrieg in Frankreich' (ibid.: vol. 17: 330). In the first draft, Marx wrote that the French ruling classes were turning the country into a 'corpse' and that proletarian government was 'in the first place' necessary 'to save France from ruin': 'the conditions of this emancipation [of the working class] are at the same time the conditions for the rejuvenation [*Erneuerung*] of France' (ibid.: 507, 516, 537, 558).
13 Ibid.: 346.

80 *Marxist patriotism*

14 See for example 'Was hat die Arbeiterklasse mit Polen zu tun?' (ibid.: vol. 16: 156–8); 'Po und Rhein' (1859), vol. 13: 267.
15 See for this point 'Revolution und Konterrevolution' (ibid.: vol. 8: 81).
16 See mainly 'Magyarische Kampf' (ibid.: vol. 6: 165–76); 'Demokratische Panslawismus' (15 February 1849, Engels) (ibid.: 270–86); 'Revolution und Konterrevolution' (ibid.: vol. 8: 49–56, 80–4). In his 9 June 1847 draft of a communist 'confession of faith', Engels asserted that the 'nationalities of the peoples who join together according to the principle of community' will merge with another. He was probably referring here to the process of assimilation of national minorities in the great nations (*CW*, vol. 25: 103).
17 'Revolution und Konterrevolution' (*MEW*, vol. 8: 3–108).
18 For Engels's reference to Hegel, see 'Magyarische Kampf' (ibid.: vol. 6: 172). For discussions of the question of (un)historic nations in Marx and Engels, see Herod, 1976: Chapter 1; Rosdolsky, 1986; Cummins, 1980: 37–46; Munck, 1986: Chapter 1; Walicki, 1995: 152–67.
19 For a selection of texts, mainly from Marx and Engels's early writings, with comments on national character, see 'Fortschritte der Sozialreform' (*MEW*, vol. 1: 480–1, 495); 'Zur Judenfrage' (ibid.: 375); 'Kritische Randglossen' (ibid.: 405); 11 August 1844 Marx to Ludwig Feuerbach (vol. 27: 426); 'Lage Englands' (vol. 1: 552–4); 'Deutsche Ideologie' (vol. 3: 73); Engels, 20 February 1846 letter to *Northern Star* (vol. 2: 580); Engels to Marx December 1846 (vol. 27: 71–2); 'Der dänisch–preussische Waffenstilstand' (Engels, 26 August 1848), vol. 5: 394–5; 'Magyarische kampf' (vol. 6: 165–76); 'Demokratische Panslawismus' (ibid.: 270–86); 23 May 1851 Engels to Marx (vol. 27: 266–8); 'Revolution und Konterrevolution', 49–56, 80–4; 'Britische Politik – Disraeli – Die Flüchtlinge – Mazzini in London – Türkei' (Marx/Engels, 7 April 1853), vol. 9: 7–10; 'Was hat die Arbeiterklasse mit Polen zu tun?' (vol. 16: 156–8); 'Die Geschichte Irlands' (Engels, written May–July 1870) (ibid.: 498); 1892 foreword to Polish edition of *Communist Manifesto* (vol. 4: 588). In 'Die deutsche Ideologie', Marx and Engels observed that states were based on family and tribal ties, 'flesh and blood' and language, as well as on class (vol. 3: 33).
20 See for example introduction to 'Lage der arbeitenden Klasse' (ibid.: vol. 2: 430–1; Marx on List (*CW*, vol. 4: 280–1); 'Fest der Nationen' (*MEW*, vol. 2: 614); 'Deutsche Ideologie' (vol. 3: 60, 70).
21 *MEW*, vol. 4: 479. Also in place of 'the old local and national self-sufficiency and secludedness' and 'national onesidedness and narrowness' would come an 'all round dependence of the nations on each other'. In literature, 'the many national and local literatures' would make room for 'one world literature' (p. 466). This latter phrase did suggest complete erasure of nations. Erica Benner (1995: Chapter 1; esp. pp. 42–3) argues that Marx and Engels distinguished between *Nation* and *Nationalität*. The latter term supposedly referred to the negative aspect of the nation, i.e. its self-assertion against other nations, rather than to its intrinsic unifying characteristics. Benner asserts that Marx and Engels expected 'nationality' not the 'nation' to disappear under communism. However, in my reading of Marx and Engels, they used these terms differently: sometimes simply interchangeably; sometimes nationality referred to the cultural identity of a nation. In Engels's 1866 'Was hat die Arbeiterklasse mit Polen zu tun?' *Nation* referred to the great and *Nationalität* to the small nations.
22 'Fest der Nationen' (*MEW*, vol. 2: 611, 614). See also 'Weltgesellschaft' (vol. 7: 553) on 'the principle of republican fraternity' that 'makes all national fences [*Schranken*] disappear'.
23 At the danger of oversimplification, three approaches on Marx, Engels and the nation can be distinguished in the scholarly literature. Some authors accept that they were inter-nationalists rather than cosmopolitans and that they saw an

important role for the nation-state: Bloom, 1941; Davis, 1967: 6–82; Cummins, 1980; Zwick, 1983: 20–3; Avineri, 1991; Nimni, 1991: 18–22; Benner, 1995. Mikhail Agursky (1987), with whom the Marxism of Marx and Engels tends to collapse into German chauvinism, represents an extreme case of this approach. Agursky has similar, in my view one-sided ideas about Lenin and Stalin as Russian chauvinists. Felix (1983), Munck (1986: Chapter 1), Nimtz (2000), and Kasprzak (2012) acknowledge that Marx accepted an important role for the struggle of nations as *Realpolitiker*. According to yet others, Marx and Engels fundamentally rejected national and patriotic principles as 'false consciousness' and merely superstructural phenomena, even though pragmatically adopting national elements in their later years (Connor, 1984: Chapter 1; Pelczynski, 1984; Szporluk, 1988: Chapters 2–5, 11).
24 See for example 'Grundsätze' (*MEW*, vol. 4: 373–4); 'Schweizer Bürgerkrieg' (ibid.: 396–7); 'Der demokratische Panslawismus' (vol. 6: 279); 'Deutsche Bauernkrieg' (vol. 7: 329, 411); 'Revolution und Konterrevolution' (vol. 8: 13, 48, 57–8).
25 'Bürgerkrieg in Frankreich' (ibid.: vol. 17: 340–1). See also 'Manifest' (vol. 4: 481); March 1850 address to Communist League (vol. 7: 252).
26 Alter, 1996: 19–23.

Part III
The socialist movement

7 Socialism as trading company

When the revolution in Central Europe proved unable to maintain itself, Marx moved to London, where he arrived in May 1849. To maintain his family he engaged in journalism. He was mostly occupied in the library of the British Museum for his study of the economics of capitalism. Engels returned to Manchester and the family firm in November 1849. Moving to Britain represented a turning point for both men. They would never move back to the continent. But Marx and Engels did not turn their backs on developments in Germany. For the rest of their lives, they would act as long-distance advisers to the socialist movement in their fatherland.

Marx and Engels were highly respected in the German party, but not everybody accepted the views about the conditions of communism that the two prophets residing in Great Britain had on offer. The idea that socialism required the joint efforts of a number of advanced countries was accepted by the German party, but important socialist theoreticians opted for an alternative model of socialism in one country.

Socialism in one country

The revolution was followed by an 'age of reaction'.[1] The League of Communists, an international not exclusively German party, was dissolved in 1852. It took more than a decade before anybody considered the establishment of a new workers' party. The towering figure in socialist Germany was Ferdinand Lassalle, a man from the circle of acquaintances of Marx and Engels but with a strong mind of his own. The year before he died, in 1863, he founded the General German Workers' Association (ADAV). The 'state socialist' Lassalle hoped to bring an end to the system of private property of the means of production through the establishment of workers' associations with the support of the existing state, so as to outcompete private firms.[2]

From the 1860s onwards those aiming for community of goods began to call themselves socialists or social democrats. In 1869 August Bebel and Wilhelm Liebknecht established the Social Democratic Workers' Party (SDAP) at Eisenach. In 1875 the two parties fused at a congress at Gotha to form the Socialist Workers' Party of Germany (SAPD).

These parties were unsure in their ideological orientation. Bebel and Liebknecht were personally close to Marx, but Lassalle's ideological influence remained equally strong.[3] The SAPD was no Marxist party. The later staunch Marxists Bebel, Liebknecht, Kautsky and Eduard Bernstein did not yet exclusively commit themselves to one line of socialist thinking. In this period of ideological eclecticism, party leaders were eagerly looking for figures of authority to clarify the new socialist doctrines for them. Next to Marx and Engels, particularly influential were the deceased Lassalle and independent socialist thinkers such as Eugen Dühring, Karl Rodbertus and Albert Schäffle.[4]

These other socialists found the idea of single-country socialism particularly appealing. Even though their arguments were obviously inspired by German patriotism, they were no narrow-minded economic nationalists: the world market was just as central in their works as with Marx and Engels. Where they differed from the latter is that they expected the superior socialist economic system to provide the isolated socialist state with predominant influence on the world market: the most powerful 'artillery' would be at the disposal of the single socialist state. As they saw it, history would reward the courageous country, preferably Germany, that made the socialist transition first. The triumphalist argument about the economic superiority of socialism, first formulated two hundred years earlier by Winstanley, returned in a new form adapted to capitalist globalisation. The 1860s and 1870s were the heydays of liberal free trade.

Lassalle expounded his thoughts on the international position of the socialist state most clearly in his last work *Mr. Bastiat-Schulze von Delitzsch* (1864). His belief that the socialist system would be a triumph of efficiency, led him to the following spectacular conclusion:

> The world market belongs to *that* nation that first decides to embark on the introduction of this social transformation on a grand scale. It will be the deserved reward for its energy and decisiveness. Because of the cheapness of concentrated production, the nation taking the lead will occupy an even more *superior* position compared to the capitalists of the other nations than *England* has occupied for so long towards the continental nations.[5]

Lassalle hoped that the introduction of socialism might allow a unified Germany to break capitalist Britain's economic dominance on the world market.

The idiosyncratic and blind professor Dühring was very popular in the SDAP and SAPD until Engels's Anti-Dühring brought his influence to an abrupt end. In his 1873 *Course of National and Social Economy*, Dühring explained that the nation that would introduce socialism first would have to defend itself arms in hand against the hostile capitalist powers, in the style of revolutionary France. Dühring also repeated after Lassalle that, with its superior economic system, the country would be able to outcompete its rivals.

It could therefore do without protective tariffs.[6] The views of the economist and political scientist Schäffle changed over the years, but during the 1870s he can best be regarded as a fellow-traveller of socialism. In the 1878 third volume of his *Construction and Life of the Social Body*, Schäffle noted that the differences in developmental levels made the simultaneous establishment of socialism in all countries impossible. Production at low cost would make the socialist state a strong player on the international market.[7]

Bebel versus Vollmar

As mentioned above, during the 1860s and 1870s, ideological preferences among party leaders remained divided over Marx and Engels on one hand and Dühring, Rodbertus and others on the other. But in September 1866 the first congress of the International Workingmen's Association (IWA) adopted rules written by Marx two years earlier. The rules classically defined the emancipation of the working class as 'neither a local nor a national, but a social problem, embracing all countries in which modern society exists, and depending for its solution on the concurrence, practical and theoretical, of the most advanced countries'.[8] The crucial point in this internationalist formula is that communism was predicated not only on the cooperation of workers' movements but on the combined efforts of the most advanced *countries*. Logically, this ruled out socialism in one country. The formula was also adopted by the 1869 founding congress of the SDAP.[9]

The party programmes did not rule out the establishment of a communist society in one country in so many words. The matter was treated neither in the programmatic documents adopted by the ADAV in 1865 and 1866, nor in the Eisenach programme.[10] Ironically, it was the Lassalleans that came closest to explicitly embracing the Marxist position. In May 1867 they decided that, since the situation of the working class was essentially the same in all civilised countries, it could 'not lastingly [*nachhaltig*] be changed for the better in one single country'.[11]

Bebel was the single most important SDAP leader to confirm the Marxist interpretation. August Bebel was born in 1840. He was a turner by trade. The first major socialist influence on him was Lassalle, but in the course of the years he became more attracted to Marx.[12] In his authoritative *Our Goals* (1871), he argued that a socialist state could only be organised on an international basis, because capitalism was also organised internationally.[13]

In March 1874 the SDAP paper *Der Volksstaat* carried Bebel's review of Dühring's *Course*.[14] Bebel was very enthusiastic about the book, but objected to Dühring's confidence about the chances of survival of a single socialist state. Bebel could not vouch for it that there would be an *absolutely* 'simultaneous transition' of the 'most advanced European civilised states' to socialism, but he insisted that it would have to be as simultaneous as possible. There were two reasons for this. First, the main civilised states were at a 'more or less equal developmental stage'. What Germany and France missed in economic terms compared to Britain was made good by the strength of the socialist movement in these countries. Second, Bebel believed that a 'socialist state closing itself off from the other states, with the capacity to defend itself effectively' was 'unthinkable'. He was convinced that the capitalist states would see that state as an 'evil example' and a source of unrest, and that they would do everything in their power to destroy it.[15]

The SAPD programme adopted at the 1875 Gotha unification congress referred to the duties following from 'the international character of the workers' movement', but the solemn formula of the joint efforts of a number of countries was missing.[16] What is more, Bebel's views did not become accepted in the party across the board. Opponents let themselves be heard. The first, October 1877 issue of the SAPD's theoretical journal, *Die Zukunft*, carried an article probably written by editor Karl Höchberg, who defined the journal's mission as being to demonstrate, among other points, that 'a socialist commonwealth [*Gemeinwesen*] of some size could more easily survive in the face of any external power than another state'.[17] In the September 1878 issue, 'V'. (almost certainly the collaborator of the journal and Bavarian social democratic leader, Georg von Vollmar) announced that, in the coming issues, he would be discussing the question of what would happen when the social democrats came to power in Germany, and of whether an '*isolated* socialist state' could exist, as well as the problem of the conditions of trade of such a state with the non-socialist countries.[18] *Die Zukunft* was soon closed down, but Vollmar's pamphlet *The Isolated Socialist State* appeared in 1878. Höchberg's new *Jahrbuch für Sozialwissenschaft und Sozialpolitik* reprinted it in July 1879.[19] It was the single most important work to be published on the subject in the German socialist party.

According to Reinhard Jansen, at the time Vollmar was equally influenced by Marx and Engels, and by Lassalle and Dühring.[20] Georg von Vollmar was born in Munich in 1850 into a noble family. He received a strict Roman Catholic education and attended a gymnasium, but turned socialist. At the time of writing the pamphlet he was on the left wing of the party.[21]

Vollmar noted that he would be covering a problem that was 'almost completely disregarded' in the socialist press. If it treated the subject at all, the press suggested that 'the socialist transformation of society must occur simultaneously in the main countries of the civilised world', but Vollmar complained that this was never proved. On the contrary, he set out to prove '*not only that the final victory of socialism in at first only one single state or several states is historically more probable, but also that nothing would get in the way of the existence and prosperity of the isolated socialist state*'. According to Vollmar the complexity of the process of socialist transition ruled out its simultaneous occurrence in all major countries. Socialism might come about near simultaneously in two or three countries, for instance in France and Germany, but 'The victory of socialism in at first only *one* country is in any case the probable scenario'.[22]

Vollmar admitted that in the modern age nations were ever more connected economically, but that would constitute no problem because rationally planned production and a state monopoly on foreign trade would create 'the most favourable position conceivable on the world market'. The socialist state would be 'the *securest* trading company [*Handelsfirma*] in the world'. Otherwise put, 'our state has a much greater influence on the world market than [the world market] on it'.[23]

Bebel quickly responded to Vollmar's challenge. In his 1879 *Woman and Socialism*, which became one of the most influential compendia of the German socialist party's world-view,[24] he predicted that the revolutionary 'explosion' would spread 'in a flash' across the whole civilised world. The civilised nations would form a socialist 'great federation'. Socialism in one country was impossible, he argued, for the prosperity of separate nations depended on the '*global economy*'. As a consequence, the 'humane existence' could not be 'the exclusive way of life [*Daseinsweise*] of a single privileged people, who, however excellent they might be, can neither found nor maintain this condition in isolation [*isolirt*]'.[25] In choosing the word '*isolirt*' Bebel was obviously taking issue with Vollmar. That the two men were close allies on the radical left wing of the party might explain why he was unwilling to attack the latter openly.[26] Hereby the two positions on the issue in the party were defined.

Notes

1 Sperber, 2013: 291.
2 For Lassalle's biography and political thought, see Na'aman, 1970.
3 On ideological conditions in the SDAP, see Mehring, 1920: 515–16; Bernstein, 1928: 46, 52; Brill, 1954: 215–17; Mehring, 1976: 420.
4 See Mehring, 1920: 515–16; Brill, 1954: 215–17; Matthias, 1957: 155–9; Lidtke, 1964; Lidtke, 1966: 59–66, 155–75; Gustafsson, 1972: 29–30; Eckert, 1974: 45–51; Adamiak, 1974: 104–7; Mehring, 1976: 420; McLellan, 1979: 22–5; Steinberg, 1979: 11–40; Steenson, 1981: 189–225; Gilcher-Holtey, 1986: 35–43, 92–100; Carsten, 1993: 12.
5 Lassalle, 1878: 199. Lassalle (1919: 89–91) suggested in his 1859 *Der Italienische Krieg und die Aufgabe Preussens* that the inevitable military conflict between a proletarian state and the capitalist powers could never end in lasting coexistence. See also Ramm, 1953: Chapter 4, 180–93. The French socialist Louis Blanc (1841: 138–43; see also pp. 79–81, 85–6) argued in his 1840 *Organisation du travail* that socialism would have the international competitive advantage and would need no protective tariffs.
6 Dühring, 1892: 346, 385; see also Dühring, 1875: 325. For Dühring's biography, see Albrecht 1927; Adamiak, 1974.
7 Schäffle, 1878: 514–28. The 1874 *Die Quintessenz des Sozialismus* did not treat the question of socialism in one country but did refer to future trade of socialism with the remaining capitalist world (Schäffle, 1877: 38–9). On Schäffle's influence in the party, see Kautsky Jr., 1971: 13, 28–30; Mehring, 1904: 436; Schippel, 1905: 1009, 1011–13. The social-monarchist Rodbertus, who died in 1875, was influential in the party until the second half of the 1880s. For Rodbertus on Germany introducing socialism first, see Rodbertus-Jagetzow, 1899: 16, 19; see also Meyer, 1882: 31–2, 325.
8 Guillaume, 1905: 12–13, 57–8; see also *MEW*, vol. 16: 14–16.
9 Dlubek, Stepanova and Bach, 1964: 408–9. See also Schröder, 1910: 465; Steenson, 1981: 243. Some of the essential texts in which Marx and Engels argued against the possibility of socialism in one country remained unpublished. *Die deutsche*

Ideologie, in which the matter was discussed most fundamentally, was published only in 1932. Engels's *Grundsätze* were published only in 1914 (Bernstein, 1914). But enough of Marx and Engels had been published to leave no room for misunderstanding here.
10 On the ADAV, see Schröder, 1910: 460.
11 Ibid.: 462. A resolution adopted by the ADAV in August 1868 proclaimed the need for the workers of all civilised countries to act 'closely together [*einheitlich zusammenhangend*]' (ibid.: 209–10).
12 For Bebel's biography, see Maehl, 1980; Seebacher-Brandt, 1988; Schmidt, 2013.
13 Bebel, 1871: 13.
14 The anonymous article in two instalments, 'Ein neuer "Communist"', was written by Bebel. See *CW*, vol. 25: 647.
15 Anonymous, 1874.
16 Schröder, 1910: 468. In his unpublished, May 1875 critique of the Gotha programme, Marx pointed to the world market context of the national state (*MEW*, vol. 19: 23–4).
17 –g, 1877: 4–5.
18 V., 1878.
19 G.V., 1879.
20 Jansen, 1958: 16, 21–3, 88.
21 For Vollmar's biography, see Jansen, 1958; Carsten, 1990.
22 Vollmar, 1878: 4, 7–8.
23 Ibid.: 19, 21–2, 24.
24 See Maehl, 1980: 124.
25 Bebel, 1891: 345–8.
26 See Jansen, 1958: 25–30; Steenson, 1978: 46–59, 84.

8 Socialism as vast state

When we now move to the Russian Empire we find ourselves in a country where, measured against the standard of industrial capitalism, conditions were even more backward than in Germany. Russia's industrial development was more rudimentary, and 'feudal' principles carried much more weight. At the risk of oversimplification, the contrast between these two nations can be conceptualised as one between pre-capitalist and early-capitalist orders. In Russia, the relevant question for socialists was not of whether a small industrial proletariat might be able to seize power and hold onto it, but of whether the capitalist stage might be skipped altogether.

The first half of the nineteenth century saw some development of consumer-goods industries. The manufacturing of cotton cloth was a modern branch, but other branches were based on relatively primitive technologies. The Urals metallurgical industry established in the eighteenth century remained stagnant. Industrial workers mostly worked on a seasonal basis and remained tied to the village. Industries such as there were cannot be simply classified as capitalist: a substantial part of the workers were serfs, either under forced labour or those who had acquired revocable permission from their masters to engage in wage work.[1]

Russia was a society of estates, social categories that went with specific legal rights, duties and privileges. The population was mainly divided into nobles, clergy, merchants, townsmen and peasants. Most of the peasants were serfs, until tsar Aleksandr II's 1861 Emancipation liberated them from this kind of bondage. The estate system in many ways limited free competition and free enterprise. The peasants could not move freely at all. In the towns, business activities, commercial as well as those of a manufacturing nature, officially were monopolies of the guilds of merchants and townsmen. In practice, businesses were often set up by individuals from estates that did not have this prerogative – from nobles to serfs. Also, some of the monopolies were curtailed in the course of time, but, overall, legal restrictions on free enterprise remained in force. Russia continued to suffer under the kind of 'feudal' regime that the Stein–Hardenberg Reforms had put an end to in Germany.[2]

The peasants were not only in bondage to their masters but also to the village commune. The so-called *obshchina* was collectively responsible for payment of taxes. Individual peasants could not travel or move away from the village without the commune's permission. The commune also had a determining voice in what individual peasants sowed, as well as in how collective resources were used. At the same time, the institution of the commune provided the peasants with important collective advantages and was therefore not without its attractions for them. Commune land was not privately owned. In many regions of the country it was subject to periodic redistribution among commune members. This is why Russian socialists were able to project their fantasies onto this institution.[3]

Russian socialism

Russian socialism took shape in the 1840s, during the reign of Tsar Nikolai I. Russian socialists believed that the conditions in their own country represented a better launching pad for the communist transition than those prevailing in the West. In their imagination, Russia could make a direct transition to communism, while bypassing capitalism. No more was required than to transform the primitive communism of the village commune into modern associations. Russian socialists also tended to believe that capitalist development created new impediments for the social revolution, through the disintegration of the commune and the emergence of an industrial bourgeoisie that would serve as a mainstay of the absolutist order. If this analysis was correct, it was tempting to predict that Russia might become the first to turn to communism, in advance of the capitalist Western nations.

At this point in the chain of argumentation the question of socialism in one country could make an appearance. With one major exception, Petr Lavrov, Russian socialists showed no interest in elaborating theoretically on this idea. Yet, the notion of single-country socialism was implicit in their hopes that Russia might establish communism in advance of other countries.

Russian socialism was formulated first and foremost by Alexander Herzen, born in Moscow in 1812. He was the son of a Russian landowner; his mother was German. Herzen studied at Moscow University. In 1835 he was exiled to Viatka on charges of seditious activities. In 1847 he left the country, never to return. Herzen lived in France, Italy, Switzerland and Great Britain.[4]

Herzen turned to socialism during the 1840s and was the first to adopt the idea of the village commune as stepping stone to communism. The failure of the Paris workers' uprising in June 1848 and the consolidation of capitalist society in France made a tremendous impression on him. He concluded that the Western nations were corrupted by bourgeois individualism and weighed down by traditions. Herzen hoped that the young and vigorous Slav nations might become the torchbearers of socialism and steal a march on the West. Another important element in Herzen's thought was his rejection of the notion of fixed historical laws and of stages of development that all countries would have to pass through. However, the same aversion to determinism that allowed him to accept the possibility of Russia's skipping capitalism also prevented him from concluding that Russia's pioneering role in socialism was a historical certainty. With Herzen, all scenarios remained open.[5]

Herzen was preoccupied with the question of where the new order, which he mostly called socialism, would strike root first, but he refused to provide definite answers to this question. In December 1851 he observed that 'communism' was 'not attached to any particular country ... Who knows where it will celebrate its victory, at this side of the ocean or at the other? In France or in Russia, in New York or precisely in Paris?'[6]

Herzen discussed various possible scenarios in a number of works written during the first years of his emigration, before he moved to London in 1852. In the first scenario, Europe, which Herzen identified mainly with France, would be able to extricate itself from its state of decay through a workers' revolution. Should France be unable to accomplish this feat, one of the young nations – Herzen was thinking either of Russia or the United States – would have the honour of establishing the new order first.[7]

Herzen was always speculating about the question of which particular country would most likely enforce the breakthrough, and become the initiator-state, but he was not unaware of mutual dependencies. In 1851 he warned that the future of Russia 'was never so closely linked to the future of Europe as today' and that it would be very difficult for the Russian peasant to force 'communist institutions' onto Russia without the support of a socialist Europe.[8] But he did not rule out this eventuality, and if the Russians failed, there were always the Americans to be handed over the torch.

Herzen furthermore hoped that a future socialist Russia would extend the already vast territory of the country even further. In his 1851 *The Russian People and Socialism*, he observed that the Slavs formed 'one single race'. Herzen therefore proposed that Russia become the nucleus of a huge state, a 'Slav federation' knit together into an 'association of free autonomous peoples'.[9] The socialist superstate would be based on the commune, which institution Herzen believed was in good harmony with the European socialist principle.[10]

Russia meanwhile stumbled on unreformed, but the weak performance of its armies in the Crimean War proved that the country could not afford to postpone serious reform for much longer. The end of the war in 1856 more or less coincided with the ascension to the throne of Aleksandr II, who seemed willing to restructure the obsolete Russian order.[11] Aleksandr's major achievement was the abolition of serfdom in 1861.

The most renowned Russian socialist of the late 1850s and early 1860s was Nikolai Chernyshevskii, author of the inspirational 1863 novel What *Is to Be done?*[12] This socialist did not show much interest in the question that preoccupied Herzen, of which part of the world, Russia or the West, would cross the threshold to the new order first.[13] That Russia would be the trailblazer was, however, a main idea of some of the activists from Chernyshevskii's circle of close acquaintances.

In 1861, government measures aimed at increasing control over the student population triggered disturbances at the universities of Moscow, St Petersburg and Kazan. Unrest among the intelligentsia took the form of a campaign of proclamations. Among the most important manifestos was Nikolai Shelgunov and Mikhail Mikhailov's *To the Younger Generation* of September 1861.[14]

Shelgunov and Mikhailov were Chernyshevskii's acquaintances, but ideologically Herzen's Slavism remained much more of an influence on them.[15] *To the Younger Generation* reads like a caricature of Herzen. Aping Europe was the worst of all sins in Shelgunov and Mikhailov's eyes. Far from arguing, as Herzen did, that the new social order based on the *obshchina* represented a Russian variety of the socialist ideal held in common with Europe, the manifesto insisted that the communal order had nothing in common with any European ideals. In Shelgunov and Mikhailov's eyes, Russia was 'summoned to introduce a new principle into history ... rather than to pass on Europe's stale news'. It would quite simply be 'a new order, unknown even in America'.[16] In this way, Shelgunov and Mikhailov suggested not only that the Russians would be the socialist initiator-people, but that their fatherland was the only country where an authentic socialism could flourish at all.

Russian Jacobinism

Another important manifesto of the period, the May 1862 Young Russia, was written by Petr Zaichnevskii. Astrid von Borcke considers him to have been the founder of the Jacobin tendency of Russian socialism.[17] In the present context, Jacobinism can be loosely defined as the revolutionary elitism that stood opposed to the populism fathered by Herzen and Chernyshevskii, and which gave precedence to the peasant masses over the revolutionary elite.[18] The texts produced by their leading personalities (Zaichnevskii, Sergei Nechaev and Petr Tkachev) indicate that the 'Jacobins' too assumed that Russia would be the first country to establish socialism. Herzen's Slav federation found a particularly favourable reception among them.

Socialist Jacobinism emerged from the radical student movement. Young Russia served as platform for a circle established by Zaichnevskii in 1859.[19] His inspiration by the French Revolution and the Mazzinian connotations of the name of his platform suggest that Zaichnevskii saw the Russian revolution, in von Borcke's terms, as part of a 'pan-European phenomenon'.[20] Even so, Zaichnevskii predicted that his fatherland was 'destined to be the first to realise the great cause of socialism'.[21]

After the suppression of the Polish rebellion in 1863, radical students lost heart for some years, but by 1868–9 the student movement was again in the ascendant, with Tkachev and Nechaev in leading roles. The former had been at St Petersburg University from 1861 and was already an author of some renown. Nechaev was an obscure teacher of religion who began to attend physics classes at St Petersburg University in 1868. Early in 1869 he fled to Switzerland, where he contacted the famous anarchist Bakunin. Later that year Nechaev returned to Russia to organise his own group, People's Reprisal. After murdering one of the group's members, he once more fled the country, only to be arrested by the Swiss police in 1872. Nechaev was extradited and spent the rest of his life in a Russian prison. Tkachev moved to Switzerland in 1873 to become editor of Petr Lavrov's journal *Vpered!*. Soon, he moved on to establish his own journal, *Nabat*, in 1875.[22]

In their 'Programme of Revolutionary Actions', Nechaev and Tkachev generously recognised the need of cooperation with the European revolutionaries, but they suggested that the Russian revolution would come first: that they set a date for that revolution in early 1870 allows hardly any other interpretation. Nechaev and Tkachev calculated that the uprising in the 'central areas' might fail, but in that case there would be room for 'a separate war along the Volga and Dnepr and for the concealment of large masses of the *narod* in the forests'.[23]

During his second emigration, Nechaev reaffirmed the need of close cooperation with European revolutionaries. He even admitted that the social problem was an 'essentially international question' that could 'not be solved by one country in isolation'.[24] However, he reaffirmed his belief in Russia's priority in a programme he authored in 1872 for the Slav circle, which he had established together with the Polish Blanquist, Kasper Turski, in Switzerland.[25] Nechaev proudly claimed that 'in solving the social question in [Russia], we will at the same time contribute to the solution of the social question in all of Europe'. Brief as it is, this formula is extremely revealing. Far from making the establishment of a socialist society in Russia dependent on a social revolution in the West, Nechaev was making the opposite point: the establishment of a socialist society in Russia would come first and serve to make things easier for social revolutionaries in the West. Echoing Herzen, Nechaev furthermore referred to the revolutionary role of the 'great Slav race'. He indicated that 'the final construction [*okonchatel'noe ustroistvo*] of a social democratic republic' in Russia depended on the unification of all Slav nations into a 'mighty revolutionary Slav union'.[26]

As mentioned above, Nechaev was arrested and shipped back to Russia. In 1873 it was Tkachev's turn to emigrate. The latter had more of a theoretical mind than Nechaev, but he was no less impatient. Tkachev argued in 1874 that it was inadmissible to postpone the revolution in Russia any longer: 'Either *now* or a very long delay, or perhaps *never*!' His point was that the conditions for the social revolution were particularly favourable in Russia, but that this situation could not last: should capitalism get the chance to develop, the advantages of having the *obshchina* and of not having a bourgeoisie would be lost.[27]

In an open letter he wrote to Engels that same year Tkachev drew the logical conclusion that, for the time being, conditions for the social revolution were more favourable in Russia than in the capitalist West: 'chances for the victory of the revolution are better with us than with you'.[28] In this way Tkachev provided the thesis of Russia's probable pioneering role with a foundation.[29] Like Nechaev before him, Tkachev joined up with Turski in the Polish–Russian Slav Circle.[30]

96 *Socialism as vast state*

Lavrov

Socialism in one country was implicit in the hypothesis of a Russian pioneering role upheld by populist as well as Jacobin socialists. It was in Lavrov's work that the question obtained serious attention. It is to him that we will now turn.

In 1869, new student circles with a populist orientation were organised in St Petersburg, as a counterweight to Nechaev and Tkachev.[31] It is from this new populist milieu that the remarkable movement of the spring of 1874 sprang. Thousands of activists from an intelligentsia background went to the countryside to establish contact with the peasant masses. The activists failed to arouse the peasants' revolutionary instincts. Their failure triggered a desire for better organisation. In 1876 Russian socialists joined up in Land and Liberty.[32] Three years later the organisation split into the two factions: Black Repartition and People's Will, the latter of which succeeded in murdering Aleksandr II in 1881.[33] The ideologies of these groups combined elements of Bakunin's anarchism, Tkachev's Jacobinism, and the populism that was most eminently represented by Lavrov.

Petr Lavrov came from a noble milieu. He studied at a military academy and became a teacher of mathematics. He was not directly involved in the student movement of 1868–9: at the time, he lived in exile in the province of Vologda, from where he managed to escape to France in 1870. The next year Lavrov travelled to London (where he met Marx and Engels) to organise support for the Paris Commune. His journal *Vpered!* began to appear in Zurich in 1873.[34]

It was Lavrov who formulated a mature concept of socialism in one country appropriate for the Russian condition. He defined Russia's vastness as the main reason why socialism could be successfully established there even if the country would initially remain alone. Herzen and Nechaev had earlier suggested that Russian socialism needed the vast scope of a Slav federation. Lavrov was uninterested in the Slav connotations. For him, the essential point was that the security of a lone socialist state in general required an extended territory.

In his *Historical Letters*, which appeared between 1867 and 1869, Lavrov presented a Darwinian interpretation of interstate relations in terms of a struggle for existence. The eleventh, twelfth and fourteenth letters are of particular importance for us. The patriot Lavrov argued that it was not uncommon for one particular nation to turn into the world's 'ideal center'.

> Progress is not an impersonal process. Someone must be its organ. Some nation must, before others, and can, better and more fully than others, become the representative of progress in a given age. The true patriot can and must desire that it be *his* nation.[35]

Lavrov furthermore explained that states must be strong to maintain themselves internationally. 'The smaller the state … or the more its geographical situation permits a predatory posture on the part of its neighbours – the greater are the dangers to which its independence is exposed.' Therefore, Lavrov found it 'perfectly natural' for societies to 'join together into large and powerful states'.[36] But, again, Lavrov insisted that 'neither vastness of territory, nor wealth of material resources' alone could guarantee security. Only a nation embodying 'progress' had the strength to defend itself against 'neighbours who occupy a lower level of civilization'.[37] Thus, the single progressive state would have two sources of strength available to ward off the onslaughts of its neighbours: territory and resources, and the superiority drawn from the progressive system itself.

Once out of the country, Lavrov was free to reformulate these views in socialist terms. In his 1875 'Socialism and the struggle for existence', he argued that a 'socialist society' could draw strength from the superior mentality of its citizenry. In an argument reminiscent of Babouvism, Lavrov felt that the best way to make a state 'powerful and strong' was to inspire its citizens with the readiness to 'sacrifice all of life's comforts and life itself for the state', which Lavrov believed gave the socialist state the advantage over capitalist societies, where egoism reigns supreme.[38]

Lavrov's 1876 *The State Element in the Future Society* can be seen as the greatest Russian tractate on socialism in one country. Lavrov discussed the hypothetical situation when 'the proletariat, having achieved victory on the banks of the Elbe, the Volga or the Michigan [River], will exist alongside bourgeois states on the banks of the Seine, the Thames or the Danube'.[39] Lavrov assumed that the single 'socialist country' would have an 'extensive enough' territory.[40] Socialism in a tiny country like Belgium would inevitably be crushed by its neighbours.[41] Lavrov furthermore believed that, at the time, of all 'large countries' only the 'workers' organisation' in Germany had the strength to make a revolution.[42] In Russia, 'workers' socialism' instead would be based on village and urban communes. According to Lavrov, the Russian revolution might be able to maintain itself even if it captured only an 'extensive enough' part of the empire's territory.[43]

If the Russian revolution came first, Lavrov expected the German and Austrian social democrats to make a major effort to prevent their governments from organising an invasion of Russia. Lavrov ruled out peaceful coexistence between 'workers' Russia' and the hostile powers: 'There *can be no* peace between the old and the new system.' The best solution for an isolated revolutionary Russia would be to support revolutionaries abroad by sending out 'emissaries and offensive detachments into hostile country'.[44]

Lavrov defined the condition of a socialist state surrounded by hostile, capitalist powers, and with an overthrown but still powerful enemy at home, as the *first stage* of socialism. That stage would also be marked by the persistence of 'old habits and propensities'.[45] However, he insisted that even in the first transitional stage capitalist property would give way to 'community of property'. The revolution:

must begin immediately and *undeviatingly* to turn all private property ... into *common* property ... The coexistence, even on a temporary basis, of the socialist system with private ownership represents the very greatest threat to the new socialist system.[46]

In other words, Lavrov's dividing socialist society into two stages must not be interpreted as if he made the establishment of communist property dependent on the spread of the revolution to other nations. Lavrov, then, left no doubt about it that common, socialist ownership could be established in a single country.

In a letter of 17 April 1877 to an acquaintance Lavrov further explained why Russia had a 'mighty socialist future': in addition to having preserved the traditional institution of the commune, the Russians had the right psychological bent, as well as being unburdened by traditions. He continued to explain his thesis of socialism in one country as follows:

You ask me: Are there countries in the world which can be victorious in Socialism? Yes, I say, there are, and a few that depend upon geography purely. I know *three* such countries ... These are the United States, Great Britain, and Russia. The geographic position of each of these is such that interference in their internal affairs by neighbours by way of invasion is quite difficult, and therefore in each of these countries victory could be achieved despite the existence of bourgeois countries on their boundaries.[47]

Under the hands of the self-styled patriot and citizen of the largest state in the world, Lavrov, socialism in one country morphed into the exclusive privilege of states equipped with the most formidable geography.

Marx, Engels and communal socialism

We have now arrived in the late 1870s. The Russian economy was changing. The Emancipation of 1861 contributed to a degree of capitalist development.[48] However, the abolition of serfdom did not liberate the peasants from all bondage. The *obshchina* preserved all of its powers over the individual peasant.[49] Having said that, those peasants who did manage to free themselves from the control of the commune, to leave the village, and to find work in a factory became more fully proletarians, though most of them preserved their connections with the village and kept their own plots.[50] Also, from 1862 to 1878, under the Minister of Finance, Mikhail Reitern, the government pursued liberal economic and financial policies based on the encouragement of free enterprise. Several important state monopolies were abolished. Estate organisations were not abolished, but controls over private economic initiative were relaxed.[51]

Results were not spectacular, though. The many ways in which the Russian state involved itself in the encouragement of private industry paradoxically resulted in 'a significant limitation of the principle of free competition'. Russian industrial capitalists remained dependent on close ties with government bureaucrats and did not develop into a powerful independent force. By the late 1870s, the government's economic policies once again became more restrictive.[52] Industrial development remained hampered by the lack of an internal mass market, which, again, resulted from the fact that the peasants were liberated under such conditions, that no well-to-do farming class could emerge.[53] Railway construction became important in the 1860s and 1870s, but the spurt of heavy industries had to wait until the mid 1880s.[54]

It is not self-evident that Russian socialists of the 1870s continued to hope that capitalism could be avoided. After all, undeniably, by this time there were capitalist industries in Russia. The industrial working class represented not much more than 1 per cent of the total population, though.[55] But one does well to realise that in 1850 Germany that class had hardly counted for more – less than 2 per cent.[56] Then again, whereas Russia shared its very depressed state of industrialisation with the Germany of the period of the *Communist Manifesto*, it differed in having retained important 'feudal' elements hampering capitalist economies. The survival of the village commune, which prevented the free movement of labour and the commercialisation of land, was the main case in point. The commune served two complementary purposes for Russian socialists. It provided them with a starting point for the communist transition as well as serving as proof that capitalism had not yet made serious inroads in Russia and was therefore still avoidable.

This is the point to turn to Engels's intervention in the debate about Russian socialism. The insulting tone in which he addressed Tkachev in an October 1874 article in *Der Volksstaat*, provoked the latter to write an open letter to Engels.[57] Engels's main response, 'Social Conditions in Russia [*Soziales aus Russland*]', appeared in April 1875, again in *Der Volksstaat*. Engels argued that the conversion of the commune into a 'higher' form of society depended on material support provided by a victorious proletarian revolution in the West. But the most likely scenario was disintegration of the village commune and 'further development of Russia in a *bourgeois* direction'.[58] For the time being, Engels added, the proletarian revolution was out of the question in Russia, where the industrial working class was in evidence only 'sporadically and on a low level of development'.[59] He furthermore pointed out that the 'final destruction of class differences' required a 'very high level of the social productive forces', and that it was the bourgeoisie that was creating these productive forces.[60]

All this, however, does not mean that Engels made the proletarian revolution in Russia dependent on the achievement of integral industrialisation. At which point in the industrialising process the Russian proletariat would be ready to assume its role as leading class of the nation remained outside the scope of his article.

When Marx began to involve himself in the question of Russian socialism, he appeared to agree with the Russian socialists about the communist potential of the commune. A suggestion made by populist sociologist Nikolai Mikhailovskii in 1877, to the effect that the Marxian view implied the disintegration of the *obshchina*, was not to Marx's liking.[61] In his unsent November 1877 letter to the editorial board of *Otechestvennye zapiski*, the journal Mikhailovskii was writing for, Marx suggested that the commune offered a non-capitalist road to modernity. Conversely, Marx warned, if Russia continued on the road it had chosen in 1861, then it would lose 'the finest chance ever offered to a people' to avoid 'the fateful vicissitudes of the capitalist system'. Marx explained that he had never meant to present capitalism as an inevitable stage for all countries. It was only that *if* Russia would aim to become 'a capitalist nation on the West-European example', *then* it:

> will not be able to achieve this without the prior transformation of a good part of her peasants into proletarians; and then ... she will have to endure the relentless laws of this system ... That's all.[62]

In his 8 March 1881 letter to a member of Black Repartition, Vera Zasulich, Marx confirmed that, if protected from capitalist disintegration, the Russian village commune might serve as 'the fulcrum of Russia's social rebirth'.[63]

Did Marx, like Engels, make a village-based development to communism in Russia dependent on the assistance of proletarian states in the West? In the first draft of his letter to Zasulich, he explained that the modern technologies that the capitalist nations had developed could help a future revolutionary Russia to transform the primitive commune into a modern cooperation with agricultural machinery.[64] What is more, he suggested that Russia did *not* need the assistance of proletarian states in the West to achieve communism:

> When the [Russian, E.v.R.] revolution ... focuses all of its energies on the securing of the free revival of the village commune, it will soon develop into an element of regeneration of Russian society and into an element of superiority over the countries enslaved by the capitalist regime.[65]

Obviously, this referred to a communist Russia in an environment of capitalist states, the only occasion for Marx ever to come close to suggesting something like socialism in one country.[66] Then again, this notion had disappeared from the letter he actually sent. In the end Marx came down to Engels's more pessimistic assessment. In their joint January 1882 foreword to the Russian edition of the *Communist Manifesto*, Russia's transition from commune to communism was made dependent on a prior 'proletarian revolution in the West'.[67]

But how could Marx have believed that Russia, even with proletarian assistance from abroad, could engage in communism – at a time when capitalism had hardly begun to strike root in that country? Marx seems to have been guided by his old insight that capitalism was a spent force, a mode of production that would be unable to bring backward countries to development. As he observed in the first draft: 'The best proof that this development of the "village commune" corresponds with the historical trend of our epoch is the fatal crisis of capitalist production in the European and American countries.' Marx assumed that the 'English capitalist' road would not do Russian agriculture any good, even 'from a purely economic point of view'. Of course, Marx understood that, in the absence of revolution, Russia would inevitably turn capitalist. But, so he believed, as capitalism no longer had the potential to make the country prosper, the commune remained the best way out for Russia.[68]

Thus, next to accepting proletarian revolutions in countries of early capitalism, Marx also came to accept that peasant revolutions in even more 'backward' countries might have communist outcomes as well. All the time, the technological preconditions for the communist transition would be created by the revolutionary government – after the revolution.

Notes

1 Blackwell, 1970: 39–42, 107–9, 189; Falkus, 1972: 31, 33–42; Ananich, 2006: 400.
2 Blackwell, 1970: 100–7, 193, 196–7; Mironov and Eklof, 2000: 75–6, 94–5, 166; Wirtschafter, 2006: 245–7.
3 Mironov and Eklof, 2000: 76; Paxton, 2001: 91. For a classic description of the workings of the commune, see Mackenzie Wallace, 1912: Chapters 8, 9.
4 For Herzen's life and thought, see: Malia, 1965; Ulam, 1977: Chapter 2; Walicki, 1979: Chapter 10; Gleason, 1980: 53–70. See also Herzen, 1974.
5 See Venturi, 1960: 1–62, 95–6; Malia, 1965: 306–27, 337, 342, 349, 356–8, 366–78, 392–410; Pomper, 1971: 48–52; Walicki, 1979: Chapter 10; Polunov, 2005: 67–8.
6 *Pis'ma iz Frantsii i Italii* (1847–52), fourteenth letter, Koz'min, Makashin and Volgin, 1956: 215–16.
7 Ibid.: 184–93, 215–17, 220–1; *From the Other Shore* [originally published in 1850 as *Vom anderen Ufer*], Herzen, 1955: 146–50, 154–7; *O razvitii revoliutsionnykh idei v Rossii* [first published in German in 1851], Koz'min, Makashin and Volgin, 1956: 390–1, 503–6; *The Russian People and Socialism. An Open Letter to Jules Michelet* (September 1851) (Herzen, 1955: 201–3).
8 *O razvitii* (Koz'min, Makashin and Volgin, 1956: 504–5).
9 Herzen, 1955: 172, 175–6.
10 Ibid.: 183 (see also p. 186).
11 See Polunov, 2005: 67, 139–40.
12 For Chernyshevskii's life and thought, see Venturi, 1960: 138–79; Woehrlin, 1971; Ulam, 1977: Chapter 3; Pereira, 1975; Walicki, 1979: Chapter 11.
13 Chernyshevskii admitted that the preservation of the commune made it easier to proceed to socialism in Russia than in the West ('Slavianofily i vopros ob obshchine' (1857)); Koz'min, 1948: 741–3; comments on August von Haxthausen's *Studien über die inneren Zustände...* (1857: 341, 347). But he believed that Russia's relative advantage was undone by the West's higher levels of socialist awareness ('O prichinakh padeniia Rima' (1861), Kirpotin, Koz'min and Lebedev-Polianskii, 1950: 643–4, 661–4). When Vera Pavlovna in *What Is to Be Done?* dreams of the future socialism, she assumes that 'New Russia' is only one socialist society among others ('Others are working in other countries': Chernyshevsky, 1982: 321–3).
14 See for the revolutionaries of the early 1860s: Billington, 1958: 44; Venturi, 1960: 241–66, 285, 292–7; Walicki, 1979: 188–9; Polunov, 2005: 140–3. For the student unrest during 1857–61, see Gleason, 1980: 123–36.

102 *Socialism as vast state*

15 See the introduction to Vilenskaia and Roitberg, 1967: 11–14; Gleason, 1980: 161.
16 'K molodomu pokoleniiu' (Vilenskaia and Roitberg, 1967: 332–50; quotations pp. 336–7, 339).
17 von Borcke, 1977: 25.
18 For a discussion of nihilism (and Jacobinism) versus populism in the Russian revolutionary movement, see Gleason, 1980: 70–6, 291–2.
19 von Borcke, 1977: 258–60. For the background of the Zaichnevskii circle, see also Pomper, 1979: 29–30, 35–9.
20 von Borcke, 1977: 255.
21 'Molodaia Rossiia': 6.
22 For these episodes in the development of Russian Jacobinism, see Pomper, 1979: 94, 97–9; von Borcke, 1977: Chapters 7 and 8; Hardy, 1977: 51–7, 75, 126–43, 186–95, 247; Gleason, 1980: 343–50. For Nechaev, see also Pomper, 1979; Gleason, 1980: Chapter 11. For Tkachev, see also Koz'min, 1922; Weeks, 1968; introduction (V. F. Pustarnakova and B. M. Shakhmatova) to Galaktionova, Pustarnakova and Shakhmatova, 1975; Rudnitskaia, 1992.
23 'A Programme of Revolutionary Actions', 1979: 57–9. Nechaev and Tkachev were responsible for the contents of this programme, produced at the time of the student movement of 1868–9. Exact authorship is uncertain. See Pomper, 1979: 54–6, 59; Koz'min, 1922: 145–9; Hardy, 1977: 135–6, 151–2.
24 Nechaev and Bakunin, 15 April 1870 to *Der Volksstaat* (Lehning, 1971: 96–7).
25 See Rudnitskaia, 1992: 107–11, 113. On Turski, see Hardy, 1977: 249–50.
26 'Osnovnye polozheniia', 1992: 248.
27 'Zadachi revoliutsionnoi propagandy v Rossii' (Koz'min, 1933: 69–70).
28 Ibid.: 89–92, 95.
29 Tkachev did not absolutely exclude the possibility that the social revolution would come first in Europe. In 1878, for example, he wrote that the 'banner' of socialism could be planted anywhere, 'either in St. Petersburg or in Kiev, either in Tiflis or in Kazan, either in Moscow or in Paris' ('Revoliutsiia i printisip natsional'nosti', Koz'min, 1933: 417, 421–4).
30 The journal *Nabat* that Tkachev founded in Geneva was a coproduction with Turski (ibid.: 462; Rudnitskaia, 1992: 123–4, 128). Nechaev had earlier insisted that everything would be declared 'social property' immediately after the revolution. See for example 'Glavnye osnovy budushchego obshchestvennogo stroia' (winter 1870), Lehning, 1971: 425, 427; 'Nasha obshchaia programma' (September 1870) (ibid.: 438–9). Tkachev, however, realised that it might take a whole post-revolutionary generation to achieve the full 'triumph of communism' ('Vozmozhnna li sotsial'naia revoliutsiia v Rossii v nastoiashchee vremia?' (1876), in Koz'min, 1933: 280–2). The post-revolutionary society would be a 'transitional society'. It could not 'be called "constructed in the complete sense [*onkonchatel'no ustroennym*]", as if it was fully incarnating the idea of the social revolution' ('Anarkhicheskoe gosudarstvo' (1876), ibid.: 342–3, 358). Again, Tkachev did not tie the progress of post-revolutionary socialist reform in Russia to the progress of the international revolution.
31 See Billington, 1958: 24–7, 58–65, 79–80; Pomper, 1971: 112–16; von Borcke, 1977: 364–72. The term populism refers either to communal and peasant socialism in general, or to a specific stage of the movement during the late 1860s and 1870s. See for various uses: Isaiah Berlin's introduction to Venturi, 1960: xvi, 1–62; Pipes, 1964; Walicki, 1969: 1–28; Hardy, 1977: 51–7; von Borcke, 1977: 362–3; Gleason, 1980: 74–5; Offord, 1986: 1–8; Polunov, 2005: 146–8.
32 For the history of Land and Freedom, see Hardy, 1987.
33 See Offord, 1986: 26–35.
34 For Lavrov's biography and ideas, see James Scanlan's introduction in Scanlan, 1967: 1–65; Pomper, 1972; Walicki, 1979: 237–44.
35 Scanlan, 1967: 212–13, 220–1.

36 Ibid.: 249–50.
37 Ibid.: 265–7.
38 Okulov, 1965: 379–80.
39 Anonymous, 1876: 6.
40 Ibid.: 55–7.
41 Ibid.: 85–95.
42 Ibid.: 191–2.
43 Ibid.: 99–102.
44 Ibid.: 131–5 (see also pp. 99–102)
45 Ibid.: 55–7 (see also pp. 82, 111–15).
46 Ibid.: 103–6 (see also pp. 99–102).
47 Pomper (1972: 178–9) gives an extensive excerpt from this letter to Aleksandra Veber.
48 See Blackwell, 1970: 183; Falkus, 1972: 20.
49 See Mironov and Eklof, 2000: 78, 97–8.
50 See for example Johnson, 1979.
51 Polunov, 2005: 125, 128–31.
52 Ibid.: 136–7; see also Ananich, 2006: 405–6.
53 Falkus, 1972: 47.
54 Ibid.: 54, 56–7; Polunov, 2005: 134–5.
55 In 1859, Russia had a total population of 74 million (Paxton, 2001: 92). In 1860 there were 860,000 industrial workers in factories and mines (to be distinguished from workers in home industries and crafts) (Crisp, 1978: 332). We would then have 1.2 per cent proletarians on the total population.
56 In 1850 Germany had 33.7 million inhabitants (Wehler, 1995: 9). For an estimate of 550,000 industrial workers in 1850, see Chapter 5, n. 5, in this volume.
57 For Engels's article, see 'Flüchtlingsliteratur', letter III (*MEW*, vol. 18: 536–46).
58 Ibid.: 563–5.
59 Ibid.: 560.
60 Ibid.: 556–7.
61 See Eaton, 1980: 110.
62 *MEW*, vol. 19: 108, 111.
63 Ibid.: 242–3.
64 Ibid.: 385, 389, 392.
65 Ibid.: 395.
66 For Marx's position on Russian socialism, see Walicki, 1969: 179–91; Walicki, 1979: 407–8; McLellan, 1979: 66–7; Kolakowski, 1981, vol. 2 : 323–4; Offord, 1986: 120–5. Several scholars have tied Marx's position in favour of a non-capitalist road to modernity in Russia to his gradual acceptance of historical multilinearity. See Löwy, 1981: 23–8; Shanin, 1983; Yassour, 1987; White, 1996: 201–10, Chapter 5, 292, 362–4; Anderson, 2010: Chapters 1, 5 and 6; Hobsbawm, 2011: 127–55. For interpretations essentially denying that Marx was open to non-capitalist modernisation, see Tucker, 1969: 100–4, 109–22; Knei-Paz, 1979: introduction, Chapter 3.
67 *MEW*, vol. 19: 296.
68 Ibid.: 385–6, 390–3 (quotations pp. 391–2).

9 Russian socialism takes a back seat

In July 1889 socialists from twenty countries met in Paris to establish a Second International.[1] The founding congress was organised by Marxists, and Marxism became the dominant ideology of the movement. However, that ideology never gained a monopoly status. Characteristically, Russia was represented at the congress by Lavrov as well as by the Marxist Georgii Plekhanov. The appeal of Marxism was strongest in East and Central Europe and tended to be weaker in the western and southern parts of the subcontinent.[2]

Marxism became particularly well entrenched in the socialist parties in Germany and Russia, but even there this ideology did not acquire a monopoly status. At its 1890 Halle congress, the SAPD rechristened itself Social Democratic Party of Germany. The SPD was the strongest member party of the International and became its 'national centre of gravity'.[3] During the years of Bismarck's *Sozialistengesetz* (1878–90), when the party was semi-outlawed, Marxism gradually marginalised rivalling ideologies in the party. With the adoption of the new programme at the 1891 Erfurt congress, Marxism became the dominant force in the SPD.[4]

Social democrats of other nations, the Russians most of all, tended highly to respect their German comrades as the 'reputed guardians of the Marxist tradition'.[5] The Russian Social Democratic Workers' Party was established in 1898. Marxism dominated the RSDRP, but that was only because socialists from the populist tradition organised themselves in a Socialist-Revolutionary Party of their own, to become the other Russian delegation to the Second International.

It was mainly in the SPD and RSDWP that developed what came to be known as 'orthodox Marxism'. Marxists defined 'orthodoxy' at the hand of what the SPD's most prominent theorist, Karl Kautsky, wrote in *Die Neue Zeit*, the journal he had founded in 1883 and which became the most prestigious Marxist journal in the world. Marxists from Russia accepted Kautsky as their guiding star, but for them orthodoxy was additionally defined by Plekhanov's writings of the 1880s and 1890s. Russian and German adherents of orthodox Marxism used the term to distinguish themselves from the 'revisionism' of Kautsky's friend, Bernstein, who in the late 1890s concluded that the creed was in need of reformulation on a number of essential points.[6]

The debate between the orthodox and revisionists need not detain us here.[7] But what the 'orthodox Marxists' had to say about the conditions of the proletarian revolution is highly relevant for us. During the 1840s Marx and Engels had injected the idea that communism required the conditions of integral industrialisation into the communist movement. But they had fine-tuned their theory to allow proletarian regimes to embark on socialist construction in industrialising countries of early capitalism after all. This escape route was closed by the 'orthodox Marxists'. The effect of this major discursive turn on revolutionary strategy was in many ways more dramatic than the original intervention by Marx and Engels had been: only now, socialism in countries with peasant or petty-bourgeois majorities was ruled out.

Plekhanov

The reformulation of Marxism began in Russia, where Georgii Plekhanov first formulated the thought that the proletarian revolution required a workers' majority in the population. Plekhanov is considered the father of Russian Marxism, a title he deserves in so far as he created Russian Marxism as a political organisation. He was born in 1856, and studied at the Voronezh Military Academy as well as at the St Petersburg Metallurgical Institute. As a leading member of Black Repartition, Plekhanov fled the country to settle in Switzerland in 1880. It was there that he was converted to Marxism. In 1883 he established the group Emancipation of Labour together with friends from Black Repartition, among whom were Zasulich and Pavel Aksel'rod. Plekhanov became an important figure in the Second International and played a key role in the struggle against revisionism.[8]

It became Plekhanov's great ambition to design his own Marxist political strategy for Russia.[9] He laid down his views in two pamphlets. His 1883 *Socialism and Political Struggle* [10] was followed in 1885 by the much longer *Our Differences.*[11] In the former pamphlet Plekhanov's views had not yet fully crystallised. He argued that the socialist revolution required the conditions of large-scale industrialisation and a politically mature working class; but, even so, the democratic revolution in Russia might turn out to become the immediate prologue of the proletarian revolution. This was in good accordance with Marx and Engels's suggestions for Germany in the *Communist Manifesto.*[12]

The permanent-revolutionary perspective was, however, lost in the second document. In *Our Differences* of 1885, Plekhanov once again explained that socialism depended on the conditions created by capitalism.[13] But in a new turn he now insisted that Russia needed the *complete* course of capitalism.[14] Plekhanov admitted that there could be a '*shortening of the duration*' of the capitalist stage, and that Russian capitalism might reach maturity in less time than its British predecessor had. What is more, 'Our capitalism will fade without having succeeded in *finally* blooming.' But this did not fundamentally change much, for he added that capitalism would nevertheless have to 'advance to its more or less complete triumph'.[15]

Plekhanov argued that a democratic revolution would obviously bring the majority to power, i.e. the peasantry. He believed that, as small commodity producers, peasants would always reject socialist economic reforms. A democratic 'peasant state' would never turn socialist.[16] In a 'country of the petty bourgeoisie', democracy could set itself only:

> the task of guaranteeing the interests of the small individual producers, because precisely this class forms the majority of the people ... the objective logic of commodity production effects the transformation of the small individual producers into wage-labourers on one hand, and bourgeois entrepreneurs on the other. *When that transformation is completed* ... the working class will occupy the place of the 'people', and the popular autocracy will turn into a dictatorship of the proletariat.[17]

The logic was impeccable: if the small producers could never be convinced of the advantages of socialism, as Marx and Engels thought they could, the only remaining option for the working class to gain a majority for the socialist revolution would be to become that majority itself. In his new book, Plekhanov discreetly avoided referring to the *Communist Manifesto* passage about the rapid succession of bourgeois and proletarian revolutions.

With Plekhanov, the democratic revolution became the introduction to a protracted period of capitalist economic development, which was to last until such time as capitalism was fully developed. Permanent revolution was off.[18] *Our Differences* represented a landslide in Marxist thinking. To my knowledge, Plekhanov was the first Marxist ever to formulate the thesis that proletarian revolutions can only occur in countries where capitalist large-scale industry has the dominating share of the economy and with a workers' majority.[19]

Plekhanov's intervention amounted to a dramatic shift in socialism. It had been quite common for socialists to cast their own nation in the role of initiator-people. Winstanley hoped the English would make the breakthrough first, and French communists from Babeuf to Pillot and Dézamy expected France to take the initiative. Marx and Engels trusted that the Germans would be among the trailblazers, in the same category as much more advanced Britain. The Russian socialists expected an *Alleingang* for their fatherland, a possibility Lavrov theoretically underpinned. On the contrary, Plekhanov made it the very essence of his strategic conception that Russia could not possibly make the move for decades to come. Other, advanced nations would come first. In relegating his own people to a back seat in socialism, Plekhanov took an extraordinary and outrageously unpatriotic position for a socialist. Strikingly, the whole Russian social democratic movement followed him.

Most likely, Plekhanov wanted to distinguish himself as sharply as possible from his former comrades and new rivals, the populists, for whom an early breakthrough to socialism in Russia was imperative. But Plekhanov's negative appreciation of the peasantry as a revolutionary factor was probably decisive. The abolishment of serfdom in 1861 had not triggered significant revolutionary stirrings in the countryside. The 1874 populist campaign of 'going to the people' had failed to stir the peasant masses as well, and neither had the peasants risen after the murder of Aleksandr II. This convinced Plekhanov that nothing much could be expected of the peasants, which, again, ruled out a socialist turn in his predominantly peasant fatherland.[20]

Russian capitalism

In the early 1880s, the question of the conditions of the proletarian revolution in Russia remained a theoretical one. However, Russia was fast changing. During the 1880s and 1890s, coal and iron mining, the metallurgical sector and the oil industry rapidly expanded. The industrial boom of the 1890s, orchestrated by Minister of Finance Sergei Witte, spawned impressive railway construction. Two remarkable aspects of Russian industrialisation were the significance of the production of capital goods (next to food processing and cotton textiles) and the high degree of concentration of production in large-scale firms.[21] Russian industry was also remarkable for the 'growth of various monopolistic devices for regulating production and sales', especially so-called syndicates.[22]

Comparatively speaking, Russia remained a 'backward' country. In 1913 agriculture still accounted for slightly over half of the national income.[23] In that year, British per capita national income was more than four times as high as Russia's. But the advances were very real. In absolute terms Russia was now the fifth industrial nation in the world.[24] For Russian social democrats it always remained important where Russia stood compared to Germany at the time of the *Communist Manifesto*. As mentioned earlier, in 1850 the German industrial working class made up less than 3.5 per cent of the economically active population. The corresponding figure for Russia in 1913 was about 6 per cent.[25] In 1906 Prime Minister Petr Stolypin gave peasants the right to leave the commune and to consolidate their individual land holdings as private property.[26]

During the 1890s and the 1900s German as well as Russian social democrats began to treat Russia as an underdeveloped capitalist nation, rather than as one that was yet to embark on the capitalist road. In his 1894 afterword to *Social Conditions in Russia*, Engels wrote that 'the foundations of the capitalist mode of production' were now in place, and that behind the absolutist–bureaucratic façade lurked the bourgeoisie in power. Russia was following the Bismarck model of 'revolutions from above'. Engels added that the commune was being undermined, and that the peasantry was rapidly being proletarianised.[27] This view of Russia as a young capitalist country was confirmed at the second congress of the RSDWP in 1903. The party programme adopted at that event had it that, although Russia preserved pre-capitalist rudiments, 'capitalism has already become the dominant mode of production'.[28]

The Plekhanov consensus

The results of rapid industrialisation plus the Russian Revolution of 1905 made it imperative for the social democrats more concretely to formulate their views on the stages of democratic and socialist revolution. The revolutionary explosion came about as a result of the firing by tsarist troops on a peaceful demonstration of workers in front of the Winter Palace in St Petersburg on 22 January, resulting in hundreds of casualties. The event triggered strikes, demonstrations, peasant uprisings, terrorist attacks and mutinies of soldiers throughout the country. The St Petersburg workers formed a council, the Soviet, with independent social democrat Trotsky as one of the leaders. By October the situation was sufficiently out of hand for Tsar Nikolai II to announce the establishment of an elected parliament based on a limited suffrage and fitted out with limited prerogatives. The revolution was finally subdued after the defeat of an armed insurrection in Moscow in December.[29]

By the time of the revolution the RSDWP was split into two factions. The radical faction of the Bolsheviks was headed by Vladimir Ul'ianov, better known as Lenin. Lenin came from a wealthy middle-class family. His father, a provincial director of public schools, acquired a noble title. Tragedy struck the family when Vladimir's elder brother, Aleksandr, was executed in 1887 for his participation in a failed plot against the life of tsar Aleksandr III. As a social democrat, Lenin became a staunch ally of Plekhanov's, but when the party split in 1903, they became political enemies.[30] The Mensheviks were most prominently represented by Plekhanov and Iulii Martov.

The two factions fundamentally differed in their understanding of the provisional government that would be thrown up by the democratic revolution, but both adhered to the Plekhanov scenario in which this revolution would culminate in an extended period of capitalist economic development.[31]

The consensus around the Plekhanov scenario remained almost absolute. Aleksandr Parvus was one of those to challenge it, but only seemingly so. Parvus was a Russian citizen who had moved to Germany. He joined the SPD and became a prominent publicist, but returned to Russia at the time of the revolution. He became close to Trotsky.[32] In January 1905, he proposed a social democratic provisional workers' government, but he did not expect it to embark on the socialist transformation of Russia but merely to radicalise the democratic revolution.[33]

Lenin, for one, did in September 1905 famously suggest:

> from the democratic revolution we will immediately begin to make the transition to the socialist revolution … to the measure of … the strength of the … proletariat. We favour an uninterrupted revolution.[34]

But this remained an exceptional remark. Both prior and subsequent to this, Lenin asserted that a proletarian minority government could never draw the peasant majority along to socialism. On the contrary, the democratic revolution would result in more capitalist development.[35]

Even the one social democrat really to challenge the Plekhanov consensus, Trotsky, in the end failed to make a clean break with it. Trotsky was born in 1879, in a Ukrainian village, in a moderately wealthy peasant family. He received an unfinished education in the city of Odessa and became involved in the revolutionary movement. From September 1904 onwards, he assumed an independent position in the RSDWP, outside the two factions.[36]

The first occasion for Trotsky to refer to the 'uninterrupted revolution' was his November 1905 'Social Democracy and Revolution'. He was thinking of a Russian workers' government resolving democratic issues and then moving on to the problems of socialism.[37] This was even more radical than Marx and Engels's proposals for Germany. The latter had mostly assumed that the workers' revolution would be triggered by a prior seizure of power by bourgeois classes. That is in any case the only sequence they referred to as permanent revolution. Trotsky reduced the two revolutions to one, proletarian revolution, which was first to see through the democratic part of the revolutionary programme.[38]

In his December 1905 foreword to a publication of Marx's comments on the Paris Commune, Trotsky defined the Russian revolution as 'a revolution *in Permanenz*, or an *uninterrupted* revolution'.[39] Most spectacularly, he suggested that there were no internal conditions standing in the way of the construction of a socialist society in backward Russia. At first, there would be created mere socialist 'oases' in certain branches of the economy. But, 'The wider the field of socialised production becomes, the more evident will its advantages be ... the bolder will the ensuing economic measures of the proletariat become.' Trotsky admitted that the Russian working class would not 'be able to carry its great cause through to the end' without the 'world victory of Labour'. But it was isolation from the world economy, not the inevitability of peasant resistance in a backward nation, which would doom isolated Russia to collapse. On the contrary: Trotsky was confident that, once in power, the Russian proletariat would 'not be driven back'. He referred to Marx's observations on workers and peasants in France to underscore that a Russian 'dictatorship of the proletariat' might rely on the peasantry, which class, he thought, could never push the workers aside.[40]

Trotsky presented the uninterrupted revolution most famously in his 1906 *Results and Prospects*. Ironically, though, this text signalled his partial return to the Plekhanov consensus. He indicated that one should not be dogmatic about the *economic* preconditions of socialism: the 'sufficient technical prerequisites for collective production have already existed for a hundred or two hundred years'.[41] Even so, without the '*direct State support of the European proletariat*', an isolated Russian workers' state would come up against insurmountable 'political obstacles'.[42] In direct contradiction with what he wrote in December 1905, he now suggested that the more determined a socialist policy the ruling proletariat would be following, 'the narrower and more shaky does the ground beneath its feet become'.[43] This is where Trotsky returned to the Plekhanov consensus: 'Left to its own resources, the working class of Russia will inevitably be crushed by the counter-revolution the moment the peasantry turns its back on it.'[44]

The crucial point here is not that Trotsky denied that countries could consolidate socialism on their own, but *why* he believed Russia could not go it alone: the allegedly inevitable peasant resistance. Marx and Engels too made permanent revolution dependent on an international follow-up to be successful. But they attributed the impossibility of socialism in one country to the world market and military intervention; they never asserted that it was inevitable for the peasants in underdeveloped capitalist countries to turn against and crush the workers' government. Trotsky was, in other words, returning to Plekhanov's negative assessment of the peasantry, rather than simply confirming his loyalty to Marx and Engels's internationalism.[45]

The Party of Socialists-Revolutionaries

Remarkably, even the Socialists-Revolutionaries, or in any case their majority faction, abandoned the nineteenth-century populist tenet that Russia was ripe for the transition to socialism. The Party of Socialists-Revolutionaries (PSR) was founded in 1902. The PSR, which in the course of the years won a substantial following among the peasantry, gained fame and notoriety for its terrorist activities.[46] Its main leader and ideologist, Viktor Chernov, was born in 1873 in the province of Saratov. He studied law, became involved in the populist movement, and in 1899 emigrated to Switzerland.[47]

In Chernov's definition, the working class included all those who drew their income exclusively from their own labour, which is to say that next to the industrial proletariat the small individual peasants were also to be counted in. This took care of the problem of the missing proletarian majority. Also, Chernov thought that in backward countries like Russia, and generally in the agricultural sector, capitalism could not fulfil its historically progressive role of concentrating production in large-scale enterprises. This train of thought should have led him to the conclusion that Russian democratic revolutionaries would have to guide their country onto the road to socialism as quickly as possible.

However, Chernov made socialism also conditional on a highly developed revolutionary consciousness among the workers, without which they would not be able to take the economy in hand. In his assessment, this condition was not met in Russia. The democratic revolution was therefore, he believed, *not* supposed to culminate in rapid socialisation of production. A revolutionary government would have to socialise the land, but socialisation of agricultural *production* would have to be postponed. Altogether, the anti-capitalist credentials of Chernov's government of industrial and agricultural workers would be only marginally more impressive than those of the post-revolutionary bourgeois government foreseen by Plekhanov.[48]

The old perspective of socialist transition in Russia was only upheld by the so-called Maximalist faction of the party, arguably the true heirs of nineteenth-century Russian socialism. First emerging in 1904, the faction established the Union of SR-Maximalists in October 1906.[49]

In his 1906 *Present Tasks*, one of the Maximalists' main ideologists, the writer and literary critic Mikhail Engel'gardt, rejected Marx's suggestion that a 'given type of economic relations' must first completely 'exhaust' itself before it can be replaced. According to Engel'gardt, the transition may as well occur 'long before or long after' that moment. He did not deny that socialism relied on the existence of large-scale factories and a market economy. But in his view these preconditions were already in evidence 'in all capitalist societies, regardless of their levels of development', *including Russia*. As for the 'subjective element', in Engel'gardt's view, unlike the workers in the West the Russian workers had the necessary 'revolutionary enthusiasm bordering on religious ecstasy'. Backward Russia was therefore the *only* country where all conditions for the 'social revolution' were in evidence. It must therefore become the 'initiator of the new era in the existence of humanity', the first country to break through to socialism and to set an example for the Western workers.[50]

Engel'gardt did not regard it as an insuperable problem if Russia transformed its 'whole economic and social system', and the workers of the West did not follow the example. He asserted that one could even 'introduce socialism' in 'one commune'. Engel'gardt's imagination of single-country socialism was markedly inward-looking: the main thing a socialist country needed to maintain herself in a hostile environment was credible defensive military power. As for the risk of the capitalist powers outcompeting socialist Russia – that could be dealt with through the establishment of import duties.[51]

Notes

1. For the history of the Second International, see Cole, 1960; Braunthal, 1961: *Geschichte*, part 3; Niemeyer, 1966; Joll, 1974; Callahan, 2010. See also: Haupt, 1964.
2. For the status of Marxism in the Second International, see Cole, 1960: vol. 3.I: xi, 7–8, 23; Braunthal, 1961: *Geschichte*, 203, 207–8; Landauer, 1966: 131, 134–6; Joll, 1974: 32–3, 41; McLellan, 1979: 20; Kolakowski, 1981: vol. 2: 1, 3–4, 18; Steenson, 1991: 7, 18–19.
3. Niemeyer, 1966: 96–7; see also Kolakowski, 1981: vol. 2: 9. For a critical discussion of the supposed role of the SPD as model party in the Second International, see Rojahn, 1991.
4. For Marxist dominance in the German socialist party, see Lidtke, 1964; Lidtke, 1966: 59–66, 155–75, 279–88; Steinberg, 1974: 52–4; Steenson, 1978: 46–59, 84; Steinberg, 1979: 11–40; McLellan, 1979: 22; Steenson, 1981: 189–225.
5. Cole, 1960: vol. 3.I: xii–xiii.
6. On the concept of 'orthodox Marxism', see Harding, 1977: Chapter 2; Kolakowski, 1981: vol. 2: 31; Gilcher-Holtey, 1986: 120; Donald, 1993: 9; Walicki, 1995: 208.
7. For revisionism, see Rikli, 1936; Gay, 1962; Gustafsson, 1972; Hirsch, 1977; Heimann and Meyer, 1978; Carsten, 1993: Chapters 3–4; Steger, 1997. For Kautsky's role in the revisionism debate, see Steenson, 1978: 116ff.

8 For Plekhanov's biography, see Baron, 1963; Tiutiukin, 1997.
9 Even though Plekhanov could not have known about the drafts, he was familiar with Marx's 1881 letter to Zasulich. Marx's unsent letter to *Otechestvennye zapiski* was known to him by 1884, when Zasulich received a copy from Engels (*MEW*, vol. 19: 558).
10 'Sotsializm i politicheskaia bor'ba' (Riazanov, *Plekhanov. Sochineniia* [*Plekhanov/Sochineniia*], 1923, vol. 2: 25–88).
11 'Nashi raznoglasiia', *Plekhanov/Sochineniia*, vol. 2: 89–356.
12 Ibid.: 86.
13 Ibid.: 122–3, 232–71, 316–17, 329–30.
14 Ibid.: 270–1.
15 Ibid.: 337–8.
16 Ibid.: Chapter 4.
17 Ibid.: 287 (emphasis added).
18 In 1901 Plekhanov confirmed that the fall of absolutism and the triumph of socialism would necessarily be separated from each other by a 'considerable stretch of time' ('O nashei taktike po otnosheniiu k bor'be liberal'noi burzhuazii s tsarizmom (Pis'mo k Tsentral'nomu Komitetu)', *Sochineniia*, vol. 13: 179). In his 'K voprosu o zakhvate vlasti (Nebol'shaia istoricheskaia spravka)' (April 1905), Plekhanov (*Sochineniia*, vol. 13: 208–10) confirmed that Marx and Engels's concept of 'revolution in permanence' was misconceived. Plekhanov asserted, wrongly, that in time they had come to acknowledge that 'the democratic system would remain dominant for a rather protracted period'.
19 Engels informed Zasulich in a 23 April 1885 letter that he had not completely read *Our Differences*. He hoped that Russia's '1789' would rapidly escalate into another '1793' (*MEW*, vol. 36: 304, 307). But even in 1891 he still saw the Russian industrial workers as too weak to make a revolution (29 September 1891 to Bebel, ibid.: vol. 38: 160). For a discussion of Engels's reference to 1793 in the letter to Zasulich, see also Löwy, 1981: 24.
20 For Plekhanov's strategic thinking, see Haimson, 1955: 21–3; Baron, 1963: Chapter 7; Keep, 1963: 20–3; Walicki, 1969: 147–59; Harding, 1977: Chapter 2; Kolakowski, 1981, vol. 2: 329–36; Löwy, 1981: 30–2; Offord, 1986: 125–31; White, 1996: 309–18; Tiutiukin, 1997: 86–95.
21 Falkus, 1972: 44–5, 54–7, 61, 68–9; Paxton, 2001: 100; Polunov, 2005: 197–8.
22 Falkus, 1972: 11–12, 77–8; see also Polunov, 2005: 197–8.
23 Gregory, 1982: 73.
24 Falkus, 1972: 11–13; Paxton, 2001: 107.
25 Russia in 1913 had 3.1 million industrial workers in factories and mines (Crisp, 1978: 332). The Russian active population of 1913 is estimated at 50 million (Munting, 1996: 331).
26 Mironov and Eklof, 2000: 99; Paxton, 2001: 89–91; Polunov, 2005: 231–2. For an analysis of the whole process of agrarian reform from 1861 to 1913, see Leonard, 2011: Chapter 1.
27 *MEW*, vol. 22: 432–5. Engels frequently noted that the *obshchina* was disintegrating and that capitalism was on the march in Russia, but he gave no indication of the preconditions of a future workers' revolution ('Über den Brüsseler Kongress und die Lage in Europa' (1891), *MEW*, vol. 22: 242); 'Der Sozialismus in Deutschland' (vol. 22: 257–8, 260); 15 March 1892 to Daniel'son (vol. 38: 305); April 1892 *L'Éclair* interview with Engels (vol. 22: 535–6); 18 June 1892 to Daniel'son (vol. 38: 366); 24 February 1893 to Daniel'son (vol. 39: 37–8); 'Kann Europa abrüsten?' (1893) (vol. 22: 390).
28 *KPSS*, vol. 1: 39.
29 Ascher, 2004.
30 For recent Lenin biographies, see Service, 2000; Read, 2005; Lih, 2011a.

31 For classical studies of early Bolshevik and Menshevik strategy, see Haimson, 1955; Keep, 1963; Schwarz, 1967; Lane, 1969. See also Larsson, 1970: Chapters 10, 11; Harding, 1977: Chapter 9; Donald, 1993: section III.
32 For Parvus's biography, see Zeman and Scharlau, 1965. For Parvus as theorist, see Scharlau, 1964.
33 'What was accomplished on the Ninth of January' (Day and Gaido, 2009: 262–72). See also Parvus's 13 November 1905 'Our tasks' (ibid.: 488–96).
34 'Otnoshenie sotsial-demokratii k krest'ianskomu dvizheniiu' (*PSS*, vol. 11: 222–3). On the exceptional nature of this passage, see Löwy, 1981: 36.
35 'Sotsial-demokratiia i vremennoe revoliutsionnoe pravitel'stvo' (April 1905) (*PSS*, vol. 10: 18); 'Dve taktiki sotsial-demokratii v demokratischeskoi revoliutsii', written June/July 1905 (vol. 11: 35). (But note the unclear passage in the same text: 90) 'Doklad ob ob"edinitel'nom s"ezde RSDRP' (May 1906, vol. 13: 17.) According to Lenin, Marx and Engels had failed to see that bourgeois revolutions in backward countries inevitably end in the 'prolonged supremacy of the democratic system', and that proletarian revolution was impossible under the 'still extremely underdeveloped' economic relations such as those reigning in Germany in the mid-nineteenth century, where there was hardly any 'large-scale industry' and 'the petty bourgeoisie was completely dominant' ('O vremennom revoliutsionnom pravitel'stve', May 1905, vol. 10: 236–9). See also 18 April (1 May) 1905 speech at the Third Party Congress (vol. 10: 132); 'Sotsialisticheskaia partiia i bespartiinaia revoliutsionnost' (vol. 12: 134).
36 For recent Trotsky biographies, see Thatcher, 2003; Swain, 2006; Service, 2009; Fel'shtinskii and Cherniavskii, 2012, 2013.
37 Day and Gaido, 2009: 455. On the fundamental difference between Parvus's and Trotsky's interpretations of permanent revolution, see Scharlau, 1964: Chapters 7–8; Larsson, 1970: 276–304; Löwy, 1981: 39–43; Donald, 1993: 69–93; Lih, 2012. On the use of the term permanent revolution in relation to Russia 1905 by Russian (Parvus, Trotsky, David Riazanov) and German (Kautsky, Luxemburg, Franz Mehring) social democrats, see Larsson, 1970: 252–304; Day and Gaido, 2009: introduction; Lih, 2012. For a discussion of Trotsky's originality, see also Thatcher, 2003: 36–42.
38 On the difference between Marx and Engels's and Trotsky's interpretation of permanent revolution, see Knei-Paz, 1979: 158.
39 'Foreword to Karl Marx, *Parizhskaya Kommuna*' (Day and Gaido, 2009: 501).
40 Ibid.: 514–20. Trotsky claimed that the workers could more easily come to power in an 'economically backward country' than in a 'country of the most advanced capitalism': it was a 'petty-bourgeois' city, Paris, that had a workers' government in 1871 (ibid.: 502).
41 Trotsky, 1978: Chapter 7 (quotation p. 91). For a discussion of this element in Trotsky's book, see Larsson, 1970: 290–2. Richard Day (1973: 6–7) observes that, given Marx's views on 1848 Germany, Trotsky was being 'not entirely unorthodox'.
42 Trotsky, 1978: 104–5.
43 Ibid.: 77.
44 Ibid.: 115. Trotsky repeated the same thesis in 'Kautsky on the Russian Revolution', written in December 1906 (Day and Gaido, 2009: 576). Trotsky believed that permanent revolution had been premature in 1848 Germany: the *Communist Manifesto* 'regarded the revolution of 1848 as the immediate prologue to the socialist revolution. Of course one does not require much penetration after 60 years to see that Marx was mistaken, because the capitalist world still exists'. In Trotsky's eyes, the Russian proletariat was much stronger than the German proletariat had been in 1848 (Trotsky, 1978: 85–6, 94). See also 'Introduction to *Ferdinand Lassalle's*' *Speech to the Jury* (July 1905) (Day and Gaido, 2009: 440); 'Social Democracy and Revolution' (ibid.: 455).

114   Russian socialism takes a back seat

45 See also Marot, 2012: 18–20.
46 For the origins of the party, see Perrie, 1976: 42–3; Hildermeier, 1978: 38–49; Gusev, 1999: 11–14.
47 For Chernov's biography, see Gusev, 1999.
48 For Chernov's programmatic thinking, see Radkey, 1958: 27, 32–4; Perrie, 1976: Chapters 2, 3; Hildermeier, 1978: 47–8, 70–1, 83–94; Immonen, 1988: 41–51, 64–6; Gusev, 1999: 15–20. See for example Chernov's presentations at the First Party Congress in December 1905–January 1906, Erofeev, 1996: 273–5, 276–8, 316–24; Chernov at the First Party Conference in August 1908 (ibid.: 2001: 137–9).
49 For the Maximalists, see Pavlov, 1989; Hildermeier, 1978: Chapter 4.
50 Engel'gardt, n.y.: 23–7. For the official Maximalist position on the objective and subjective conditions for the socialist transition in Russia, see the report of the October 1906 founding conference: Pavlov, 2002: 36.
51 Tag-in, 1906: 85–6. Such a 'commune' – it might be a single city – would find itself in the position of an 'invested fortress' ('Osnovnye zadachi Trudovoi respubliki', *Volia truda*, 1907: 94–5).

10 Marxism in industrialised Germany

Just like their Russian comrades, the German social democrats profoundly changed their understanding of the conditions of the proletarian revolution in the late nineteenth century. They too made the workers' revolution dependent on integral industrialisation and a workers' majority. One important factor contributing to this dramatic shift in German social democratic opinion was the long 'delay' of the proletarian revolution.

Eric Hobsbawm lets the 'Age of Revolution' end with 1848. After the Springtime of the Peoples, popular revolution was on the way out. There was, of course, the 1871 Paris Commune, but Adam Zamoyski aptly notes that there was something of the 'convulsive spasm' about this event, 'the final manifestation of the religious cult of the nation, whose cause had expired back in 1848'.[1] But the social democrats had more to worry about than the winding down of the petty-bourgeois 'democratic revolution': the *proletarian* revolution almost completely failed to materialise. The Paris workers rose in June 1848, but their attempt at establishing a proletarian dictatorship, which is how Marx interpreted their actions, failed.[2] The Commune, the first workers' government in his eyes, was drowned in blood. In all of fifty years no other workers' government emerged anywhere.

Given their 'materialist' bias, the Marxists were bound to interpret history's disconcerting lack of readiness to sing to their tune, in terms of lacking socio-economic conditions. As we saw, in 1895 Engels finally admitted that he and Marx had been mistaken in assuming that capitalism was on the way out. Engels admitted that a true 'industrial revolution' had been sweeping through Europe in the course of the second half of the century, turning Germany into an 'industrial country of the first order'. The collapse of the Paris Commune proved that working-class rule had been 'impossible' in 1871.[3]

The German social democrats accepted this essentially economic interpretation of the proletariat's failures. The 23 September 1896 lead article of *Die Neue Zeit* pointed to the many impressive economic and technological strides made by capitalism, only to conclude in an obvious reference to Engels:

> Marx has often overestimated the speed of the process of disintegration to which capitalist society is subjected; this is his one big mistake … We

now know from the experience of half a century that the collapse of the bourgeoisie takes place much more slowly than Marx assumed in 1850.[4]

The person who, after Plekhanov, contributed most to formulating the new 'orthodox Marxist' formula predicating the socialist transition on integral industrialisation was Karl Kautsky, the man who, after Engels's death, many saw as the greatest living Marxist thinker. Kautsky was born in Prague in 1854 and studied at the University of Vienna. He joined the SDAP in 1874. As SPD leader, he never involved himself in the party organisation, but concentrated on his work as journalist and Marxist theorist.[5]

In his 1899 Bernstein und the Social Democratic Program, Kautsky wrote that it was impossible sharply to determine the degree of capital concentration required for the socialist transition.[6] Nonetheless, he formulated some sort of minimum requirement. Experience teaches, Kautsky asserted, that 'communist colonies' established by socialists and 'founded on the basis of the production of artisans and small peasants' always failed: the 'desire for private property' sooner or later overrules any 'socialist enthusiasm'.

> The matter will turn out very differently *where individual production is the exception rather than the rule*, where economic conditions make social production ever more general and advantageous and influence the feelings and thought of the toiling classes ever more in the direction of social cooperation. There, socialist organisation will also become possible without that extremely powerful enthusiasm.[7]

In other words, in countries with a preponderance of small-scale production, attempts at socialist transition will be in vain. The petty bourgeoisie will prevent it.[8] In his important 1909 brochure *The Road to Power*, Kautsky confirmed that economic conditions in a country like Russia were too 'unripe' to allow a socialist transition. Nationalisation of the economy was feasible only in 'industrially highly developed' Germany and England.[9]

> Only there where the capitalist mode of production is highly developed, the opportunity could be found to use economic state power to transform capitalist ownership of the means of production into social ownership.[10]

Thus the perspective of minority workers' governments creating the economic conditions for the transition after the revolution, to be found with Marx and Engels, was lost.[11]

Germany, industrial superpower

Fortunately for the German social democrats, the conclusion that proletarian revolution required highly developed, fully industrialised capitalism did not have the dramatic implications that it had for their Russian comrades. The immediate socialist perspective for their country remained intact, for the newly formulated conditions of socialism were actually in the process of being created.

By the end of the century Germany was rapidly overcoming its backwardness and becoming an industrial superpower. German state unification in 1871, under 'iron chancellor' Bismarck, had been accompanied by an industrial growth spurt in the early years of the decade. During the so-called *Gründerzeit* numerous new industrial firms were established. The Great Depression of the 1870s and 1880s reduced growth rates or even led to declines in production, but between 1895 and the outbreak of the Great War growth was again spectacular. Germany became an *Industriestaat* and an especially strong player in the new technologies of the 'second industrial revolution' (chemistry, electricity and advanced machine tools), as well as in the production of steel. By 1913 the empire had become the second industrial power of the world, leaving only Great Britain ahead of it.[12] In 1907 the industrial sector accounted for 43 per cent of Germany's gross domestic product, far surpassing agriculture's 25 per cent.[13] With a share close to 25 per cent of Germany's economically active population in 1907, the industrial working class had become the numerically strongest social formation. It was, of course, nothing like a majority, but a share of wage-earners of 76 per cent gave the social democrats ample scope for creative arithmetic.[14]

Altogether, although history hadn't been smiling on them, the German social democrats became increasingly optimistic about the prospects for the socialist transition in their country. Engels even suggested that the new industrialised conditions would turn the socialist transition into a routine operation: the increasing scale of production, the creation of joint-stock companies, nationalisations and state intervention, trusts and other organisational arrangements, were facilitating and directly preparing the transition to the planned socialist economy.[15]

Around the turn of the century, a certain light-heartedness took hold of the German social democrats. Not long before his death, Engels wrote that in Germany 'the transformation of the capitalist enterprise into a social one has already been completely prepared and can be effected *overnight*'![16] According to Parvus, *half a year* in power would suffice for the workers' party to put an end to capitalism.[17] The famous Austrian economist Rudolf Hilferding, who lived in Germany since 1906, argued that abolishing capitalism had become 'extraordinarily' easier. Under the new conditions, he believed, 'it suffices for society ... to seize finance capital so as to immediately [*sofort*] establish direction over the main branches of production'.[18]

The petty bourgeoisie lost as ally

The new 'orthodox Marxism' can be regarded, quite simply, as an adaptation to the new, more advanced conditions emerging in Germany at the end of the century. But the new formula also emerged out of Kautsky's deception with, as he saw it, the counter-revolutionary development of the petty-bourgeois masses and political parties in Germany. This made successful proletarian revolution directly dependent on the presence of a workers' majority, an argumentation quite similar to Plekhanov's.

In Volker Berghahn's interpretation, the Reich Constitution of April 1871 'brought together three features – absolute monarchy, representative parliament, and democratic plebiscite', but the balance of power remained tipped in favour of the emperor. Nonetheless, Germany now had a national assembly with some important prerogatives and elected by universal male suffrage.[19] The SPD could not afford to ignore this national arena. The impressive results the party scored in the elections greatly added to its focus on the *Reichstag*. This was the most impressive result socialists achieved anywhere in the world before the Bolsheviks seized power in Russia. In 1890, the year when Bismarck's *Sozialistengesetz* was annulled, the SPD achieved a 20 per cent share of the votes, and jumped to 23 per cent in 1893. With a result of 110 seats in the elections of 1912, the party became the largest in the country.[20]

Since the establishment of the Reich in 1871 the state structure had been upheld by an alliance of the agrarian Junker interest and the industrial bourgeoisie. Political power mostly remained concentrated in the hands of the Junkers, but, in exchange for accepting this, the capitalist element could count on the state facilitating their economic interests.[21] In the *Reichstag*, the government mostly relied on the support of the conservative parties as well as on the National-Liberals. Some opposition could be expected from the Catholic Centre, which for mainly religious reasons was not fully integrated in the Empire. In social terms, the Centre relied mostly on what the Marxists called the petty-bourgeois element, branching out towards the bourgeoisie and working class. Since 1893 the *Reichstag* knew two Left-Liberal parties, the Liberal [*Freisinnige*] Association and the more radical Liberal People's Party. The Liberals of various denominations drew their votes mainly from the protestant bourgeois, petty bourgeois and peasant strata.[22]

The economic recovery setting in in 1895, Germany's growing economic power, its rivalry with Great Britain, and the new enthusiasm for colonialism and imperialism combined to produce a shift in the Reich's foreign policy. What Germany needed, thought Emperor Wilhelm II and his Foreign Secretary Bernhard von Bülow, was a 'world politics [*Weltpolitik*]'. In von Bülow's words, it was high time for Germany to secure its 'place in the sun'. To secure the new German ambitions, the government presented a bill allowing the construction of a powerful navy to the Reichstag in November 1897. In the eyes of the government, the plan served the additional purpose of restoring a nationwide parliamentary coalition to deal with the social democratic threat.[23] The bill presented a major challenge for the SPD. The party mobilised all its forces to prevent its adaptation. To have any chance of success, the social democrats needed the support of the 'petty bourgeois' Liberal and Centre parties.

In the early 1890s the German social democrats had not yet given up on the petty bourgeoisie, which class in the classic permanent revolution would play a decisive role as trigger of the proletarian revolution. The social democrats continued to deny that the petty bourgeoisie formed one 'reactionary mass'. It was not impossible, they thought, that the petty-bourgeois parties would turn away from the Junkers, thus setting in motion a dynamic that might end with the workers' party in power.[24]

Social democratic disappointment was immense when in late March 1898 the Reichstag accepted the *Flottengesetz* with the support of the National-Liberals, the majority of the Centre, and the Liberal Association.[25] It was this event, more than anything else, which triggered the SPD's leading theorist's loss of faith in the petty bourgeoisie. Kautsky interpreted the navy vote as the closing of the ranks of the bourgeois parties against the proletariat. He drew the momentous conclusion that the petty-bourgeois radicals were lost for the democratic revolution.

On 30 March 1898 the lead article of Die Neue Zeit observed that a year ago the party had hoped for the 'bourgeois opposition' to brace itself 'just once more' for resistance against the absolutist state. Unfortunately, though, the Centre and Liberal parties had decided in support of the *Flottengesetz*. There followed this remarkable conclusion: 'The working class has no other support in the whole world but itself, and the more exclusively it seeks its salvation in its own ranks, the more surely it will prevent all attacks by its mortal enemies.'[26]

According to Kautsky, the vote revealed that the petty-bourgeois classes were lost as allies in the struggle for democracy. Instead, they had turned into a force of reaction.[27] Kautsky was not afraid to cross the taboo line and to establish in a direct challenge to Marx: 'the slogan of the "reactionary mass" has come true'.[28] The reason for the unfortunate development was, he suggested in his 1902 *The Social Revolution*, that under the new and relatively more democratic conditions the petty bourgeois class knew themselves to be represented by the state. They had become a satisfied class.[29] Kautsky went so far as to conclude that already by June 1848 the hope of an uprising of bourgeois classes triggering the proletarian revolution had been misguided. It was the failed uprising of the Paris workers that had definitely frightened away the petty bourgeoisie.[30]

The supposed loss of the democratic-revolutionary potential of the non-proletarian masses would, again, make it imperative for the workers to have the majority. This was precisely the conclusion Kautsky drew in the 1907 edition of his *The Social Revolution*. He characterised the 'bourgeois classes, i.e. those standing on the basis of private ownership of the means of production' as follows:

> Ever more, all of them form a closed phalanx against the proletariat. Under such circumstances this [class] can remain confident of its victory only in the case when it becomes the mass of the nation itself.[31]

Under these terms, proletarian revolution would be ruled out under circumstances where the petty bourgeoisie was in the majority, i.e. among the less developed nations such as the Russian Empire.

Kautsky and Russia

Kautsky's comments on the revolution that broke out in Russia in January 1905 confirmed that this was the drift of his thinking. On several occasions he mentioned 'revolution in permanence' as the most apt strategic formula for Russia.[32] But with Kautsky, permanent revolution had a fundamentally more modest orientation than with either Marx and Engels or Trotsky. Kautsky acknowledged that the industrial proletariat was the leading force of the democratic revolution. He also accepted that the success of the revolution depended on an alliance with the Russian peasants, who, in contrast to the German petty bourgeoisie, had preserved their democratic orientation. But Kautsky firmly denied the peasantry could have any socialist aspirations. The Russian workers would have to commit themselves forcefully to the democratic revolution, stretching it to the limit, but without overstepping that limit. Kautsky adopted the 'permanent revolution', but without the socialist sting that was in its tail.[33] Most aptly, Lars Lih calls his conception: 'Democratic Revolution *in Permanenz*'.[34]

Kautsky's fullest presentation of his Russian strategy of democratic worker–peasant alliance came in 1907: socialism was 'unthinkable' in backward Russia – even if the Russian social democrats 'temporarily' would come to power:

> It is ... not to be expected that the peasants become socialists. Socialism can only be constructed on the basis of large-scale enterprise; it contradicts the conditions of small-scale enterprise too much to be able to arise and assert itself among a predominantly peasant population.[35]

Kautsky's Russian strategy differed from Plekhanov's in some essential ways, but he too saw the democratic revolution ending in a protracted period of capitalist development. The bottom line of 'orthodox Marxism', German and Russian, was that the petty bourgeois and peasant masses were never socialists. Everything else followed from this. Only in 1917, would Lenin break the spell.

Notes

1. Zamoyski, 1999: 443.
2. See 'Klassenkämpfe in Frankreich' (*MEW*, vol. 7: 33, 35, 89).
3. Ibid.: vol. 22: 515–17. Note, however, that Engels indicated in his *Anti-Dühring*, written in the late 1870s, that the present level of production in Germany could sustain a classless society: 'This point has now been reached' (vol. 20: 261–4).
4. Anonymous, 1897a: 3.
5. For Kautsky's biography and thought, see Steenson, 1978; Salvadori, 1979; Hünlich, 1981; Gilcher-Holtey, 1986; Donald, 1993.
6. Kautsky, 1976: 54, 185.
7. Ibid.: 53–4 (emphasis added).
8. In his 1899 *Die Agrarfrage* Kautsky (1966: 295) explained that human society functions as an integrated organism and could therefore only move 'in *one*

direction'. That direction would be determined by the leading segment of society. Thus, if 'large-scale industry' was the 'ruling power', small-scale agriculture could never prevent society from moving towards socialism. For Kautsky's 'Socialist organism theory', see also Larsson, 1970: 53–5.
9 Kautsky, 1972: 25, 46.
10 Ibid.: 16.
11 See Kolakowski (1981, vol. 2: 43–7) for the 'principle of "maturity"' with Kautsky, who made the proletarian revolution dependent on the 'ripening of economic conditions'.
12 See Tipton, 2003b: 131–3, 137; Fairbairn, 2008: 62, 69, 73–5.
13 Fontana, 2006a: 139.
14 In 1907, Germany had an economically active population of 28.1 million people. There were 10.1 million industrial workers and artisans employed in the industrial sector. Artisans made up 11.3 per cent of all *Erwerbstätigen* (Wehler, 1995: 680–1, 773–4). This would make for an industrial working class of 6.9 million people. For the figure of 76 per cent, see ibid.: 773. Compare: Fontana (2006a: 139), who gives 41 per cent of the economically active population as employed in the industrial sector in 1907.
15 See for example 'Anti-Dühring' (*MEW*, vol. 20: 258–9). 'Die Entwicklung des Sozialismus von der Utopie zur Wissenschaft' (1891 edition), vol. 19: 220–8; passage inserted by Engels in the third volume of *Das Kapital*, 1894 (vol. 25: 453–4). Engels could rely on Marx's notes from the 1860s, which he included in that volume (ibid.: 451–7).
16 'Die Bauernfrage', 1894 (ibid.: vol. 22: 504; emphasis added).
17 Parvus wrote this in the *Sächsische Arbeiterzeitung* of 6 March 1898 (cited in Scharlau, 1964: 98). I have not been able to view this newspaper first-hand. For the new capitalism preparing socialism, see also Parvus's (n.y.) 1910 *Der Staat, die Industrie und der Sozialismus*. See also Tudor and Tudor, 1988: Chapter 6.
18 *Das Finanzkapital* (1910): Hilferding, 1973: 503–7. For a discussion of this aspect of Hilferding's work, see Gronow, 1986: 19–21. For discussions of *Das Finanzkapital*, see Wagner, 1996: Chapter 4; Smaldone, 1998: Chapter 2; Bottomore and Goode, 1978: 22–5. For Hilferding on the increasing capitalist state intervention facilitating the socialist transition, see ibid.: 25–9; Kowalski, 1991: 26–7; Smaldone, 2014: 184.
19 Berghahn, 1994: 190–3; see also Mommsen, 1995.
20 Berghahn, 1994: 335–6. For the electoral process in imperial Germany, see also Sperber, 1997.
21 See Willms, 1983: 428–9.
22 For the party landscape in the 1890s, see ibid.: Chapters 18–20; Berghahn, 2003: 312–13; Hewitson, 2008: 46.
23 Berghahn, 1971: 129–57; Willms, 1983: 602–3, 623–61; Fesser, 1996: 25–38.
24 See for example Anonymous, 1891: 751–2; Kautsky, 1897: 584–9; Bebel, 1897: 610–11.
25 Berghahn, 1971: 155–7; Fesser, 1996: 38–40.
26 Anonymous, 1898a: 33, 35–6.
27 See for example Kautsky, 1899: 292–5.
28 Kautsky, 1972: 111. According to Gilcher-Holtey (1986: 229), this was the first instance of Kautsky accepting the 'one reactionary mass' formula. For her comments on Kautsky's turn to proletarian isolationism, see ibid.: 223ff.
29 Kautsky, 1907a: 30–5, 52–3. See also: Kautsky, 1903: 389–98; Kautsky, 'To what extent is the *Communist Manifesto* obsolete?' (original 1903 version) (Day and Gaido, 2009: 173–4).
30 Kautsky, 'To what extent' (Day and Gaido, 2009: 178). For Kautsky on Marx and Engels's supposed overestimation of the revolutionary potential of the bourgeois

classes, see also ibid.: 19. See on Kautsky's interpretation of how the west European petty bourgeoisie became satisfied classes in the period 1846–70, and on the impossibility of the model of the 'petty bourgeois-proletarian revolution', see also Kautsky, 1972: 18, 71–3. See also Salvadori (1979: 79–90, 100–8, 128–30) on Kautsky, the petty bourgeoisie and the permanent revolution; Hobsbawm, 2011: 66.

31 Kautsky, 1907a: 59–60. In his 1909 *Road to Power*, Kautsky was less straightforward, referring to the proletariat in highly developed countries both as the majority and as the most numerous class, without clearly indicating what would be the minimum requirement for the revolution (Kautsky, 1972: 18, 32–3, 46, 63, 89).

32 See for example Kautsky, 1905b: 461–2; Anonymous, 1906: 169, 171. Unsigned lead articles were mostly written by Franz Mehring.

33 See also Kautsky, 1905c: 615 [cf. Kautsky, 1904: 623–7]; Kautsky, 1905a: 675–6; Kautsky, 'Old and New Revolution' (December 1905) Day and Gaido, 2009: 532–4; Kautsky, 1906a: 414; 'To what extent' (Day and Gaido, 2009: 174, 179).

34 Lih, 2012. On the 'democratic' character of Kautsky's permanent revolution, see Larsson, 1970: 252–304; Salvadori, 1979: 88, 100–6; Löwy, 1981: 39–43. Donald (1993: 70–84, 95–102) accepts that Kautsky's permanent revolution did not include the socialist transition, but nonetheless sees it as groundbreaking radicalism compared to Marx and Engels. For Kautsky as forerunner of Trotskii, see Day and Gaido, 2009: xi, 40–4.

35 Kautsky, 1907b: 331–3. Kautsky recognised that the conditions in Russia in the early twentieth century were in many ways similar to those in Germany at the time of the *Communist Manifesto*, which text therefore continued to be relevant for Russian socialists. But he insisted that the quick transition from bourgeois to proletarian revolution had proved impossible ('To what extent', Day and Gaido, 2009: 174, 177, 183–4).

11 Socialism as autarky

During the 1880s and 1890s government policies of the capitalist great powers took a new turn. The Great Depression of 1873 to 1895 led to the demise of liberal free trade. With the exception of Great Britain, one power after another decided to shield its home market from foreign competition through the establishment of protective tariffs. In Germany, Bismarck initiated the process in 1879.[1]

In a concomitant process, the European powers greatly expanded their colonial holdings. The bulk of the remaining free areas of the world outside the Americas were occupied and put under direct European administration. Imperialism climaxed in the scramble for Africa. The German ruling classes realised that their country, a latecomer in the struggle for global dominance, could acquire its own 'place in the sun' only in the face of stiff British and French competition. German colonialism always remained a comparatively weak force, but a good beginning was made in 1884, with the acquirement of extensive territories in Western Africa. Germany engaged in the power game in other parts of the world as well, for example when it acquired Jiaozhou Bay on the Chinese coast in 1898.[2]

Protectionism and imperialism significantly impacted on how the social democrats conceptualised capitalism. Social democrats speculated about the emergence of large-scale and supposedly more or less autarkic capitalist economic spaces. That, again, impacted on the social democratic imagination of the socialist *Zukunftsstaat*. During the heydays of liberal free trade, the 1860s and 1870s, socialists like Lassalle and Vollmar had expected much of the supposed superiority of the socialist economic system. Its higher efficiency would allow an isolated socialist state to engage in an offensive survival strategy on the international market: the capitalist rivals would be outcompeted. In the era of imperialism and protectionism, the question was reformulated fundamentally. Now, social democrats tended to find the solution for an isolated socialist state in withdrawal into self-sufficiency, a survival strategy more reflective of the communitarian instincts of communism. Yet, in a paradox, social democrats of the right wing of the party argued that, to be truly self-sufficient, an isolated socialist Germany needed a colonial empire to secure markets and sources of raw materials. Thus, in the revisionist imagination, inward-looking autarky acquired an expansionist orientation.

Kautsky's autarkic socialism

According to the new programme adopted by the SPD at its 1891 Erfurt congress, the workers of the world were ever more mutually dependent. 'The liberation of the working class is therefore a work in which the workers of all civilised countries are equally engaged.'[3] This formula made proletarian internationalism essential but it did not define cooperation of proletarian *countries* as indispensable. Strictly speaking, single-country socialism was not ruled out here. Even so, the text was surely not intended as a departure from the view that socialism required the joint efforts of a number of advanced countries. The 1899 Hannover SPD congress adopted a resolution in favour of a federation of the 'civilised countries'.[4]

However, old certainties were gradually evaporating. In practice, the Marx–Engels formula of the alliance of advanced countries no longer carried much weight. Though the idea was never formally withdrawn, the *Dreibund* was not often referred to anymore. Even the 'orthodox Marxists' were beginning to look at the socialist *Zukunftsstaat* in new ways.

The main theorist of 'orthodox Marxism' seems to have been very much of two minds. On several occasions Kautsky predicted a cascade of proletarian revolutions ending in the establishment of a 'United States of Europe' (USE), which in 1911 he called the 'state foundation of the coming socialist society'.[5] The ideal of the United States of Europe had been formulated in 1867, in the programme for the first Geneva congress of the radical International League of Peace and Freedom.[6] On occasion Engels had positively referred to it.[7] The socialist United States of Europe became a more popular idea in the SPD than the old *Dreibund*.[8]

However, even though the USE was the ideal to which socialism tended, socialism was not made dependent on achieving that European scale. To be sure, Kautsky remained committed to the idea of proletarian revolution as a contagious phenomenon, rapidly spreading from one country to another. In Massimo Salvadori's words, Kautsky's thinking remained stamped by the 'hypothesis of revolutionary chain reactions'.[9] Around the turn of the century Kautsky wrote: 'social democracy could not be victorious in Germany without making the socialist movement irresistible in all of Europe'.[10]

But Kautsky did not take it for granted absolutely that the revolution would rapidly spread beyond the initiator-state. In his very important 'Various Revolutionary Issues [*Allerhand Revolutionäres*]', he explained that no 'lasting socialist regime within a capitalist environment' could be established in a 'small territory' such as Belgium, but that it would be an altogether different story if the 'victory of socialism' came first in the USA. According to Kautsky, there was no absolute guarantee that the European proletariat would follow suit. And, should the European workers fail to follow the shining American example, this would not result in the demise of socialism in the USA but, on the contrary, in the degradation of European society.[11] In other words, Kautsky did not rule out the possibility that the socialist system might at first flourish on the territory of a single great power after all.[12]

Unfortunately, we do not know whether Kautsky placed Germany in the Belgium or in the USA category, but the most plausible interpretation of his thinking in the years before the Great War is that any proletarian revolution would most likely quickly be followed by others, but that in case the revolutionary chain reaction did cool off it was not impossible for a single socialist great power to persist within a hostile capitalist environment.

Kautsky's main contribution to the question of socialism in one country lies in his autarkic conception of the socialist economy. He was a convinced opponent of colonialism, imperialism and protectionism, but he could not help being fascinated by the idea of autarky. In his 1892 *The Erfurt Program*, Kautsky defined socialism as 'cooperative [*genossenschaftliche*] production for one's own needs [*Selbstbedarf*]', as opposed to production for the market. Socialism, Kautsky explained, would function like a primitive peasant household, but on an incomparably more sophisticated, modern technological basis. The question was how extended the socialist 'self-sufficient co-operative [*Genossenschaft*]' must be to function effectively. This was Kautsky's answer: 'Only *one* presently existing social organisation has the necessary dimensions for the development of a socialist co-operative, and that is the *modern state*.' But wasn't there good reason to doubt 'whether even the framework of the state would be spacious enough to encompass the socialist co-operative'? *There was not*, Kautsky insisted, for the impressive expansion of international trade had more to do with capitalism than with real needs. Under socialism international trade would be 'sharply reduced'. 'The dimensions of the modern state', Kautsky concluded, 'suffice to allow each socialist co-operative to produce everything it *needs* for its existence'.[13]

In envisioning the *Zukunfsstaat* as an autarky, Kautsky was building on the tradition of the 'state socialists'.[14] This tradition again built on the work of the philosopher Johann Gottlieb Fichte, who was highly regarded in socialist circles as a humanist and forerunner of socialism.[15] Fichte's argument in *The Closed Commercial State* (1800) was that a state that wants to regulate its economy, as it should in order to protect the welfare of its people, must sever the unpredictable economic links with the world abroad as much as possible.[16]

This argument was easily translated into Marxist terms. In March 1900 Kautsky wrote that a socialist economy was necessarily a 'rounded [*in sich abgerundetes*] area of production' because 'The more products the economy of a socialist commonwealth must procure from outside, the more commodity trading will be preserved within the socialist society.'[17] In other words, it was the Marxist ideal of a society without commodity production (i.e. production for the purpose of trade) that led Kautsky to the conclusion that a socialist state should be self-sufficient.

126 *Socialism as autarky*

Kautsky was in his *Erfurt Program* not necessarily referring to an isolated socialist state. What he would have found more likely to emerge was an international community of socialist states, each of which was to be organising its own autarkic economy. Even so, he couldn't have been more explicit that it *was* possible to have a functioning socialist economy within the confines of a single state. The significance of this for party ideology can hardly be overestimated, for the *Erfurt Program* was the most authoritative compendium of SPD ideology. Through Kautsky, the idea that a socialist economy could function on the scale of one country entered the 'orthodox' mainstream of German socialism. Importantly, Kautsky never took the trouble to explain how state autarky could be reconciled with the Marx–Engels notion that a socialist economy required the input of several countries.

Kautsky took the ambivalent position that, *economically*, socialism in one country was a viable proposition but *politically* it was an unlikely one – but again not impossible. But even on the economic aspect, he could never really make up his mind. In June 1905 he wrote that a socialist economy 'cannot be restricted to one nation, one country'. He explained that, with the emergence of the capitalist world market, no nation could exist 'for itself alone', which is why socialism 'in the end necessarily leads ... to the establishment of an organism of social production that encompasses the whole world market'.[18] Oddly, Kautsky failed to explain why the capitalist world market would necessarily undo an autarkic economy.

Despite all of this ambiguity, Kautsky's acceptance of the viability of a single socialist great power and of autarkic socialist economies proves that he no longer took the official view that socialism required the cooperation of a number of states at face value. It was a bridge too far for him to discard the official dogma in so many words.

Socialism in one country: the imperialist variety

As mentioned earlier, even after the symbolic triumph of Marxism at the 1891 Erfurt congress, the SPD never became an ideologically monolithic party. The adherents of 'revisionism', who were competing with Kautskyan 'orthodoxy', straightforwardly adapted their agenda to the German *Weltpolitik*. 'Social imperialism' has been analysed in depth in the scholarly literature. The revisionists had their own theoretical journal, the *Sozialistische Monatshefte*, to which they all contributed, but they were internally deeply divided, the main division being that between the editor of the *Monatshefte*, Joseph Bloch, on the one hand and Bernstein on the other. Roger Fletcher sees Bloch's comrades-in-arms – Max Schippel, Richard Calwer, Gerhard Hildebrand and others – as authoritarian nationalists and champions of protectionism. At the same time, they were preoccupied with the view that the nation-state was getting obsolete. The future belonged to large economic spaces. More concretely, the whole world was in the process of being divided up into a small number of great empires, mainly Britain, France, America, Russia and an

East-Asian zone. Germany would have to establish an autarkic hegemonic zone of its own, in the form a continental-European bloc with colonial ramifications in Africa and the Middle East.[19] Bernstein's sympathies lay more in the liberal direction. As a long-term resident of Great Britain and an Anglophile, he advocated free trade, but he was also known for his spirited defence of colonialism.[20]

The revisionists furthermore argued that socialist economies, no less than the capitalist, required large, autarkic zones for their survival. Perhaps the first to make this point was Kārlis Balodis, an independent Latvian socialist scholar who lived in Germany since 1895, under the name of Carl Ballod. He was writing under the pseudonym 'Atlanticus'. Balodis's *Production and Consumption in the Social State* was published by Dietz Verlag in 1898.[21] Balodis found it 'completely unthinkable that the whole earth will turn socialist in one blow'. One should rather reckon with the possibility that one state would come first. In that case, 'such a state will acquire nothing from the rest of the world', and it would have no choice but to become a 'closed state, which produces all it requires on its own territory'. That again, Balodis continued, was only possible through the contributions provided by colonial territories, which is why the 'victory of socialism' in Germany required a colonial empire to fall back on.[22] In his foreword to the book, Kautsky rejected Balodis's colonialist aspirations, but he considered it a serious contribution to the debate about socialism.[23]

Bernstein covered more or less the same ground in his famous 1899 *Preconditions of Socialism*. The father of revisionism observed that the SPD might possibly come to power in the near future. The neighbouring peoples were however not yet that advanced, and Bernstein was afraid that the German social democrats would have to defend their country in the revolutionary–patriotic way of the Jacobins. Germany might move fast, but 'in many other countries it will still take a considerable period of time until they will be introducing socialism'. Like Balodis, he concluded that a solitary German advance to socialism would make colonial expansion essential, for 'one day the time might come when it may be desirable for us to be able to procure at least part of these products from our own colonies'.[24]

A similar viewpoint was again defended in December 1899 by the unknown social democrat Erich Rother. Rother hoped to show that it was in the interest of the proletariat for Germany to have a powerful navy. This instance of social democratic support for the *Flottengesetz* was embarrassing enough for Bebel to inform the Reichstag that the *Sozialistische Monatshefte*, in which 'On the theory of the naval question' had appeared, was not representing official party positions.[25] For Rother, socialism meant an 'organised, closed economy, producing all its essential consumer goods on its own territory and for itself, without dependence on the world abroad'. Economically closed territories, Rother believed, were already under formation, in particular the British and French empires, Russia's continental colonialism, and the United States, dominating the American continent. What is more, these 'large areas of production' were, in effect, according to Rother, the 'nuclei [*Keime*] of future socialist organisations'. From the point of view of the development of 'single [*einzelner*], rounded socialist societies', Germany needed a colonial empire of its own to cover its imports. Rother did not rule out the possibility of a proletarian triumph on an international scale, but, alternatively, a socialist Germany might have to fight for a colonial empire with the capitalist world: 'who can say whether one day we will not have to eke out the secure basis for the socialist society with armour and torpedoes?'[26]

Thus there emerged a new, imperialist variety of socialism in one country among the right wing of German socialism: Germany, the initiator-state hosting a socialist mode of production, would be kept afloat by a colonial empire. The underlying principle of socialist autarky was sharply at odds with Marx and Engels's thinking. Ironically, though, it was the 'pope of orthodox Marxism' himself that had paved the way for the revisionists on this score.

The classic Marx–Engels idea of a league of socialist states returned among German social democrats of the right wing in a new context. In 1894, *Die Neue Zeit* carried a remarkable article suggesting that Germany, Italy, France and Austria-Hungary join forces to ward off the competition of the extra-European powers: Great Britain, Russia, the USA and China. What is more, the European countries, H. M. suggested, were much closer to the new 'more harmonious economic order' than those outside Europe. The continental association was to introduce that new order.[27] In 1898, the economist and SPD member of the Reichstag, Richard Calwer, advanced the idea of a Central-European tariff union, which in his view would not only help the Central powers to survive international competition, but would also expedite a future socialist transition.[28] It was Calwer who developed this thought into a full-blown conception of continental-European socialism.

In his September 1905 article 'World policy and Social Democracy', Calwer urged Germany to fortify itself against the four supposedly autarkic empires that were in the process of formation: Britain, the USA, Russia and the Japanese sphere in East Asia. Calwer found the solution in continental European unification. Whereas, he believed, neither Britain nor America would soon move 'in a socialist direction', in France and Germany the conditions for the transition were much better.

> Economies cannot be made subject to socialist regulation within a narrow national framework ... Things will be very different when the Central- and West-European countries ... create a large, sufficiently broad basis that can be closed off ... Given the economic and political power of such an aggregate of countries [*Länderkomplexes*] it will be comparatively easy to overcome the international problems facing socialist measures.[29]

The Great War and socialism

The speculations about a German socialist breakthrough in advance of other countries were inspired by the fact that the SPD was much more influential than socialist parties in other countries. It seemed very likely that it would be the first party to seize the helm of state. The Great War fuelled speculations that the increasing state regulation of the wartime economies was further improving the prospects of socialist transition.[30]

The most interesting wartime speculations about an early German breakthrough were undertaken by the 'Lensch–Cunow–Haenisch group', as Robert Sigel calls them. The journalists and editors Paul Lensch and Konrad Haenisch, and high schoolteacher and ethnologist Heinrich Cunow formed a distinct faction in the party. They had been on the radical left and were close to Parvus, but, like the latter, swung to the revisionist right after the outbreak of the war.[31] The members of the faction argued that German political culture was more conducive to socialism than the French and British, and that state capitalism was further advanced in Germany than in those other countries. They even suggested that the transition was already an ongoing process in their fatherland.

Haenisch did not deny that, for the time being, Germany remained a capitalist country, but in his eyes the 'foundations' of the socialist state had already been laid. He did not hesitate to call Germany a *'workers' state in the process of formation* [werdenden Arbeiterstaat]'.[32] And even though the process of socialisation was ongoing on both sides of the front, Haenisch believed that Germany was much further advanced than Britain.[33] In his *German Social Democracy and the World War* (1915), Lensch too admitted that Germany was still a capitalist country, but he insisted that the contemporary 'organisation of economic life' 'in principle' already represented socialism.[34] In his 1916 *Sozial Democracy. Its Passing* [Ende] *and Its Auspiciousness* [Glück], he called the ongoing war a *'revolutionary world war'*.[35] Whereas Britain represented reactionary individualism, the Prussian tradition stood for the revolutionary principle of 'social organisation'.[36] Germany was therefore the country closest to socialism: 'it is the historical task of Germany to create the unfolding conditions of this socialised society'.[37] Haenisch and Lensch were suggesting that their German fatherland might become the pioneer of 'organised' socialism.

It was impossible, though, for right-wing social democrats during the war to speculate too openly about the socialist transition– for obvious reasons. At the outbreak of the war, when it came to a vote on 4 August, the Reichstag faction, notoriously, unanimously supported the war credits. For the duration of the war, the majority of the German social democrats accepted the regime of the *Burgfrieden*. Class struggle and open challenges to the system that might endanger national defence and rattle the government were avoided.

It proved impossible to keep the party united behind this position. The SPD was led by two co-chairmen, the lawyer Hugo Haase and the former saddle-maker, Friedrich Ebert, who had replaced Bebel after his death in 1913. On 2 December 1914, Karl Liebknecht became the first German social democrat courageously to vote against the credits. In January 1916, he, Rosa Luxemburg and others from the left wing of the party formed the Spartakus League. In late 1915, Haase's centrists decided to withdraw their support for the war credits. This rebellion led to the formation of the Independent Social Democratic Party of Germany in April 1917. Kautsky and Bernstein, as well as the Spartakists, joined the USPD. The party majority led by Ebert, now calling themselves the MSPD (Majority Social Democratic Party of Germany), however, continued to support the government.[38] Inevitably, the self-imposed acceptance of the *Burgfrieden* made the MSPD reluctant to engage in explicit discussions about the socialist transition, which could only harm national unity.

This clearly showed through at the October 1917 MSPD congress in Würzberg, where Ebert and Philipp Scheidemann were elected co-chairmen of the party. According to Susanne Miller, Scheidemann's speech and the four main reports presented at the congress made up the first systematic reflection concerning post-war policies on the part of the MSPD.[39] The presenter on economic policy, Cunow, described the war as an 'immense revolutionary factor' in German economic life.[40] He proposed socialisation of the mining sector, iron and steel, and the armaments industries, in an ever widening process resulting in 'socialisation of the state'. But in a paradoxical counterpoint he also asserted that such reforms would open up a new 'stage of capitalist development'.[41] Similarly, Scheidemann referred favourably to the 'etatisation' of the economy, but warned that no attempt be made to establish socialism in a single 'jump'.[42]

If we now return to Kautsky, a member of the rival USPD, we find him pessimistic about an early breakthrough to socialism as well. In his *Social Democratic Comments on the Transitional Economy*, written in 1918 sometime before the revolutionary storm broke loose in his fatherland, Kautsky denied that state and monopoly–capitalist regulation significantly facilitated the socialist transition.[43] Another problem was that the war had ruined the economy. The conditions for socialism were 'unfavourable': socialism needed prosperity, not 'general shortages'. The social democrats had therefore better *not* seek power in the immediate aftermath of the war, Kautsky thought.[44]

But Kautsky would not be Kautsky if he did not leave all scenarios open. He did not rule out the possibility that the German socialists or the comrades in another developed capitalist state in the wake of the war would find themselves in power after all. What was to be done in that case? Kautsky began by saying that socialism would be 'realised simultaneously' in several countries: the 'starting point of a proletarian commonwealth' could only be a developed country in which the proletariat forms the great majority of the population, but socialism was bound to spread rapidly to other countries. This is how the contagious mechanism would work:

> once the proletariat in such a state has successfully taken up the organisation of production in its own way, the example will work as a detonator [*zündend*]. No country with capitalist production will be able to ignore the impact of the pioneering state [*des bahnbrechenden Staatswesens*].[45]

Ironically, Kautsky hereby confirmed that the introduction of socialism would *not* be simultaneous! The time lapse would be short, but that makes no fundamental difference: Kautsky was not simply arguing here that one proletarian revolution would trigger another, but that the establishment of a *socialist economy in one country* would trigger socialist ambitions elsewhere. It was the successful creation of a socialist economy in one initiator-state that would create the attractive example to draw other nations towards revolution.[46] Kautsky described this mechanism in terms of state-to-state 'object-lessons [*Anschauungsunterricht*]'.[47]

Kautsky still saw the world revolution as a compact process playing itself out over a number of countries in a short period of time, but the world-revolutionary mechanism depended on the successful prior construction of a socialist order in one trailblazing state. Essentially, he adopted the conception of revolution by example pioneered by Winstanley.

Notes

1 On the emergence of protectionism, see Hobsbawm, 1987: 38–43. For protectionism in Germany, see Willms, 1983: 467–472, 549–58, 602–3, 650; Berghahn, 2003: 283–4.
2 Hobsbawm, 1987: Chapter 3. For the history of German colonialism, see Fröhlich, 1994; Fesser, 1996.
3 Schröder, 1910: 470–1.
4 Ibid.: 88.
5 Kautsky, 1908: 36; 1911: 105–7.
6 See van der Linden, 1987: Chapters 21 and further; Cooper, 1991: Chapters 2, 3; Cherubini, 2004. Kautsky (1916: 526–30) traced back the ideal of a European league of states to Cloots, the International Workingmen's Association, as well as to the ILPF. According to Kautsky, after the era of bourgeois revolutions had ended in the 1870s, the ideal had been mostly forgotten. On the IWA and the slogan of European confederation, see also Guillaume, 1905: 37.
7 See 1893 interview with the *Daily Chronicle* (*MEW*, vol. 22: 547).
8 For the popularity of the slogan among the party centre (Kautsky, Bebel and others), see Fletcher, 1984: 40. The European confederation was also on Bernstein's agenda. See Fletcher, 1983: 86, 89; Fletcher, 1979b: 230. For Parvus and the idea of a United States of Europe, see also Zeman and Scharlau, 1965: 42, 105. In his *Die Erschütterung der Industrieherrschaft*, Gerhard Hildebrand (1910: 238) advocated a 'United States of Western Europe' based on a tariff union. See also the discussions about Hildebrand at the 1912 Chemnitz SPD congress: *Handbuch*, n.y.: 200–23. Luxemburg rejected the United States of Europe, which she believed was inevitably tainted with imperialism: 'Friedensutopien' (May 1911), Luxemburg, 1981: 498–503; 'Perspektiven und Projekte' [1915], Luxemburg, 1983: 33–4, 40. 'Entwurf zu den Junius-Thesen', adopted 1 January 1916 by the 'Gruppe "Internationale"', predecessor to the *Spartakusbund* (ibid.: 45); *Die Krise* (ibid.: 138).
9 Salvadori, 1979: 89.
10 Kautsky, 1900: 815–16.
11 Kautsky, 1904: 653, 655–6.
12 Kautsky also discussed the possibility of America establishing a 'socialist society' in advance of Europe in 'Der amerikanische Arbeiter' (1906b: 787). For other

132 Socialism as autarky

social democrats vaguely hinting at socialism in one country, see also Kolb, 1903: 908; Emil, 1907: 243; Hildebrand, 1910: 81 (see also p. 6); Däumig, 1912: 682–3, 744; see also Vollmar, 1893: 198. To counter the argument that the fatherland needed imperialism and colonialism to survive, Franz Mehring wrote in a remarkable March 1897 editorial of *Die Neue Zeit*: 'If Germany wants to get ahead of richer nations, only one road is available to her, the road of a "social revolution, which ... allows the creation of new productive forces cancelling out the disadvantages of the geographical situation". Marx expressed this thought already fifty years ago ... and Lassalle later formulated that the world market will belong to that nation whose working class first manages to emancipate itself' (Anonymous, 1897b). See also Anonymous, 1898b: 514–15; Anonymous, 1900: 68; Anonymous, 1904: 651–2.

13 Kautsky, 1919: 111–16. For the comparison of a communist economy with a peasant household, see also Kautsky, 1887: 30; Kautsky, 1900: 778. On the question of the primacy of the internal market under socialism, see also Kautsky, 1898: xvii–xxiv; Kautsky, 1966 (originally published 1899): 442; Kautsky, 1901: 7, 91–5. See also Schröder, 1978: 175–6. On socialist autarky in Kautsky, see also Kelsen, 1920: 58–9; Cole, 1961, vol. 2: 434.

14 Dühring (1892: 89–90), Rodbertus-Jagetzow (1884: 101–2, 124, 159, 223, 275, 285–6) and Schäffle (1877: Chapters 3–5) imagined the *Zukunftsstaat* as a self-sufficient economy matching its own needs. For Carl August Schramm, defender of Rodbertus's heritage in the party, on an autarkic socialist Germany, see C. A. S., 1878. Cole (1961, vol. 2: 434) suggests that Petr Kropotkin inspired Kautsky in suggesting that international trade would decrease under socialism.

15 The editorial of the first issue of *Die Neue Zeit* mentioned Fichte as a source of inspiration (Anonymous, 1883: 2, 4).

16 Fichte, 1979. According to Cole (1977: 225), Fichte anticipated 'Socialism in one country'. For a discussion of Fichte's *Handelsstaat*, see Szporluk, 1988: 101; Harada, 1989: 37, 56–62.

17 Kautsky, 1900: 777–8; see also Kautsky, 1902: 199.

18 Kautsky, 1905d: 345–7.

19 On this form of social democratic imperialism, see Fletcher, 1984: esp. 61–2, 91; O'Boyle, 1949: 291–4, 297; Landauer, 1959: 361; Ascher, 1961; Bloch, 1974: esp. 261–2; Fletcher, 1980; Fletcher, 1982; Fletcher, 1988. For the term 'social imperialism', see Eley, 1976: 265–9.

20 For Bernstein's imperialism, see Fletcher, 1979a: 240–1; Fletcher, 1983: 86, 89; Fletcher, 1984: 39–40, Chapters 6–8. See also Gay, 1962: 252; Mommsen, 1978; Schröder, 1978.

21 For Balodis's biography, see Balabkins, 1978.

22 Atlanticus, 1898a: 17–18. Atlanticus (1898b) assumed that Germany would precede the other countries in the socialisation of society.

23 Kautsky, 1898.

24 Bernstein, 1899: 144–5, 149–50. According to Schröder (1978: 170–1) and Fletcher (1983: 84; 1984: 162–3), Bernstein defended the same standpoint at the August 1907 Stuttgart congress of the Second International. However, while advocating a 'positive-socialist colonial policy', Bernstein did not refer to the possibility of an isolated German socialism (*Internationaler Sozialisten-Kongress*, 1907: 28–9).

25 See Probert, 2003: 130.

26 Rother, 1899: 639–42.

27 H. M., 1894: 167–70.

28 Calwer, 1898: 328–30.

29 Calwer, 1905: 744–6, 748. Calwer confessed that, as a German socialist, he hoped for the conditions of socialisation to mature in Germany earlier than elsewhere. See for example Calwer, 1906: 356; Calwer, 1907a: 105, 107; Calwer, 1907b: 195–6,

198. In the last-mentioned article, Calwer insisted that a socialist Germany must not disarm in the face of foreign threats.
30 The Austrian Marxist Karl Renner was the most influential promoter of the idea of the wartime 'etatisation [*Durchstaatlichung*] of the economy', 'war socialism' and 'war capitalism'. In Renner's eyes, the 'quintessence of socialism' consisted in organisation and administration. The state was gradually turning into a 'lever of socialism'. The workers need only take over the state apparatus. See Renner, 1917 *Marxismus, Krieg und Internationale*: 9–10, 12, 28, 30. See also Leser, 1968: 280; Bottomore and Goode, 1978: 25–9; Anton Pelinka's (1994: 59) comments; Saage, 2008: 70; Stöger, 2008: 124.
31 For the classical study of the group, see Sigel, 1976; see also O'Boyle, 1949; Ascher, 1961; Cole, 1961, vol. 4.1: 111, 117; Schröder, 1978: 204.
32 Haenisch, 1916: 110, 125, 128–9.
33 Ibid.: 130–1.
34 Lensch, 1915: 54–64.
35 Lensch, 1916: 124.
36 Ibid.: v.
37 Ibid.: 217. For the whole argument about Germany and socialism, see especially: v–viii, 124–5, 158, 177, 183–8, 194–7, 217.
38 For the SPD during the war, see Fülberth and Harrer, 1974: 112–35; Miller, 1974; Fülberth, 1975; Miller and Potthoff, 1986: 55–63; Faulenbach, 2012: Chapter 4. On the establishment of the USPD, see Ryder, 1967: 93–9; Morgan, 1975: Chapter 1; Berlin, 1979: 62; Broué, 2005: Chapter 5.
39 See Miller, 1974: 339.
40 *Protokoll*, 1973: 145.
41 Ibid.: 159–60.
42 Ibid.: 408.
43 Kautsky, 1918b: 159–62.
44 Ibid.: 164–6.
45 Ibid.: 163.
46 It bears mentioning that, at this point, Kautsky (1918a: 42–3) saw Bolshevik Russia as a bourgeois country.
47 Ibid.: 42.

12 Socialism as war economy

Among the Russian social democrats, the paradigm of the dependence of socialism on the combined efforts of a number of advanced countries was well entrenched. Given that the Plekhanov consensus in any case ruled out a socialist transition in their fatherland for the foreseeable future, there would not have been much point in exploring the territorial and state preconditions of socialism. The Russian social democrats stuck to the Marx–Engels paradigm as a matter of course. Plekhanov wrote in the 1884 programme of Emancipation of Labour: 'The modern development of international commerce [*obmena produktov*] makes *the participation of all civilised societies* in this [impending economic] revolution imperative [*neobkhodimim*].'[1]

The manifesto adopted at the 1898 First Party Congress did not include a similar passage ruling out single-country socialism.[2] And the RSDWP programme adopted at the second congress in 1903 confined itself to saying that international commerce had welded such close ties between the civilised nations that the 'liberation struggle of the proletariat' had become international.[3] But that the Russian Marxists were not always unambiguous is not because they would have wanted to keep the option of the nationally confined breakthrough open. With socialism relegated to the distant future, they were simply not very interested in the question.[4]

Remarkably, prior to the Great War even Trotsky showed only sporadic interest in the problem of socialism in one country outside of the Russian context. Only in his 1906 *Results and Prospects* did he make the following important observation:

> The development of the social division of labour, on the one hand, and machine production on the other, has led to the position that nowadays the only co-operative body which could utilise the advantages of collective production on a wide scale is the State. *More than that, socialist production, for both economic and political reasons, could not be confined within the restricting limits of individual states.*[5]

Trotsky rejected socialism in one country, on economic grounds, not only in backward Russia but in any country. What makes this passage particularly interesting is that he described the position rejected by him – that a single state could hold a cooperative of socialist production – in the terms Kautsky had used in his comments on the Erfurt programme. Without mentioning him by name, Trotsky was rebuking the number-one 'orthodox Marxist'. *Results and Prospects* highlighted the growing apart of the German social democrats, who did not feel strictly bound to the Marx–Engels paradigm, and the Russians, who did.[6]

Russian internationalism

Initially, the Great War stiffened the Russian social democrats in their principled internationalism. The RSDWP was one of the few socialist parties that did not fall for the shrill patriotism prevalent in Europe in those days. This may have reflected the marginalised social position Russian workers occupied compared to their better integrated German and French colleagues. In August 1914, neither of the social democratic factions in the State Duma supported the war budget. With some exceptions, most prominently Plekhanov, the Bolshevik and Menshevik leaders embraced anti-defencism. Lenin took the most radically anti-patriotic position of all: he called for the transformation of the imperialist war into civil war and openly expressed the hope that his country would be defeated.

During the war the idea gained popularity among Russian social democrats that the proletarian revolution would take the form of a single, concerted action by the European proletariat, resulting in the immediate abolishment of state borders. The Menshevik internationalists hoped for an early peace arrangement. They shared neither Lenin's hopes that Russia would be defeated nor his hopes for the transformation of the war into a Europe-wide revolutionary civil war. Nonetheless, when they speculated about the possible course of the revolution, they tended to think in radically internationalist scenarios.[7] In his 'The War and the Russian Proletariat', published early in 1915, Martov argued that the Russian proletarian movement could not be 'locked up in "national frameworks [*natsional'nye ramki*]"'.[8] In his 1915 *The Crisis and the Tasks of the International Social-Democracy*, Aksel'rod asserted that the communist revolution would be an international joint venture aiming for the 'blasting of the state frameworks in several capitalistically highly developed countries'. He even posited that the development of the productive forces made the world economy interconnected to the point of ruling out the establishment of 'national and state property in separate parts of the world'.[9]

In the early period of the war, the independent social democrat Trotsky served with Martov on the editorial board of the Paris daily *Golos/Nashe slovo*.[10] In his 1914 *The War and the International* (originally written in German), he argued that the most fundamental reason why war had broken out was that the productive forces had outgrown 'the *national state* as an independent economic zone'. Instead, the world economy had become a single, interdependent whole. That is why fatherland defence had become pointless for the proletariat. Trotsky set his hopes on the creation of a 'much more powerful and robust fatherland – *the republican United States of Europe*'. But even that seemed not enough: the only real alternative to capitalist chaos was, Trotsky insisted, the 'socialist organisation of the world economy'.[11]

The Bolshevik faction was never a monolith. Among those most forcefully advocating radical internationalism was the left-wing Bolshevik Nikolai Bukharin. Bukharin, born in 1888, had been a member of the Moscow party organisation and a student at the juridical faculty in that city. The year 1914 found him in Lausanne, where he teamed up with a few other Bolsheviks living in the nearby village of Baugy.[12] In his seminal work *Imperialism and the World Economy*, written for the most part in 1915, Bukharin claimed that the national state had become a fetter on the productive forces. The world economy was increasingly becoming an interdependent whole, as well as being subject to a process of levelling. In a paradox, however, Bukharin saw the imperialist states at the same time turning themselves into 'state-capitalist trusts' and forming autarkic, closed national units, locked in mutual competition and war.[13] The latter tendency might have helped Bukharin to underpin an argument for socialism in one country, but that was far from his intention. As he saw it, socialism was heir to the first, internationalisation tendency. Bukharin's proletarian revolution would have the 'destruction of state borders' and the 'combination of the nations into one socialist community' as necessary elements.[14] Like Trotsky, Bukharin supported the slogan of the United States of Europe as the goal of the proletarian struggle.[15]

In short, during the war many Russian social democrats concluded almost in so many words that socialist economies were incompatible with the preservation of state borders and at a minimum required the framework of the United States of Europe. Until early 1915 Lenin remained part of this radical consensus. In his November 1914 'War and the Russian Social Democracy' he proposed the formation of a 'republican United States of Europe', emerging from a 'revolutionary war of the proletarians of all countries against the bourgeoisie of all countries'.[16] Lenin described the nation-state as obsolete and contrasted it with socialism as a necessarily supranational system: 'It is impossible to make the transition from capitalism to socialism without breaking the national frameworks.'[17] Whereas seizing power in single countries had been possible at the time of the *Communist Manifesto*, Lenin asserted that such an eventuality was now to be ruled out.[18]

Lenin breaks ranks

Yet Lenin was too intelligent a man to get lost in extremes. For one, however fiercely he was denouncing patriotism, he did not want to create the impression that he was rejecting the sentiment for all time. In December 1914, the revolutionary defeatist Lenin famously declared that he shared the 'national pride of the Great Russians'. Not only did he take pride in Russian revolutionary achievements, he also admired the beauty of the Russian language and of 'our wonderful motherland'. In an especially illuminating passage he indicated that his hatred of Russia's reactionary social order was inspired precisely by this 'feeling of national pride'. This is extremely revealing – Lenin was admitting that one of his reasons for being a revolutionary in the first place was that he wanted the best for his country.[19]

This avowal of Russian patriotism might seem difficult to square with the defeatism that Lenin displayed so openly. But as a socialist patriot he would have regarded the proletarian revolution to represent his country's true and deepest interest. From a revolutionary–patriotic point of view, his country's defeat on the battlefield would be a price well worth paying to achieve the larger good of bringing the revolution nearer.

Lenin's writings furthermore suggest that in the course of 1915 he began to realise that the way he and other Russian social democrats were imagining the European revolution represented an irresponsible radicalisation of the contagious-revolution scenario. Essentially, he accused his comrades of not taking into account that the world revolution might seize hold of one country and then grind to a halt. What was then to be done? Lenin's answer was that, in that case, the single revolutionary state would have to restart the world revolution by resorting to revolutionary war. It was in this context that Lenin developed his own conception of socialism in one country.

At the February–March 1915 Bern conference of foreign sections of the Bolshevik organisation, Lenin was informed that Luxemburg was an opponent of the slogan of the United States of Europe. He decided to omit it from the conference decisions.[20] The conference resolution confirmed that the productive forces had outgrown the nation-state, and that in the imperialist era justified national wars became rare. Even so, the conference did not completely rule out 'revolutionary wars', for example wars 'for the protection of the achievements of a proletariat victorious in the struggle with the bourgeoisie'.[21] This referred to the Russian proletariat triumphing in the democratic revolution as well as to the socialist proletariat of developed nations. In October 1915 Lenin wrote that, should the Russian proletarian party seize power and establish a democracy, it would have to submit peace proposals that neither Germany nor Britain nor France could accept; 'revolutionary war' would then become inevitable.[22]

On 23 August 1915 Lenin's 'On the Slogan of the United States of Europe' appeared in the Bolshevik publication *Sotsial-Demokrat*. Lenin asserted that the socialist revolution would *not* take the form of 'one act', but of a whole epoch of revolutions and counter-revolutions. One of the reasons for withdrawing the slogan was this:

> It might lead to an incorrect interpretation concerning the impossibility of the victory of socialism in one country and concerning the relationship of such a country with the others. The unevenness of economic and political development is an unconditional law of capitalism. It follows

from this that the victory of socialism initially in several or even in one, separately taken capitalist country is possible. Having expropriated the capitalists and having organised socialist production at home, the victorious proletariat of this country would rise *against* the remaining capitalist world ... in case of need even coming out with military force against the exploiting classes and their states ... The free unification of nations in socialism is impossible without a more or less prolonged, stubborn struggle of socialist republics against the backward states.[23]

Historians have correctly pointed out that Stalin later misinterpreted the article as if it concerned Russia. Lenin had capitalistically developed states in mind, not Russia, where at that time he believed socialism was not on the agenda. The second point made by many historians – that Lenin was only referring to socialist *revolution*, not to the construction of a socialist *society* in a single country – is however much less convincing.[24] The problem is that Lenin clearly indicated that, before engaging in revolutionary war, the single revolutionary state would have to organise 'socialist production at home' – a point oddly ignored in the scholarly literature.

Unsurprisingly, Trotsky reacted sharply to Lenin's speculations. In his 'The Programme of Peace', he reiterated the idea that the world was tending towards a *'unified world economy*, free from national frameworks', which is why he warmly supported the slogan of the United States of Europe. For political as well as economic reasons, Trotsky believed that the establishment of a 'stable regime of proletarian dictatorship' was 'only conceivable across the whole of Europe'. Trotsky furthermore took issue with Lenin's interpretation of the unequal development of capitalism. He, Trotsky, discerned a levelling out of developmental levels within Europe. Trotsky accepted that one proletariat should not wait for the others to make revolution, but neither a 'revolutionary Russia' nor a 'socialist Germany' could survive in isolation against conservative Europe.[25]

Lenin stuck to his guns. He did not deny the possibility that European revolutions might occur essentially simultaneously.[26] But the other scenario could not be ruled out either. In the short period up to December 1916 he repeated the socialism in one country thesis at least three times. In September 1916 he wrote that the uneven development of capitalism made it inevitable that socialism 'will be victorious at first in one or several countries'. This would inevitably provoke the 'straightforward aspiration of the bourgeoisie of the other countries to crush the victorious proletariat'. That, again, would make it inevitable for the 'socialist state' to fight wars 'for socialism, for the liberation of other peoples from the bourgeoisie'. Lenin cautioned: 'Only after we will have overthrown, finally vanquished and expropriated the bourgeoisie in the whole world, and not only in one country, will wars become impossible.'[27] This passage is especially significant, for it can only mean that, even though this would not yet make wars impossible, expropriating the bourgeoisie in one country *was* possible.

In a December 1916 article Lenin once again wrote: 'There is the possibility of wars of socialism victorious in one country against other bourgeois or reactionary countries.'[28] In the same month, he explained in yet another article that militarised capitalist Germany proved that it was possible to lead a huge economy *from one centre*. This proved that 'socialist revolution' was no utopian enterprise even with a 'small people' like the Swiss. Switzerland's 'very high level of capitalism' would allow the expropriation of the country's '30,000 bourgeois', who would be forced to hand over their property to the 'socialist workers' government'. Under the present condition of World War, Lenin did not expect the imperialists to intervene in a revolutionary Switzerland, which country could survive even in the absence of revolution abroad – provided that an international proletarian solidarity movement emerged.[29] This article represents strong additional proof that Lenin found the project of an isolated socialist economy a realistic one.

Finally, Lenin was not the only Russian social democrat to advocate the idea of socialism in one country. In his 'The Russian Social Democracy and Russian Social Chauvinism', published in 1915 in the Bolshevik theoretical journal *Kommunist*, his close comrade Grigorii Zinov'ev mentioned the possibility of a 'war of a *proletariat* that has been victorious in some country, and that defends the socialist system [*stroi*] gained by it, against other states attempting to vindicate the capitalist regime'.[30] The term *stroi* leaves little doubt that Zinov'ev was not merely talking about a workers' government but about a socialist economy.

Militarised Marxism

Disappointingly, Lenin did not explain why it was that a socialist economy could be established on the scale of a single country. It is as if he took this for granted. He was neither obviously attracted to the idea of the socialist state as strong player on the world market nor to the autarkic scenario.[31] Lenin's acceptance of socialism in one country mainly speaks to the enormous influence of the Great War on his thinking. Revolution and war tended to get conflated ever more narrowly in his mind. James Ryan aptly calls Lenin's mentality 'militarized Marxism'.[32]

Lenin was so much under the spell of the scenario of revolutionary war that he began to warn fellow internationalists not to drive anti-patriotism too far, lest it might turn into an ideological obstacle, were such wars to be waged in the future. He repeatedly took Luxemburg and Karl Radek to task for rejecting 'defence of the fatherland' under all conditions and for failing to see that revolutionary 'national' wars would remain possible.[33]

The single socialist economy would be a war economy, geared to the project of expanding socialism through military means. Lenin's scenario rested on the assumption that socialism was the superior, more efficient economy compared to capitalism, offering the best infrastructure for an effective army. Oddly as it may sound now, far from conceiving it as a problem, Lenin saw socialism in one country as the solution for the isolated revolutionary state. Given his expectation that war with the imperialist states would not be long in waiting, Lenin's scenario crucially depended on the assumption that socialisation would be accomplished in an extremely short period of time. As we saw earlier, it was a commonly held view among socialists that trustification and capitalist state intervention turned socialisation into a routine operation to be accomplished in a matter of weeks or months.

But Lenin also indicated that 'no separate solution of the revolutionary tasks in any single country is possible'.[34] What was this supposed to mean if single-country socialism *was* possible? Lenin accepted that a socialist economy could function within the confines of a single country, but he refused to believe that the imperialists would allow such a state to persist. They would not rest before they had crushed the source of revolutionary infection. For its survival the socialist state therefore depended on the destruction of the imperialist powers. The inevitable war with the imperialists would end either in victory and the expansion of socialism to other countries or in defeat and the destruction of the socialist state. In either case, socialism in one country would soon come to an end. At the same time, however, this scenario implied that the isolated socialist state was *not* passively dependent for its salvation on the world revolution. The socialist state could *create* the required international conditions for its own survival by defeating the imperialists on the battlefield.

A socialist perspective for Russia

In 1917 Lenin finally concluded that in Russia too the socialist transition was on the agenda after all. He even allowed the possibility that Russia would become the first state to embark on the transition. And if the world revolution did not come to its assistance, revolutionary Russia would have to embark on revolutionary war to guarantee its own survival.

On the Gregorian calendar, the so-called 'February Revolution' in Russia occurred in March. On that calendar Tsar Nikolai II abdicated on 15 March 1917. In September 1915, Nikolai Romanov had been foolish enough to assume personal command of the army. In the eyes of the people this made him responsible for the less than successful course of the war. The legitimacy of the monarchy took a nose dive. The millions of casualties at the front and declining living conditions in the hinterland proved too much of a strain on Russian society for the people to put up with.

The fall of the tsar was directly triggered by violent demonstrations in Petrograd in early March. When the capital's garrison disobeyed orders to fire on the demonstrators, the end of the Romanov dynasty had arrived. A provisional government of liberal and conservative parties was formed from among the Duma. At the same time, a soviet of workers and soldiers was established in Petrograd, with a majority of Mensheviks and Socialists-Revolutionaries, resulting in the creation of a situation of dual power. In May,

Mensheviks and Socialists-Revolutionaries joined the coalition government, which continued the war under a revolutionary flag.[35] Neither of these two parties considered socialism to be on the agenda in Russia.[36]

The Bolsheviks refused to join the government. They insisted that, given the participation of 'capitalist' parties in the coalition, the war had *not* turned into revolutionary defence but preserved its imperialist character. Upon his return from Switzerland in April, Lenin called for the establishment of a new provisional government exclusively consisting of socialist parties and based on the soviets. Quite unexpectedly for his Bolshevik comrades, Lenin furthermore argued that the soviet government would have to make a beginning with the socialist transition.

The collapse of tsarism and the creation of the Petrograd Soviet shocked Lenin into a new understanding of the situation. In their days, Marx and Engels had made communism dependent on integral industrialisation, but they had not been prepared to accept the consequence that this would exclude an early march to socialism for their own fatherland. They found a solution in fine-tuning their theories so as to allow a proletarian revolution in 'backward' Germany after all. Lenin found himself in a similar dilemma and he reacted likewise: given the real possibility for power to devolve upon the radicalised workers and soldiers, the taboo on socialist transition in Russia established by Plekhanov had to go.

The first indication that his thinking was shifting came in the famous 'Farewell Letter to the Swiss Workers', written in March. The Bolshevik leader confirmed that the Russian proletariat 'cannot *complete* [*zavershit'*] the socialist revolution when it uses only its own forces', for which purpose the support of the European and American workers remained indispensable. But the socialist revolution could nonetheless 'be *begun* in a certain way'. Russia could engage in nationalisation of the land and in the establishment of '*control over* production and distribution' in industry. The 'poorest peasants' would support this.[37]

Once back in Petrograd, Lenin revealed to his comrades what he had in mind: a 'transition from the first stage of the revolution, which gave power to the bourgeoisie ... to its *second* stage, which will hand over power to the proletariat and the poorest layers of the peasantry'. An immediate '"introduction" of socialism' remained out of the question, but a 'transition to *control* by the [soviets] over social production and the distribution of products' *was* feasible. Immediate nationalisation was in store only for the banks and the land. The land would continue to be tilled by individual peasant households as state tenants, but large model farms might be established on land expropriated from the landlords.[38] Such measures were 'steps in the direction of socialism' in agriculture.[39] Thus, Lenin at last embraced permanent revolution.

At the seventh Bolshevik conference running from 7 to 12 May, Aleksei Rykov observed that the 'objective conditions' for socialism were lacking in Russia.[40] Lenin disagreed. In Russia as well as in other, more advanced countries, the war had set in motion a process of transition from trusts and syndicates to 'state monopoly', which carried the following implication:

> Usually one draws the ... conclusion ... 'Russia is a backward, peasant, petty bourgeois country, and therefore one should not speak of the social revolution', but one forgets that the war put us in unusual conditions and that next to the petty bourgeoisie there is big capital ... Russia will come to stand with one foot in socialism, with one – because the peasant majority leads the other economic side of the country.

The poor peasants would again provide this programme with a majority in the population.[41]

Lenin gave the 'orthodox Marxist' idea predicating socialism on capitalist modernisation, a new reading: if Russian industries were as large scale and as modern as its British and German counterparts, why couldn't they be reorganised on a socialist footing?[42] That is why, Lenin thought, it was so fortunate that the tsarist government had been following the German capitalists in establishing economic regulation, to be referred to by him either as 'war capitalism', 'state capitalism' or 'state-monopoly capitalism'. A Soviet government would have a ready-made apparatus for socialisation at its disposal.[43] In his famous *State and Revolution*, written in August–September, Lenin concluded optimistically that the introduction of socialism was an 'urgent and burning question of *today's* politics' and that it could be taken in hand 'immediately, overnight [*s segodnia na zavtra*]'.[44]

It did not take long for Lenin to begin to suggest nationalisation of Russia's large-scale industries.[45] As regards the peasantry, Lenin did not reconfirm the old idea that a socialist workers' government would be overthrown by a *Jacquerie*.[46] To be sure, he accepted that peasant owners were averse to socialism.[47] But he also suggested that, given time, the Russian peasants might be made to see the light of socialism after all. As he argued, in a country of small peasants socialism cannot be introduced 'until the overwhelming majority of the population has come to understand the necessity of socialist revolution'.[48] This finally exploded the Plekhanov consensus.

Russia first

But could backward Russia initiate the socialist transition even in the case that the advanced countries in the West remained in capitalist hands? Lenin thought his fatherland might indeed play the role of initiator-state. At the May conference, he indicated the following: 'Comrade Rykov says that socialism must come from other countries with a more developed industry. But that is not true. It is impossible to say who'll begin and who will end.'[49] This was the first occasion for Lenin to suggest that the socialist revolution in his backward fatherland might indeed *anticipate* the more developed countries.

It appeared at the Sixth Party Congress, convening in August, that Lenin's suggestion of Russia as pioneer of socialism was too much to stomach for some Bolsheviks, but the majority supported his bold position. Not long before the congress convened, the provisional government had accused the Bolsheviks of an attempted *coup d'état* and issued warrants for the arrest of some of their leaders. With Lenin and Zinov'ev in hiding and Trotsky, who now joined the Bolsheviks, under arrest, the defence of Lenin's line fell to Stalin and Bukharin. The latter supported Lenin's view that the coming revolution needed a socialist orientation, but he remained under Plekhanov's spell in expecting the peasant masses to turn away from the proletariat once the latter class would embark on socialist construction.[50]

The manifesto written by the Central Committee on behalf of the congress made the 'success of the Russian revolution' dependent on the 'insurrection … of the proletarians of Europe'.[51] The possible role of Russia as initiator of socialism was addressed in a resolution tabled by Joseph Stalin. Stalin was born Dzhugashvili, in the Georgian town of Gori in 1878. He made a career in the Bolshevik party as a so-called *praktik*. Rather than emigrating to one of the cities of Western Europe, as so many other Bolshevik leaders did, he preferred to work in the underground. He was co-opted into the Bolshevik Central Committee in 1912, and in 1917 became one of Lenin's confidants.[52] In his resolution he proposed that the revolution was to aim for a 'socialist reconstruction of society, in union with the revolutionary proletariat of the advanced countries'. Evgenii Preobrazhenskii proposed another editing, with the revolution oriented 'to peace and, in case of a proletarian revolution in the West, to socialism'. This would have made Russian moves towards socialism dependent on proletarian revolution in Europe. Stalin countered that socialist revolution had a broader basis in Russia than in the West: whereas the west European workers were alone, their Russian comrades were supported by the poor peasants. It was, Stalin thought, 'not impossible that precisely Russia will be the country to pave the way to socialism'. And he concluded: 'We must reject the obsolete view that only Europe can point us the way. There exists a dogmatic and a creative Marxism. I stand on the basis of the latter.'[53] The Bolshevik congress supported Stalin's editing and thereby officially accepted that even an isolated revolutionary Russia could embark on socialist construction.

Robert Tucker correctly perceived in Stalin's remark the shadow of 'the future party debate over the possibility of building a socialist society in Soviet Russia without revolutions in Europe'. In Tucker's view, 'the notion of socialism in one country was embryonic in Stalin's "creative Marxism" of 1917'.[54] But it needs also to be acknowledged that Stalin was merely echoing Lenin's remarks at the May conference. His 'creative Marxism' was Lenin's – which explains why the congress supported Stalin not Preobrazhenskii.

But what if socialist revolution struck Russia but the proletariat of the West did not follow the example?[55] Lenin did not retreat from his conviction that the World War had bound up humanity in one 'bloody lump [*komok*]', from which no single country could possibly find an 'exit'. The single exit remained unthinkable: 'either the proletariat breaks free as a whole, or it will be strangled'.[56] The crucial point here is that an isolated revolutionary Russia would not be passively dependent on the world revolution for its survival. World revolution was not the only option Lenin saw for a Soviet Russia to break out of its confinement. He kept reminding his comrades of his October 1915 statement that an isolated revolutionary state would have to resort to revolutionary war.[57] In the absence of world revolution, the way out for it would be to destroy the imperialist threat on the battlefield.

Beginning in May a patriotic note had begun to creep into Lenin's argumentation: workers' control and nationalisation were needed *to save the country*: 'The capitalists' were leading 'the whole country' to 'collapse' and 'catastrophe', and 'salvation' could only come from workers' power and proletarian discipline in the economy.[58] The workers would be 'Rescuing the country'.[59] Lenin's point was that the capitalists and bankers were sabotaging the Russian economy, which led him to the conclusion that only a complete break with them could 'save our revolution and our country, squeezed in the iron grip of imperialism'.[60]

This hope that the workers' revolution might contribute to the strengthening of the country merged with Lenin's expectations of revolutionary war. The train of thought reached a climax in Lenin's September 'The Impending Catastrophe and How to Combat It'. In this stunning statement Lenin catapulted backward Russia into a position of military and economic superiority. The revolution would raise Russia to an 'immeasurably higher level of economic organisation'. What is more, 'The military power of a country with nationalisation of the banks is *higher* than of a country with banks remaining in private hands.' Russia would have to emulate the 'heroic patriotism and miracles of military courage' displayed by the French revolutionaries of 1792–3, which Lenin attributed to their imposition of a 'higher mode of production' onto France. He added that, likewise, 'in order to make Russia capable of defence' it was necessary to 'regenerate Russia *economically*'. Revolutionary war would place a Soviet Russia before the question of:

> either to perish or to catch up with the advanced countries and to overtake them *economically*. This is possible, for we have before us the ready-made experience of a large number of advanced states, the ready-made results of their technology and culture.[61]

Evidently, Lenin hoped that socialist economic reforms would provide an isolated revolutionary Russia with economic superiority vis-à-vis the West, which would again translate into superiority on the battlefield. Thus, if the German proletarians failed to destroy imperialism, the Russian revolutionary state would step in and remove the danger herself.

Notes

1 *Pervyi s"ezd*, 1958: 231 (emphasis added). In his second draft of the social democratic programme (1887), Plekhanov wrote that the '*consolidation of* this revolution' required the participation of '*all or at least several civilised societies*' (ibid.: 235, emphasis added).
2 *KPSS*, vol. 1: 12–14.
3 Ibid.: 37.
4 The Russian Marxists admitted that a socialist revolution in the West, sparked off by democratic revolution in Russia, might help the Russians to establish socialism prematurely, a scenario to be found with Marx and Engels: Engels's 1875 'Soziales aus Russland' (*MEW*, vol. 18: 565); foreword by Marx and Engels to the 1882 Russian edition of *Communist Manifesto* (vol. 19: 296); Engels's 1894 afterword to 'Soziales aus Russland' (vol. 22: 429). Kautsky (1904: 622–3, 626) adopted the same viewpoint. Both Mensheviks and Bolsheviks officially adopted it in 1905. For the Mensheviks, see their April–May 1905 Geneva conference: 'O zavoevannii vlasti i uchastii vo vremennom pravitel'stve' (Tiutiukin, 1996: 124). For the Bolshevik Third Party Congress convened at the same time: 'Izveshchenie o III s"ezde Rossiiskoi sotsial-demokraticheskoi rabochei partii' (*KPSS*, vol. 1: 73, 75). According to Baruch Knei-Paz (1979: 18–19), the model of the Russian revolution triggering revolutions in the West with socialist repercussions in Russia, was not taken seriously by Russian Marxists except for Parvus and Trotsky. However, the model was in fact generally accepted by social democrats. But if that scenario ever came true, the question of socialism in one country would, of course, not come up either.
5 Trotsky, 1978: 90 (emphasis added). Trotsky (ibid.: 122) also advocated the revolutionary slogan of the 'United States of Europe'. Day (1973: 6–11) argues that Trotsky did not deny the possibility of creating a socialist economy in Russia alone. According to Day, Trotsky argues in the seventh chapter of *Results and Prospects* that the economic prerequisites of socialism were present in Russia. However, it would not follow that a socialist economy could have been constructed in Russia alone: Trotsky was precisely arguing in *Results and Prospects* that such a thing would be impossible in *any* country, even in those ripe for socialism.
6 The only other discussion of socialism in one country that I found in Russian social democratic writings prior to the Great War was in the left-wing Bolshevik, Aleksandr Bogdanov's, science-fiction novel *Red Star* (1908). The Martian Sterni mentions the uneven character of the struggle for socialism and the creation of isolated socialist states (Bogdanov, 1984: 113–14, 117–18). See also Loren Graham, 'Bogdanov's Inner Message' (ibid.: 245–6); Richard Stites, 'Fantasy and Revolution' (ibid.: 13). James White drew my attention to the fact that the idea of socialism in one country may have been more widespread in the Bogdanov circle (Gel'fond, 1908).
7 For the Menshevik internationalists (Martov, Aksel'rod and others), see Gankin and Fisher, 1940: 162–4; Martow and Dan, 1973: 276–9; Thatcher, 2003: 75–6; Savel'ev and Tiutiukin, 2006: 39–48; Service, 2009: 147.
8 'Voina i rossiiskii proletariat' (in Martov, 2000: 339–43).
9 Axelrod, 1915: 10–11, 13, 43.
10 See Martow and Dan, 1973: 279; Daniels, 1960: 29–30; Savel'ev and Tiutiukin, 2006: 40, 43–4, 48; Service, 2009: 138, 142.
11 Trotsky, n.y.a: 3, 6, 84. In his July 1915 'Natsiia i khoziaistvo', Trotsky (1927: 214–15) repeated that the state 'has become too narrow for the economy', and that the only solution is a 'broad democratic federation of the advanced states', i.e. the 'European United States'. See also Day, 1973: 13–14; Thatcher, 2003: 71–2; Service, 2009: 147–8.

12 For Bukharin's early life, see Cohen, 1974: 6–25. On the Baugy group, see also Gankin and Fisher, 1940: 173–82; Daniels, 1960: 32.
13 See Bukharin, 1929: 15, 45, 86, 116, 189 (quotation p. 131). For *Imperialism and the World Economy*, see Nove, 1992b: 27; Cohen, 1974: 25–34; Haynes, 1985: 53, Chapters 2, 3; Kowalski, 1991: 30–2.
14 Bukharin, 1929: 188–9. Left-wing Bolshevik Georgii Piatakov and the Polish social democrat Karl Radek too observed close integration of the world economy and imagined the proletarian revolution in terms of a united action breaking down state frontiers (Kowalski, 1991: 33–5).
15 For Bukharin's theses for the February–March 1915 Bern Bolshevik conference, see Gankin and Fisher, 1940: 188. See also the resolution of the Baugy group for that conference (ibid.: 190). See also Kowalski, 1991: 32–3. The November 1915 theses of the 'Bukharin–Piatakov group' held: 'The imperialist epoch is an epoch of the absorption of small states by the large state units'. Correspondingly, the 'proletarian forces' should be mobilised 'on an international scale for their international activities' for the overthrow of capitalism (Gankin and Fisher, 1940: 219–20).
16 'Voina i rossiiskaia sotsial-demokratiia' (*PSS*, vol. 26: 20–2).
17 Notes about Lenin's October 1914 presentation on the proletariat and war (ibid.: 35). Kowalski (1991: 46) interprets this as an 'implicit rejection of the possibility of socialist revolution in one country'. In June–July 1915 Lenin wrote in 'Glavnyi trud nemetskogo opportunizma o voine' that a proletarian revolution breaking the 'frameworks' of the national state was the only way out (*PSS*, vol. 26: 281). See also 'Pod chuzhim flagom' (1915) (ibid.: 145).
18 'Polozhenie i zadachi sotsialisticheskogo Internatsionala' (November 1914) (ibid.: 39–40). See also 'Karl Marks', written 1914 (ibid.: 75).
19 'O natsional'noi gordosti velikorossov' (*PSS*, vol. 26: 107–8). See also: 'Kriticheskie zametki po natsional'nomu voprosu' (December 1913), vol. 24: 120–1.
20 For the Bern conference, see Gankin and Fisher, 1940: 179–80; Tiutiukin, 1972: 165–7; Nation, 1989: 42–4.
21 *KPSS*, vol. 1: 329.
22 'Neskol'ko tezisov', *PSS*, vol. 27: 50–1.
23 'O lozunge soedinennykh shtatov Evropy' (ibid.: vol. 26: 352–5). Hilferding (1973: Chapter 22; quotation p. 452) had argued in 1910 that the larger the organised economic zone, the higher its growth rate and the better its developmental potential. Differences in size of imperialist zones therefore created 'unevenness [*Ungleichheit*] of the industrial development', which again led to war. Whereas Hilferding acknowledged that there were counteracting tendencies, Lenin absolutised the 'law of uneven development'.
24 See for example Meyer, 1957: 220f.; Carr, 1970, vol. 2: 49–51; Daniels, 1960: 251–2; Daniels, 1962: 30, 174. Marek, 1969: 74; Leonhard, 1970: 98–9, 125, 142; Nation, 1989: 159; White, 2001: 120–1. Trotsky pioneered the interpretation according to which Lenin was only referring to the establishment of a 'proletarian dictatorship' in a single country (Trotsky, 1970: 12, 43–4). Other historians leave unanswered the question of whether Lenin referred to socialist revolution or to socialism. See for example Harding, 1981: 67; Kowalski, 1991: 49. To my knowledge only Robert Tucker (1969: 130–1) acknowledged that Lenin was indeed referring to the construction of a socialist economy in one country.
25 'Programma mira' (made up of a number of articles published in 1915–16 in *Nashe slovo*) (Trotsky, 1923a: 471–9. On Trotsky's position during the Great War, the 'simultaneity of modern revolutions', their interconnectedness, and their operation in terms of a 'chain reaction', see Knei-Paz, 1979: 303, 306–10. On Trotsky's debate with Lenin in 1915–16, see also Thatcher, 1991: 253–4; Thatcher, 2003: 74–5.
26 'Porazhenie Rossii' (*PSS*, vol. 27: 27); 'O karikature na marksizm i ob "imperialisticheskom ekonomizme"' (August–October 1916), vol. 30: 110–12, 122–3.

Russian historian S. V. Tiutiukin (1972: 172) suggested that Lenin was alternating between 'two lines', now rejecting then accepting the possibility of socialism in a single country.
27 'Voennaia programma proletarskoi revoliutsii' (*PSS*, vol. 30: 133–4).
28 'O lozunge "razoruzheniia"' (*PSS*: 152). See also 'O broshiure Iuniusa' (October 1916) (ibid.: 13).
29 'Printsipal'nye polozheniia k voprosu o voine' (ibid.: 218–30). See also Tiutiukin, 1972: 174.
30 Zinov'ev, 1915: 129.
31 Some of Lenin's formulations are strikingly reminiscent of Vollmar, but I found no indication that he read the latter's work on the isolated socialist state. Lenin did read Balodis's book on socialism. See his second cahier on imperialism, written in 1915–16 (*PSS*, vol. 28: 111). The book was popular among the intelligentsia in pre-revolutionary Russia and had several Russian translations (see Balabkins, 1978: 217, 229). Lenin referred to Balodis in his speech to the Comintern on 5 July 1921 (ibid.: vol. 44: 51).
32 Ryan, 2012: 26.
33 Letter to Zinov'ev, written in August 1916 (*PSS*, vol. 49: 288); 'O broshiure Iuniusa' (vol. 30: 8). To underscore the idea of a revolutionary war waged by either one or several developed socialist countries against the rest of the world, Lenin referred to Engels's 12 September 1882 letter to Kautsky (in which Engels however did not mention the possibility of *one* country turning socialist). See for example: 'Itogi diskussii o samoopredelenii' (1916) (ibid.: 30: 50–1); 'O karikature' (ibid.: 111–12); 'Voennaia programma' (ibid.: 133). In 'Krakh II Internatsionala' (June 1915), Lenin fantasised about a war of Japan and China against either a socialist Europe or a socialist America (*PSS*, vol. 26: 226f.).
34 'Porazhenie Rossii i revoliutsionnyi krizis' (September 1915) (ibid.: vol. 27: 27).
35 For the history of the February and October Revolutions, see for example Rabinowitch, 1976; Acton, 1990; Pipes, 1990; Pipes, 1996; Figes, 1996; Kowalski, 1997; Wade, 2000; Miller, 2001; Smith, 2002; Read, 2013; Ascher, 2014.
36 For the PSR, see Chernov's speeches at the third party congress in June (Erofeev, 2000, vol. 3.1: 199–212, 227–38, 311–30). Chernov feared that, unless it spread to other European countries, 'the Russian revolution would begin to choke in its narrow, cramped frameworks, within the walls of purely national life' (Erofeev, 2000, vol. 3.1: 210; see also 229–31). The transition to socialism in Russia depended on the spread of the revolution to other European nations (ibid.: 237). For a brief overview of the PSR in 1917, see Smith, 2011: xvi–xix. The classic work on the March–November 1917 period for the PSR is Radkey, 1958.
37 'Proshchal'noe pis'mo k shveitsarskim rabochim' (*PSS*, vol. 31: 92–3).
38 'O zadachakh proletariata v dannoi revoliutsii' (17 April) (ibid.: 113–16).
39 'Iz dnevnika publitsista' (11 September) (ibid.: vol. 34: 111). For an interpretation of Lenin's 1917 strategy in terms of 'steps toward socialism', see Lih, 2011b.
40 *Sed'maia (aprel'skaia) vserossiiskaia konferentsiia*, 1958: 107.
41 Ibid.: 76, 235–6.
42 On 7 July Lenin pointed to the 'presence of the material foundations for the movement to socialism' in Russia: 'Mozhno li zapugat' rabochii klass "iakobinstvom"?' (*PSS*, vol. 32: 374).
43 On the term 'war capitalism', see 'Doklad na sobranii bol'shevikov' (17 April) (ibid.: vol. 31: 111); 'state-monopoly capitalism': 12 May speech as seventh conference (ibid.: 443); 'state capitalism': 'Razrukha i proletarskaia bor'ba s nei' (17 June), vol. 32: 293. See further 'Zadachi proletariata v nashei revoliutsii' (23 April 1917) (ibid.: vol. 31: 168); 7 May speech at seventh conference (ibid.: 355); 'Proekt izmenenii teoreticheskoi, politicheskoi i nekotorykh drugikh chastei programmy' (May 1917) (ibid.: 139); 'Groziashchaia katastrofa i kak s nei

148 Socialism as war economy

borot'sia' (September 1917), vol. 34: 163, 168, 191–2; 'Uderzhat li bol'sheviki gosudarstvennuiu vlast?' (written September–October) (ibid.: 306–7). In *State and Revolution*, Lenin defined socialism as a society directed by workers' soviets and armed workers, but the economy would still be run like a syndicate or a post office, using the economic apparatus developed by the bourgeoisie: 'Gosudarstvo i revoliutsiia' (vol. 33: 50, 92–101). On Lenin and German war–capitalism, see Carr, 1952: 91, 360–2; Nove, 1992a: 35; Lih, 2011a: 136–7. See for Lenin in 1917 on socialism in Russia, Marek, 1969: 67–83, Harding, 1981: Chapters 4, 7; Kowalski, 1991: 44–56. Bogdanov rejected Lenin's interpretation of state capitalism as a progressive phenomenon facilitating socialist transition (see White, 2013: 60–1).

44 'Gosudarstvo i revoliutsiia', *PSS*, vol. 33: 49–50, 97–101. According to Nation (1989: 190, 194–5), Lenin argued in *State and Revolution* that a soviet democracy could only exist on a multi-state or even global scale. I don't think Lenin made this point.

45 For nationalisation of banks, syndicates and trusts, see 'Zadachi proletariata' (*PSS*, vol. 31: 168); 'Proekt izmenenii' (vol. 32: 143). On nationalisation of large-scale industries, see 'Rezoliutsiia ob ekonomicheskikh merakh bor'by s razrukhoi' (7 June) (ibid.: 196); 'Zadachi revoliutsii' (written 9–10 October), vol. 34: 235. On Lenin's ambivalence about nationalisation of industry shortly before the revolution, see Nove, 1992a: 35–7.

46 For the essential likeness of Lenin's and Trotsky's 1917 positions, see Carr, 1970, vol. 2: 46; Thatcher, 2003: 86–7. Hildermeier (1998: 180–1) points to the differences between the two men in respect to the peasants. See for the 1905–6 background, Swain, 2006: 30.

47 7 May 1917 speech at Seventh Party Conference (*PSS*, vol. 31: 357).

48 'Zadachi proletariata' (ibid.: 168).

49 *Sed'maia (aprel'skaia) vserossiiskaia konferentsiia*, 1958: 112.

50 *Shestoi s"ezd*, 1958: 138.

51 *KPSS*, vol. 1: 389.

52 For recent Stalin biographies, see Service, 2004; Kuromiya, 2005; McDermott, 2006; Creuzberger, 2009. See also Davies and Harris, 2005. For Stalin's political thought, see van Ree, 2002.

53 *Shestoi s"ezd*, 1958: 250, 257. For Stalin on the socialist character of the Russian revolution, see also 14, 111–12, 142–3.

54 Tucker, 1974: 175.

55 Trotsky and Bukharin rejected the idea of a single socialist economy. In May 1917, the former republished *The Programme of Peace*. This may be taken as an indication that he still rejected the idea of a viable isolated socialist state. Bukharin shared Lenin's confidence that the Russian capitalist industry was ready for socialisation, but insisted, with Marx, that socialism could not be constructed within national walls: 'Klassovaia bor'ba i revoliutsiia v Rossii' [July 1917], in Bukharin, 1923: 7–8. He furthermore wrote that 'final' and 'lasting [*prochnaia*]' victory would evade the Russian proletariat without proletarian revolution in the West (Bukharin, 1917 (May–June)); 'Klassovaia bor'ba', in Bukharin, 1923: 7–8. For Bukharin's pre-October position in 1917, see also Cohen, 1974: 56; Haynes, 1985: 51; Kowalski, 1991: 36–9.

56 7 May speech at seventh conference, *PSS*, vol. 31: 353–4, also 358. See also 'Uroki krizisa' (5 May) (ibid.: 326); 'Rezoliutsiia o voine', seventh conference (ibid.: 405).

57 'Proshchal'noe pis'mo' (ibid., *PSS*, vol. 31: 90–1; 'O zadachakh' (ibid.: 113–14); 'Nashi vzgliady' (1 May) (ibid.: 281); 'Kakie zaiavleniia delala nasha partiia o voine pered revoliutsiei' (26 May), vol. 32: 72; 'Voina i revoliutsiia' (27 May) (ibid.: 99–100). Bukharin too advocated revolutionary war in case the Russian proletariat would seize power in advance of the workers in the West (*Shestoi s"ezd*, 1958: 103–5).

58 'Grozit razrukha' (May 1917) (*PSS*, vol. 32: 76).
59 7 June resolution on measures against collapse (ibid.: 196).
60 'Groziashchaia katastrofa' (*PSS*, vol. 34: 157, 197).
61 'Groziashchaia katastrofa' (ibid.: 194–8). See also 22 June speech at first Soviet Congress (vol. 32: 287–9, 291); 'Zadachi revoliutsii' (vol. 34: 233–4); 'Uderzhat li' (ibid.: 307); 'K peresmotru partiinoi programmy' (written October) (ibid.: 373, 375). Later in September 1917, Lenin wrote that, once they had taken the economic apparatus of the bourgeoisie in hand, the Bolsheviks would be able to build a state sufficiently strong to carry on until the victory of the socialist world revolution: 'Uderzhat li' (ibid.: 332–3). For another occasion of Lenin referring to the wars of revolutionary France as example for a Soviet Russia, see 'Voina i revoliutsiia' (vol. 32: 78–9).

＃ Part IV
Revolution

13 Socialisation of the national economy

The last attempts actually to realise the ideal of community of goods on any significant scale, i.e. at a minimum of a town or city, had been undertaken by sixteenth-century Anabaptists.[1] The nineteenth-century modern socialists and communists believed that community of goods required the territory of a nation-state or even of an amalgam of countries. Communism made itself dependent on the seizure of power by workers' parties. This proved much harder to realise than Marx and Engels expected. The result was paradoxical: precisely at a time when the ideal of community of goods gained much wider currency than ever before through the spectacular expansion of the social democratic workers' movement, actual attempts at its realisation were no longer undertaken.

The Great War changed everything, however. The Romanov, Hohenzollern, Habsburg and Ottoman empires proved insufficiently robust to survive. The war brought social democrats to power, first in Russia and then in Germany and Austria. Before turning to the November 1917 Bolshevik revolution, we will first explore the revolutions striking the latter two countries in the following year.

The German revolution

Kautsky's hypothesis of the autarkic, one-country socialist economy irreversibly undermined the seeming self-evidence of the Marx–Engels postulate that socialism required the joint efforts of a number of advanced countries. As we saw earlier, by the time of the Great War the German social democrats no longer took this postulate much into account when they were formulating their various scenarios. At the end of the war, an opportunity of actually establishing a socialist economy in Germany presented itself – or so it seemed to the USPD leadership. These radical social democrats recognised the many obstacles to be met on the way to a socialised economy, but, given the opportunity of the moment, it did not occur to them to let an obsolete dogma stand in the way. The Marx–Engels paradigm was conveniently forgotten.

According to Ulrich Kluge, the revolutionary movement that swept through Germany in November 1918 was the product of military disaster and

154   *Socialisation of the national economy*

socio-economic crisis.[2] The collapse of the July Offensive convinced the German army leadership that the war was lost. When the naval command ordered a last and obviously futile offensive to save the national honour, sailors in the port of Kiel rebelled and took hold of the town on 4 November. The rebellion precipitated a spontaneous workers' revolution that took the major cities of Germany by storm. Within a few days, effective power fell into the hands of workers' and soldiers' councils.[3] On 10 November a provisional government was formed under *Reichskanzler* Ebert. The nucleus of the 'Council of People's Delegates [*Rat der Volksbeauftragten*]' consisted of a small cabinet evenly divided over MSPD and USPD. The Berlin workers' and soldiers' council appointed an Executive Council (*Vollzugsrat*) to supervise Ebert and his team.[4]

On 10 November this Berlin council adopted a declaration, written by USPD chairman and People's Delegate Haase, defining Germany as a 'socialist republic'. The council demanded 'speedy and consistent socialisation [*Vergesellschaftung*] of the capitalist means of production'. The council was convinced that similar measures were being prepared 'in the whole world', and trusted that the proletariat of other countries would make every effort to prevent the German people from being assaulted. The Russian Revolution provided special cause for hope.[5]

But was this the time to embark on the socialist transition? Economically, the country was in dire straits. Even though an armistice was reached, the country was still at war. The Berlin council could however not be ignored. On 12 November the Council of People's Delegates issued a proclamation to announce that it set itself 'the task to realise the socialist programme'. Socialisations were not announced, though.[6] The fact of the matter is that Ebert and the MSPD never seriously considered socialisation.[7]

The other government party, the USPD, however, did. Even moderates like Haase and editor of the party daily *Die Freiheit*, Hilferding, believed that a beginning with the socialist transition should be made. On 16 November *Die Freiheit* made a passionate appeal to the government to nationalise mining, metallurgy, textile, chemical and many other industries without delay.[8] William Smaldone calls Hilferding 'a leader in the socialist effort to transform German society'.[9] Hilferding realised that socialisation required caution, and that without improvement of the material conditions of the workers the project would fail. Bolshevik recklessness was to be avoided. But he did write on 23 November: 'the *hour of socialism has arrived*'. Hilferding admitted that 'the economy has been ruined and paralysed by the war', but he insisted that 'the difficulties *must* be overcome ... The socialisation of those productive branches that are ripe must be confirmed [*festgestellt*]. The measures of socialisation in other economic areas must be stipulated [*festgesetzt*].' For the time being Hilferding wanted to confine socialisation to the raw-materials sector, though.[10]

The government reached a compromise on 18 November, to the effect that, for a start, some branches would be socialised, based on recommendations of a newly to be appointed Socialisation Commission. Kautsky (chairman), Cunow and Hilferding were included in the commission. Ballod was another interesting name on the member list. The commission's preliminary report published on 11 December defined socialisation as a process of long duration, predicated upon economic effectiveness. For now, the commission was considering iron industries and coal mining. Ebert agreed to ask the commission to make a concrete plan for the socialisation of the coal mines.[11]

On the Spartakist left wing of the USPD, Liebknecht was troubled by the slowness of the process. He insisted on socialisation of all large-scale production without delay. He believed this had effectively been prepared by wartime centralisation and regulation and that socialisation would be a relatively easy operation. Also, in his eyes, Germany's economic distress made socialisation the best solution to save the country.[12] Liebknecht's comrade, Luxemburg, agreed.[13]

On 20 December 1918, Hilferding presented the report on socialisation to the first national congress of councils. He acknowledged that Germany's economic problems made socialisation extremely difficult, but with sufficient caution it was realisable. Socialising the mines and some of the iron industries would allow the socialist government to acquire 'control over a large part of industry' as well as over the banks.[14] Even though it had a preponderance of MSPD delegates, the congress accepted a motion ordering the government 'to begin with the *socialisation* of all industries that are ripe for this, in particular *mining*, without delay'.[15]

Socialisation proved a mirage, though. Later in December, the USPD resigned from the government. The failed attempt at revolution in Berlin early in January 1919, in which activists of the new Communist Party of Germany (Spartakus League) and the USPD, as well as the so-called Revolutionary Shop Stewards cooperated, was drowned in blood. Luxemburg and Liebkbnecht were murdered by a Freikorps unit. The 19 January elections for the National Assembly gave the USPD only 8 per cent of the vote. The question of socialisation remained under discussion in the new government coalition of MSPD, Centre and left-liberals, and an important issue among radical workers, but the momentum was lost.

Hilferding

But when the matter still lay open, how did USPD theorists interpret the chances for socialisation of the German economy in light of the world revolution? Bolshevik Russia could not be of much assistance. Radicals in the party, for example the Spartakists and member of the Berlin Executive Council, Ernst Däumig, acknowledged the Bolsheviks as bona fide socialists, but they saw Russia as a country in need of saving by socialist Germany rather than as socialist Germany's potential saviour.[16] For all practical purposes, Germany was alone.

Liebknecht was adamant that the 'eradication of capitalism, the introduction of the socialist social order, is only possible on an international scale', through a 'world social revolution'. He imagined the revolutionary chain reaction moving from Russia to Germany to the Entente countries. Only the German example could tempt the British, French and American workers to seize power.[17] Liebknecht did not make socialisation of the German economy dependent on revolutions abroad: he was all the time demanding socialisation without delay, under the obvious assumption that Germany could in principle function as a single socialist economy. Liebknecht was, however, convinced that the capitalist powers would team up to strangle socialised Germany. His writings from the period suggest that he was particularly concerned about the 'terrible dangers' arising from a blockade and the lack of foodstuffs and raw materials.[18]

The most prominent Spartakist theoretician, Rosa Luxemburg, was born in a Jewish family in the Russian-occupied part of Poland. She had started her political career as a leader of the internationalist faction of the Polish social democracy. In 1897 she received a doctorate of law from the University of Zurich. The next year she moved to Berlin. As an SPD member, she engaged prominently in the struggle against Bernstein's revisionism.[19] Like Liebknecht, Luxemburg was emphatic that 'the future of the German revolution is anchored only in the world revolution'.[20] Her main fear seems to have been that an isolated socialist Germany would not be able to stand up to military intervention of the Entente Powers.[21]

It was not that the Spartakists regarded socialisation of Germany as a single economy an inherently impossible proposition. That they rejected it as a realistic option was because they expected external factors, from economic blockade to military intervention, to come into play and to lead to the demise of an isolated socialist Germany.

Somewhat more to the right in the party, Daümig was more optimistic. He argued at the December 1918 congress of councils that the British and French workers were bound to follow the German example: '*world war must lead to world revolution*, here earlier, there later'.[22] But the security of German socialism did not depend on revolution in the Entente countries. Daümig trusted that a Council Germany would be able successfully to defend itself on the battlefield.[23] What is more, he was confident that the Entente Powers would be willing to sign a peace treaty with a Council Germany. He only conceded that, in defining Germany's borders and its remaining economic potential, the treaty might put certain limits on the socialisation of the German economy.[24]

Hilferding recognised the possibility of socialism in one country in so many words. He concluded the socialisation debate on 20 December 1918 as follows:

> socialism is a challenge [*eine Schwierigkeit*] for a single country; and many of our hesitations precisely come from the fact that, when I forget about Russia for a moment, Germany is for the time being facing the task alone. But, party comrades, precisely that makes this task not only difficult but also promises that its solution will carry an extremely high reward.

In a sequence we found earlier in Kautsky's work, Hilferding trusted that socialist construction in Germany would spawn a 'tremendous spiritual, propagandistic force' that would help socialism to spread to other states in the West.[25] Far from depending on the emergence of other socialist countries, socialism could emerge in Germany independently, while in the process creating the attractive example other nations were bound to want to emulate.

Otto Bauer: the Austrian case

Austria was another country in the wake of the war to be governed by social democrats. The Austrian Social Democratic Workers' Party [SDAP] was founded in 1889, under the leadership of the physician, Victor Adler, who remained the unrivalled leader of the party. Adler's Marxism was close to Kautsky's, with whom he was personally close as well, but after the outbreak of the revisionism struggle in Germany, the SDAP assumed a centrist position between the 'orthodox' and 'revisionist' wings. In the early years of the twentieth century a distinct 'Austromarxist' group of theorists emerged, with Hilferding, Max Adler, Otto Bauer and Karl Renner as main proponents.[26]

Bauer and Renner made an impressive name for themselves as socialist specialists in the nationality question. They believed the Habsburg Empire exemplified the trend of capitalist economies to recast themselves into large, supranational economic spaces, in which separate nations would remain embedded.[27] But before the war they did not pay systematic attention to the question of the viability of socialism in single countries. In his 1907 *The National Question and Social Democracy*, Bauer referred to the ideal of the United States of Europe.[28] He furthermore suggested that the proletariat would first seize power 'in one of the large capitalist states of the European cultural milieu', and that socialism would spread to the rest of the world within a few decades, but he did not explore the question of whether the initiator-state could independently construct a socialist economy.[29]

During the war, the SDAP came out strongly in support of the war effort.[30] The patriotic wave powerfully boosted the party's right wing led by Renner.[31] Renner saw a great future for the multinational Habsburg framework. He was also insistent that socialism was incompatible with 'Kleinstaaterei' and depended on the expanded territory of the Habsburg state.[32]

Bauer shared Renner's aversion to *Kleinstaaterei* – yet his conclusions diverged widely from the latter's. Otto Bauer was born in Vienna. His father owned a textile factory. In 1906 Otto obtained a doctorate of law. He became one of the leading Marxist theoreticians of the day. Bauer served as army officer in the Great War, but fell into Russian captivity, only to return to his fatherland in 1917.[33] In late October 1918 the army began to disintegrate. When Polish and Czech delegates withdrew from parliament, the empire was on the verge of collapse.[34] Bauer's return reinforced the left wing of the party. In April 1918 he worked out a new national programme. In a sharp break with the Habsburg multinationalism championed by Renner, the programme accepted the right of nations to secede from the empire and to form their own national states. The German-Austrians might join a democratised Germany.[35]

In mid-October, Bauer wrote three articles for the SDAP daily *Arbeiter-Zeitung* to win over the membership for an *Anschluss*. Bauer believed that an independent German-Austria, small as it was, would not be able feed itself, and that its internal markets could not absorb the output of its own industries. The best solution would be for it to join the large, integrated economic space of Germany.[36]

Bauer suspected that the Austrian social democratic workers would be less than enthusiastic about the prospect of joining the reactionary German state. To deal with such doubts, he argued in the 16 October article that no other country was 'as ripe for socialism as Germany'. Compared to Russia, it had a majority of workers. And compared to Great Britain, state intervention in its economy was much further advanced. The 'enormous organizational apparatus of state control over the economy' set up in wartime Germany needed only to change hands to turn into an 'instrument of socialism'. Bauer concluded that, 'unlike in other countries', establishing socialism in Germany remained 'only a matter of [acquiring] power'. 'The decisive battles between capital and labour will be fought on German soil and they will be fought in the near future.' Integration into Germany would lead Austria straight to socialism.[37] Bauer expected Germany to establish a socialist economy on its own, in advance of the other great European nations.

Despite the fact that the soldiers were out of control and in the streets, and notwithstanding the many demonstrations and mass meetings, the Austrian revolution was not decided on the streets. The process was essentially directed by politicians.[38] When the Habsburg Empire disintegrated around them, the SDAP accepted the national programme of the Left. On 21 October the German-Austrian rump parliament proclaimed itself a provisional national assembly. A provisional coalition government under Chancellor Renner and dominated by the social democrats signed an armistice on 3 November. On 12 November the assembly proclaimed German-Austria a democratic republic and an integral part of the German republic. After Victor Adler's sudden death on 11 November, Bauer succeeded him as minister of Foreign Affairs and as de facto party leader.[39]

German-Austria was cut off from its traditional sources of foodstuffs and coal. This carried the threat of famine, cold and widespread unemployment. Only the Entente powers were in a position to provide assistance.[40] Bauer continued to nail his colours to an *Anschluss* with Germany. In the early weeks of 1919 he wrote a number of articles in *Arbeiter-Zeitung*, later to be collected in *The Road to Socialism*. Bauer admitted that the disastrous state of Austria's economy made the country completely dependent on foreign credits for imports of foodstuffs and coal, and thereby on the forbearance of the Entente Powers. Until the country had made a full recovery, radical steps towards socialisation were out of the question.[41] Joining up with the 'large German republic' remained the sure way out to socialism in Austria.[42]

The SDAP acquired a very substantial plurality at the February 1919 elections. Renner formed a new coalition government together with the Christian Socials. A law pertaining to the preparation of socialisation was adopted. Bauer became chairman of the commission to work out the proposals, but the commission was unable to achieve any substantial results.[43] Unfortunately, the *Anschluss* too proved a vain dream. The September 1919 Treaty of Saint-Germain between Austria and the Entente Powers prohibited it.[44] From Bauer's perspective, the road to socialism in Austria was now cut off. He resigned in July, even before the treaty was signed.

In his July 1919 *Eight Months of Foreign Policy*, Bauer repeated that Austria was no economically viable state. 'We are too small, too helpless to be free on our own.' Separated from Germany, Austria was doomed to 'a *life of smallness and pettiness*, a life in which nothing big can flourish, least of all the biggest thing we know, socialism'.[45] By now, however, Bauer was also losing confidence in the prospects of socialisation in Germany. He admitted that the deplorable state of the German economy, and its dependence on the Entente Powers, ruled out quick progress towards the great goal in that country as well.[46] In his 1920 *Bolshevism or Social Democracy?*, Bauer wrote that the war-ravaged economies of Western and Central Europe would remain dependent on the capital contributions and credits provided by the victors. Until these countries, including Germany, had restored their own financial health, socialisation could only be 'incremental' and only in those branches where it would not hinder economic recovery. Bauer called this a 'limit on the proletarian revolution on a *national* scale'.[47]

Yet, Bauer just could not bring himself to discard his faith in Germany's exemplary agency. He admitted that the future of the German nation lay only in the 'international revolution, which destroys the imperialist system of domination', but he still insisted that the German nation would become 'a vanguard of the world revolution'. 'German socialism' would transform the country and create an 'example' for the Western nations to follow. The 'propaganda of the creative act' would lead the workers of the West towards proletarian revolution, which would again break the imperialist stranglehold on Germany.[48] In other words, against all odds Bauer continued to hope that Germany would be the first to establish a socialist order and to trigger the revolution in other countries through its example.

Importantly, in his 1921 introduction to *The Road to Socialism* Bauer confirmed the general idea that a single country could make the breakthrough to the socialist system, even in an environment of hostile capitalist countries: he indicated that successful socialisation required the seizure of power by the proletariat not in a 'small, economically and politically dependent country, but at any rate in a large economic area that has a strong economic and political position in the face of the other states'.[49]

In summing up, the German Independents and Otto Bauer's Austrian socialists no longer made the creation of a socialist economy dependent on socialisation in a number of countries. The German economy was in ruins,

160 Socialisation of the national economy

but neither Hilferding nor Bauer doubted that the country possessed the economic prerequisites to establish a socialist economy on its own. Even Liebknecht and Luxemburg accepted this. What worried all of these socialists most was the imperialist threat. For the Spartakists the destruction of an isolated socialist Germany through economic blockade or military intervention was a certainty. But Hilferding and Bauer were fundamentally more optimistic. They dreamed of a socialised Germany and exemplary state that other nations would want to emulate, a scenario strikingly reminiscent of the one Kautsky had been developing in his *Social Democratic Comments*.

Notes

1 I am not counting experiments with small-scale 'intentional communities'. See for this term Leopold, 2007: 221–2.
2 Kluge, 1985: 51.
3 See Ryder, 1967: 119–24, 132–3; Winkler, 1984: Chapter 3; Kluge, 1985: 51–3; Broué, 2005: Chapter 8. For a recent collection of essays on the German revolution, see Gallus, 2010.
4 See Ryder, 1967: 167; Morgan, 1975: 122–3; Winkler, 1984: Chapter 4; Broué, 2005: 172–9. See also Matthias, 1970. On the councils and the social democrats, see Waldman, 1958; Morgan, 1975; Broué, 2005.
5 Full text in Berlin, 1979: 167–8.
6 Full text in Ebert, 1926: 96–7.
7 For Ebert's motives to reject early socialisation, see Mühlhausen, 2007: 107, 117–18, 155–6. A few MSPD functionaries argued that socialisation would only work on a global scale: MSPD member of the Socialisation Commission, O. Hue, on 8 December (Berlin, 1979: 257). See also MSPD functionary and *Staatssekretär im Reichswirtschaftsamt*, August Müller, 28 December 1918 press conference (ibid.: 258).
8 'Nicht stehenbleiben' (large extract), Ritter and Miller, 1975: 259–60. A 19 November *Die Freiheit* article based the realism of immediate nationalisation of the '*large-scale industrial monopolies*' on the wartime state regulation of the economy. See Berlin (1979: 250) for a large extract.
9 Smaldone, 1998: 76.
10 'Klarheit!', in Stephan, 1982: 93–4. For Hilferding's combination of carefulness and decisiveness in the socialisation question, see Wagner, 1996: 119–20; Smaldone, 1998: 76–7.
11 See Waldman, 1958: 117–18; Ryder, 1967: 167–8; Schieck, 1972: 147–9; Winkler, 1984: 79–82; Kluge, 1985: 91–100; Wagner, 1996: 121–2. For the socialisation question in general, see Miller, 1978: 141–63. For a transcript of the discussion in the government on 18 November, see Berlin, 1979: 254. For an extract of the preliminary report, see ibid.: 255–6.
12 'Klarheit über Weg und Ziel' (27 November), Liebknecht, 1982: 621–3; 'Leitsätze' (ibid.: 632–3); 'Was will der Spartakusbund?' (ibid.: 655–7).
13 According to Luxemburg, Marx and Engels had been wrong to assume that Germany was economically ripe for socialist revolution in 1848. Engels acknowledged the mistake in 1895. But now the German economy was ripe for socialisation: speech to the 30 December/1 January founding congress of the communist party (Luxemburg, 1983: 486–90). In her 1916 *Die Krise der Sozialdemokratie*, she had referred to Marx's *Die Klassenkämpfe in Frankreich* to underscore the impossibility of socialism within national walls (ibid.: 56–7).

Socialisation of the national economy 161

14 *Allgemeiner Kongress*, 1919: 312–17.
15 Ibid.: 344. For the treatment of the socialisation question at the congress, see also Ryder, 1967: 182; Winkler, 1984: 100–4.
16 For USPD views on Bolshevik Russia, see Ströbel, 1920: 187–8; Morgan, 1975: 98–103; Wheeler, 1975: 45–61. For Däumig's revolutionary career, see Morgan, 1982.
17 'Klarheit', Liebknecht, 1982: 622–4; 'Leitsätze' (28 November) (ibid.: 635); 'Was will der Spartakusbund?' (23 December) (ibid.: 659–60). Liebknecht saw the German revolution, *not* revolution in Britain or France, as the event on which the world revolution depended. See 'Die Aufgabe der deutschen Arbeiter nach dem Kriege' (notes written mid 1917) (ibid.: 341); 'Taktisches zum Prinzip' (October/November 1917) (ibid: 365–6); 'Zur Lage' (ibid.: 560–2).
18 'Klarheit', Liebknecht, 1982: 623. See also 'Leitsätze' (ibid.: 635); 'Was will der Spartakusbund?' (ibid.: 657–8).
19 For Luxemburg's biography, see Nettl, 1966; Abraham, 1989.
20 'Der Anfang' (18 November), Luxemburg, 1983: 398. See also 'An die Proletarier aller Länder' (25 November) (ibid.: 415–16).
21 'An die Proletarier', Luxemburg, 1983: 417–18; 'Was will der Spartakusbund?' (14 December) (ibid.: 444). Luxemburg made the success of the Russian revolution crucially dependent on the German workers coming to the assistance of their comrades. See for example 'Der alte Maulwurf' (May 1917) (ibid.: 259); 'Brennende Zeitfragen' (August 1917) (ibid.: 277–81). In her 'Zur russischen Revolution' (no date), Luxemburg (ibid.: 332–3, 341, 370) accepted that Russia was ripe for socialism. Lenin's formula of workers and poor peasantry had solved 'the famous question of the "majority of the people"', which had bothered the German social democrats for so long. But the problem of socialism could only be 'solved internationally'. For the impossibility of a stable proletarian dictatorship and socialism in Russia alone, see also 'Die russische Tragödie' (September 1918), 391. Liebknecht (1982: 386) concurred that a socialist Russia could not exist in isolation: 'Aufgabe' (late 1917/early 1918). See also 'Zur Lage der russischen Revolution' (August 1918) (ibid.: 560, 562).
22 *Allgemeiner Kongress*, 1919: 230–1.
23 Ibid.: 234.
24 Ibid.: 234–5, 280–1.
25 Ibid.: 344. In an October 1920 speech, Hilferding advocated expropriation of the capitalist owners, but as long as socialism has not been introduced in the whole world, the German economy would remain subjected to the 'capitalist laws of price formation': 'Die politischen und ökonomischen Machtverhältnisse und die Sozialisierung', in Stephan, 1982: 117–18.
26 For the SDAP before the war, see Knapp, 1980. See for Austromarxism, Cole, 1960, vol. 3.II: 546–58; Stadler, 1966: 20–2; Leser, 1968: 177; Low, 1974: 55; Tom Bottomore's, introduction in Bottomore and Goode, 1978: esp. 1–36; Knapp, 1980: 189–93; Panzenböck, 1985: Chapter 1.
27 Springer, 1902: 57, 78–9, 209–10; Bauer, 1907: 177–82, 441. See also Cole, 1960, vol. 3.II: 636–7; Bottomore and Goode, 1978: 32–3; Leser, 1968: 34–5, 97.
28 Bauer, 1907: 519–20.
29 Ibid.: 507–15.
30 See Braunthal, 1963: 31–3, 74–5.
31 See Low, 1974: 55–6.
32 Renner, 1915: 20–3; see also Renner, 1917: 19–20.
33 For Bauer's biography, see Leichter, 1970; Hanisch, 2011.
34 See Rauchensteiner, 2008; Maderthaner, 2008: 192.
35 See Braunthal's introduction in *Otto Bauer*, 1961: 29–30; Stadler, 1966: 22; Low, 1974: 53–67; Saage, 2008: 70, 72–3; Maderthaner, 2008: 188–9.

36 O. B., 1918a and O. B., 1918b.
37 O. B., 1918c. On Bauer's mid-October articles, see also Low, 1974: 62–7; Hanisch, 2008: 216–17.
38 See Maderthaner, 2008: 195–9. For a history of the Austrian council movement, see Hautmann, 1987.
39 Braunthal's introduction in *Otto Bauer*, 1961: 31; Stadler, 1966: 70; Low, 1974: 57–67, 83, 90, 101; Saage, 2008: 73–5.
40 See Saage, 2008: 76; Hanisch, 2008: 213–14.
41 Bauer, 1921: 8–9, 34.
42 Ibid.: 35–6.
43 For the events in Austria in the spring and for the commission, see Hautmann, 1987: 314–24, 330–4, 418–21; Maderthaner, 2008: 202–3, 205; Stöger, 2008: 129–34.
44 See Stadler, 1966: 62–80; Low, 1974: 187, 192–3; Panzenböck, 1985: Chapter 3.
45 Bauer, 1919a: 4–5. For Bauer's view that socialism can only exist in large countries, see also Braunthal's introduction in *Otto Bauer*, 1961: 44; Leser, 1968: 325–6; Bottomore and Goode, 1978: 32–3; Hanisch, 2008: 217.
46 In his 1919 *Weltrevolution*, Bauer suggested that Britain and America, not Germany, might play the decisive role in the worldwide socialist transition.
47 Bauer, 1920: 81–4 (see also p. 118). According to Hautmann (1987: 326), Bauer implied that socialism on the European continent would have to await the establishment of socialism in America, Australia and Africa, where Europe drew its foodstuffs and raw materials from. However, in my opinion Hautmann reads too much into Bauer here.
48 Bauer, 1920: 117–20. In the same book, Bauer argued that proletarian rule in backward Russia was doomed eventually to make way for peasant rule (ibid.: 70).
49 Bauer, 1921: 5.

14 Socialism in one country

Whereas the German and Austrian revolutions failed to fulfil their socialist promises, the Bolshevik regime put in a major effort actually to realise the utopian system. In October 1917 the Bolsheviks obtained majorities in the Petrograd and Moscow Soviets. Chairman of the Petrograd Soviet, Trotsky, secured the support of the troops stationed in the capital. On the night of 6 and 7 November Lenin ordered the occupation of strategic locations. The Second Congress of Soviets confirmed the Bolshevik Council of People's Commissars as the new provisional government. When it appeared that the Socialists-Revolutionaries scored the best results in the November elections, Lenin dispersed the Constituent Assembly when it met on 18 January 1918.

The Bolsheviks defended their dictatorship in a horrendous Civil War. They controlled the European–Russian heartland with Petrograd and Moscow. The White Army's backbone was made up of former tsarist officers, but it was a motley company that engaged the Bolsheviks – from the Czechoslovak Legion and the Cossacks to socialists who refused to accept the dictatorship. At different times, the Red Army faced Ukrainian, Polish, Baltic and anarchist forces. British, French, American, Japanese and other capitalist powers intervened, albeit weakly, on the side of the Whites. During 1918 and 1919 Soviet rule was under serious threat at various times, but by the beginning of 1920 the tables were definitely turned. The end came in November of that year, when baron Vrangel' evacuated his troops from the Crimea.[1]

The Civil War was won, but the world revolution never materialised. Germany remained the arena of localised communist rebellions until 1923. In March 1919 the Hungarian communists established a short-lived proletarian dictatorship. Their Red Army established a satellite regime in Slovakia. The Bulgarian communists rose in 1923, and their Estonian comrades in the following year. But by then the revolutionary engine had run out of steam. Not counting Mongolia, communism failed to hold onto any country outside Soviet Russia.[2]

The Bolshevik regime almost immediately nationalised the banks, but in the spring of 1918 Lenin proposed not immediately to expropriate Russian industry but merely to bring it under state control. In June the large-scale industries were expropriated after all. What was later called 'war communism' combined nationalised industry with rationing and the withering away of money. Private grain trade was not allowed. Peasants were forced to hand over their surpluses to state procurement detachments. Collectivised and state-run farms, however, remained exceptional. The individual peasant household remained the basic unit of production. With the introduction of the New Economic Policy in March 1921, money was restored, and peasants were allowed to sell their grain and to pay taxes. Industry and trade were partly reprivatised. Large-scale industries were not, but state companies too were redirected towards profit and the market. The goal of complete socialisation of the economy, including agriculture, was however not given up. The NEP was still in force when Lenin passed away in January 1924.[3]

Confidence to despair

The scholarly consensus has it that, when he seized power, Lenin assumed that the socialist regime 'would be unable to maintain itself in Russia at all unless a proletarian revolution occurred in the more advanced European countries'.[4] In Craig Nation's dramatic words, Lenin looked to the European revolution for Soviet Russia's 'salvation'. 'The Russian revolution's capacity to inspire the proletariat of industrial Europe was presumed to be the key to its survival.'[5] This interpretation seems to be confirmed by Lenin himself. In July 1921 he reminisced that, at the time of the revolution, he had been thinking: 'the revolution will begin in other, capitalistically more developed countries ... or, in the opposite case, we'll perish'.[6]

The interpretation is, however, true only as far as it goes. It is a radical simplification. Lenin surely believed that the imperialists would never tolerate a socialist state in their midst. They would crush the deviant.[7] Soviet Russia's survival therefore depended on the destruction of the imperialist threat by proletarian revolution in the West. But the crucial point is that Lenin had an alternative, emergency scenario available to destroy the threat in case the world revolution failed to arrive: revolutionary war. Furthermore, he saw the key to the organisation of a revolutionary army powerful enough to be victorious in the rapid creation of a superior socialist economy. It would therefore have been absurd for Lenin to make the creation of a socialist economy in Soviet Russia dependent on the world revolution. Socialisation of the economy was precisely what he depended on in case the world revolution would *not* come.

Lenin optimistically assumed that it would only require a couple of months of peace to realise the socialist transformation of the Russian economy and prepare the army. In a set of theses on the question of peace, written on 20 January 1918, he explained why, for now, he rejected revolutionary war and favoured peace with imperialist Germany. Briefly, as matters stood, the Russian army would be unable to repulse a German attack. However, far from advising his comrades to bet on the German revolution, Lenin advised them to seek security in their own forces. As he saw it, the 'success of socialism in

Russia' required 'several months'. Once socialism would be consolidated, the country would be unbeatable.

> The reorganisation of Russia ... on the basis of nationalisation of the banks and of large-scale industry, with *barter* between town and ... consumer associations of small peasants, is economically completely feasible, provided we have a guarantee of a few months of peaceful work. And such a reorganisation will make socialism invincible in Russia and in the whole world, while in the process creating the firm economic basis for a powerful worker-peasant Red Army.[8]

In January 1918, then, Lenin did not seek the salvation of Soviet Russia in the world revolution. It was precisely the other way around: the faltering world revolution would be made invincible through the triumph of the socialist order in Russia.

But wasn't all this mere rhetoric? That Lenin was deadly serious comes to us from the most unsuspected of sources: Trotsky, who later commented on Lenin's January 1918 words:

> Shouldn't it have been a few years or decades? But no – this was no slip of the pen ... I remember very well how ... Lenin repeated time and again ... half a year from now we'll have socialism and we'll be the most powerful state on earth ... *He believed what he said.*[9]

In February 1918 Lenin confirmed that in case of 'the victory of socialism in one country and the preservation of capitalism in the neighbouring countries', revolutionary war would become inevitable. The point was only that, as for revolutionary France in the past, Russia should first have the superior new economic order in place before it could engage in that kind of war.[10]

But Lenin's boldness did not last. As he had expected, when the Germans broke the armistice and resumed their offensive in late February 1918 the Russian army could not offer any meaningful resistance. On 3 March Soviet Russia was forced to sign the humiliating Peace of Brest-Litovsk. Worse, the peace did not allay the fears of the Soviet government that Germany might once again take to the offensive.[11]

These events left Lenin shattered. The utter helplessness vis-à-vis the German army produced a significant shift in his appreciation of the situation. Lenin realised that he had suffered from irresponsible optimism. His hopes to establish a vibrant socialist economy and a powerful army in a few months time had been deeply misguided. Should the Germans resume their offensive, Soviet Russia would almost certainly collapse. Only the German revolution could now save the country. Lenin would not remain in this downcast state of mind for very long, but this was the time when he came closest to the views historians usually attribute to him. In his 7 March speech to the Seventh Party Congress, Lenin concluded in an obvious state of shock that the

German offensive had put an end to the period of continuous revolutionary triumphs begun in November 1917. History, the speaker bitterly informed his audience, 'taught you a good lesson': even if they withdrew to Vladivostok, the Bolsheviks still would not be safe – 'if the German revolution fails to come, we'll perish'.[12]

Lenin solemnly vowed that he would see to it that the national humiliation would be overcome, in the hope that one day 'Mother Russia' would be 'mighty and abundant' again.[13] He also indicated how unfortunate it was that the concessions made at Brest had made the Bolsheviks look like anti-patriots – which they were not.[14] But there was not very much he could do.

In May 1918 Lenin took the further step of formulating the following general principle: until the international revolution comprises a group of states powerful enough 'to defeat *international imperialism*', it is the duty of 'the socialists victorious in one country, especially if it is a backward one,' to *avoid* the fight with the 'imperialist giants' and to adopt a policy of 'waiting'. The imperialists would have to be decisively weakened and be tottering on the brink of collapse to make revolutionary war feasible.[15] In effect, Lenin asserted that a single socialist country as a rule would be the militarily *weaker* party, which made nonsense of everything he had been writing about revolutionary war since 1915. He was truly and thoroughly sobered up.

Despair to confidence

In March 1919 Lenin classically formulated the view that the Soviet state existed in a '*system of states*', and that its prolonged existence next to the imperialist states was 'unthinkable'. 'In the end, either the one or the other will be victorious.'[16] But when the Bolsheviks were winning the Civil War in late 1919, Lenin's despondency reverted to buoyancy. That is not to say that he regained his confidence in revolutionary war as the solution for Soviet Russia to break out of its confinement. The disastrous ending of the Red Army's march into Poland in August 1920 would have destroyed his last illusions on this score. Rather, he now formulated a new scenario of peaceful coexistence, in which Soviet Russia would be secured for an indefinite period of time.

Lenin asked himself how the Bolsheviks could have been victorious when the Entente powers obviously had the troops to crush them. Why didn't they make a more serious attempt? His answer was that, given the Bolshevik sympathies of the British, French and American workers, the risk of sending soldiers out to fight against them would have been unacceptably high. The 'world revolution' *had* saved Soviet Russia, Lenin argued, through the 'sympathy of the workers of the whole world' that prevented the imperialists from bringing their military superiority into play.[17]

At a conference of the Moscow party organisation on 21 November 1920, Lenin observed that Soviet Russia had gained much more than a mere 'breathing space': it had entered a whole 'new phase', in which 'our fundamental international existence in the system of capitalist states' was confirmed. The Bolshevik leader now accepted 'the possibility of the existence of proletarian power and of the Soviet republic, even if the socialist revolution in the whole world is delayed'.[18] Thus Lenin more or less officially acknowledged that the Soviet state might persist without the triumph of the world revolution.

On 23 December 1921 Lenin confirmed at the Ninth Congress of Soviets that it was feasible 'for a socialist republic to exist in a capitalist encirclement'.[19] The direct support of victorious proletariats for Soviet Russia had not come, but 'support of another kind' *had* come. Soviet Russia was kept safe from invasion through the 'sympathy for us among the toiling masses ... in the whole world'. And even though this support remained 'insecure', Lenin was confident that 'we can now already rely on it'.[20]

No question that Lenin still ardently wanted Soviet Russia to break out of its confinement. Now that revolutionary war had largely been discredited, he fell back on the scenario of revolutionary contagion. He pointed out that the construction of a socialist economy in Russia would serve as a means of 'setting the example'. According to the Bolshevik leader, 'all works of the greatest socialist writers' testified to the importance of building socialism in one's own country as a means of attracting the admiring attention of the rest of the world. Other countries would thus be convinced of the superiority of the communist order and be infused with the desire to emulate it.[21] Briefly, Lenin fell back on the fantasy of revolution through example we met earlier with socialists from Winstanley to Kautsky, Hilferding and Bauer.

Socialism in one country

What does all this tell us about Lenin's views on socialism in one country? Reduced to the basics, the idea of single-country socialism means two things that both have to be the case, i.e. a revolutionary country surrounded by hostile capitalist states must be able to organise its own socialist economy, and it must be able to prevent or survive military intervention.

That Soviet Russia could maintain itself in the face of the imperialist threat was a conclusion Lenin drew in late 1919 under the influence of Civil War victories. International proletarian solidarity was deemed the essential factor. That Russia could create its own socialist economy even without the support of other proletarian states had been taken for granted by Lenin since 1917. Even when he was most desperate about his regime's chances of survival, in March 1918, his loss of faith exclusively concerned the country's military effectiveness. He could in one and the same article make the point that 'salvation is *only* possible by way of the international socialist revolution', *and* that Russia possessed the territory and natural resources to become strong again and to lay the 'durable foundation of the socialist society'.[22]

It is true that in the spring of 1918 Lenin argued against Left communists Bukharin and N. Osinskii that Soviet Russia better not expropriate large-scale industry all at once. In his eyes, 'state capitalism' – private enterprise under state control – would be a step forward for backward Russia. Soviet Russia would do well first to introduce the methods of the German state-capitalist war economy before advancing any further.[23] But this scenario amounted to postponement rather than cancellation of the socialisation of industry. In May 1918 Lenin predicted that if state capitalism could be established in half a year, this would guarantee that 'in one year socialism will be finally consolidated and invincible with us'.[24] As we saw, in June the large-scale industries were expropriated after all.

The main problem with constructing a socialist economy remained the agricultural sector, which, from a Marxist point of view, was not ready for the transition. Lenin admitted that in backward Russia the socialisation of agriculture would be a gradual process. It required various transitional, intermediary organisational schemes in order finally to arrive at large-scale socialist forms.[25] But he trusted that industry could function as the motor of the process, by providing electricity and tractors.[26] Most significantly, Lenin repeatedly indicated that agriculture could be socialised even if there were no other proletarian states available to help out with their technologies. Thrown back on their own resources, it would only take the isolated Bolsheviks more time.[27]

Thus, for all practical purposes, Lenin accepted socialism in one country for Soviet Russia. This conclusion seems to be at odds, though, with his monotonously repeated assertions that a 'complete' socialist society could never emerge in one country, that the 'victory of socialism' in one country was impossible, or that, in any case, 'complete' and 'final' victory could not be achieved in a single country. For that, the joint efforts of a number of advanced countries were required.[28] What could this possibly mean, if the Bolsheviks were socialising the economy, if Lenin was confident that this could be done irrespective of the world revolution, and if he came to trust that international solidarity likely would keep Soviet Russia afloat?

There was ambiguity and complexity to Lenin's thinking. He accepted that a socialist economy could be constructed in a single country, but, confined to one country, socialism would display all kinds of imperfections that only the cooperation with a number of other socialist states could fix. That is why Lenin denied that a 'complete' socialist society could emerge in one country, but never, to my knowledge, flatly asserted that 'socialism in one country is impossible'. Also, it was self-evident for Lenin that any single country that had the temerity to introduce socialism was in danger of being crushed by the imperialists – which is why he would say that the 'victory of' socialism could never be achieved in a single state. But on this point Lenin's views were subject to profound change over time. In his darkest hours, between Brest-Litovsk and late 1919, he indeed assumed that the imperialists would crush Soviet Russia if the proletariat of the West did not rise. But earlier he had suggested the alternative solution of the revolutionary war, and from late 1919 onwards he trusted that international proletarian solidarity could guard

Soviet Russia from intervention. Then again, as military intervention could, of course, never be completely ruled out, 'final' victory would evade the single socialist state as long as the main imperialist states had not been destroyed.

Altogether, confined to a single country, the socialist economy would remain incomplete, and victory could never be considered finally assured. But that isolated Russia was in the process of establishing a socialist economy and that she had gained a reasonable degree of international security was unquestionably accepted by Lenin. With final victory still dependent on the world revolution, socialism in one country nonetheless could work.

Lenin's confidence in the ability of isolated Russia to establish a socialist economy is the more remarkable if we regard it in a comparative perspective. In the early months of their regime, the Bolsheviks had one ally, the Party of Left Socialists-Revolutionaries, split off from the PSR in November 1917.[29] The PLSR joined the government in December, only to leave it again in March 1918 in protest against the Peace of Brest-Litovsk.[30] When the Left SR rose against the Bolshevik regime in July their party was destroyed.[31]

The PSR position was that, for the time being, socialism represented no real option in backward Russia.[32] On the contrary, the Left SR argued, like Lenin, that Russia's backwardness shouldn't be an obstacle for the socialist transition.[33] Yet, the Left SR were not as optimistic as Lenin. In his *Two Tactics*, written in early 1918, one of their main theorists, Boris Kamkov, confirmed that socio-economic backwardness would not prevent Russia from achieving 'complete socialism', but without the class support from the West the Russian Revolution was bound to remain locked in 'some kind of preliminary stage'.[34] The other main theorist of the party, Vladimir Trutovskii, argued in his 1918 *The Transitional Period* that the conditions for establishing socialism in backward Russia were even better than in the developed capitalist states.[35] But would revolutionary Russia be able to persist as an 'isolated state'? Trutovskii thought Russia had the vast territory and natural resources to become a 'self-sufficient economic unit'. It was therefore 'possible for a society of the 'transitional period' to exist in an environment of capitalist states'.[36] But whether a *socialist* economy could emerge in case Russia remained isolated was a question Trutovskii left unanswered.[37] In light of the Left SR's views, Lenin's confidence was indeed remarkable.

In the last period of his life Lenin became even more optimistic. On 20 November 1922 he informed the Moscow Soviet that 'NEP Russia will become socialist Russia' in just a couple of years.[38] The leader's optimism was fed by a new appreciation of peasant cooperatives, which he had originally regarded as state capitalist institutions.[39] In his 'On the Cooperation', dictated in early January 1923, Lenin redefined peasant cooperatives working with state-owned means of production as 'socialist enterprises'.[40] This led him to the conclusion that the combination of proletarian state power and peasant cooperatives would allow Russia to create a 'complete socialist society'.[41]

Finally, Lenin was also reconsidering the question of the preconditions of the socialist transition. In 'On our revolution' dictated on 16 and 17 January, he mentioned the 'endlessly trite' argument that had emerged in 'the period of development of West-European social democracy', to the effect that Russia did not have the 'objective economic preconditions' to advance towards socialism. But couldn't one make revolution first and then create the conditions? To underscore the point, Lenin referred to Marx's hopes expressed in 1856 that the German proletarian revolution would be precipitated by a new Peasants' War.[42]

Lenin's last turn has been interpreted as more reminiscent of the Baron Münchhausen than of Marx.[43] However, it would be better to say that Lenin was finally returning to the original Münchhausen, Marx. Lenin was beginning to understand that Marx had accepted the notion of proletarian revolution in weakly industrialised France and Germany all along, and that the idea that such a thing was not possible had emerged only in the Second International.

The views of Lenin's comrades

This interpretation of Lenin's views gains plausibility if we see the other Bolshevik leaders also accepting a socialism in one country perspective. Stalin had been nominated People's Commissar of Nationalities in 1917. In 1922 he became the party's General Secretary, an important position that however did not yet have the significance it would later acquire. Not surprisingly in view of his performance at the August 1917 party congress, Stalin closely followed Lenin's lead.

In a speech delivered at Vladikavkaz in October 1920, Stalin explained that Soviet Russia's survival proved that the socialist revolution could be 'crowned with success' and become 'durable [*prochnym*]', even in the absence of revolutions abroad. Russia was turning into 'some kind of oasis of socialism', serving as an 'example for the capitalistically developed countries'. Stalin mentioned two main reasons for the staying power of the revolution in Russia: the country's vastness and its abundant natural resources, which strong points distinguished it from countries like Hungary, Italy and Germany. Finally, the revolutionary movement in the West effectively prevented military intervention.[44]

Bukharin was another important case in point. Earlier, he had insisted on the necessarily international and simultaneous character of proletarian takeovers.[45] But he shifted his position. In 1920, he and Preobrazhenskii published *The ABC of Communism*, which Stephen Cohen characterises as 'the best-known and most widely circulated of all pre-Stalinist expositions of Bolshevism'.[46] What did this compendium of bolshevism have to say about the prospects of socialism in Russia?

The authors predicted world revolution based on the interconnectedness of the economies of the important countries of the world.[47] 'The communist revolution can be victorious only as a world revolution', Bukharin and Preobrazhenskii insisted, because if the workers seized power only in one country, then 'in the end the great robber States would crush the workers' State'.

But this was not to be taken too literally, for the book continued that the imperialists had been 'unable to crush Soviet Russia'. Fear of revolution in their own countries had paralysed them. Just like Lenin, Bukharin and Preobrazhenskii did not make Soviet Russia's security dependent on the triumph of the world revolution but on the 'international solidarity of the working class'. Nonetheless, if Soviet Russia remained alone, she would be in a precarious position:

> when the workers have gained the victory in only one country, the organisation of economic life ... is a very difficult matter. Such a country receives little or nothing from abroad; it is blockaded on all sides.[48]

But, again, if Russia's isolation made it 'difficult' to organise a communist economy, it was not impossible.[49] As regards industry, the problems were not even all that great. State-capitalist centralisation during the war had effectively prepared the ground for 'socialist organisation'. Despite 'all difficulties', the Russian workers would be able to maintain their grip on industry 'until help comes from the west'.[50] Agriculture represented more of a problem. The assistance from proletarian states in the West would allow the Bolsheviks to set up 'a general and immense cooperative organisation.'[51] Without such assistance, it would be 'very difficult' to convince the peasants.[52] Difficult but not impossible:

> the principal task of communism in Russia is to bring it to pass that ... the peasants upon their own initiative, shall destroy the counter-revolution. When that has been achieved, there will no longer remain any insuperable obstacles in the way of the socialisation of agriculture.[53]

Bukharin and Preobrazhenskii thus looked eye to eye with Lenin in accepting that international proletarian solidarity effectively shielded Soviet Russia from military intervention, and in trusting that a socialist economy could emerge even without proletarian assistance from the West.

Richard Day discovered that even the staunchly internationalist Trotsky came to accept the feasibility of the socialist economy in one country.[54] Trotsky was on record that single-country socialism was impossible economically as well as for military reasons. Also, an isolated backward proletarian state would be overturned in a *Jacquerie*. But at the 1920 Ninth Party Congress, he presented the outlines of a plan for the 'organisation of labour on new socialist foundations' that seemed to call into question these pessimistic assumptions.[55] Of all prominent Soviet leaders, War Commissar Trotsky was the one most taken by the spirit of civil war. He proposed the autarky of the besieged fortress: even under blockade, he argued, Soviet Russia would be able to produce everything it needed itself, including sophisticated machinery. Militarised labour would make up for capital deficiencies.[56] In another speech, Trotsky explained that the outlook of the world revolution was uncertain, but, regardless, 'We can't rule out the possibility that we'll arrive at [*pereidem k*] a more or less developed socialist economy in the course of three, four or five years.' The socialisation of agriculture would take more time.[57]

The introduction of the New Economic Policy made Trotsky think again. In the January 1922 preface to the new edition of his *1905*, he mentioned the permanent revolution and his old thesis of peasant rebellion against socialist government in Russia. Trotsky added that his interpretation of permanent revolution had turned out 'completely justified'.[58] In the afterword to a new edition of 'The Program of Peace', reissued that same year, Trotsky mentioned the 'impossibility of isolated socialist construction in a national, state framework'. The point was that Soviet Russia could not do without economic interaction with the capitalist countries; but that interaction was bound to harm Russia's economic development. A 'genuine upsurge of the socialist economy in Russia' would become possible only after the 'victory of the proletariat in the main countries of Europe'.[59]

But did Trotsky really discard his hopes for an autarkic socialist Russia? According to Iurii Fel'shtinskii and Georgii Cherniavskii, he abandoned the single-country socialism perspective only in 1926. Even in the spring of 1923 Trotsky still argued in a lecture that, given its vastness and natural resources, Russia was exceptional in possessing the conditions for constructing socialism 'on its own', without any outside support.[60]

Altogether, by the end of the Civil War it was quite common for party leaders to accept that isolated Russia might establish and maintain a socialist order.[61] This hardly seems to have been the fruit of theoretical considerations. It would be better to say that the Bolsheviks were adaptive to circumstance. The Red Army had stood its ground, and there was no reason to assume that there would be insurmountable obstacles to further socialisation of the economy. In any case, the Great Debate after Lenin's death, which supposedly decided the question of socialism in one country, can better be regarded as having solemnly confirmed what had already been decided.

Notes

1. For recent studies of the Civil War, see Pipes, 1994; Brovkin, 1994; Figes, 1996; Swain, 1996; Wade, 2001: Chapters 4, 5; Mawdsley, 2011.
2. See for the revolutionary era of 1917–23, Brown, 2009: 79–84; Priestland, 2009: 104–24.
3. For economic policies from 1917 to 1923, see Carr, 1952; Malle, 1985; Nove, 1992a: Chapters 3 and 4; Suny, 2011: Chapters 1.3 and 2.5; Hildermeier, 1998: 134–58. For this period, see also Raleigh, 2006: 157–63; Ball, 2006. For the state farms (*sovkhozy*) and the collective farms (*kolkhozy*, coming as *kommuny* and *arteli*), see Malle, 1985: 410–18; Suny, 2011: 105.
4. Carr, 1970, vol. 2: 46.
5. Nation, 1989: 211. See also for example Suny, 2011: 72.
6. Speech at the Third Congress of the Comintern, 5 July 1921 (*PSS*, vol. 44: 36).
7. On 14 December 1917 Lenin wrote that peace between capitalism and socialism would be a mere 'armistice' ('Za khleb i za mir', ibid.: vol. 35: 169). See also speech at Seventh Extraordinary Party Congress, 7 March 1918 (vol. 36: 8).

8 Ibid.: vol. 35: 244, 248, 250–1.
9 Trotsky, 1964: 106.
10 'O revoliutsionnoi fraze' (*PSS*, vol. 35: 343–6). For the debate between Lenin and the Left Bolsheviks on peace and revolutionary war, see Cohen, 1974: 63–9; Kowalski, 1991: 60–82.
11 See Swain, 1996: 127, 132–49.
12 *PSS*, vol. 36: 11, 15. See also 14 March speech at the Fourth Congress of Soviets (ibid.: 109). Compare: 'O 'levom' rebiachestve i o melkoburzhuaznosti' (May 1918) (ibid.: 290–1); 23 April speech (ibid.: 235). Lenin also concluded that it was easier for the proletariat of a backward country to seize power (because the elite of the workers in the imperialist West could be bribed and the bourgeoisie in the West represented a much more powerful and sophisticated ruling class), though more difficult for it to establish socialism than in advanced states. See for example speech 24 January 1918 at Third Congress of Soviets (vol. 35: 279); 7 March speech at Seventh Party Congress (vol. 36: 10, 15–16); 14 March 1918 speech at Fourth Congress of Soviets (ibid.: 97); 29 April 1918 speech at Central Executive Committee (ibid.: 252); 1 March 1920 speech at congress of toiling Cossacks (vol. 40: 170). For the fullest exposé of Lenin's ideas about the workers' aristocracy in the imperialist countries, see 'Imperializm i raskol sotsializma' (October 1916), vol. 30: 163–79. Thus Lenin established that a semi-industrialised country like his own country would be the more likely candidate to initiate the proletarian world revolution.
13 'Glavnaia zadacha nashikh dnei' (11 March 1918), *PSS*, vol. 36: 78–9.
14 'Tsennye priznaniia Pitirima Sorokina' (20 November 1918), vol. 37: 190.
15 'O "levom" rebiachestve' (*PSS*, vol. 36: 287). See also 29 April speech at the All-Union CEC (ibid.: 251, 253); 9 May 1918 theses (ibid.: 277).
16 Speech at Eighth Party Congress (*PSS*, vol. 38: 139).
17 2 December 1919 speech at the Eighth Party Conference (ibid.: vol. 39: 343, 346). See also speech at Seventh Congress of Soviets (ibid.: 388–400); 1 March 1920 speech (vol. 40: 166–73); 15 October 1920 speech (ibid.: 348, 356).
18 *PSS*, vol. 42: 20–2. In a 5 July 1921 speech Lenin however once again spoke of a 'brief breathing-space' (vol. 44: 37).
19 Ibid.: 301.
20 Ibid.: 293. Compare 5 July 1921 speech (ibid.: 36–7).
21 21 November 1920 (*PSS*, vol. 42: 27–9).
22 'Glavnaia zadacha' (ibid.: vol. 36: 80). See also 'Ocherednye zadachi sovetskoi vlasti' (28 April 1918), (ibid.: 171); 9 May theses (ibid.: 278).
23 29 April speech (ibid.: 254–60); 'O "levom" rebiachestve' (ibid.: 295–302). Lenin's argumentation shifted compared to 1917, when he had been arguing that state capitalism already had prepared Russia for the socialist transition. Now he argued that Russia did *not yet have* state capitalism. See for example 29 speech (ibid.:, vol. 36: 255, 258–9). In May 1918 Lenin suggested that Russia did not yet have the economic preconditions of socialism: 'O "levom" rebiachestve' (ibid.: 300–1). But, crucially, in his scenario the introduction of state capitalism precisely served to create these conditions. For Lenin's spring 1918 views on state capitalism, see also Carr, 1952: 88–93; Kowalski, 1991: Chapter 5; Nove, 1992b: 30; Suny, 2011: 74–6. For the Left-communist views of state capitalism and socialism, see Kowalski, 1991: 19, 39–43; Cohen, 1974: 69–78.
24 'O "levom" rebiachestve' (*PSS*, vol. 36: 295).
25 See for example 1 December 1917 letter to *Pravda* (ibid.: vol. 35: 102–3); 'Proletarskaia revoliutsiia i renegat Kautskii' (1918), vol. 37: 316, 321; 11 December 1918 speech (vol. 37: 356, 361–2); February 1919 drafts for party programme (vol. 38: 102, 123); 'Ekonomika i politika v epokhu diktatura proletariata' (30 October 1919), vol. 39: 273; 15 March 1921 speech to Tenth Party Congress (vol. 43: 57–9).

174 *Socialism in one country*

26 See for example 23 March 1919 speech (*PSS*, vol. 38: 204); 15 March 1921 speech (vol. 43: 60); theses for the June–July 1921 Third Congress of the Comintern (vol. 44: 9). See also 24 January 1918 speech to the Third Congress of Soviets (vol. 35: 263–4); 21 November 1920 speech (vol. 42: 28–9).

27 See for example 23 March 1919 speech (ibid.: vol. 38: 204); 'O prodovol'stvennom naloge' (21 April 1921) (ibid.: vol. 43: 228–9); 'Plany broshiury "O prodovol'stvennom naloge"' (ibid.: 383). See also first draft of 'Ocherednye zadachi' (vol. 36: 138–9).

28 For some of the most important and most often quoted examples, see theses 20 January 1918 (ibid.: vol. 35: 245); speech at Third Congress of Soviets, 24 January 1918 (ibid.: 271, 277); 24 February 1918 speech at the All-Union Central Executive Committee (ibid.: 378); 23 April 1918 speech at Moscow Soviet (vol. 36: 234); 21 June 1918 speech at the *Sokol'nycheskii klub* (ibid.: 427); 8 November 1918 speech to the Sixth Congress of Soviets (vol. 37: 153); 'Uspekhi i trudnosti sovetskoi vlasti' (1919), vol. 38: 42; 4 December 1919 speech (vol. 39: 388); 15 October 1920 speech (vol. 40: 348); 6 November 1920 speech (vol. 42: 1–3); 21 November 1920 speech (vol. 42: 20); 6 February 1921 speech (vol. 42: 311); 15 March 1921 speech on Tenth Party Congress (vol. 43: 58); 'Zametki publitsista' (written February 1922), vol. 44: 417–18. Such observations concerned any hypothetical isolated country – 'backward' or 'advanced': in a 26 May 1918 speech Lenin remarked: 'one cannot completely [*vsetselo*] fulfil the socialist revolution in one country with one's own forces ... even if [the country] would be much less backward than Russia' (vol. 36: 382).

29 For the history of the PSR Left faction prior to November 1917, see Häfner, 1994: 23–117.

30 Ibid.: Chapter 7.

31 See for this episode, ibid.: 535–71.

32 See decision of Fourth PSR Congress of late 1917: Erofeev, 2000: vol. 3.2: 184; Chernov's speech at the Constituent Assembly in January 1918 (ibid.: 286–93); 'Ko vsem partiinym organizatsiiam. Obraschchenie TsK PSR' (1918) (ibid.: 316). For the Socialists-Revolutionaries after the October Revolution, see Radkey (1963) and Smith (2011). For Chernov during this period, see Gusev, 1999: Chapters 6, 7.

33 See for example: resolution adopted at founding congress: 'Rezoliutsiia po politicheskoi programme': *Rezoliutsii i postanovleniia*, 1918: 20. See also for that congress: 'Tezisy i osnovnye polozheniia ekonomicheskoi politiki' (ibid.: 21).

34 Kamkov, 1918: 13–15, 19–20, 26–7 (quotations pp. 20, 15). In his 'Organicheskii nedug', written in January 1919, Kamkov (n.y.: 13) observed retrospectively that the PSLR in the past had advocated a 'whole series of transitional measures' on the road to socialism, which they had considered realisable even 'in the most unfavourable international situation'. But they had also recognised that 'the socialist transformations in our country can be delayed, fettered in their advance, by the presence of bourgeois–capitalist relations in all of the rest of the world'.

35 Trutovskii, 1918: 7–18.

36 Ibid.: 70–7 (quotations pp. 71, 72, 77). For military intervention see also ibid.: 36–8.

37 On the question of the PLSR and 'socialism in one country', see also Häfner, 1994: 172.

38 *PSS*, vol. 45: 309.

39 'O prodovol'stvennom naloge' (ibid.: vol. 43: 225–6). With the New Economic Policy Lenin had once again become enthusiastic about 'state capitalism'. See the whole article, ibid.: 203–45. See also: 16 March 1921 speech at Tenth Party Congress (ibid.: 157–61); 11 April 1921 speech (ibid.: 163–82). For Lenin on state capitalism in 1921, see Suny, 2011: 153–5.

40 'O kooperatsii' (written 4 and 6 January 1923), *PSS*, vol. 45: 375.

41 Ibid.: 370, 377. Carr (1952: 279) comments that Lenin foresaw a development from NEP to socialism, 'whose fulfilment seemed to depend exclusively on the ingenuity and strength of Soviet policy'. Under Stalin, 'Lenin's insistence on NEP as the true road to socialism was revealed as an unavowed forerunner of the doctrine of "socialism in one country"'. Cohen (1974: 138) agrees that Lenin's cooperative socialism 'implied that socialism in an isolated Soviet Russia was possible'.
42 'O nashei revoliutsii' (*PSS*, vol. 45: 380–1). For a briefer version of the argument, see 'O kooperatsii' (ibid.: 376–7).
43 Lih, 2011a: 84.
44 Stalin, *Sochineniia* [*Sochineniia*], 1947, vol. 4: 374–80. See also 'O politicheskoi strategii i taktike russkikh kommunistov' (written July 1921), vol. 5: 83; 'Perspektivy' (December 1921) (ibid.: 117–18).
45 In his pamphlet 'Ot diktatury imperializma k diktature proletariata', published in early 1918, Bukharin (1923: 78) observed that 'the permanent revolution in Russia is transforming itself into a European revolution of the proletariat'. See also ibid.: 144. This did not reveal, though, what would happen to Russia should the European revolution fail. For Bukharin's position on the viability of an isolated Soviet Russia, see Cohen, 1974: 55–6; Haynes, 1985: 52, 54.
46 Cohen, 1974: 83.
47 Bukharin and Preobrazensky, 1966: 136.
48 Ibid.: 138–9.
49 Ibid.: 130. See also Bukharin's (1979: 170) 1920 *The Politics and Economics of the Transition Period*.
50 Bukharin and Preobrazensky, 1966: 160–1.
51 Ibid.: 161.
52 Ibid.: 165.
53 Ibid.: 318.
54 Day, 1973: Chapter 2; see also Swain, 2006: 2, 159.
55 *Deviatyi s"ezd*, 1960: 91, 93, 95–6.
56 Ibid.: 191–2.
57 Ibid.: 395.
58 Trotsky, 1923b: 4.
59 Trotsky, 1923a: 481–2.
60 Fel'shtinskii and Cherniavskii (2013: 116–17) quote archival materials.
61 According to Marot (2012: 18–20), after 1917 all Bolsheviks including Trotskii accepted socialism in one country.

15 The Great Debate

The debate about socialism in one country began in late 1924. As argued earlier, the whole debate was, really, an afterthought. Yet, having a debate about it and turning 'socialism in one country' into party dogma, did add a new dimension. Neither in Germany nor in Russia had the matter ever been object of an official party debate. Before the Bolsheviks turned the matter into the touchstone of Marxist orthodoxy and heresy, it never had that charge. Before social democrats came to power no practical purpose would have been served by including the question in the struggles over revisionism and orthodoxy. In Germany and Austria socialisation of the economy was seriously considered, but only for a short while. The question soon lost the acuteness it might otherwise have acquired. The Soviet communists formally put the matter on the agenda only after the German revolution in October 1923 had failed and the conclusion became unavoidable that the world revolution would be very long in waiting.

Apart from questions of principle, the debate was also marked by the power struggle that broke out after Lenin's death in January 1924. Each of the major party leaders hoped to establish his own legitimacy by formulating the supposedly most orthodox Leninist position. What Stalin, Bukharin, Kamenev, Zinov'ev and Trotsky – to mention the main contestants – would say was to a certain extent predictable. Inevitably, Lenin's 1915–16 articles would be made the object of their particular scrutiny. It was also to be expected that, in dealing with Lenin's 1917–23 contributions, all of the contestants would engage in cherry picking, so as to create a Lenin closest to their own particular views. The significant changes in Lenin's views over the course of the years left ample space for selective and out-of-context quoting for both parties.

Stalin was cheating on important issues, but his fundamental position in the quest for Leninist legitimacy was the stronger one: it was undeniable that Lenin had accepted that isolated Russia could host a socialist economy, and neither could it be plausibly denied that, in the course of the years, Lenin had convinced himself that Soviet Russia could achieve a relatively secure existence even without revolution in Europe. Compared to this, the bickering about whether Lenin had been referring to Russia in 1915, or what exactly he had meant with 'complete and final victory' were points of the second order.

The Great Debate: first round

When illness incapacitated Lenin, power was taken in hand by a troika consisting of Stalin, Zinov'ev and Kamenev. In late 1923 a Left Opposition (Trotsky, Preobrazhenskii and others) began to advocate more ambitious industrial investment policies and heavier taxation of the top layers of the peasantry, the so-called kulaks. Bukharin, who for the time being remained outside the leading inner circle, objected that healthy industrial development required an orientation on the peasant market. This would guarantee slow but steady growth of the socialist element, including peasant cooperatives. At the January 1924 Thirteenth Party Conference the troika easily defeated the Left Opposition.[1]

Lenin's death on 21 January 1924 became the occasion for Bukharin to hammer out his proposals for a gradualist road to socialism. In a 2 February speech, 'Lenin as Marxist', he referred to a process of *'growing into socialism'*, with the reservation: 'it goes without saying that I am only looking at one country in isolation'.[2] Sometime later Bukharin elaborated on an evolutionary road based on electrification and peasant cooperatives, only to conclude: 'The victory in this type of class struggle (we are here abstracting from the problems of the world abroad [*vneshnego poriadka*]) represents the final victory of socialism.'[3]

According to Cohen, Bukharin's suggestions of socialism in isolated Russia were indebted to Lenin's last writings.[4] More importantly, Cohen added that 'the whole controversy over the novelty of "socialism in one country" was in some respects a misleading one. Bukharin and the party leadership had thought of war communism as leading to socialism quite separate from the prospects of European revolution.'[5] Far from making a new departure, Bukharin was following the drift of earlier Bolshevik thinking.

At this point, Stalin was mostly focusing not on the question of isolated socialism but on the related but distinct issue of workers' revolution in backward countries. He was in fact concluding the train of thought of Lenin's 'On our revolution'. In his April–May 1924 *On the Foundations of Leninism*, Stalin pointed out that in the 1850s, when Marx was advocating proletarian revolution in Germany, 'there were relatively less proletarians in Germany than for example in Russia in 1917'. It seems, Stalin concluded, that the conditions for the socialist transition might as well be created *after* the revolution.[6] He furthermore ascribed the idea that the proletarian revolution would be separated from its bourgeois predecessor by a protracted period of capitalist economic development, to the 'Heroes of the Second International'. In Stalin's own model of preference, 'uninterrupted revolution', the two revolutions would be rapidly following upon each other. Stalin accused Trotsky, not mentioned by name, of having dished up a garbled version of the 'permanent revolution' that essentially skipped the bourgeois revolution.[7]

The significance of these passages is hard to overestimate. They represented the final confirmation of Marx and Engels's assumption that rapid, permanent-revolutionary transition from bourgeois–democratic to proletarian revolution was possible even in backward countries with a proletarian minority. That Stalin used the Russian word *nepreryvnaia* rather than Trotsky's term of preference *permanentnaia* is immaterial. It means the same thing. From Trotsky's perspective, Stalin's division of the revolution into two stages might have been problematic. In Trotsky's version, there would not be two revolutions but only one, workers' revolution, consecutively carrying out the democratic and socialist tasks. But Stalin was correct in suggesting that this kind of compact sequence was not what Marx and Engels had been referring to when they discussed permanent revolution.[8]

As regards the other question, of what would happen if the proletariat came to power but remained alone, Stalin opined that the 'organisation of socialist production' would be inconceivable without the 'joint efforts of the proletarians of several advanced countries', especially in backward Russia. In that sense 'final victory of socialism' was impossible to achieve in one country.[9] Given Stalin's own earlier statements as well as the general drift of Bolshevik thinking over the preceding years, this was an exceedingly odd remark, which he later much regretted having entrusted to paper.

When Bukharin and Stalin made their observations the struggle with the Left Opposition had abated, but in October 1924 Trotsky returned to the attack. In his *Lessons of October*, he accused Zinov'ev and Kamenev of having rejected proletarian revolution as a scenario unsuitable for backward Russia in 1917.[10] Trotsky was subjected to a blistering counter-attack. The campaign began on 18 November with Kamenev's speech at the Moscow Party Committee and lasted for two months.[11] Kamenev alleged that Trotsky's version of permanent revolution had no place for the peasantry, which is why in Trotsky's scenario peasant Russia supposedly was unable to construct a socialist society independently.[12]

Kamenev's accusation was historically misleading, in so far as in 1905–6, when Trotsky's theory emerged, *all* 'orthodox Marxists', including Lenin, had been of this opinion.[13] But Trotsky had been foolish enough in 1922 to confirm his adherence to the vision of the inevitable peasant rebellion, by then an eccentric view among Bolsheviks. The irony was that, in all likelihood, Trotsky himself no longer really expected Soviet Russia to fall victim to a *Jacquerie* either. But even if he recanted now, his stature would be seriously diminished. He chose simply not to respond to the point.

Stalin turned the issue of socialism in one country into the main line of attack on Trotsky. In his 'October and Comrade Trotsky's Theory of Permanent Revolution', signed 17 December, he accused him of not acknowledging the 'possibility of the victory of socialism in one country even in a capitalistically weakly developed one'.[14] Stalin admitted that 'the *complete* victory of socialism, the *complete* guarantee against the restoration of the old order' depended on the prevention of military intervention, but the 'solidarity of the European workers with our revolution' would suffice to secure this.[15] As we saw, during the Civil War, Trotsky had been offering a powerful conception of an autarkic socialist economy himself. Once again, he chose not to respond to Stalin and to remain silent.

The affair ended in January 1925 with Trotsky's resignation as War Commissar. The Politburo decided to settle the matter once and for all at the Fourteenth Party Conference, convening on 27–29 April. At one of the preparatory Politburo meetings Zinov'ev and Kamenev defended the position that 'we won't be able completely to build [*stroit' do kontsa*] socialism because of our *technical backwardness*'.[16] But after some discussion a unanimous decision was taken in line with Stalin and Bukharin's proposals.[17]

In his opening speech at the conference, chairman Kamenev assured his audience that the Bolsheviks could successfully build [*postroim*] a socialist society in Russia.[18] In his 29 April report, Zinov'ev confirmed that only the international revolution could make victory 'solid' and 'final'; but not counting 'international interference [*vmeshatel'stva*]', it *was* possible to construct a 'complete socialist society' in backward Russia.[19]

> Notwithstanding the whole technological backwardness of our country, we can and must ... *completely build* [postroit'] *socialism, despite the delay in tempo of the international revolution* ... *final* victory is a matter of the international arena, but ... the delay in tempo of the revolution does not put off victory itself, only its date.[20]

The resolution tabled by Zinov'ev confirmed that 'the victory of socialism ... is unconditionally possible in one country'. At the same time, the presence of a 'permanent threat of capitalist blockade, of other forms of economic pressure, of armed intervention, of restoration' made it impossible for a single country to declare '*final*' victory.

> The only guarantee of the *final victory of socialism*, i.e. guarantees against restoration, is therefore the victorious socialist revolution in several countries. From this it does not follow at all that the building [*postroika*] of a complete socialist society in a backward country like Russia without 'state support' (Trotsky) by technologically and economically more developed countries, is impossible.[21]

The socialist USSR would be serving as the 'fundamental centre [*bazoi*] of the international revolution' and as her 'powerful lever and support'.[22]

The only element in the resolution hard to reconcile with Lenin's pronouncements over the preceding years was that of a *complete* socialist society crystallising in one country, the point Zinov'ev and Kemenev had been weakly objecting to during the preparation of the conference. But, arguably, even on that point Lenin's thinking had been shifting in the very last period of his life. Essentially, the resolution was merely dotting the ideological i's. This helps us to understand the very odd fact that the conference accepted the resolution that supposedly represented a momentous break in Bolshevik ideology without discussion and unanimously.[23] The best explanation for this is that the participants did not experience the resolution as momentous at all. Rather, it confirmed what they had been thinking all along.[24]

Once in place, the doctrine of socialism in one country underwent no further essential development. Stalin and Bukharin only narrowed it down somewhat further when they concluded that only military intervention – not economic blockade – might prove fatal for Soviet Russia.[25]

The Great Debate: second round

The Fourteenth Party Conference agreed on a number of new concessions to the peasants. The 1925 harvest was a very good one, but the government was nonetheless faced with a grain procurement crisis. Fearing that differentiation in the countryside was empowering the 'kulaks', Zinov'ev and Kamenev now began to argue that the concessions had gone too far. Early in September they formed a New Opposition. Bukharin moved into the centre of power as Stalin's main ally.[26]

The debate on economic policy is not of much direct interest here, but Zinov'ev also returned to the theoretical issue of socialism in one country. He discussed it at length in the rambling chapter 14 of his September 1925 book, *Leninism*.[27] Zinov'ev confirmed that it was possible to be constructing socialism, but socialism could not be finally established and consolidated 'within the confines of one country'. If Russia remained alone, only a 'large measure' of socialism could be preserved.[28] Thus Zinov'ev committed himself to the idea that a socialist economy could emerge in a single isolated country but not in any complete, rounded form, an idea Lenin would probably have subscribed to if we discount his very last observations.[29]

Trotsky did not join the New Opposition. After his resignation from the War Commissariat he was employed at the Supreme Council of the National Economy, which added to his already strong preoccupation with industry. Trotsky was less nervous than Zinov'ev and Kamenev about the growing strength of the kulaks, whom he appreciated as the producers of the marketable grain that provided the funds for the import of machinery. He did not trust the opposition to share his taste for rapid industrialisation.[30]

In his September 1925 *Towards Capitalism or Towards Socialism?*, Trotsky commented on recent figures of the State Planning Commission indicating that the socialist sectors of the Soviet economy were achieving a 'growing preponderance' over the capitalist ones. For the future, he was optimistic about the 'socialist transformation of agriculture' as well. Trotsky concluded in high spirits that the Gosplan tables 'lead forward to the future socialist society'. He believed that 'the socialist tendencies are assured of victory'.[31] Trotsky still preferred not to inform his comrades about his views on socialism in one country, but the pamphlet leaves no doubt about it that he saw a socialist economy emerging in isolated Soviet Russia.

Trotsky did break with the autarkic ideals he espoused during the Civil War years, though. Instead, he now saw participation in the international division of labour as essential for driving up the growth rate of the Soviet economy.[32] Trotsky warned that Soviet Russia was not a 'closely knit self-sufficing economy', but participated in the 'system of the world division of labour'. And under the conditions of the capitalist world market 'the rate of our economic development determines the force of our resistance to the economic pressure of world capital, and to the military–political pressure of world imperialism'.[33] This carried the implication that, should the Soviet economy fall behind those of its capitalist competitors, the Soviet state might yet come to a bad end through economic pressure or military intervention. But that kind of eventuality had been allowed for in the April 1925 resolution.[34]

At the December 1925 Fourteenth Party Congress, Kamenev confirmed that it was possible to complete the process of building socialism [postroim] in the Soviet Union despite the 'delay of the world revolution'.[35] Zinov'ev admitted that 'we are building [stroim] socialism', but it was impossible to 'finally completely build [postroit'] *socialism and to consolidate the socialist system in one country*'.[36] In other words, though complete socialisation was unachievable in the absence of the world revolution, the socialist transition was an ongoing process.[37] Until the end of 1925, then, Trotsky, Kamenev and Zinov'ev each accepted a version of socialism in one country.

The December 1925 congress decided that Russia must turn itself from an importer into a producer of machinery, from an 'appendage of the capitalist world economy' into an 'independent economic entity'.[38] Trotsky could only welcome the recognition of the primacy of industry, but, given his new integrationist economic preferences, he would have been appalled by a strategy of import substitution. Ignoring comparative advantages on the world market would likely lower the growth tempo, and thereby endanger the survival of the Soviet state. Bukharin's observation that the 'growth of socialism' would proceed at a 'snail's pace' would have confirmed these fears. In the summer of 1926 Trotsky finally teamed up with Zinov'ev and Kamenev. The United Opposition worked out a programme that combined industrialisation with heavier taxation of the kulaks.[39]

This was the occasion for Trotsky to turn against the formula of socialism in one country. The first occasion for him to do so was in a 28 June 1926 statement intended for the Soviet delegation to the Comintern.[40] But even now the only reason Trotsky could mention to reject the 'theory of socialism in one [*odnoi*] country' was that the 'complete victory of socialism in our country' depended on the 'course of the revolution in other countries', which was in full accordance with the April 1925 resolution![41]

Richard Day has famously argued that Trotsky never stopped accepting the single socialist economy. The latter 'objected, not so much to the notion of Socialism in *One* Country ... as to Stalin's concept of Socialism in a *Separate* Country'. In Day's interpretation, Trotsky's real point was to guarantee socialism in one country through an economic strategy based on world-market integration.[42] It seems to me that a valid point is overstated here: Trotsky would soon conclude that even integrationism couldn't save socialist Russia if it remained alone for too long.

The October–November 1926 Fifteenth Party Conference was the most important occasion for the two factions to cross swords. Kamenev and Zinov'ev had nothing new to say. The former defended the position laid down in the April 1925 resolution. He confirmed that the construction of a 'complete socialist society' in Russia did not depend on European revolutions. But military intervention was not the only potentially fatal external threat. The Soviet economy's survival also depended on the achievement of a higher growth rate than the capitalist nations. This was required to avoid fatal economic pressures, as well as to show the 'real superiority of the socialist economy' to the workers of the world.[43] Zinov'ev explained that unfavourable developments on the world market could lead to Soviet collapse: as the *Communist Manifesto* had it, low prices served capitalist industries as 'heavy artillery' to force other nations into submission.[44] All this remained in perfect accordance with the April 1925 resolution.

But whereas for Kamenev and Zinov'ev defeat on the economic battlefield could not be ruled out, Trotsky newly suggested that collapse was inevitable in the case of a long delay of the world revolution. This is where we begin to see that Day unduly simplifies Trotsky's position.

Trotsky insisted that 'our whole constructive activity is internationally determined', in the sense that survival depended crucially on achieving a higher growth rate than the capitalist states. But *could* that be achieved? What if against all expectations international capitalism would strengthen itself and the world revolution failed to arrive? If 'we proceed from the assumption that European capitalism will gain strength in the course of the next 30–50 years', Trotsky answered, 'then we would have to conclude that we would be strangled or shattered'.[45] Essentially, Trotsky said that socialism in one country could indeed be established but that it could not be maintained if its isolation continued for too long.

In defence of his own views, Stalin explained that socialism in one country did not imply reduced attention to the world revolution. Quite the contrary, successful socialist construction in Soviet Russia would drive the world revolution forward through the power of its example and the sympathetic enthusiasm that it generated. The international proletariat, Stalin said:

> will look to our economic construction and to our successes ... with the hope that we will emerge from this struggle as victors, that we'll succeed in constructing socialism. So many workers' delegations visiting us from the West ... tell us that our struggle at the front of construction has huge international significance in revolutionising the proletarians of all countries.[46]

Like Lenin before him, Stalin came down to the view that the world revolution depended on the example of the successful construction of a socialist order in the initiator-state.

The United Opposition stood no chance. The conference not only confirmed socialism in one country, but additionally decreed that *only* 'military intervention of imperialism' could prevent the Soviet proletariat from establishing a 'complete socialist society'. Collapse through economic pressure, a point the April 1925 resolution had allowed and that the Opposition leaders had been emphasising, was now ruled out.[47] The loophole was closed.

One last occasion for the matter to be debated at length was the Seventh Enlarged Plenum of the Comintern Executive Committee, to assemble from 22 November to 16 December 1926.[48] Stalin was particularly incensed by Trotsky's assertion that it was possible to 'completely construct [*postroit*'] an isolated socialist state', but that maintaining this isolated socialist economy depended on reaching a higher productivity of labour than the capitalist world, which, again, might take a whole century. Stalin retorted that the planned and 'concentrated' socialist economy had the potential to establish its 'superiority over the capitalist system' in a much shorter period of time.[49]

The best interpretation of Trotsky's position is that he still regarded a socialist economy in a single country as a viable scenario. But this assumed that, to maintain itself in an international competitive environment, that economy would have to achieve superiority in terms of productivity compared to its capitalist opponents. And if, Trotsky argued, capitalism was not overthrown by the workers, that could only mean that it had preserved its economic strength and thus also its capacity to outcompete Soviet Russia. This is another way of saying that a long delay of the world revolution would make it impossible for socialist Russia to survive. In his 12 December 'The Theory of Socialism in a Separate Country' Trotsky wrote that if European capitalism would be allowed to grow stronger, the Soviet socialist economy would be bombarded with cheap products. Europe's military strength would grow accordingly. 'We would land in a hopeless situation with our socialist construction.'[50]

The most dramatic turn in Trotsky's thinking came in 1928, when he defined the ideal of the 'isolated socialist society' as a foolish attempt 'to construct a socialist paradise as some kind of oasis in the hell of world capitalism', an ideal that reminded him of the archaic Utopias.[51] In his final argumentation, Trotsky returned to the view that the modern productive forces had outgrown the framework of the national state, and that the world division of labour ruled out such a thing as a socialist economy in one country as a matter of principle.[52] Even for the short run, there seemed to be little point, then, in socialist construction: '*genuine* socialist construction' in Soviet Russia could only begin after the proletariat seized power in a number of developed states.[53] Without the world revolution, collapse was inevitable:

> In an isolated proletarian dictatorship, the internal and external contradictions grow inevitably along with the successes achieved. If it remains isolated, the proletarian state must finally fall victim to these contradictions. The way out for it lies only in the victory of the proletariat of the advanced countries.[54]

184 The Great Debate

In concluding, Edward Carr was on the mark when he noted that the Great Debate had an 'air of unreality' about it.[55] There was actually something approaching a consensus on the socialism in one country scenario. Only the factional struggles prevented the contenders from admitting this. Zinov'ev only differed from Stalin and Bukharin in that he denied that a *complete* socialist society could emerge in a single country. He and Kamenev also insisted that military intervention was not the only remaining threat to Soviet Russia, but that economic pressure might also prove fatal. Prior to 1928 even Trotsky regarded the single socialist economy as a viable scenario. He was only convinced that an isolated Soviet Russia could not indefinitely survive capitalist competition.

There was surprisingly little awareness among the Bolsheviks of the historical depth of the question of socialism in one country. Stalin seems to have been largely unaware of German and Austrian Marxist thinking over the years. At the Fifteenth Party Conference, he asserted that 'all of us Marxists, beginning with Marx and Engels' had self-evidently rejected the notion of single-country socialism, until the genius Lenin had set everybody on the right track.[56] At a June 1927 plenary session of the Central Control Commission, Trotsky revealed that Vollmar had created the theory of the isolated socialist state. Stalin's comrade-in-arms, Sergo Ordzhonikidze, confirmed this: 'We read it'.[57] But Stalin and his comrades had no interest in pursuing the question of historical antecedents any further. To refer to Vollmar, to Kautsky or to any other social democrat who had anticipated them in exploring the theme of single-country socialism, could only have detracted from their own Bolshevik legitimacy. There was no gain to be had in referring to what, in Bolshevik eyes, were revisionists and renegades. The history of socialism in one country was reduced to Lenin's 1915–16 observations.

Notes

1. For a classical analysis of the industrialisation debate, see Erlich, 1960. For the 1923–4 struggle with the Left Opposition, see Carr, 1969: 23–4, 114–16, 134–9; Cohen, 1974: 150–1, 156–7; Swain, 2006: 144–56; Suny, 2011: 169–71. For the question of cooperatives, see Carr, 1970, vol. 1: 239, 279–84, 295–303; Danilov, 1992: 73–6. For Preobrazhenskii's ideas, see Carr, 1970, vol. 1: 219–22; Tucker, 1974: 374–7; Cohen, 1974: 163–5; Nove, 1992a: 121–3. For Bukharin's views on economic policy, see Carr, 1970, vol. 1: 223–6, 264–5, 279–81; Cohen, 1974: 165–83; Nove, 1992b: 35; Ferdinand, 1992: 45–57; Nove, 1992a: 118–21.
2. 'Lenin kak marksist', Smirnov, 1988: 77–8.
3. 'O likvidatorstve nashikh dnei' (*Bol'shevik*, 1924, no. 2), Abalkin, 1990: 256.
4. Cohen, 1974: 147–8; see also Tucker, 1974: 371–4.
5. Cohen, 1974: 418.
6. 'Ob osnovakh leninizma', *Sochineniia* (vol. 6: 83). Stalin deduced the possibility of a socialist breakthrough in weakly industrialised countries from the integrated nature of the world economy, which, *as a whole*, was ripe for the socialist transition. Weakly industrialised countries represented the weakest links in the chain (ibid.: 93–9). Stalin also referred to Engels's *Die Bauernfrage* to underscore the idea that peasants could be made to see the advantages of socialist cooperativisation (ibid.: 133–4).

7 Stalin also accused Trotsky of underestimating the 'revolutionary energy of the peasantry' (*Sochineniia*, vol. 6: 99, 103–6). To prove that Lenin had always proposed uninterrupted revolution, Stalin unconvincingly pointed to Lenin's 1905 *Two Tactics* and other texts (ibid.: 100–3). See also 'K voprosam leninizma' (January 1926) (ibid.: vol. 8: 19–20).
8 In 1926 Bukharin called the view that proletarian revolution cannot be attempted in countries lacking a majority proletariat, a deviation introduced by social democrats: 'O kharaktere nashei revoliutsii i o vozmozhnosti pobedonosnogo sotsialisticheskogo stroitel'stva v SSSR', Smirnov, 1988: 277–304.
9 See 'K voprosam leninizma' (*Sochineniia*, vol. 8: 61). This passage was later omitted from *On the Foundations of Leninism*.
10 'Uroki oktiabria' (Trotsky, 1991: esp. 74–88). For proletarian revolution in backward countries Trotsky referred to Engels's 1870 preface to the *Deutsche Bauernkrieg*. Also, Marx's dictum that advanced countries show the less advanced ones their own [capitalist] future, according to Trotsky must not be taken as an unconditional law (ibid.: 74).
11 Introduction by V. Startsev, Trotsky, 1991: 49–50.
12 'Leninizm ili trotskizm' (ibid.: esp. 161–73). Zinov'ev made essentially the same point: 'Bol'shevizm ili trotskizm?' (ibid.: esp. 232–3). See also Bukharin in: 'Novoe otkrovenie o sovetskoi ekonomike ili kak mozhno pogubit' raboche-krest'ianskii blok' (12 December 1924), Smirnov, 1988: 88.
13 On Kamenev's point, see also Carr, 1970, vol. 2: 45; Day, 1973: 10; Tucker, 1974: 382–3.
14 'Oktiabr'skaia revoliutsiia i taktika russkikh kommunistov' (article was renamed): *Sochineniia* (vol. 6: 371–2).
15 *Sochineniia* (ibid.: 374–5). For the Lenin quotes Stalin provided to prove his case, see ibid.: 369–72, 377–8. In his 25 January 1925 'Letter to c. D-ov' Stalin came round to the point of view that 'complete, final' victory had to await the lifting of the 'capitalist encirclement' (ibid.: vol. 7: 17). Stalin remained of the opinion that the solidarity of the international working class was the key to the survival of the Soviet state (10 February 1926 letter to comrade Pokoev, vol. 8: 96).
16 Cited in Bukharin at the December Fourteenth Party Congress, *XIV s"ezd*, 1926: 135–6. Neither Kamenev nor Zinov'ev denied the truth of this account, though the latter scathingly remarked that there was no point in citing 'conversations in the Politburo that have been recorded nowhere' (ibid.: 430). Zinov'ev said he never turned economic backwardness into an *insuperable* obstacle (*XV konferentsiia*, 1927: 574).
17 According to Klim Voroshilov (*XIV s"ezd*, 1926: 397–8), Zinov'ev (ibid.: 431) and Kamenev (*XV konferentsiia*, 1927: 471), the resolution had represented a compromise formula.
18 Ibid.: 1925: 5–6.
19 Ibid.: 237–8. For the Lenin quotes provided by Zinov'ev, see ibid.: 236–8, 241.
20 Ibid.: 244.
21 'O zadachakh Kominterna i RKP(b) v sviazi s rasshirennym plenumom IKKI' (*KPSS*, 1953, vol. 2: 48–9). The resolution provided a string of Lenin quotations running from 1915 to 1923 to support the thesis (ibid.: 46–50).
22 Ibid.: vol. 2: 50.
23 *Chetyrnadtsaiaia konferentsiia*, 1925: 246.
24 For an analyses of this early stage of the debate, see Carr, 1970, vol. 2: 45–61; Cohen, 1974: 186–7; Tucker, 1974: 368–83; Suny, 2011: 168–73.
25 See 'K itogam rabot XIV konferentsii RKP(b)' (9 May 1925), *Sochineniia*, vol. 7: 118. For Stalin's treatment of Lenin's views, see ibid.: 114–19. In his 18 June 1925 comment on the Fourteenth Party Conference, Bukharin (1925: 10) remained closer to the resolution: the Soviet regime might be overthrown through

'intervention, blockade, attack etc.'. But in his December 1925 'Put' k sotsializmu i raboche-krest'ianskii soiuz' he too suggested that only military intervention might prove fatal (Smirnov, 1988: esp. 226–7). Bukharin admitted that the socialist transition would be slow and initially produce a 'backward socialism', but Soviet Russia was *not* condemned to perish because of its '*economic backwardness*' and in the end it could achieve 'complete socialism' relying exclusively on its own forces (ibid.: 227–30).
26 See Carr, 1970, vol. 1: 259–336; vol. 2: 62–86; Day, 1973: 114–17; Ferdinand, 1992: 56; Nove, 1992a: 124; Davies, 2008: 183–4.
27 For Zinov'ev's list of Lenin quotations to support his case, see Zinov'ev, 1926: 249–74.
28 Ibid.: 248, 275–6. Zinov'ev (ibid.: 270–1; see also: 275) seemed even more pessimistic than this when he observed that 'to prevent our revolution from undergoing a restoration of bourgeois relations, we need a socialist revolution in several countries'. He furthermore identified the 'final victory of socialism' with the establishment of the higher, communist stage of the new society (ibid.: 241–8). This is the only occasion when Marx's distinction between first- and second-stage communism was injected into the debate. The debate really concerned the question of whether socialism, i.e. first-stage communism, could or could not be 'completely' realised in a single country. Bukharin responded that complete socialism could be built, offering a string of Lenin quotations ('O kharaktere': Smirnov, 1988: 304–10).
29 For an analysis of Zinov'ev's views, see Korey, 1950; Day, 1973: 108, 113.
30 For Stalin's and Trotsky's position on industrialisation in 1925, see Day, 1973: 111–18; Swain, 2006: 163.
31 Trotsky, 1925: 5–14.
32 For Trotsky's transformation from champion of autarky to world market involvement, see Day, 1973: 6, 119, 126–48. See also Thatcher, 2003: 142–4; Swain, 2006: 159–60; Suny, 2011: 168–9.
33 Trotsky, 1925: 5–6.
34 For a comparative analysis of Bukharin's and Trotsky's positions on socialism in one country, see also Haynes, 1985: 74–9.
35 *XIV s"ezd*, 1926: 273.
36 Ibid.: 98.
37 Zinov'ev also subscribed to Stalin's early 1924 statement that it was impossible to construct a socialist economy in a single country (ibid.: 429–30). For Stalin's critique of Zinov'ev, see 'K voprosam leninizma' (*Sochineniia*, vol. 8: 60–75).
38 *KPSS*, vol. 2: 75. For the economic policies of the congress, see di Biagio, 1992: 120. According to Day (1973: 124), the congress served to identify the principle of socialism in one country with one particular policy, i.e. with 'economic autarchy'. Day (ibid.: 121) regards Stalin as the driving force behind industrial autarky. See Stalin's 18 December speech at the Fourteenth Party Congress: *Sochineniia* (vol. 7: 298–300). According to David Woodruff (2008: 210–15), Stalin aimed for a positive trade balance to avoid dependence on foreign markets. He was prepared to restrict imports even if this would lower the tempo of industrialisation. Sanchez-Sibony (2014: 34–5) argues that Stalin was not only a champion of austerity but also a 'staunch integrationist'. Trotsky stood for 'forcing exports' to boost industrialisation.
39 For the development of Trotsky's position, see Day, 1973: 118–20, 153, 162; Thatcher, 2003: 144–5; Swain, 2006: 164–9; Davies, 2008: 189–90; Fel'shtinskii and Cherniavskii, 2013: 190–1. For Bukharin's remark, see *XIV s"ezd*, 1926: 135. According to Ferdinand (1992: 41–2, 56–61), Bukharin's views shifted towards more rapid industrialisation after 1925.
40 Fel'shtinskii and Cherniavskii, 2013: 190.
41 'Voprosy Kominterna' (Fel'shtinskii, 1990, vol. 1: 242–3).

42 Day, 1973: 4–6 (see also pp. 136, 161). Swain (2006: 159–60) follows Day in this analysis.
43 *XV konferentsiia*, 1927: 469–72. Kamenev paid particular attention to proving that Lenin's 1915 socialism in one country thesis did not refer to Russia (ibid.: 474–5).
44 *XV konferentsiia*, 1927: 565–77. Zinov'ev presented a large number of quotations to prove that Marx and Engels ruled out socialism in one country.
45 Ibid.: 531–3. Trotsky suggested, but did not say so unequivocally, that he no longer shared the view that the workers' government would be faced with insurmountable peasant rebellions (ibid.: 516–19). For Trotsky on Lenin and socialism in one country, see ibid.: 523–7. For Bukharin on Trotsky's Lenin interpretation, see ibid.: 585–91.
46 1 November speech, *Sochineniia* (vol. 8: 280–1). For Stalin's treatment of Lenin quotations, see ibid.: 251–66. For Stalin on Lenin also his concluding remarks, see ibid.: 328–9. Unable to deny that Marx and Engels had ruled out socialism in one country, Stalin proposed in his 1 November speech that Lenin's 'law of uneven development' had not yet been in operation in their days of pre-monopolist capitalism (ibid.: 247–51). See also Stalin's 15 September 1925 letter to comrade Ermakov (vol. 7: 232–3). For Stalin on Engels, see also his concluding remarks at the conference (vol. 8: 298–303).
47 *KPSS*, vol. 2: 210–11. Once again, the main relevant Lenin and Trotsky quotations were listed (ibid.: 211–12).
48 Again Zinov'ev (see *Puti mirovoi revoliutsii*, 1927: 59ff.) and Stalin (*Sochineniia*, vol. 9: 29–36, 86–144) gave lengthy overviews of Marx, Engels and Lenin quotations.
49 13 December concluding remarks (ibid.: 136–7). In his 7 December speech Stalin admitted that Montenegro or Bulgaria couldn't have socialism in one country. In view of its having a 'certain minimum of large-scale industry' and a 'certain minimum of proletariat', Russia could (ibid.: 20).
50 'Teoriia sotsializma v otdel'noi strane', Fel'shtinskii, 1990, vol. 2: 142–3. For this article, see also Fel'shtinskii and Cherniavskii, 2012, vol. 3: 217–18.
51 'Kritika programmy Kommunisticheskogo Internatsionala' (written June 1928), Trotsky, 1993: 107, 115.
52 Ibid.: 103; 1929 Russian edition of *The Permanent Revolution* (Trotsky, 1978: 279–80).
53 Trotsky, 1993: 113. In discussing Lenin's 1915 references to a socialist economy in one country, Trotsky argued that Lenin had merely referred to a nationalised economy, not to a developed socialist society (ibid.: 72–3, 82–9).
54 Trotsky, 1978: 133.
55 Carr, 1970, vol. 1: 327.
56 1 November 1926 speech, *Sochineniia* (vol. 8: 247–50).
57 Fel'shtinskii, 1990, vol. 3: 101. See also Trotsky (1993: 96) in his 'Kritika programmy Kommunisticheskogo internatsionala'.

Conclusion

The scenario of socialism in one country has a long and respectable history. Its prehistory can be traced back to Plato. Before the 1840s, it was held to be self-evident that a utopian order based on common ownership could work in a single city, region or country. It was only with Marx and Engels, with Moses Hess, really, that this scenario was rejected as unrealistic.

Marx and Engels assumed that a single state could not survive the pressures of the world market, nor would it be able to mobilise sufficient military power to survive the onslaught of a capitalist coalition. They also regarded an autarkic economy as incompatible with a cultured life, for it would cut off citizens from what the world at large had on offer. But the break that Marx and Engels enforced with earlier communist thinking was less dramatic than has been commonly assumed. Their confederacy of socialist nations (Britain, France and Germany) would still have been a little corner of the world, an island in a sea of capitalist hostility.

Moreover, Marx and Engels's theoretical position was vulnerable. The SPD and the RSDWP officially adopted their view that the socialist order depended on the contribution of a number of advanced countries, but there always remained rivalling visions, each of which took advantage of certain weak points in Marx and Engels's argumentation.

To begin with, given the supposed superiority of the socialist economy, it was not self-evident why a socialist state would be unable to stand up to capitalist competitors on the world market. During the 1860s and 1870s, Ferdinand Lassalle, Eugen Dühring and Georg von Vollmar suggested that a single socialist state would be able to operate as a successful trading company. The latter expounded the concept most systematically in his 1878 pamphlet *The Isolated Socialist State*. The argument that a single state could survive in a hostile capitalist environment was also made by Petr Lavrov. Instead of focusing on the competitiveness of the socialist economy, Lavrov argued that a country's vast scope and abundant natural resources could provide it with the necessary staying power.

Another moot point in Marx and Engels's argumentation concerned the assumption that international circumstances were levelling out and that the revolution would be a contagious process. What if the conditions for socialism were much more favourable in one particular country than in all others? The idea that one country, in this case Russia, would most likely become the sole pioneer was defended by nineteenth-century Russian socialists Nikolai Shelgunov, Mikhail Mikhailov, Petr Zaichnevskii, Sergei Nechaev and Petr Tkachev. In their view, the Russian village commune provided better revolutionary conditions than Western capitalism. The Slav spirit outpaced the decadent West. These ideas received a follow-up in the work of Maximalist Mikhail Engel'gardt.

That the uniquely strong German social democratic party would most likely come to power long before their counterparts in other countries was reason enough for Eduard Bernstein, Carl Ballod and Erich Rother to conclude that socialism in one country was on the cards. In their view, an isolated socialist Germany would only need an overseas colonial empire to survive. Richard Calwer expected France and Germany, together, to anticipate Britain and America, for which reason he explored the option of an alliance of continental socialist countries. Paul Lensch and Konrad Haenisch deduced the possibility of Germany's pioneering socialism from their country's superior political culture and from its remarkable advances in the process of state capitalist organisation.

Marx and Engels not only feared that a single socialist state would be confronted with the overwhelming economic and military power of the neighbouring capitalist states – they also assumed that a single country would lack the *internal* preconditions for successfully operating a socialist economy: a cultured economy required the input of at least several civilised countries. Karl Kautsky fundamentally challenged that assumption when he suggested that socialist economies would be autarkic. In his view, one country sufficed as framework for the socialist economy.

It was more difficult for Kautsky to trust that the single socialist economy could be *maintained* in the face of the inevitable response of the enraged imperialists. He hoped that the spread of the revolution would rapidly eliminate the external threat. But, as we have seen, Kautsky's world-revolutionary scenario depended precisely on the attractive example of the first socialist economy: one single state would precipitate other nations into revolution by showing them in practice the advantages of the socialised economy. Paradoxically, in this model of revolution by example socialism in one country became the lever of world revolution.

Rudolf Hilferding's and Otto Bauer's fantasies closely resembled Kautsky's. At the end of the war and in the immediate post-war period, they expressed the hope that, despite the prevailing adverse conditions, Germany might become the state that would show other nations how to build the new society.

Among Russian social democrats socialism in one country initially found little support. During the Great War, Pavel Aksel'rod, Nikolai Bukharin, Leon Trotsky and others even took the Marx–Engels argument a step further when they suggested that socialist economies could not be confined within state borders at all and could only be realised on a pan-European or even a global scale.

But in 1915 Lenin concluded that socialism could be established on the scale of one country after all. Like Kautsky, he accepted the real possibility of a socialist economy confined to a single country. At the same time, it seemed obvious to Lenin that the imperialists would do everything in their power to destroy the isolated state. At the time, this way of conceptualising the dilemma had become widespread. Even the Spartakists Liebknecht and Luxemburg accepted it as a matter of course that socialisation could work in an isolated Germany, but they nonetheless rejected the single-country scenario, because they expected the isolated state to be strangled or crushed from the outside by the imperialists.

Lenin, however, discovered a solution in revolutionary war: the isolated socialist state might be able to crush the imperialists before they could crush it. Lenin never doubted that a socialist economy could be constructed in an isolated Soviet Russia, but developments on the battlefield in early 1918 made him lose faith in revolutionary war as an effective defence. He concluded that Soviet Russia was lost without a workers' revolution in Germany. But when the civil war took a turn for the better he reconsidered that the international workers' solidarity with Soviet Russia would suffice to reign in imperialist aggression and to allow the isolated socialist state to persist. During the civil war, the whole Bolshevik leading team, including Trotsky, accepted some version of socialism in one country.

Essentially, the Great Debate did no more than solemnly to confirm conclusions already drawn. None of the contestants saw anything inherently impossible in having a socialist economy in isolated, backward Soviet Russia. None took the position that the delay of the world revolution would prevent socialisation of the economy. Zinov'ev insisted only that an isolated socialism would inevitably be stained with imperfections. All of the contestants agreed that the potentially fatal threat could only come from abroad. Differences were only about the seriousness of the threat. For the optimists, Stalin and Bukharin, only military intervention might possibly bring the Soviet experiment to an end. Kamenev, Zinov'ev and Trotsky were more pessimistic in pointing to the additional risk that the imperialists might outcompete socialist Russia or strangle her through an economic blockade.

It was only in 1926 that Trotsky began to argue that prolonged isolation would make the collapse of the Soviet state inevitable. Two years later he finally rejected the whole idea of isolated socialist economies. However, he was not returning to an imaginary earlier Bolshevik consensus ruling out the single-country scenario. From the October Revolution onwards the Bolsheviks had taken it for granted that they were constructing a socialist economy in their isolated country and from the late Civil War period onwards they accepted the possibility that international solidarity would protect them against the foreign threat. It was in fact Trotsky who was breaking with the Bolshevik consensus, while returning to the ultra-Marxist, globalist conceptions that had been popular among Russian social democrats during the Great War.

Why has this not been recognised before?

Why have the many schemes of single-country socialism all too often been overlooked? Marx and Engels successfully projected an image of themselves as scientific, sober and non-utopian thinkers. Compared to them, other socialists seemed hardly in need of being taken seriously. Marxism cast a shadow of naivety over the idea of socialism in one country. This reached the point that researchers discovering that notion in the works of other socialists easily ignored it. It couldn't be taken seriously anyhow. This might explain why Vollmar's pamphlet has not received the attention that it deserves, and why, to my knowledge, Lavrov's *The State Element in the Future Society* has never been scrutinised for its views on single-country socialism. The scholarly literature has equally failed to discuss Kautsky's well-known *Erfurt Programme* definition of autarkic socialism confined to one state, as foundational for socialism in one country.

The fact that, prior to the Soviet 1920s, socialists almost never engaged in debate about the issue did not help in bringing the matter to the attention of historians. In 1874 Bebel took issue with Dühring and in 1879, by innuendo, with Vollmar. Trotsky fired away at Lenin when the latter suggested the one-country scenario during the Great War. But that was more or less it. As long as the socialists were not in power, the issue remained too theoretical to merit polemics. This may have helped to consolidate the false impression of a consensus against socialism in one country.

Lenin's desperation in the period of the German military offensive of early 1918 and its aftermath – all will be lost without the German revolution! – easily created the impression that he could not have accepted the prospect of socialism in one country at all. The ambivalences in his and Kautsky's works most likely contributed further to the scholarly myopia. During the Great War, both men recognised that the establishment of a socialist economy in a single country might have crucial significance for the world revolution. But they never believed the exemplary state could withdraw in splendid isolation. Their strong emphasis on the world-revolutionary process to a certain extent masked the fact that Kautsky and Lenin did accept the idea of the single socialist state.

Stalin and Trotsky did the rest. Stalin had no interest in pointing out that other socialists had preceded him in accepting the one-country scenario. References to what he regarded as revisionists could only hurt his Marxist legitimacy. Trotsky was a master in making other people, academics included, see the world through his eyes. He was very influential with his assertion that real Marxists had always shied away from socialism in one country, and that it was defended only, and very incidentally, by revisionists such as Vollmar.

Trotsky's success in convincing later generations of his own views cannot be attributed solely to his qualities as a writer and thinker, though. For those sympathetic to the socialist project it was only too attractive to follow his lead and to write socialism in one country out of the socialist discourse. In this way, Stalin's crimes could be taken out of their socialist context and be interpreted, quite to the contrary, as the product of an alien influence in socialism.

Continuity

There is a striking element of continuity between early communism and socialism on the one hand and Stalinist ideology on the other. Socialists had been imagining communism on the scale of a single country all along. What is more, those like Marx and Engels who considered this too narrow a framework, still envisioned communism as an island in a capitalist world sea. Whether this would be a single city, a country or an alliance of great states, the principle remained the same. The modern socialists neither copied Thomas More, nor were they even inspired by him, but his spirit hovered over them.

Even before the October Revolution Lenin had been contemplating how the Soviet state could possibly survive the inevitable confrontation with all-powerful imperialism. The Civil War and foreign intervention confirmed his fears that the Bolsheviks would have to fight for their survival. The sense of being an embattled community became a permanent feature of the Bolshevik mind. One of the main findings of the present study is that imagining communism in this way long antedated the Bolshevik seizure of power. Utopian communists and socialists had been imagining communism as an embattled commonwealth all along. They had always been preoccupied with the threats that the new order would be subjected to, as well as with the question of how to deal with such threats.

The socialist imagination was shot through with anxiety. A siege mentality characterised socialists all along. But fears of the capitalist encirclement were balanced with a self-assured confidence that capitalism was no match for the superior socialist system. Two kinds of survival strategies were designed to deal with the imperialist threat, reflecting the two main drives inherent in the communist project. The first, communitarian option was withdrawal and fortification. The economy could be made autarkic, and defences could be bolstered through unyielding citizen commitment. The second, universalist option saw salvation in expansion – defence in the attack. The capitalist competitor could be outcompeted on the world market or, more decisively, be subdued through offensive revolutionary war. Revolution by example, building an ideal community that other nations would want to emulate, was another way for the commonwealth to break out of its confinement.

The Soviet communists took recourse to all of these strategies to save their isolated state. Stalin and Trotsky's differences over economic policies – would Soviet Russia profit most from engaging in or disengaging from the world division of labour? – classically reflected the dilemma of autarky and market competitiveness. We have seen Lenin fantasising about revolutionary war, and in 1920 unsuccessfully practising it, later to turn to less aggressive hopes of unleashing revolution abroad through the shining example of socialist construction in Soviet Russia.

As we have seen, these survival strategies for the embattled commonwealth had been foreshadowed in the imagination as far back as More's Utopia. We met the autarky option with eighteenth-century French communists, and we saw it return with Kautsky and with the socialist colonialists. Winstanley, Marx and Engels, as well as Vollmar surmised that the superior communist economy would provide the commonwealth with predominant power on the world market. That the communist commonwealth would be shored up by exemplary citizen commitment and unsurpassed military valour went back to the myth of Sparta and was taken for granted by all communists from Campanella onwards. The scenario of revolution by example was suggested by Winstanley, later picked up by French utopian communists and Babouvists, and German social democrats Kautsky, Hilferding and Bauer returned to it once again.

Another finding of this study is that Stalin's prideful boasting about the pioneering role of his own country was no innovation either. To be sure, not all socialists had expected their own country to become the initiator-state. Kautsky, for example, was largely immune to the patriotic sentiment. He was never particularly keen on seeing socialism established in his fatherland in advance of other countries; he merely formulated the general thought that it would be possible for some advanced nation, not necessarily Germany, to fulfil that exemplary role. Plekhanov assumed an even more dramatically unpatriotic position when he ruled out an early breakthrough to socialism in his country and thereby effectively asked the Russian people to take a back seat.

Most socialists, however, did dream of a pioneering role for their own people. Even Marx and Engels included Germany among the path-breaking nations, notwithstanding the country's socio-economic backwardness.

The main reason why socialists wanted their own country to be among the first to break the path seems to have been that they expected huge gains for the fatherland from the introduction of a new social system that they regarded as obviously superior. Winstanley was the first communist explicitly to make the point that England must establish community of goods in advance of other nations in order to acquire predominant world power. French communist republicans, from Mably to Dézamy, were jubilant at the military potential of communism that would make France invincible. Marx and Engels hoped that the communist revolution would restore Germany's power, prestige and honour, as well as help it to shake off British economic domination. Lassalle, Dühring and Vollmar promised that being the first to have socialism would give Germany a competitive edge on the world market. Lenin represented an extreme case in claiming preposterously that the socialist economy would regenerate backward Russia and turn it into the superior economic and military world power in a few months' time.

Marxism

The element of continuity between early communism and socialism on the one hand and Bolshevism on the other becomes even more pronounced if we now, finally, turn to the question of the socio-economic conditions of the socialist transition. The idea that socialism could be established in 'backward' countries too was prefigured in the socialist imagination, long before the Bolsheviks decided to undertake the experiment in practice.

Before the 1840s, communist utopians seldom asked themselves whether community of goods depended on certain socio-economic conditions. If it were desirable for their town or country to have it, it did not occur to them seriously to question the feasibility of the project. Otherwise put, before modern industry came into the world, the question of whether communism depended on it couldn't emerge.

The question arose only with Marx and Engels. Not all socialists turned an industrialisation deficit into an insuperable obstacle. Nineteenth-century Russian socialists did not see a problem. Marx and Engels did, though. They pictured communism as an affluent society with a planned economic infrastructure, both of which elements made it dependent on the predominance of large-scale industrial production. But, as argued in this book, they fine-tuned such insights with an eye to allowing the proletariat to create the necessary industrial conditions *after* the revolution through a process of state-directed industrialisation. The real caesura occurred only in the years 1885–95, when Plekhanov and Engels concluded that the proletarian revolution required the conditions of *highly developed* capitalism. Kautsky quickly adopted Engels's conclusions. Thus the Marxists became more Marxist than Marx, and the Russian social democrats cut themselves off, theoretically, from the socialist revolution for decades.

It is almost a commonplace that Marxism was intended for highly industrialised countries but that, in a paradox, it came to power in countries that were only in the process of industrialising and for which it was never intended. In this interpretation, Bolshevik Russia was the first in a long row of premature experiments. This thesis must be discarded as fundamentally flawed. The paradox of Marxism – the ideology that, supposedly, found a home so far away from its place of birth that it couldn't possibly remain true to itself – is a myth.

Twentieth-century communist theory and practice surely diverged widely from the 'orthodox Marxism' of the Second International, but if we reach back somewhat further things look very differently. Taking the whole flow of Marx and Engels's writings into account, it is quite clear that they were *not* specifically, or even mainly, designed for highly industrialised countries. They were meant to apply not only to Britain, but also to countries that were industrialising rather than industrialised and that for the time being remained predominantly agrarian, peasant nations – like Germany.

In 1924 Stalin claimed that the Bolsheviks had recovered the original, revolutionary Marxism that been hidden from view by the leaders of the Second International. The idea that minority proletariats must postpone their revolution until industrialisation turns them into the majority was attributed to the 'opportunist' likes of Plekhanov and Kautsky, who in the era of the Second International dominated the scene. The findings of the present book suggest that, for all his mudslinging, Stalin was essentially correct in making this claim.[1]

This conclusion gives pause to think again about twentieth-century communist strategies, in the context of the history of Marxism. The communists staged successful revolutions in 'backward' countries with small industrial proletariats and predominantly agrarian economies, like Russia, China, Cuba and Vietnam. Democracy was rudimentary in these countries, or even lacking altogether, and the state was in such a weak condition that foreign powers could ride roughshod over them. The communists tended to respond to these conditions by moving democracy and the nation to the top of their list. They defined it as their priorities to enforce the convocation of a constituent assembly, to remove 'feudal rudiments', and to put up a patriotic fight to end all foreign interference in the life of their nations. Subsequently, the proletarian party would have to make sure to seize the helm of state and to embark on an intense process of industrialisation and national development, in order to prepare the conditions of the socialist society.

This two-stage model of revolution resembled the Marx–Engels original to a striking degree. Because of its association with Trotsky, the communists avoided the term permanent revolution, but they were in fact reproducing that strategy to be found with Marx and Engels.

The reason why the solutions Marx and Engels came up with suited the needs of their successors so well is that the conditions they were writing in were very similar to theirs. At the danger of overstating my point: Marxism was written precisely for the kind of circumstances in which the twentieth-century communists came to power.

Marxism emerged in the 1840s, when mass poverty and the suffering of the proletarian classes had become acute. The 'social question' created an outburst of utopian longing. Communism became an attractive ideal for a growing number of artisans and proletarians. The trailblazers were the German, French, English, Swiss, Swedish, Belgian and other journeymen that travelled from country to country, as a true International, and who joined the League of the Just and its successor, the League of Communists. Marx and Engels were authentic representatives of this milieu of internationally oriented workers and artisans. Their fundamental goal was the abolition of capitalism worldwide, and their main commitment lay with the international working class.

But there was more to mid-nineteenth-century Europe than class struggle and the social question. At least as important were the issues of monarchical absolutism and democratisation, issues that concerned nations as a whole. The European continent was furthermore rife with national frustrations and ambitions. Depressed, fragmented nations were striving to coalesce into nation-states; populations integrated in large empires hoped to break free and to establish an independent existence for themselves. Economically, the states on the European continent stood in awe of British industrial and commercial power. How to get things going, to catch up with Britain, and to create a strong, modern economy were matters of urgent concern.

Germany epitomised all of these European conditions: a poor country, a tiny industrial working class, and industrialisation just beginning. Marx's and Engels's land of birth was a confederacy of independent princely states ruled by absolute monarchs. The democratic nation-state was something people could only dream of. Internationally, Germany was completely outclassed by Great Britain's economic power.

Marxism was an answer to *all* of these concerns – not merely to class and social issues. Marx and Engels's suggestion to the proletarian party of their 'backward' fatherland was to focus all efforts on the creation of a democratic, unified nation-state. When that issue would have been resolved, the workers were advised not to let their own minority status stand in the way of the seizure of power. With power in their hands, they would tackle the problem of backwardness, industrialise their country and lay the foundations for the socialist transition. This was the permanent revolution, and it was this course that communists followed a century later. Once again, they did this not because they felt obligated to Marx and Engels's holy book, but because similarity of condition demanded similar policies. Being determines consciousness.

The fundamental conclusions historians have drawn about twentieth-century communism are mostly correct. Where they go wrong is in assuming that there was something new under the sun. No less than twentieth-century communism, the original Marxism had been an ideology attuned to conditions of backwardness. The young Marx and Engels were despairing about the backward conditions of their fatherland and groping for a solution, to finally discover it in communism. In their book, communism stood not only for the universal liberation of humankind, it also represented an alternative model of modernisation to draw stagnating Germany from its slumber: the shortcut to national resurrection.

Note

1 The communists did, of course, not follow Marx and Engels in making socialist construction in one country dependent on revolution in other countries, but that is another matter entirely and essentially unrelated to the question of economic development: in Marx and Engels's conception even developed countries couldn't make the breakthrough to socialism on their own.

References

Primary Literature

–g., 'Der Socialismus und die Wissenschaft', in *Die Zukunft*, 1877, vol. 1, no. 1: 1–9.
Abalkin, L.I., Ia. V. Iaremenko, S.L. Leonov, L.M. Larina (eds) *N.I. Bukharin. Izbrannye proizvedeniia* (Moscow: Ekonomika), 1990.
d'Allais, D.V., *The History of the Sevarambians. A People of the South Continent. Containing an Account of the Government, Laws, Religions, Manners* (London: John Noon), 1738.
Allgemeiner Kongress der Arbeiter- und Soldatenräte. Berlin 16. bis 21. Dezember 1918. Stenographische Berichte (Berlin: Zentralrat der sozialistischen Republik Deutschlands), 1919.
Andreae, J.V., *Christianopolis. Utopie eines christlichen Staates aus dem Jahre 1619* (Leipzig: Koehler & Amelang), 1977.
Anonymous, *Gosudarstvennyi element v budushchem obshchestve* (London: Vpered!), 1876.
Anonymous, 'Ein neuer "Communist". Schluss', in *Der Volksstaat*, 20 March 1874.
Anonymous, 'An unsere Leser!', in *Die Neue Zeit*, 1883, vol. 1, no. 1: 1–8.
Anonymous, 'Der Entwurf des neuen Parteiprogramms. Schluss', in *Die Neue Zeit*, 1891, vol. 9.II, no. 50: 749–758.
Anonymous, 'Arbeiter und Gewerbeausstellung', in *Die Neue Zeit*, 1897a, vol. 15.I, no. 1: 1–4.
Anonymous, 'Weltpolitik', in *Die Neue Zeit*, 1897b, vol. 15.I, no. 26: 801–804.
Anonymous, 'Flottengesetz und Zentrum', in *Die Neue Zeit*, 1898a, vol. 16.II, no. 28: 33–36.
Anonymous, 'Kiao-Tschau', in *Die Neue Zeit*, 1898b, vol. 16.I, no. 17: 513–516.
Anonymous, 'Demokratie und Kaiserthum', in *Die Neue Zeit*, 1900, vol. 18.II, no. 30: 65–69.
Anonymous, 'Die gelbe Gefahr', in *Die Neue Zeit*, 1904, vol. 22.I, no. 21: 649–652.
Anonymous, 'Die Revolution *in Permanenz*', in *Die Neue Zeit*, 1906, vol. 24.I, no. 6: 169–172.
'A Program of Revolutionary Actions', in Pomper, P., *Sergei Nechaev* (New Brunswick, NJ: Rutgers University Press), 1979: 56–59.
Archbishop of Cambray, *The Adventures of Telemachus, the Son of Ulysses. Translated into English. A New Edition, Revised and Corrected* (Paris: Théophile Barrois), 1798.
Atlanticus, *Produktion und Konsum im Sozialstaat. Mit einer Vorrede von Karl Kautsky* (Stuttgart: Dietz Verlag), 1898a.

198 References

Atlanticus, 'Produktion und Konsum im Sozialstaat. Eine Selbstanzeige von Atlanticus', in *Die Neue Zeit*, 1898b, vol. 16.II, no. 47: 661–666.

Axelrod, P., *Die Krise und die Aufgaben der internationalen Sozialdemokratie* (Zurich: Druck und Verlag der Genossenschaftsdruckerei), 1915.

Bauer, O., *Die Nationalitätenfrage und die Sozialdemokratie* (Vienna: Wiener Volksbuchhandlung Ignaz Brand), 1907.

Bauer, O., *Acht Monate auswärtiger Politik. Rede, gehalten am 29. Juli 1919* (Vienna: Wiener Volksbuchhandlung Ignaz Brand), 1919a.

Bauer, O., *Weltrevolution* (Vienna: Wiener Volksbuchhandlung Ignaz Brand), 1919b.

Bauer, O., *Bolschewismus oder Sozialdemokratie?* (Vienna: Verlag der Wiener Volksbuchhandlung), 1920.

Bauer, O., *Der Weg zum Sozialismus* (Vienna: Verlag der Wiener Volksbuchhandlung), 1921.

Bebel, A., *Unsere Ziele. Eine Streitschrift gegen die 'Demokratische Korrespondenz'. Separatabdruck aus dem 'Volksstaat'. Zweite Aulage* (Leipzig: Volksstaat), 1871.

Bebel, A., *Die Frau und der Sozialismus (Die Frau in der Vergangenheit, Gegenwart und Zukunft). Zehnte Auflage* (Stuttgart: Dietz Verlag), 1891.

Bebel, A., 'Unsere Betheiligung an den preussischen Landtagswahlen', in *Die Neue Zeit*, 1897, vol. 15.II, no. 46: 609–617.

Berlin, J. (ed.), *Die deutsche Revolution 1918/19. Quellen und Dokumente* (Cologne: Pahl-Rugenstein), 1979.

Bernstein, E., *Die Voraussetzungen des Sozialismus und die Aufgaben der Sozialdemokratie* (Stuttgart: Dietz Verlag), 1899.

Bernstein, E., 'Die internationale Politik der Sozialdemokratie', in *Sozialistische Monatshefte*, 1909, vol. 15, no. 10: 613–624.

Bernstein, E. (ed.), *Grundsätze des Kommunismus. Eine gemeinverständliche Darlegung von Friedrich Engels. Aus dessen Nachlass herausgegeben von Eduard Bernstein* (Berlin: Paul Singer), 1914.

Bernstein, E., *Sozial-Demokratische Lehrjahre* (Berlin: Der Bücherkreis), 1928.

Blanc, L., *Organisation du travail* (Paris: Administration de Librairie), 1841.

Bogdanov, A., *Red Star. The First Bolshevik Utopia* (Bloomington, IN: Indiana University Press), 1984.

Braunthal, J. (ed.), *Otto Bauer. Eine Auswahl aus seinem Lebenswerk* (Vienna: Verlag der Wiener Volksbuchhandlung), 1961.

Bronterre (ed.), *Buonarotti's History of Babeuf's Conspiracy for Equality* (London: H. Hetherton), 1836.

Bukharin, N., 'The Russian revolution and its significance', in *The Class Struggle*, 1917, vol. 1, no. 1. Available at: www.marxists.org/archive [retrieved 29 September 2014].

Bukharin, N., *Ot krusheniia tsarizma do padeniia burzhuazii* (Khar'kov: Krympoligraftresta), 1923.

Bukharin, N., *Tekushchii moment i osnovy nashei politiki. O resheniiakh TsK RKP(b) i XIV partkonferentsii. Doklad na plenume MK RKP(b)* (Moscow: Moskovskii rabochii), 1925.

Bukharin, N., [Bucharin, N.], *Imperialismus und Weltwirtschaft. Mit einem Vorwort von N. Lenin* (Vienna and Berlin: Verlag für Literatur und Politik), 1929.

Bukharin, N., *The Politics and Economics of the Transition Period* (London: Routledge & Kegan Paul), 1979.

References 199

Bukharin, N., E. Preobrazhensky, *The ABC of Communism. A Popular Explanation of the Program of the Communist Party of Russia* (Ann Arbor, MI: University of Michigan Press), 1966.

Cabet, E., *Travels in Icaria* (Syracuse, NY: Syracuse University Press), 2003.

Calwer, R., 'Die Vorbereitung neuer Handelsverträge. Schluss', in *Die Neue Zeit*, 1898, vol. 16.II, no. 37: 323–329.

Calwer, R., 'Weltpolitik und Sozialdemokratie', in *Sozialistische Monatshefte*, 1905, vol. 11, no. 9: 741–749.

Calwer, R., 'Das Fazit der Marokko-Affäre', in *Sozialistische Monatshefte*, 1906, vol. 12, no. 5: 355–360.

Calwer, R., 'Der 25. Januar', in *Sozialistische Monatshefte*, 1907a, vol. 13, no. 2: 101–107.

Calwer, R., 'Kolonialpolitik und Sozialdemokratie', in *Sozialistische Monatshefte*, 1907b, vol. 13, no. 3: 192–200.

Campanella, T., *The City of the Sun* (London and New York: Journeyman Press), 1981.

C.A.S., 'Die Vermehrung der Producte durch socialistisch organisirten Betrieb', in *Die Zukunft*, 1878, vol. 1, no. 14: 401–411.

Chernyshevsky, N., *What Is to Be Done?* (London: Virago), 1982.

Chetyrnadtsataia konferentsiia Rossiiskoi kommunisticheskoi partii (bol'shevikov). Stenograficheskii otchet (Moscow and Leningrad: Gosudarstvennoe izdatel'stvo), 1925.

Cloots, A., 'La république universelle ou adresse aux tyrannicides', in *Écrits révolutionnaires 1790–1794* (Paris: Éditions Champ Libre), 1979: 243–318.

Cohen, M., 'Mitteleuropa', in *Die Glocke*, 1916, vol. 1, no. 10: 575–583.

Comte, A., *General View of Positivism* (London: Trübner), 1865.

Condorcet, *Esquisse d'un tableau historique des progrès de l'espirit human. Suivi de Fragment sur l'Atlantide* (Paris: Flammarion), 1988.

Däumig, E., 'Die Neue Armee', in *Die Neue Zeit*, 1912, vol. 30.II, no. 45: 681–687; 'Schluss', no. 46: 733–744.

Day, R.B., D. Gaido (eds), *Witnesses to Permanent Revolution: The Documentary Record* (Leiden: Brill), 2009.

Deviatyi s"ezd RKP(b). Mart–aprel' 1920 goda. Protokoly (Moscow: Gosudarstvennoe izdatel'stvo politicheskoi literatury), 1960.

Dézamy, T., *Code de la Communauté* (Paris: Prévost, Rouannet), 1842.

Dlubek, R., E. Stepanova, I. Bach (eds), *Die I. Internationale in Deutschland (1864–1872). Dokumente und Materialien* (Berlin: Dietz Verlag), 1964.

Dommanget, M. (ed.), *Pages choisies de Babeuf receuillies, commentées, annotées* (Paris: Librairie Armand Colin), 1935.

Dühring, E., *Cursus der Philosophie als streng wissenschaftlicher Weltanschauung und Lebensgestaltung* (Leipzig: Erich Koschny), 1875.

Dühring, E., *Cursus der National- und Socialökonomie, nebst einer Anleitung zum Studium und zur Beurtheilung von Volkswirthschaftslehre und Socialismus. Dritte, theilweise umgearbeitete Auflage* (Leipzig: O.R. Reisland), 1892.

Ebert, F., *Schriften, Aufzeichnungen, Reden*, vol. 2 (Dresden: Carl Reissner), 1926.

Emil, K., 'Antimilitarismus', in *Die Neue Zeit*, 1907, vol. 25.II, no. 34: 241–245.

Engel'gardt, M.A., *Zadachi momenta* (St Petersburg and Moscow: Zarnitsa), n.y.

Erofeev, N.D. (ed.), *Partiia sotsialistov-revoliutsionerov. Dokumenty i materialy. 1900–1925 gg.*, vol. 1, *1900–1907 gg.* (Moscow: ROSSPEN), 1996; vol. 2, *Iiun' 1907 g.–fevral' 1917 g.*, 2001; vol. 3.I, *Fevral'–oktiabr' 1917 g.*, 2000; vol. 3.II, *Oktiabr' 1917 g.–1925 g.*, 2000.

Fel'shtinskii, I., *Arkhiv Trotskogo. Kommunisticheskaia oppozitsiia v SSSR. 1923–1927*, 3 vols (Moscow: Terra), 1990.
Fichte, J.G., *Der geschlossene Handelsstaat. Ein philosophischer Entwurf als Anhang zur Rechtslehre und Probe einer künftig zu liefernder Politik* (Hamburg: Meiner), 1979.
Galaktionova, A.A., V.F. Pustarnakova, V.M. Shakhmatova (eds), *Petr Nikitich Tkachev. Sochineniia v dvukh tomakh*, vol. 1 (Moscow: Izdate'lstvo sotsial'no-ekonomicheskoi literatury 'Mysl'), 1975.
Gankin, O.H., H.H. Fisher, *The Bolsheviks and the World War. The Origin of the Third International* (Stanford, CA: Stanford University Press), 1940.
Gel'fond, D., 'Filosofiia Ditsgena i sovremennyi pozitivizm', in *Ocherki po filosofii marksizma. Filosofskii sbornik* (St Petersburg: Bezobrazov), 1908: 243–290.
Guillaume, J., *L'Internationale. Documents et Souvenirs (1864–1878)*, vol. 1 (Paris: Société nouvelle de librairie et d'édition), 1905.
G.V., 'Der isolirte sozialistische Staat', in *Jahrbuch für Sozialwissenschaft und Sozialpolitik*, 1879, vol. 1, no. 1: 54–74.
Haenisch, K., *Die deutsche Sozialdemokratie in und nach dem Weltkriege* (Berlin: Schwetschke), 1916.
Handbuch der sozialdemokratischen Parteitage von 1910 bis 1913 (Munich: Birk), n.y.
Herzen, A., *From the Other Shore and The Russian People and Socialism* (London: Weidenfeld & Nicolson), 1955.
Herzen, A., *My Past and Thoughts. The Memoirs of Alexander Herzen* (London: Chatto & Windus), 1974.
Hess, M., *Philosophische und sozialistische Schriften, 1837–1850. Eine Auswahl* (Berlin: Akademie-Verlag), 1961.
Hildebrand, G., *Die Erschütterung der Industrieherrschaft und des Industriesozialismus* (Jena: Gustav Fischer), 1910.
Hilferding, R., *Das Finanzkapital* (Frankfurt M.: Europäische Verlagsanstalt), 1973.
Hill, C. (ed.), *Winstanley: The Law of Freedom and Other Writings* (Cambridge: Cambridge University Press), 1983.
H.M., 'Weltpolitik', in *Die Neue Zeit*, 1894, vol. 12.II, no. 32: 165–170.
Höppner, J., W. Seidel-Höppner (eds), *Von Babeuf bis Blanqui. Französischer Sozialismus und Kommunismus vor Marx*, vol. 2, *Texte* (Leipzig: Philipp Reclam), 1975.
Internationaler Sozialisten-Kongress zu Stuttgart, 18. Bis 24. August 1907 (Berlin: Vorwärts), 1907.
Kamkov, B., *Dve taktiki* (Moscow: Revoliutsionnyi Sotsializm), 1918.
Kamkov, B., 'Organicheskii nedug', in *Respublika sovetov* (Berlin and Milan: Izdatel'stvo 'Skify'), n.y.: 5–27.
Kant, I., *Zum ewigen Frieden. Ein philosophischer Entwurf* (Königsberg: Friedrich Nicolovius), 1795.
Kautsky, K., 'Kommunistische Kolonien', in *Die Neue Zeit*, 1887, vol. 5, no. 1: 28–33.
Kautsky, K., 'Die preussischen Landtagswahlen und die reaktionäre Masse', in *Die Neue Zeit*, 1897, vol. 15.II, no. 45: 580–590.
Kautsky, K., 'Vorrede', in Atlanticus, *Produktion und Konsum im Sozialstaat. Mit einer Vorrede von Karl Kautsky* (Stuttgart: Dietz Verlag), 1898: v–xxiv.
Kautsky, K., 'Das böhmische Staatsrecht und die Sozialdemokratie', in *Die Neue Zeit*, 1899, vol. 17.I, no. 10: 292–301.
Kautsky, K., 'Schippel, Brentano und die Flottenfrage. Fortsetzung', in *Die Neue Zeit*, 1900, vol. 18.I, no. 25: 772–782; 'Schluss', no. 26: 804–816.

Kautsky, K., *Handelspolitik und Sozialdemokratie. Populäre Darstellung der handelspolitischen Streitfragen* (Berlin: Vorwärts), 1901.
Kautsky, K., 'Der Wiener Parteitag', in *Die Neue Zeit*, 1902, vol. 20.I, no. 7: 197–203.
Kautsky, K., 'Was nun?', in *Die Neue Zeit*, 1903, vol. 21.II, no. 39: 389–398.
Kautsky, K., 'Allerhand Revolutionäres', in *Die Neue Zeit*, 1904, vol. 22.I, no. 20: 620–627; no. 21: 652–657.
Kautsky, K., 'Die Bauern und die Revolution in Russland', in *Die Neue Zeit*, 1905a, vol. 23.I, no. 21: 670–677.
Kautsky, K., 'Die Folgen des japanischen Sieges und die Sozialdemokratie', in *Die Neue Zeit*, 1905b, vol. 23.II, no. 41: 460–468.
Kautsky, K., 'Die zivilisierte Welt und der Zar', in *Die Neue Zeit*, 1905c, vol. 23.I, no. 19: 614–617.
Kautsky, K., 'Patriotismus, Krieg und Sozialdemokratie', in *Die Neue Zeit*, 1905d, vol. 23.II, no. 37: 343–348.
Kautsky, K., 'Die Agrarfrage in Russland', in *Die Neue Zeit*, 1906a, vol. 24.I, no. 13: 412–423.
Kautsky, K., 'Der amerikanische Arbeiter. Schluss', in *Die Neue Zeit*, 1906b, vol. 24.I, no. 24: 773–787.
Kautsky, K., *Die soziale Revolution. Zweite, durchgesehene Auflage* (Berlin: Buchhandlung Vorwärts), 1907a.
Kautsky, K., 'Triebkräfte und Aussichten der russischen Revolution. Schluss', in *Die Neue Zeit*, 1907b, vol. 25.I, no. 10: 324–333.
Kautsky, K., 'Nationalität und Internationalität', in *Ergänzungshefte zur Neuen Zeit*, 1908, no. 1: 1–36.
Kautsky, K., 'Krieg und Frieden. Betrachtungen zur Maifeier', in *Die Neue Zeit*, 1911, vol. 29.II, no. 30: 97–107.
Kautsky, K., 'Mitteleuropa. Fortsetzung', in *Die Neue Zeit*, 1916, vol. 34.I, no. 17: 522–534.
Kautsky, K., *Die Diktatur des Proletariats* (Vienna: Ignaz Brand), 1918a.
Kautsky, K., *Sozialdemokratische Bemerkungen zur Uebergangswirtschaft* (Leipzig: Verlag der Leipziger Buchdruckerei Aktiengesellschaft), 1918b.
Kautsky, K., *Das Erfurter Programm in seinem grundsätzlichen Teil erläutert* (Stuttgart: Dietz Verlag), 1919.
Kautsky, K., *Die Agrarfrage. Eine Uebersicht über die Tendenzen der modernen Landwirthschaft und die Agrarpolitik der Sozialdemokratie* (Hanover: Dietz), 1966.
Kautsky, K., *Der Weg zur Macht* (Frankfurt M.: Europäische Verlagsanstalt), 1972.
Kautsky, K., *Bernstein und das Sozialdemokratische Programm. Eine Antikritik* (Berlin: Dietz Verlag), 1976.
Kautsky, K. Jr. (ed.), *August Bebels Briefwechsel mit Karl Kautsky* (Assen: Van Gorcum), 1971.
Kirpotin, V.I., B.P. Koz'min, P.I. Lebedev-Polianskii (eds), *N.G. Chernyshevskii. Polnoe sobranie sochinenii*, vol. 7, *Stat'i i retsenzii 1860–1861* (Moscow: Gosudarstvennoe izdatel'stvo khudozhestvennoi literatury), 1950.
Kolb, W., 'Theorie und Taktik', in *Socialistische Monatshefte*, 1903, vol. 9, no. 12: 902–909.
Kommunisticheskaia partiia Sovetskogo soiuza v rezoliutsiiakh i resheniiakh s"ezdov, konferentsii i plenumov TsK, 1898–1953. Izdanie sed'moe, vol. 1, *1898–1925*; vol. 2, *1925–1953* (Moscow: Gosudarstvennoe izdatel'stvo politicheskoi literatury), 1953 [*KPSS*].

Koz'min, V.P., (ed.), *N.G. Chernyshevskii. Polnoe sobranie sochineii*, vol. 4, *Stat'i i retsenzii, 1856–1857* (Moscow: OGIZ), 1948.

Koz'min, V.P. (ed.), *P.N. Tkachev. Izbrannye sochineniia na sotsial'no-politicheskie temy v chetyrekh tomakh*, vol. 3, *1873–1879* (Moscow: Izadatel'stvo vsesoiuznogo obshchestva politkatorzhan i ssyl'no-poselentsev), 1933.

Koz'min, V.P., S.A. Makashin, V.P. Volgin (eds), *A.I. Gertsen. Sochineniia*, vol. 3, *Pis'ma iz Frantsii i Italii. S togo berega. O razvitii revoliutsionnykh idei v Ross* (Moscow: Gosudarstvennoe izdatel'stvo khudozhestvennoi literatury), 1956.

Lassalle, F., *Herr Bastiat-Schulze von Delitzsch, der Oekonomische Julian, oder: Capital und Arbeit* (Berlin: Druck und Verlag der Allg. Deutschen Associations-Buchdruckerei), 1878.

Lassalle, F., *Gesammelte Reden und Schriften*, vol. 1, *Der Italienische Krieg. Franz von Sickingen* (Berlin: Paul Cassirer), 1919.

Lehning, A. (ed.), *Michel Bakounine et ses relations avec Sergej Nečaev, 1870–1872. Écrits et matériaux* (Leiden: Brill), 1971.

Lenin, V.I., *Polnoe sobranie sochinenii. Izdanie piatoe* (Moscow: Gosudarstvennoe izdatel'stvo politicheskoi literatury), 56 vols, 1958–1965 [*PSS*].

Lensch, P., *Die deutsche Sozialdemokratie und der Weltkrieg* (Berlin: Verlag Buchhandlung Vorwärts Paul Singer), 1915.

Lensch, P., *Die Sozialdemokratie. Ihr Ende und ihr Glück* (Leipzig: G. Hirzel), 1916.

Liebknecht, K., *Gesammte Reden und Schriften*, vol. 9, *Mai 1916 bis 15. Januar 1919* (Berlin: Dietz Verlag), 1982.

Luxemburg, R., *Gesammelte Werke*, vol. 2, *1906 bis Juni 1911* (Berlin: Dietz Verlag), 1981; vol. 4, *August 1914 bis Januar 1919*, 1983.

Mably, l'Abbé de, *De la législation ou principes des loix*, vol. 1 (Amsterdam), 1776.

Mably, l'Abbé de, 'Doutes proposés aux philosophes économistes sur l'ordre naturel et essentiel des sociétés politiques', in *Œuvres completes de l'abbé de Mably*, vol. 11 (London), 1789: 3–247.

Martov, Iu.O., *Izbrannoe* (Moscow: Vneshtorgizdat), 2000.

Marx, K., F. Engels, *Werke*, 43 vols (Berlin: Dietz Verlag), 1964–1973 [*MEW*].

Marx, K., F. Engels, *Collected Works*, 50 vols (London and New York: Lawrence & Wishart), 1975–2005 [*CW*].

Matheson, P. (ed.), *The Collected Works of Thomas Müntzer* (Edinburgh: T&T Clark), 1988.

Mehring, F., 'Albert Schäffle', in *Die Neue Zeit*, 1904, vol. 22.I, no. 14: 434–437.

Meslier, J., *Œuvres complètes*, 3 vols (Paris: Éditions Anthropos), 1970, 1971, 1972.

Meyer, R. (ed.), *Briefe und Socialpolitische Afsaetze von dr. Rodbertus-Jagetzow* (Berlin: Adolf Klein's Verlag), 1882.

'Molodaia Rossia'. Available at: www.hist.msu.ru/ER/Etext/molrus.htm [retrieved 26 January 2012].

More, T., *Utopia* (Harmondsworth: Penguin), 1984.

Morelly, *Code de la Nature, ou le véritable esprit de ses lois, 1755* (Abbeville: F. Paillart), 1950.

Mr. M, *Naufrages des isles flottantes ou Basiliade du célèbre Pilpai. Poème héroique* (Paris: Messine), 1753.

O.B., 'Der deutschösterreichische Staat', in *Arbeiter-Zeitung*, 13 October 1918a.

O.B., 'Selbstbestimmungsrecht und Wirtschaftsgebiet', in *Arbeiter-Zeitung*, 15 October 1918b.

O.B., 'Deutschland und wir', in *Arbeiter-Zeitung*, 16 October 1918c.

Okulov, A.F. (ed.), *P.L. Lavrov. Filosofiia i sotsiologiia. Izbrannye proizvedeniia v dvukh tomakh*, vol. 2 (Moscow: Mysl'), 1965.
'Osnovnye polozheniia', in Rudnitskaia, E.L., *Russkii blankizm: Petr Tkachev* (Moscow: Nauka), 1992: 246–248.
Oxford Annotated Bible with the Apocrypha. Revised Standard Version, The (Oxford: Oxford University Press), 1965 [*OAB*].
Paine, T., *Rights of Man* (New York: Penguin), 1985.
Parvus, *Der Staat, die Industrie und der Sozialismus* (Dresden: Von Kaden), n.y.
Pavlov, D.B. (ed.), *Soiuz eserov-maksimalistov. Dokumenty, publitsistika, 1906–1924 gg* (Moscow: ROSSPEN), 2002.
Pelinka, A. (ed.), *Karl Renner. Schriften* (Salzburg and Vienna: Residenz Verlag), 1994.
Pervyi s"ezd RSDRP. Mart 1898 goda. Dokumenty i materialy (Moscow: Gosudarstvennoe izdatel'stvo politicheskoi literatury), 1958.
Pillot, J.-J., *Histoire des Égaux, ou moyens d'établir l'égalité absolue parmi les hommes* (Paris: La Tribune du Peuple), 1840.
Plato, *The Republic* (Harmondsworth: Penguin), 1983.
Protokoll über die Verhandlungen des Parteitages der Sozialdemokratischen Partei Deutschlands Abgehalten in Würzburg vom 14. bis 20. Oktober 1917 (Berlin: Dietz Verlag), 1973.
Puti mirovoi revoliutsii. Sed'moi rasshirennyi plenum Ispolnitel'nogo komiteta Kommunisticheskogo internatsionala. 22 noiabria–16 dekabria 1926. Stenograficheskii otchet (Moscow: Gosudarstvennoe izdatel'stvo), 1927.
Ramm, T. (ed.), *Der Frühsozialismus. Quellentexte. Zweite erweiterte Auflage* (Stuttgart: Alfred Kröner), 1968.
Renner, K., 'Der Krieg und die Wandlungen des nationalen Gedankens', in *Der Kampf*, 1915, vol. 8, no. 1: 8–23.
Renner, K., *Marxismus, Krieg und Internationale. Kritische Studien über offene Probleme des wissenschaftlichen und des praktischen Sozialismus in und nach dem Weltkrieg* (Stuttgart: Dietz Verlag), 1917.
Restif de la Bretonne, *Monsieur Nicolas ou la cœur humain dévoilé*, vols 1, 5, 6 (Paris: Jean-Jacques Pauvert), 1959.
Restif de la Bretonne, *La découverte australe par un homme-volant ou le Dédale français* (Paris: France Adel), 1977.
Rezoliutsii i postanovleniia I i II vserossiiskikh s"ezdov partii levykh sotsial.-revoliutsionerov (internatsionalistov) (Moscow: Revoliutsionnyi Sotsializm), 1918.
Riazanov, D. (ed.), *G.V. Plekhanov. Sochineniia*, 24 vols (Moscow and Leningrad: Gosudarstvennoe izdatel'stvo), 1923–1927 [*Plekhanov/Sochineniia*].
Ritter, G.A., S. Miller (eds), *Die deutsche Revolution. 1918–1919. Dokumente. Zweite, erheblich erweiterte und überarbeitete Ausgabe* (Hamburg: Hoffmann und Campe), 1975.
Rodbertus-Jagetzow, C., *Das Kapital. Vierter Socialer Brief an Von Kirchmann* (Berlin: Puttkammer & Mühlbrecht), 1884.
Rodbertus-Jagetzow, C., *Zur Beleuchtung der socialen Frage. Theil II. Neue wohlfeile Ausgabe* (Berlin: Puttkammer & Mühlbrecht), 1899.
Rother, E., 'Zur Theorie der Flottenfrage', in *Socialistische Monatshefte*, 1899, vol. 5, no. 12: 639–644.
Sabine, G.H. (ed.), *The Works of Gerrard Winstanley* (Ithaca, NY: Cornell University Press), 1941.

204 References

de Saint-Simon, C.-H., *Oeuvres de Claude-Henri de Saint-Simon*, 6 vols (Paris: Éditions Anthropos), 1966.
Salvemini, G., *Mazzini* (London: Jonathan Cape), 1956.
Scanlan, J.P. (ed.), *Peter Lavrov. Historical Letters* (Berkeley, CA: University of California Press), 1967.
Schäffle, A., *Die Quintessenz des Sozialismus. Zweite unveränderte Auflage* (Gotha: Friedrich Andreas Perthes), 1877.
Schäffle, A., *Bau und Leben des socialen Körpers. Encyclopädischer Entwurf einer realen Anatomie, Physiologie und Psychologie der menschlichen Gesellschaft mit besonderer Rücksicht auf die Volkswirthschaft als socialen Stoffwechsel*, vol. 3, *Specielle Socialwissenschaft, erste Hälfte. (Kapitalismus und Sozialismus mit besonderer Rücksicht auf Geschäfts- und Vermögensformen. Zweite gänzlich umgearbeitete Auflage)* (Tübingen: Verlag der H. Laupp'schen Buchhandlung), 1878.
Schippel, M., 'Schäffles Lebensbild', in *Sozialistische Monatshefte*, 1905, vol. 11, no. 12: 1009–1015.
Schröder, W., *Handbuch der sozialdemokratischen Parteitage von 1863 bis 1909* (Munich: Birk), 1910.
Sed'maia (aprel'skaia) vserossiiskaia konferentsiia RSDRP (bol'shevikov). Petrogradskaia obshchegorodskaia konferentisiia RSDRP (bol'shevikov). Aprel' 1917. Protokoly (Moscow: Gosudarstvennoe izdatel'stvo politicheskoi literatury), 1958.
Sharp, A. (ed.), *The English Levellers* (Cambridge: Cambridge University Press), 1999.
Shestoi s"ezd RSDRP (bol'shevikov). Avgust 1917 goda. Protokoly (Moscow: Gosudarstvennoe izdatel'stvo politicheskoi literatury), 1958.
Smirnov, G.L., V.V. Zhuravlev, L.F. Morozov, V.P. Naumov (eds), *N.I. Bukharin. Izbrannye proizvedeniia* (Moscow: Izdatel'stvo politicheskoi literatury), 1988.
Springer, R., *Der Kampf der oesterreichischen Nationen um den Staat* (Leipzig and Vienna: Franz Deuticke), 1902.
Stalin, I.V., *Sochineniia*, 13 vols (Moscow: Gosudarstvennoe izdatel'stvo politicheskoi literatury), 1946–1951 [*Sochineniia*].
Stephan, C. (ed.), *Zwischen den Stühlen. Oder über die Unvereinbarkeit von Theorie und Praxis. Schriften Rudolf Hilferdings 1904 bis 1940* (Berlin: Dietz Verlag), 1982.
Tag-in, E., *Printsipy trudovoi teorii (Posviashchaetsia pamiati N.K. Mikhailovskogo i P.L. Lavrova)* (St Petersburg: Tipo-Litografiia S.M. Muller), 1906.
Thomas, J., F. Venturi (eds), *Dom Deschamps, Le vrai système ou le mot de l'énigme métaphysique et morale* (Geneva: Librairie Droz), 1963.
Tiutiukin, S.V. (ed.), *Men'sheviki. Dokumenty i materialy 1903–1917gg* (Moscow: ROSSPEN), 1996.
Trotsky, L. [Trotskii, L.], *Voina i revoliutsiia. Krushenie Vtorogo internatsionala i podgotovka Tret'ego*, vol. II, *Izdanie vtoroe* (Moscow and Petrograd: Gosudarstvennoe izdatel'stvo), 1923a.
Trotsky, L., *1905* (Paris: Librairie de l'Humanité), 1923b.
Trotsky, L., 'Towards capitalism or towards socialism?' (1925). Available at: www.marxists.org/archive/trotsky/1925/11/towards.htm [retrieved 7 March 2014].
Trotsky, L. [Trotskii, L.], *Sochineniia*, vol. 9, *Evropa v voine* (Moscow and Leningrad: Gosudarstvennoe izdatel'stvo), 1927.
Trotsky, L. [Trotzki], *Über Lenin. Material für einen Biographen* (Frankfurt M.: Europäische Verlagsanstalt), 1964.
Trotsky, L., *The Third International after Lenin* (New York: Pathfinder Press), 1970.

Trotsky, L., *The Permanent Revolution & Results and Prospects* (New York: Pathfinder Press), 1978.
Trotsky, L. [Trotskii, L.], *Uroki oktiabria (s prilozheniem kriticheskikh materialov 1924 goda)* (St Petersburg: Leninizdat), 1991.
Trotsky, L. [Trotskii, L.], 'Kritika programmy Kommunisticheskogo internatsionala', in Trotskii, L., *Kommunisticheskii internatsional posle Lenina. Velikii organizator porazhenii* (Moscow: Spartakovets, Printima), 1993: 64–118.
Trotsky, L. [Trotzki], *Der Krieg und die Internationale* (Munich: Futurus-Verlag), n.y.a.
Trotsky, L. [Trotzki], *Verratene Revolution. Was ist die Sowjetunion und wohin treibt sie (1936)?* (Verlag Ergebnisse & Perspektiven/n.p.), n.y.b.
Trutovskii, V., *Perekhodnyi period (mezhdu kapitalizmom i sotsializmom)* (Petrograd: Pervaia Gosudarstvennaia Tipografiia), 1918.
V., book review of *Der Zukunftsstaat. Zwölf Briefe eines Arbeiterfreundes* (Weigmann: Schweidnitz, C.F.), 1878, in *Die Zukunft*, 1878, vol. 1, no. 23: 734–735.
Vilenskaia, E., L. Roitberg (eds), *N.V. Shelgunov, L.P. Shelgunova, M.L. Mikhailov. Vospominaniia v dvukh tomakh*, vol. 1, *Vospominaniia N.V. Shelgunova* (Moscow: Izdatel'stvo 'Khudozhestvennaia literatura'), 1967.
Volia truda (Sbornik statei) (St. Peterburg: Tipo-Litografiia I. Lur'e), 1907.
Vollmar, G., *Der isolirte sozialistische Staat. Eine sozialökonomische Studie* (Zurich: Verlag der Volksbuchhandlung), 1878.
Vollmar, G., 'Zur Streitfrage über den Staatssozialismus', in *Die Neue Zeit*, 1893, vol. 11.I, no. 7: 196–210.
von Dülmen, R. (ed.), *Das Täuferreich zu Münster 1534–1535. Berichte und Dokumente* (Munich: Deutscher Taschenbuch Verlag), 1974.
Vtoroi s"ezd RSDRP. Iul'–avgust 1903 goda. Protokoly (Moscow: Gosudarstvennoe izdatel'stvo politicheskoi literatury), 1959.
Weitling, W., *Die Menschheit wie sie ist und wie sie sein sollte* (Munich: Verlag für Gesellschaftswissenschaft), 1895.
Weitling, W., *Garantien der Harmonie und Freiheit. Jubiläums-Ausgabe* (Berlin: Vorwärts), 1908.
Wolfe, D.M. (ed.), *Leveller Manifestoes of the Puritan Revolution* (New York: Humanities Press), 1967.
XIV s"ezd Vsesoiuznoi kommunisticheskoi partii (b.). 18–31 dekabr' 1925. Stenograficheskii otchet (Moscow and Leningrad: Gosudarstvennoe izdatel'stvo), 1926.
XV konferentsiia Vsesoiuznoi kommunisticheskoi partii (b.). 26 oktiabria–3 noiabria 1926 g. Stenograficheskii otchet (Moscow and Leningrad: Gosudarstvennoe izdatel'stvo), 1927.
Zinov'ev, G., 'Rossiiskaia sotsial-demokratiia i russkii sotsial-shovinizm', in *Kommunist*, 1915, nos. 1–2: 102–155.
Zinov'ev, G., [Zinoviev, G.], *Le Léninisme. Introduction à l'étude du léninisme* (Paris: Bureau d'édition, de diffusion et de publicité), 1926.

Secondary Literature

Abraham, R., *Rosa Luxemburg. A Life for the International* (Oxford and New York: Berg), 1989.
Acton, E., *Rethinking the Russian Revolution* (London: Edward Arnold), 1990.
Adamiak, R., 'Marx, Engels, and Dühring', in *Journal of the History of Ideas*, 1974, vol. 35, no. 1: 98–112.

References

Agursky, M., *The Third Rome. National Bolshevism in the USSR* (Boulder, CO: Westview), 1987.

Albrecht, G., *Eugen Dühring. Ein Beitrag zur Geschichte der Sozialwissenschaften* (Jena: Gustav Fischer), 1927.

Alsop, J.D., 'Gerrard Winstanley: what do we know of his life?', in Bradstock, A. (ed.), *Winstanley and the Diggers, 1649–1999* (London: Frank Cass), 2000: 19–36.

Alter, P., *Nationalism* (London: Edward Arnold), 1996.

Ananich, B., 'The Russian economy and banking system', in Lieven, D. (ed.), *The Cambridge History of Russia*, vol. 2, *Imperial Russia, 1689–1917* (Cambridge: Cambridge University Press), 2006: 394–425.

Anchor, R., *The Enlightenment Tradition* (Berkeley, CA: University of California Press), 1967.

Anderson, K.B., *Marx at the Margins. On Nationalism, Ethnicity, and Non-Western Societies* (Chicago, IL: University of Chicago Press), 2010.

Anderson, M.S., *Europe in the Eighteenth Century 1713–1783. Third Edition* (London: Longman), 1989.

Andress, D., 'The course of the Terror, 1793–94', in McPhee, P. (ed.), *A Companion to the French Revolution* (Oxford and Cambridge, MA: Wiley-Blackwell), 2013: 293–309.

Angenot, M., *L'utopie collectiviste. Le grand récit socialiste sous la Deuxième Internationale* (Paris: Presses Universitaires de France), 1993.

Anonymous, 'Einführung', in *Karl Marx Friedrich Engels Gesamtausgabe (MEGA)*, vol. 3.9, *Karl Marx–Friedrich Engels Briefwechsel. Januar 1858 bis August 1859. Apparat* (Berlin: Akademie Verlag), 2003: 577–667.

Armstrong, S.W., 'The internationalism of the early social democrats of Germany', in *American Historical Review*, January 1942, vol. 47, no. 2: 245–258.

Ascher, A., 'Imperialists within German social democracy prior to 1914', in *Journal of Central European Studies*, 1961, vol. 20, no. 4: 397–422.

Ascher, A., *The Revolution of 1905. A Short History* (Stanford, CA: Stanford University Press), 2004.

Ascher, A., *The Russian Revolution. A Beginner's Guide* (London: Oneworld), 2014.

Audisio, G., *The Waldensian Dissent. Persecution and Survival, c.1170–1570* (Cambridge: Cambridge University Press), 1999.

Avineri, S., *The Social and Political Thought of Karl Marx* (Cambridge: Cambridge University Press), 1968.

Avineri, S., *Moses Hess. Prophet of Communism and Zionism* (New York: New York University Press), 1985.

Avineri, S., 'Marxism and nationalism', in *Journal of Contemporary History*, September 1991: 637–657.

Aylmer, G., 'The Diggers in their own time', in Bradstock, A. (ed.), *Winstanley and the Diggers, 1649–1999* (London: Frank Cass), 2000: 8–18.

Balabkins, N.W., 'Der Zukunftsstaat: Carl Ballod's vision of a leisure-oriented socialism', in *History of Political Economy*, 1978, vol. 10, no. 2: 213–232.

Ball, A., 'Building a new state and society: NEP, 1921–1928', in Suny, R.G. (ed.), *The Cambridge History of Russia*, vol. 3, *The Twentieth Century* (Cambridge: Cambridge University Press), 2006: 168–191.

Baron, H., *The Crisis of the Early Italian Renaissance. Civic Humanism and Republican Liberty in an Age of Classicism and Tyranny* (Princeton, NJ: Princeton University Press), 1966.

Baron, S., *Die politische Theorie Ferdinand Lassalle's* (Leipzig: Hirschfeld), 1923.

Baron, S.H., *Plekhanov. The Father of Russian Marxism* (Stanford, CA: Stanford University Press), 1963.
Beaud, M., *Histoire du capitalisme de 1500 à nos jours* (Paris: Éditions du Seuil), 1981.
Benner, E., *Really Existing Nationalisms. A Post-Communist View from Marx and Engels* (Oxford: Clarendon), 1995.
Bensing, M., 'Idee und Praxis des "Christlichen Verbündnisses" bei Thomas Müntzer', in Friesen, A., H.-J. Goertz (eds), *Thomas Müntzer* (Darmstadt: Wissenschaftliche Buchgesellschaft), 1978: 299–338.
Berghahn, V.R., *Der Tirpitz-Plan. Genesis und Verfall einer innenpolitischen Krisenstrategie unter Wilhelm II* (Düsseldorf: Droste Verlag), 1971.
Berghahn, V.R., *Imperial Germany, 1871–1914. Economy, Society, Culture, and Politics* (Oxford and Providence, RI: Berghahn), 1994.
Berghahn, V.R., *Das Kaiserreich, 1871–1914. Industriegesellschaft, bürgerliche Kultur und autoritärer Staat* (Stuttgart: Klett-Cotta), 2003.
Bestor, A.E., 'The evolution of the socialist vocabulary', in *Journal of the History of Ideas*, 1948, vol. 9, no. 3: 259–302.
Billington, J.H., *Mikhailovsky and Russian Populism* (Oxford: Clarendon), 1958.
Billington, J.H., *Fire in the Minds of Men. Origins of the Revolutionary Faith* (London: Temple Smith), 1980.
Blackwell, W.L., *The Beginnings of Russian Industrialization 1800–1860* (Princeton, NJ: Princeton University Press), 1970.
Blickle, P., 'The popular Reformation', in Brady *et al.* (eds), *Handbook of European History, 1400–1600*, vol. 2, *Visions, Programs and Outcomes* (Leiden: Brill), 1995: 161–192.
Bloch, C., 'Der Kampf Joseph Blochs und der "Sozialistischen Monatshefte" in der Weimarer Republik', in *Jahrbuch des Instituts für Deutsche Geschichte*, 1974, vol. 3: 257–287.
Bloom, S.F., *The World of Nations. A Study of the National Implications in the Work of Karl Marx* (New York: Columbia University Press), 1941.
Bödeker, H.E., P. Friedemann (eds), *Gabriel Bonnot de Mably. Politische texte 1751–1783* (Berlin and Baden: Nomos), 2000.
Bottomore, T., P. Goode (eds), *Austro-Marxism* (Oxford: Clarendon), 1978.
Bouman, P.J., 'De theorie van den internationalen handel in de socialistische literatuur', in *De Economist*, 1933, vol. 82, no. 1: 461–480.
Bouvier, B.W., *Französische Revolution und deutsche Arbeiterbewegung. Die Rezeption des revolutionären Frankreich in der deutschen sozialistischen Arbeiterbewegung von den 1830er Jahren bis 1905* (Bonn: Verlag Neue Gesellschaft), 1982.
Bouvier, B.W., 'The influence of the French Revolution on socialism and the German socialist movement in the nineteenth century', in *History of European Ideas*, 1992, vol. 14, no. 1: 101–113.
Bradstock, A., *Faith in the Revolution. The Political Theologies of Müntzer and Winstanley* (London: SPCK), 1997.
Bradstock, A. (ed.), *Winstanley and the Diggers, 1649–1999* (London: Frank Cass), 2000.
Bradstock, A., *Radical Religion in Cromwell's England. A Concise History from the English Civil War to the End of the Commonwealth* (London and New York: I.B. Tauris), 2011.
Brady, T.A., H.O. Doberman, J.D. Tracy (eds), *Handbook of European History, 1400–1600*, vol. 2, *Visions, Programs and Outcomes* (Leiden: Brill), 1995.

Brandenberger, D., *National Bolshevism. Stalinist Mass Culture and the Formation of Modern Russian National Identity, 1931–1956* (Cambridge, MA: Harvard University Press), 2002.
Brandenberger, D., *Propaganda State in Crisis. Soviet Ideology, Indoctrination, and Terror under Stalin, 1927–1941* (New Haven, CT: Yale University Press), 2011.
Braunthal, J., *Geschichte der Internationale* (Hanover: Dietz Verlag), vol. 1, 1961; vol. 2, 1963.
Brecht, M., *Johann Valentin Andreae 1586–1654. Eine Biographie* (Göttingen: Vandenhoeck & Ruprecht), 2008.
Brill, H., 'Karl Kautsky. 16. Oktober 1854–17. Oktober 1938', in *Zeitschrift für Politik*, 1954, vol. 1, no. 3: 211–240.
Broué, P., *The German Revolution 1917–1923* (Leiden: Brill), 2005.
Brovkin, V.N., *Behind the Front Lines of the Civil War. Political Parties and Social Movements in Russia, 1918–1922* (Princeton, NJ: Princeton University Press), 1994.
Brown, A., *The Rise and Fall of Communism* (London: Bodley Head), 2009.
Bruce, S., 'More's *Utopia*. Colonialists, refugees and the nature of sufficiency', in Ramiro, A. *et al.*, *Utopian Moments. Reading Utopian Texts* (London and New York: Bloomsbury), 2012: 8–14.
Callahan, K.J., '"Performing inter-nationalism" in Stuttgart in 1907: French and German socialist nationalism and the political culture of an International Socialist Congress', in *International Review of Social History*, 2000, vol. 45, no. 1: 51–87.
Callahan, K.J., *Demonstration Culture. European Socialism and the Second International, 1889–1914* (Leicester: Troubadour), 2010.
Campbell, P., 'Rethinking the origins of the French Revolution', in McPhee, P. (ed.), *A Companion to the French Revolution* (Oxford and Cambridge, MA: Wiley-Blackwell), 2013: 3–23.
Carr, E.H., *The Bolshevik Revolution. 1917–1923*, vol. 2 (London: Macmillan), 1952.
Carr, E.H., *The Interregnum. 1923–1924* (Harmondsworth: Penguin), 1969.
Carr, E.H., *Socialism in One Country 1924–1926*, 2 vols (Harmondsworth: Penguin), 1970.
Carsten, F.L., 'Georg von Vollmar: A Bavarian Social Democrat', in *Journal of Contemporary History*, 1990, vol. 25, no. 2: 317–335.
Carsten, F.L., *Eduard Bernstein, 1850–1932. Eine Politische Biographie* (Munich: C.H. Beck), 1993.
Carver, T., *Marx & Engels. The Intellectual Relationship* (Brighton: Harvester Press), 1983.
Carver, T., *Friedrich Engels. His Life and Thought* (Basingstoke: Palgrave Macmillan), 1989.
Cherubini, D., 'Si vis pacem para libertatem et justitiam. Les Etats-Unis d'Europe, 1867–1914', in Petricioli, M., D. Cherubini, A. Anteghini (eds), *Les Etats-Unis d'Europe. The United States of Europe. Un Projet pacifiste. A Pacifist Project* (Berne: Peter Lang), 2004: 3–47.
Christianson, P., *Reformers and Babylon. English Apocalyptic Visions from the Reformation to the Eve of the Civil War* (Toronto: University of Toronto Press), 1978.
Claeys, G., '"Individualism", "socialism", and "social science": further notes on a process of conceptual formation, 1800–1850', in *Journal of the History of Ideas*, 1986, vol. 47, no. 1: 81–93.
Claeys, G., 'Socialism and utopia', in Schaer, R. *et al.* (eds), *Utopia. The Search for the Ideal Society in the Western World* (New York and Oxford: New York Public Library, Oxford University Press), 2000: 206–247.

Claydon, T., I. McBride, 'The trials of the chosen peoples. Recent interpretations of Protestantism and national identity in Britain and Ireland', in Claydon, T., I. McBride (eds), *Protestantism and National Identity. Britain and Ireland, c.1650–c.1850* (Cambridge: Cambridge University Press), 1998: 3–29.
Cochrane, E., *Italy, 1530–1630* (London: Longman), 1988.
Coe, R.N., *Morelly. Ein Rationalist auf dem Wege zum Sozialismus* (Berlin: Rütten & Loening), 1961.
Cohen, G.A., *Karl Marx's Theory of History. A Defence* (Oxford: Clarendon), 1982.
Cohen, G.A., *Self-Ownership, Freedom and Equality* (Cambridge: Cambridge University Press), 1995.
Cohen, S.F., *Bukharin and the Bolshevik Revolution. A Political Biography, 1888–1938* (London: Wildwood House), 1974.
Cohn, N., *The Pursuit of the Millennium. Revolutionary Messianism in Medieval and Reformation Europe and its Bearing on Modern Totalitarian Movements. Second Edition* (New York: Harper), 1961.
Cole, G.D.H., *A History of Socialist Thought*, vol. 1, *Socialist Thought. The Forerunners 1789–1850* (London: Macmillan), 1977; vol. 2, *Socialist Thought. Marxism and Anarchism 1850–1890* (London: Macmillan), 1961; vol. 3.I and II, *The Second International 1889–1914* (London: Macmillan), 1960; vol. 4.I, *Communism and Social Democracy 1914–1931* (London: Macmillan), 1961.
Confino, A., *The Nation as a Local Metaphor. Württemberg, Imperial Germany, and National Memory, 1871–1918* (Chapel Hill, NC: University of North Carolina Press), 1997.
Connor, W., *The National Question in Marxist-Leninist Theory and Strategy* (Princeton, NJ: Princeton University Press), 1984.
Conze, W., D. Groh, *Die Arbeiterbewegung in der nationalen Bewegung. Die deutsche Sozialdemokratie vor, während und nach der Reichsgründing* (Stuttgart: Ernst Klett Verlag), 1966.
Cooper, S.E., *Patriotic Pacifism. Waging War on War in Europe, 1815–1914* (Oxford: Oxford University Press), 1991.
Coward, D., *The Philosophy of Restif de la Bretonne* (Oxford: Voltaire Foundation), 1991.
Creuzberger, S., *Stalin. Machtpolitiker und Ideologe* (Stuttgart: Kohlhammer), 2009.
Crisp, O., 'Labour and industrialization in Russia', in Mathias, P., M.M. Postan (eds), *The Cambridge Economic History of Europe*, vol. 7, *The Industrial Economies. Capital, Labour, and Enterprise*, part 2, *The United States, Japan, and Russia* (Cambridge: Cambridge University Press), 1978: 308–415.
Crocker, L.G., *Nature and Culture. Ethical Thought in the French Enlightenment* (Baltimore, MD: John Hopkins Press), 1963.
Crouzet, F., *A History of the European Economy, 1000–2000* (Charlottesville, VA: University Press of Virginia), 2001.
Cummins, I., *Marx, Engels and National Movements* (London: Croom Helm), 1980.
Daniels, R.V., *The Conscience of the Revolution. Communist Opposition in Soviet Russia* (Cambridge, MA: Harvard University Press), 1960.
Daniels, R.V., *The Nature of Communism* (New York: Random House), 1962.
Danilov, V.P., 'Bukharin and the countryside', in Kemp-Welch, A. (ed.), *The Ideas of Nikolai Bukharin* (Oxford: Clarendon), 1992: 69–81.
Davidson, N., *How Revolutionary Were the Bourgeois Revolutions?* (Chicago, IL: Haymarket Books), 2012.

Davies, N., *Europe, a History* (London: Pimlico), 1997.
Davies, R.W., 'Grain, class, and politics during NEP. The Politburo meeting of December 10, 1925', in Gregory, P.R., N. Naimark (eds), *The Lost Politburo Transcripts. From Collective Rule to Stalin's Dictatorship* (New Haven, CT: Yale University Press), 2008: 181–198.
Davies, S., J. Harris (eds), *Stalin. A New History* (Cambridge: Cambridge University Press), 2005.
Davis, J.A. (ed.), *Italy in the Nineteenth Century* (Oxford: Oxford University Press), 2000.
Davis, J.C., *Utopia and the Ideal Society. A Study of English Utopian Writing, 1516–1700* (Cambridge: Cambridge University Press), 1981.
Davis, J.C., 'The Levellers and Christianity', in Gaunt, P. (ed.), *The English Civil War. The Essential Readings* (Oxford and Cambridge, MA: Blackwell), 2000: 279–302.
Davis, H.B., *Nationalism & Socialism. Marxist and Labor Theories of Nationalism to 1917* (New York and London: Monthly Review Press), 1967.
Day, R.B., *Leon Trotsky and The Politics of Economic Isolation* (Cambridge: Cambridge University Press), 1973.
Delaporte, A., *L'idée d'égalité en France au XVIIIe siècle* (Paris: Presses Universitaires de France), 1987.
Deppermann, K., *Melchior Hoffman. Soziale Unruhen und apokalytische Visionen im Zeitalter der Reformation* (Göttingen: Vandenhoeck & Ruprecht), 1979.
Deprun, J., R. Desné, A. Soboul, 'Avant-propos', in Meslier, J., *Œvres complètes* (Paris: Éditions Anthropos), vol. 1, 1970: xi–xiv.
Desné, R., 'L'homme, l'œuvre et la renommée', in Meslier, J., *Œvres complètes* (Paris: Éditions Anthropos), vol. 1, 1970: xvii–lxxxix.
Desroches, H.-C., 'Notes sociales à propos de Lamennais et du mot "communisme"', in *L'actualité de l'histoire*, 1955, no. 11: 28–32.
Deutscher, I., *The Prophet Outcast. Trotsky: 1929–1940* (Oxford: Oxford University Press), 1963.
di Biagio, A., 'Bukharin's international alternative', in Kemp-Welch, A. (ed.), *The Ideas of Nikolai Bukharin* (Oxford: Clarendon), 1992: 113–127.
Dietzel, H., *Karl Rodbertus. Darstellung seines Lebens und seiner lehre*, vol. 2, *Darstellung seizer Socialphilosophie* (Jena: Gustav Fischer), 1888.
Dommanget, M., *Le curé Meslier. Athée, communiste et révolutionaire sous Louis XIV* (Paris: Julliard), 1965.
Donald, M., *Marxism and Revolution. Karl Kautsky and the Russian Marxists, 1900–1924* (New Haven, CT: Yale University Press), 1993.
Draper, H., *Karl Marx's Theory of Revolution*, vol. 2, *The Politics of Social Classes* (New York and London: Monthly Review Press), 1978.
Eagleton, T., *Why Marx Was Right* (New Haven, CT: Yale University Press), 2011.
Eaton, H., 'Marx and the Russians', in *Journal of the History of Ideas*, 1980, vol. 41, no. 1: 89–112.
Eckert, G., 'Die Konsolidierung der sozialdemokratischen Arbeiterbewegung zwischen Reichsgründung und Sozialistengesetz', in Mommsen, H. (ed.), *Sozialdemokratie zwischen Klassenbewegung und Volkspartei* (Frankfurt M.: Athenäum), 1974: 35–51.
Eigner, P., 'Der Weg in die Industriegesellschaft', in Cerman, M., F.X. Eder, P. Eigner, A. Komlosy, E. Landsteiner (eds), *Wirtschaft und Gesellschaft. Europa 1000–2000* (Innsbruck: Studienverlag), 2011: 104–133.
Eley, G., 'Defining social imperialism: use and abuse of an idea', in *Social History*, 1976, vol. 1, no. 3: 265–290.

Eliav-Feldon, M., *Realistic Utopias. The Ideal Imaginary Societies of the Renaissance 1516–1630* (Oxford: Clarendon), 1982.
Elliger, W., *Thomas Müntzer. Leben und Werk* (Göttingen: Vandenhoeck & Ruprecht), 1975.
Emmerson, R.K., B. McGinn (eds), *The Apocalypse in the Middle Ages* (Ithaca, NY: Cornell University Press), 1992.
Erlich, A., *The Soviet Industrialization Debate, 1924–1928* (Cambridge, MA: Harvard University Press), 1960.
Fairbairn, B., 'Economic and social developments', in Retallack, J. (ed.), *Imperial Germany, 1871–1918* (Oxford: Oxford University Press), 2008: 61–82.
Falkus, M.E., *The Industrialisation of Russia 1700–1914* (Basingstoke: Palgrave Macmillan), 1972.
Faulenbach, B., *Geschichte der SPD. Von den Anfängen bis zur Gegenwart* (Munich: C.H. Beck), 2012.
Felix, D., *Marx as Politician* (Carbondale, IL: Southern Illinois University Press), 1983.
Fel'shtinskii, I., G. Cherniavskii, *Lev Trotskii*, (Moscow: Tsentrpoligraf), 2012, vol. 1–2; 2013, vol. 3.
Ferdinand, P., 'Bukharin and the New Economic Policy', in Kemp-Welch, A. (ed.), *The Ideas of Nikolai Bukharin* (Oxford: Clarendon), 1992: 40–68.
Ferguson, J., *Utopias of the Classical World* (Ithaca, NY: Cornell University Press), 1975.
Ferguson, K., *Pythagoras. His Lives and the Legacy of a Rational Universe* (London: Icon Books), 2011.
Fesser, G., *Der Traum vom Platz an der Sonne. Deutsche 'Weltpolitik' 1879–1914* (Bremen: Donat Verlag), 1996.
Fetscher, I., *Der Marxismus. Seine Geschichte in Dokumenten. Philosophie, Ideologie, Ökonomie, Soziologie, Politik* (Munich: Piper), 1967.
Figes, O., *A People's Tragedy. The Russian Revolution, 1891–1924* (London: Pimlico), 1996.
Fitzpatrick, M., 'The age of Louis XIV and early Enlightenment in France', in Fitzpatrick, M. *et al.* (eds), *The Enlightenment World* (London and New York: Routledge), 2004: 134–155.
Fitzpatrick, M., P. Jones, C. Knellwolf, I. McCalman (eds), *The Enlightenment World* (London and New York: Routledge), 2004.
Fitzsimmons, M.P., 'The principles of 1789', in McPhee, P. (ed.), *A Companion to the French Revolution* (Oxford and Cambridge, MA: Wiley-Blackwell), 2013: 75–90.
Flannery, K.V., J. Marcus, *The Creation of Inequality. How our Prehistoric Ancestors Set the Stage for Monarchy, Slavery and Empire* (Cambridge, MA: Harvard University Press), 2012.
Fletcher, R., 'A revisionist looks at imperialism: Eduard Bernstein's critique of imperialism and *Kolonialpolitik*, 1900–1914', in *Central European History*, 1979a, vol. 12, no. 3: 237–271.
Fletcher, R., 'World power without war. Eduard Bernstein's proposals for an alternative Weltpolitik, 1900–1914', in *Australian Journal of Politics and History*, 1979b, vol. 25, no. 2: 228–236.
Fletcher, R., 'Revisionism and empire: Joseph Bloch, the *Sozialistische Monatshefte* and German Nationalism, 1907–1914', in *European Studies Review*, 1980, vol. 10: 459–485.

Fletcher, R., 'Socialist nationalism in Central Europe before 1914: the case of Karl Leuthner', in *Canadian Journal of History*, 1982, vol. 17, no. 1: 27–57.

Fletcher, R., 'In the interest of peace and progress: Eduard Bernstein's socialist foreign policy', in *Review of International Studies*, 1983, vol. 9, no. 2: 79–93.

Fletcher, R., *Revisionism and Empire. Socialist Imperialism in Germany 1897–1914* (London: Allen & Unwin), 1984.

Fletcher, R., 'Revisionism and Wilhelmine Imperialism', in *Journal of Contemporary History*, 1988, vol. 23, no. 3: 347–366.

Fontana, G.L., 'The economic development of Europe in the nineteenth century (I). Growth and transformation of the economy', in Di Vittorio, A. (ed.), *An Economic History of Europe. From Expansion to Development* (London and New York: Routledge), 2006a: 135–153.

Fontana, G.L., 'The economic development of Europe in the nineteenth century (III). The process of industrialization', in Di Vittorio, A. (ed.), *An Economic History of Europe. From Expansion to Development* (London and New York: Routledge), 2006b: 176–207.

Fontana, G.L., 'The economic development of Europe in the nineteenth century (V). International exchanges and monetary systems', in Di Vittorio, A. (ed.), *An Economic History of Europe. From Expansion to Development* (London and New York: Routledge), 2006c: 222–238.

Förder, H., M. Hundt, 'Zur Vorgeschichte von Engels' Arbeit "Grundsätze des Kommunismus". Der "Entwurf des Kommunistischen Glaubensbekenntnisses" vom Juni 1947', in *Beiträge zur Geschichte der Arbeiterbewegung*, 1970, vol. 12, no. 1: 60–85.

Friesen, A., 'Thomas Müntzer in Marxist thought', in *Church History: Studies in Christianity and Culture*, 1965, vol. 34, no. 3: 306–327.

Fröhlich, M., *Imperialismus. Deutsche Kolonial- und Weltpolitik 1880–1914* (Munich: Deutscher Taschenbuch Verlag), 1994.

Frye, N., 'Varieties of literary utopias', in Manuel, F.E. (ed.), *Utopias and Utopian Thought* (Boston, MA: Houghton Mifflin), 1966: 25–49.

Fudge, T.A., '"Neither mine nor thine": communist experiments in Hussite Bohemia', in *Canadian Journal of History*, 1998a, vol. 33, no. 1: 25–47.

Fudge, T.A., *The Magnificent Ride. The First Reformation in Hussite Bohemia* (Aldershot: Ashgate), 1998b.

Fudge, T.A., *The Crusade against Heretics in Bohemia, 1418–1437* (Aldershot: Ashgate), 2002.

Fülberth, G., 'Die deutsche Sozialdemokratie im Ersten Weltkrieg 1914–1918', in von Freyberg, J. (ed.), *Geschichte der deutschen Sozialdemokratie 1863–1975* (Cologne: Pahl-Rugenstein), 1975: 51–64.

Fülberth, G., J. Harrer, *Die deutsche Sozialdemokratie 1890–1933* (Darmstadt and Neuwied: Luchterhand), 1974.

Fukuyama, F., *The Origins of Political Order. From Prehuman Times to the French Revolution* (London: Profile Books), 2012.

Furet, F., *Interpreting the French Revolution* (Cambridge: Cambridge University Press), 1981.

Gallus, A. (ed.), *Die vergessene Revolution von 1918/19* (Göttingen: Vandenhoeck & Ruprecht), 2010.

Gaunt, P. (ed.), *The English Civil War. The Essential Readings* (Oxford and Cambridge, MA: Blackwell), 2000.

Gay, P., *The Dilemma of Democratic Socialism. Eduard Bernstein's Challenge to Marx* (New York: Collier Books), 1962.
Gay, P., *The Enlightenment. The Science of Freedom* (New York and London: W.W. Norton), 1969.
Geoghegan, V., *Utopianism and Marxism* (New York and London: Methuen), 1987.
Gilbert, A., *Marx's Politics. Communists and Citizens* (Oxford: Martin Robertson), 1981.
Gilcher-Holtey, I., *Das Mandat des Intellektuellen. Karl Kautsky und die Sozialdemokratie* (Berlin: Siedler Verlag), 1986.
Girsberger, H. *Der utopische Sozialismus des 18. Jahrhunderts in Frankreich* (Wiesbaden: Focus Verlag), 1973.
Gleason, A., *Young Russia. The Genesis of Russian Radicalism in the 1860s* (New York: Viking Press), 1980.
Goldie, M., R. Wokler (eds), *The Cambridge History of Eighteenth-Century Political Thought* (Cambridge: Cambridge University Press), 2006.
Goodman, E.R., *The Soviet Design for a World State* (New York: Columbia University Press), 1960.
Goodman, J., K. Honeyman, *Gainful Pursuits. The Making of Industrial Europe 1600–1914* (London: Edward Arnold), 1988.
Gouldner, A.W., *The Two Marxisms. Contradictions and Anomalies in the Development of Theory* (London: Macmillan), 1980.
Grabes, H., '"Elect Nation": The founding myth of national identity in early modern England', in Grabes, H. (ed.), *Writing the Early Modern English Nation. The Transformation of National Identity in Sixteenth- and Seventeenth-Century England* (Amsterdam: Rodopi), 2001: 173–189.
Graeber, D., *Debt. The First 5,000 Years* (New York: Melville), 2012.
Grandjonc, J., *Communisme/Kommunismus/Communism. Origine et développement international de la terminologie communautaire prémarxiste des utopistes aux néo-babouvistes, 1785–1842*, vol. 1, *Historique* (Trier: Schriften aus dem Karl-Marx-Haus, no. 39,1), 1989.
Gregory, P.R., *Russian National Income, 1885–1913* (Cambridge: Cambridge University Press), 1982.
Gregory, P.R., N. Naimark (eds), *The Lost Politburo Transcripts. From Collective Rule to Stalin's Dictatorship* (New Haven, CT: Yale University Press), 2008.
Groh, D., *Negative Integration und revolutionärer Attentismus. Die deutsche Sozialdemokratie am Vorbend des Ersten Weltkrieges* (Berlin and Vienna: Ullstein), 1973.
Groh, D., P. Brandt, *'Vaterlandslose Gesellen'. Sozialdemokratie und Nation 1860–1990* (Munich: C.H. Beck), 1992.
Gronow, J., *On the Formation of Marxism. Karl Kautsky's Theory of Capitalism, the Marxism of the Second International and Karl Marx's Critique of Political economy* (Helsinki: Societas Scientiarum Fennica), 1986.
Gurney, J., 'Gerrard Winstanley's The Law of Freedom: context and continuity', in Ramiro, A. et al. (eds), *Utopian Moments. Reading Utopian Texts* (London and New York: Bloomsbury), 2012: 4–52.
Gusev, K.V., *V.M. Chernov. Shtrikhi k politicheskomu portretu* (Moscow: ROSSPEN), 1999.
Gustafsson, B., *Marxismus und Revisionismus. Eduard Bernsteins Kritik des Marxismus und ihre ideengeschichtlichen Voraussetzungen*, vol. 1 (Frankfurt M.: Europäische Verlagsanstalt), 1972.

Guy, J., *Tudor England* (Oxford: Oxford University Press), 1988.
Haakonssen, K., *Natural Law and Moral Philosophy. From Grotius to the Scottish Enlightenment* (Cambridge: Cambridge University Press), 1996.
Häfner, L., *Die Partei der Linken Sozialrevolutionären in der russischen Revolution von 1917/18* (Cologne: Böhlau Verlag), 1994.
Haimson, L.H., *The Russian Marxists and the Origins of Bolshevism* (Cambridge, MA: Harvard University Press), 1955.
Haller, W., *The Elect Nation. The Meaning and Relevance of Foxe's Book of Martyrs* (New York: Harper & Row), 1963.
Hamm, B., 'The urban Reformation in the Holy Roman Empire', in Brady, T.A. *et al.* (eds), *Handbook of European History, 1400–1600*, vol. 2, *Visions, Programs and Outcomes* (Leiden: Brill), 1995: 193–228.
Hampson, N., *The Enlightenment. An Evaluation of Its Assumptions, Attitudes and Values* (London: Penguin), 1987.
Hanagan, M.P., *Nascent Proletarians. Class Formation in Post-Revolutionary France* (Oxford and Cambridge, MA: Blackwell), 1989.
Hanisch, E., 'Im Zeichen von Otto Bauer. Deutschösterreichs Aussenpolitik in den Jahren 1918 bis 1919', in Konrad, H., W. Maderthaner (eds), *Das Werden der Ersten Republik...der Rest ist Österreich* (Vienna: Carl Gerold's Sohn Verlagsbuchhandlung KG), 2008, vol. 1: 207–222.
Hanisch, E., *Der grosse Illusionist. Otto Bauer (1881–1938)* (Vienna: Böhlau Verlag), 2011.
Hankins, J., 'The "Baron thesis" after forty years and some recent studies of Leonardo Bruni', in *Journal of the History of Ideas*, 1995, vol. 56, no. 2: 309–338.
Hanlon, G., *Early Modern Italy, 1550–1800. Three Seasons in European History* (London: Macmillan), 2000.
Hanschmidt, A., *Republikanisch-demokratischer Internationalismus im 19. Jahrhundert. Ideeen – Formen – Organisierungsversuche* (Husum: Matthiesen Verlag), 1977.
Harada, T., *Politische Ökonomie des Idealismus und der Romantik. Korporatismus von Fichte, Müller und Hegel* (Berlin: Duncker & Humblot), 1989.
Harding, N., *Lenin's Political Thought*, vol. 1, *Theory and Practice in the Democratic Revolution* (London: Macmillan), 1977; vol. 2, *Theory and Practice in the Socialist Revolution*, 1981.
Hardy, D., *Petr Tkachev, the Critic as Jacobin* (Seattle, WA: University of Washington Press), 1977.
Hardy, D., *Land and Freedom. The Origins of Russian Terrorism, 1876–1879* (New York: Greenwood Press), 1987.
Haupt, G., *La Deuxième Internationale 1880–1914. Essai bibliographique* (Paris), 1964.
Hautmann, H., *Geschichte der Rätebewegung in Österreich, 1918–1924* (Vienna and Zurich: Europaverlag), 1987.
Haynes, M., *Nikolai Bukharin & the Transition from Capitalism to Socialism* (London: Croom Helm), 1985.
Headley, J.M., *Tommaso Campanella and the Transformation of the World* (Princeton, NJ: Princeton University Press), 1997.
Hearder, H., *Italy in the Age of the Risorgimento, 1790–1870* (London and New York: Longman), 1990.
Heimann, H., T. Meyer (eds), *Bernstein und der Demokratische Sozialismus* (Berlin: Dietz Verlag), 1978.
Henning, F.-W., *Deutsche Wirtschafts- und Sozialgeschichte im 19. Jahrhundert* (Paderborn: Ferdinand Schöningh), 1996.

Herod, C.C., *The Nation in the History of Marxist Thought. The Concept of Nations with History and Nations without History* (The Hague: Martinus Nijhoff), 1976.
Hewitson, M., 'Wilhelmine Germany', in Retallack, J. (ed.), *Imperial Germany 1871–1918* (Oxford: Oxford University Press), 2008: 40–60.
Heymann, F.G., *John Žižka and the Hussite Revolution* (Princeton, NJ: Princeton University Press), 1955.
Hildermeier, M., *Die Sozialrevolutionäre Partei Russlands. Agrarsozialismus und Modernisierung im Zarenreich (1900–1914)* (Cologne: Böhlau Verlag), 1978.
Hildermeier, M., *Geschichte der Sowjetunion 1917–1991. Entstehung und Niedergang des ersten sozialistischen Staates* (Munich: C.H. Beck), 1998.
Hill, C., *Puritanism and Revolution. Studies in Interpretation of the English Revolution of the 17th Century* (London: Secker & Warburg), 1958.
Hill, C., *Lenin and the Russian Revolution* (London: English Universities Press), 1965.
Hill, C., *The World Turned Upside Down. Radical Ideas during the English Revolution* (London: Temple Smith), 1972.
Hill, C., *The Religion of Gerrard Winstanley* (Oxford: Past and Present Society), 1978.
Hill, C., 'A bourgeois revolution?', in Gaunt, P. (ed.), *The English Civil War. The Essential Readings* (Oxford and Cambridge, MA: Blackwell), 2000: 324–346.
Hirsch, H., *Der 'Fabier' Eduard Bernstein. Zur Entwicklungsgeschichte des evolutionären Sozialismus* (Berlin: Dietz Verlag), 1977.
Hobsbawm, E.J., *The Age of Revolution. Europe 1789–1848* (London: Weidenfeld & Nicolson), 1975.
Hobsbawm, E.J., *The Age of Empire, 1875–1914* (New York: Pantheon Books), 1987.
Hobsbawm, E.J., *How to Change the World. Marx and Marxism 1840–2011* (London: Little, Brown), 2011.
Höppner, J., W. Seidel-Höppner, *Von Babeuf bis Blanqui. Französischer Sozialismus und Kommunismus vor Marx*, vol. 1, *Einführung* (Leipzig: Philipp Reclam), 1975.
Hünlich, R., *Karl Kautsky und der Marxismus der II. Internationale* (Marburg: Verlag Arbeiterbewegung und Gesellschaftswissenschaft), 1981.
Hundt, M., 'Zur Entwicklung der marxistischen Revolutionstheorie nach der Revolution von 1848/49', in *Marx–Engels–Jahrbuch*, vol. 10 (Berlin: Dietz Verlag), 1987: 31–64.
Hundt, M., *Geschichte des Bundes der Kommunisten 1836–1852* (Frankfurt M.: Peter Lang), 1993.
Hunley, J.D., *The Life and Thought of Friedrich Engels. A Reinterpretation* (New Haven, CT: Yale University Press), 1991.
Hunt, R.N., *The Political Ideas of Marx and Engels. Marxism and Totalitarian Democracy, 1818–1850* (Pittsburgh, PA: University of Pittsburgh Press), 1974.
Hunt, T., *The Frock-Coated Communist. The Revolutionary Life of Friedrich Engels* (London: Allen Lane), 2009.
Immonen, H., *The Agrarian Program of the Russian Socialist Revolutionary Party, 1900–1914* (Helsinki: SHS), 1988.
Israel, J., *Revolutionary Ideas. An Intellectual History of the French Revolution from The Rights of Man to Robespierre* (Princeton, NJ: Princeton University Press), 2014.
Jansen, R., *Georg von Vollmar. Eine politische Biographie* (Düsseldorf: Droste Verlag), 1958.
Johnson, C.H., *Utopian Communism in France. Cabet and the Icarians, 1839–1851* (Ithaca, NY: Cornell University Press), 1974.
Johnson, P., *A History of Christianity* (London: Penguin), 1990.

216 References

Johnson, R.E., *Peasant and Proletarian. The Working Class of Moscow in the Late Nineteenth Century* (Leicester: Leicester University Press), 1979.

Joll, J., *The Second International 1889–1914* (London: Routledge & Kegan Paul), 1974.

Jowitt, C., '"The consolation of Israel": representations of Jewishness in the writings of Gerrard Winstanley and William Everard', in Bradstock, A. (ed.), *Winstanley and the Diggers, 1649–1999* (London: Frank Cass), 2000: 87–100.

Jung, W., *August Bebel. Deutscher Patriot und internationaler Sozialist. Seine Stellung zu Patriotismus und Internationalismus* (Pfaffenweiler: Centaurus Verlagsgesellschaft), 1986.

Kaminsky, H., *A History of the Hussite Revolution* (Berkeley, CA: University of California Press), 1967.

Kaminsky, H., 'From lateness to waning to crisis. The burden of the Later Middle Ages', in *Journal of Early Modern History*, 2000, vol. 4. no. 1: 85–125.

Kasprzak, M., 'To reject or not to reject nationalism: debating Marx and Engels' struggles with nationalism, 1840s–1880s', in *Nationalities Papers*, 2012, vol. 40, no. 4: 585–606.

Kautz, S., *Liberalism and Community* (Ithaca, NY: Cornell University Press), 1995.

Keep, J.L.H., *The Rise of Social Democracy in Russia* (Oxford: Clarendon), 1963.

Kelsen, H., *Sozialismus und Staat. Eine Untersuchung der politischen Theorie des Marxismus* (Leipzig: C.L. Hirschfeld), 1920.

Kemp, T., *Industrialization in Nineteenth-century Europe* (London: Longman), 1969.

Kemp-Welch, A. (ed.), *The Ideas of Nikolai Bukharin* (Oxford: Clarendon), 1992.

Kenyon, T., *Utopian Communism and Political Thought in Early Modern England* (London: Pinter), 1989.

Klassen, J.M., *The Nobility and the Making of the Hussite Revolution* (New York: Columbia University Press), 1978.

Kluge, U., *Die deutsche Revolution 1918/1919. Staat, Politik und Gesellschaft zwischen Weltkrieg und Kapp-Putsch* (Frankfurt M.: Suhrkamp), 1985.

Knapp, V.J., *Austrian Social Democracy, 1889–1914* (Washington, DC: University Press of America), 1980.

Knei-Paz, B., *The Social and Political Thought of Leon Trotsky* (Oxford: Clarendon), 1979.

Kolakowski, L., *Main Currents of Marxism*, vol. 1, *The Founders*, vol. 2, *The Golden Age* (Oxford: Oxford University Press), 1981.

Konrad, H., W. Maderthaner (eds), *Das Werden der Ersten Republik…der Rest ist Österreich*, vols 1 and 2 (Vienna: Carl Gerold's Sohn Verlagsbuchhandlung KG), 2008.

Korey, W., 'Zinov'ev's critique of Stalin's theory of socialism in one country, December 1925–December 1926', in *American Slavic and East European Review*, 1950, vol. 9, no. 4: 255–267.

Koselleck, R., 'Bund. Bündnis, Föderalismus, Bundesstaat', in Brunner, O., W. Conze, R. Koselleck (eds), *Geschichtliche Grundbegriffe. Historisches Lexikon zur politisch-sozialen Sprache in Deutschland*, vol. 1, *A–D* (Stuttgart: Ernst Klett Verlag), 1972: 582–671.

Kowalski, R.I., *The Bolshevik Party in Conflict. The Left Communist Opposition of 1918* (London: Macmillan), 1991.

Kowalski, R.I. (ed.), *The Russian Revolution, 1917–1921* (London and New York: Routledge), 1997.

Koz'min, B., *P.N. Tkachev i revoliutsionnoe dvizhenie 1860-kh godov* (Moscow: Novyi mir), 1922.
Kulke, H., D. Rothermund, *A History of India. Fifth Edition* (London and New York: Routledge), 2010.
Kumar, K., *The Making of English National Identity* (Cambridge: Cambridge University Press), 2003.
Kuromiya, H., *Stalin* (Harlow: Pearson), 2005.
Kuznets, S., *Modern Economic Growth. Rate, Structure, and Spread* (New Haven, CT: Yale University Press), 1967.
Lademacher, H., *Moses Hess in seiner Zeit* (Bonn: Ludwig Röhrscheid Verlag), 1977.
Lake, P., 'Calvinism and the English church 1570–1635', in Todd, M. (ed.), *Reformation to Revolution. Politics and Religion in Early Modern England* (London and New York: Routledge), 1995: 179–207.
Lambert, M., *The Cathars* (Oxford and Cambridge, MA: Blackwell), 1998.
Lambert, M., *Medieval Heresy. Popular Movements from Gregorian Reform to the Reformation. Third Edition* (Oxford and Cambridge, MA: Blackwell), 2010.
Lamont, W.M., *Godly Rule. Politics and Religion, 1603–60* (London: Macmillan), 1969.
Landauer, C., *European Socialism. A History of Ideas and Movements from the Industrial Revolution to Hitler's Seizure of Power*, vol. 1, *From the Industrial Revolution to the First World War and Its Aftermath* (Stanford, CA: Stanford University Press), 1959.
Landauer, C., 'Social democracy', in Drachkovitch, M.M., *The Revolutionary Internationals, 1864–1943* (Stanford, CA: Stanford University Press), 1966: 128–155.
Landes, D.S., *The Unbound Prometheus. Technological Change and Industrial Development in Western Europe from 1750 to the Present* (Cambridge: Cambridge University Press), 1969.
Lane, D., *The Roots of Russian Communism. A Social and Historical Study of Russian Social-Democracy 1898–1907* (Assen: Van Gorcum), 1969.
Lane, M., *Greek and Roman Political Ideas* (London: Penguin), 2014.
Larsson, R., *Theories of Revolution. From Marx to the First Russian Revolution* (Stockholm: Almqvist & Wiksell), 1970.
Lawday, D., *The Giant of the French Revolution. Danton, a Life* (New York: Grove), 2009.
Leff, G., *Heresy in the Later Middle Ages. The Relation of Heterodoxy to Dissent c.1250–c.1450*, vols 1 and 2 (Manchester: Manchester University Press), 1967.
Lehmann, H.G., *Die Agrarfrage in der Theorie und Praxis der deutschen und internationalen Sozialdemokratie. Vom Marxismus zum Revisionismus und Bolschewismus* (Tübingen: J.C.B. Mohr (Paul Siebeck)), 1970.
Leichter, O., *Otto Bauer. Tragödie oder Triumph* (Vienna and Zurich: Europa Verlag), 1970.
Leonard, C.S., *Agrarian Reform in Russia. The Road from Serfdom* (Cambridge: Cambridge University Press), 2011.
Leonhard, W., *Sowjetideologie heute*, vol. 2, *Die politischen Lehren* (Frankfurt M.: Fischer Bücherei), 1962.
Leonhard, W., *Die Dreispaltung des Marxismus. Ursprung und Entwicklung des Sowjetmarxismus, Maoismus und Reformkommunismus* (Düsseldorf: Econ Verlag), 1970.
Leopold, D., 'Socialism and (the rejection of) utopia', in *Journal of Political Ideologies*, 2007, vol. 12, no. 3: 219–237.

Leser, N., *Zwischen Reformismus und Bolschewismus. Der Austromarxismus als Theorie und Praxis* (Vienna and Zurich: Europa Verlag), 1968.
Levine, N., *The Tragic Deception. Marx Contra Engels* (Oxford: Clio), 1975.
Lichtheim, G., *Marxism. An Historical and Critical Study* (London: Routledge & Kegan Paul), 1961.
Lidtke, V.L., 'German social democracy and German state socialism, 1876–1884', in *International Review of Social History*, 1964, vol. 9, no. 2: 202–225.
Lidtke, V.L., *The Outlawed Party. Social Democracy in Germany, 1878–1890* (Princeton, NJ: Princeton University Press), 1966.
Lidtke, V.L., *The Alternative Culture. Socialist Labor in Imperial Germany* (Oxford: Oxford University Press), 1985.
Lieven, D. (ed.), *The Cambridge History of Russia*, vol. 2, *Imperial Russia, 1689–1917* (Cambridge: Cambridge University Press), 2006.
Lih, L.T., *Lenin* (London: Reaktion), 2011a.
Lih, L.T., 'The ironic triumph of Old Bolshevism: the debates of April 1917 in context', in *Russian History*, 2011b, vol. 38, no. 2: 199–242.
Lih, L.T., 'Democratic Revolution in Permanenz', in *Science & Society*, 2012, vol. 76, no. 4: 433–462.
Linton, M., *Choosing Terror. Virtue, Friendship, and Authenticity in the French Revolution* (Oxford: Oxford University Press), 2013.
List, G., *Chiliastische Utopie und radikale Reformation. Die Erneuerung der Idee vom tausendjährigen Reich im 16. Jahrhundert* (Munich: Wilhelm Fink), 1973.
Löwy, M., *The Politics of Combined and Uneven Development. The Theory of Permanent Revolution* (London: Verso), 1981.
Löwy, M., *The Theory of Revolution in the Young Marx* (Leiden: Brill), 2003.
Loades, D., *Power in Tudor England* (New York: St Martin's Press), 1997.
Logan, G.M., *The Meaning of More's 'Utopia'* (Princeton, NJ: Princeton University Press), 1983.
Loubère, L.A., 'The intellectual origins of French Jacobin socialism', in *International Review of Social History*, 1959, vol. 4, no. 3: 415–431.
Low, A.D., *The Anschluss Movement 1918–1919 and the Paris Peace Conference* (Philadelphia, PA: American Philosophical Society), 1974.
McDermott, K., *Stalin* (Basingstoke: Macmillan), 2006.
Macek, J., *The Hussite Movement in Bohemia. Second, Enlarged Edition* (Prague: Orbis), 1958.
McGinn, B., *Visions of the End. Apocalyptic Traditions in the Middle Ages* (New York: Columbia University Press), 1979.
McGowen, R., 'Law and Enlightenment', in Fitzpatrick, M. *et al.* (eds), *The Enlightenment World* (London and New York: Routledge), 2004: 502–514.
Mackenzie Wallace, D., *Russia. Revised and Enlarged Edition* (London: Cassell), 1912.
McLellan, D., *Karl Marx. His Life and Thought* (London: Macmillan), 1973.
McLellan, D., *Engels* (Hassocks: Harvester), 1977.
McLellan, D., *Marxism after Marx. An Introduction* (London: Macmillan), 1979.
McPhee, P. (ed.), *A Companion to the French Revolution* (Oxford and Cambridge, MA: Wiley-Blackwell), 2013.
Maddison, A., *Dynamic Forces in Capitalist Development. A Long-Run Comparative View* (Oxford: Oxford University Press), 1991.
Maddison, A., *Monitoring the World Economy, 1820–1992* (Paris: Development Centre of the OECD), 1995.

Maderthaner, W., 'Die eigenartige Grösse der Beschränkung. Österreichs Revolution im mitteleuropäischen Spannungsfeld', in Konrad, H., W. Maderthaner (eds), *Das Werden der Ersten Republik...der Rest ist Österreich* (Vienna: Carl Gerold's Sohn Verlagsbuchhandlung KG), 2008, vol. 1: 187–206.

Maehl, W., 'The triumph of nationalism in the German socialist party on the eve of the First World War', in *Journal of Modern History*, 1952, vol. 24, no. 1: 15–41.

Maehl, W., *August Bebel. Shadow Emperor of the German Workers* (Philadelphia, PA: American Philosophical Society), 1980.

Magraw, R., *A History of the French Working Class*, vol. 1, *The Age of Artisan Revolution, 1815–1871* (Oxford and Cambridge, MA: Blackwell), 1992.

Malia, M., *Alexander Herzen and the Birth of Russian Socialism* (New York: Grosset & Dunlap), 1965.

Malle, S., *The Economic Organization of War Communism, 1918–1921* (Cambridge: Cambridge University Press), 1985.

Manuel, F.E., *The New World of Henri Saint-Simon* (Cambridge, MA: Harvard University Press), 1956.

Manuel, F.E. (ed.), *The Enlightenment* (Englewood Cliffs, NJ: Prentice-Hall), 1965.

Manuel, F.E., 'Toward a psychological history of utopias', in Manuel, F.E. (ed.), *Utopias and Utopian Thought* (Boston, MA: Houghton Mifflin), 1966: 69–98.

Manuel, F.E. (ed.), *Utopias and Utopian Thought* (Boston, MA: Houghton Mifflin), 1966.

Manuel, F.E., *A Requiem for Karl Marx* (Cambridge, MA: Harvard University Press), 1995.

Marek, F., *Philosophy of World Revolution. A Contribution to an Anthology of Theories of Revolution* (London: Lawrence & Wishart), 1969.

Marot, J.E., *The October Revolution in Prospect and Retrospect. Interventions in Russian and Soviet History* (Leiden: Brill), 2012.

Martow, J., T. Dan, *Geschichte der russischen Sozialdemokratie* (Erlangen: Politladen Erlangen), 1973.

Mason, L., 'The Thermidorian Reaction', in McPhee, P. (ed.), *A Companion to the French Revolution* (Oxford and Cambridge, MA: Wiley-Blackwell), 2013: 313–327.

Mastnak, T., 'Abbé de Saint-Pierre: European union and the Turk', in *History of Political Thought*, 1998, vol. 19, no. 4: 570–598.

Matthias, E., 'Kautsky und der Kautskyanismus. Die Funktion der Ideologie in der deutschen Sozialdemokratie vor dem ersten Weltkriege', in *Marxismusstudien. Zweite Folge* (Tübingen: J.C.B. Mohr (Paul Siebeck)), 1957: 151–197.

Matthias, E., *Zwischen Räten und Geheimräten. Die deutsche Revolutionsregierung 1918/19* (Düsseldorf: Droste), 1970.

Mawdsley, E., *The Russian Civil War* (Edinburgh: Birlinn), 2011.

Mehring, F., *Karl Marx. Geschichte seines Lebens* (Leipzig: Verlag der Leipziger Buchdruckerei), 1920.

Mehring, F., *Geschichte der deutschen Sozialdemokratie*, vol. 2, *Von Lassalles 'Offenem Antwortschreiben' bis zum Erfurter Programm 1863 bis 1891* (Berlin: Dietz Verlag), 1976.

Merriman, J., *A History of Modern Europe. From the Renaissance to the Present. Second Edition* (New York and London: W.W. Norton), 2004.

Mevius, M., 'Reappraising communism and nationalism', in Mevius, M. (ed.), *The Communist Quest for National Legitimacy in Europe, 1918–1989* (London and New York: Routledge), 2011: 1–24.

Meyer, A.G., *Leninism* (Cambridge, MA: Harvard University Press), 1957.
Miller, M.A. (ed.), *The Russian Revolution. The Essential Readings* (Oxford and Cambridge, MA: Blackwell), 2001.
Miller, S., *Burgfrieden und Klassenkampf. Die deutsche Sozialdemokratie im Ersten Weltkrieg* (Düsseldorf: Droste Verlag), 1974.
Miller, S., *Die Bürde der Macht. Die deutsche Sozialdemokratie 1918–1920* (Düsseldorf: Droste Verlag), 1978.
Miller, S., H. Potthoff, *A History of German Social Democracy from 1848 to the Present* (New York: Berg), 1986.
Mironov, B.N., B. Eklof, *The Social History of Imperial Russia, 1700–1917*, vol. 2 (Boulder, CO: Westview), 2000.
Mommsen, H., 'Nationalismus und nationale Frage im Denken Eduard Bernsteins', in Heimann, H., T. Meyer (eds), *Bernstein und der Demokratische Sozialismus* (Berlin: Dietz Verlag), 1978: 131–148.
Mommsen, H., *Arbeiterbewegung und Nationale Frage. Ausgewählte Aufsätze* (Göttingen: Vandenhoeck & Ruprecht), 1979.
Mommsen, W.J., *Imperial Germany, 1867–1918. Politics, Culture, and Society in an Authoritarian State* (London: Arnold), 1959.
Morgan, D.W., *The Socialist Left and the German Revolution. A History of the German Independent Social Democratic Party, 1917–1922* (Ithaca, NY: Cornell University Press), 1975.
Morgan, D.W., 'Ernst Däumig and the German Revolution of 1918', in *Central European History*, 1982, vol. 15, no. 4: 303–331.
Morrill, B. Manning, D. Underdown, 'What was the English Revolution?', in Gaunt, P. (ed.), *The English Civil War. The Essential Readings* (Oxford and Cambridge, MA: Blackwell), 2000: 14–32.
Moss, B.H., *The Origins of the French Labor Movement, 1830–1914. The Socialism of Skilled Workers* (Berkeley, CA: University of California Press), 1976.
Mühlhausen, W., *Friedrich Ebert 1871–1925. Reichspräsident der Weimarer Republik* (Berlin: Dietz Verlag), 2007.
Mumford, L., *The Story of Utopias* (Gloucester, MA: Peter Smith), 1959.
Munck, R., *The Difficult Dialogue. Marxism and Nationalism* (London: Zed Books), 1986.
Munting, R., 'Industrial revolution in Russia', in Teich, M., R. Porter (eds), *The Industrial Revolution in National Context. Europe and the USA* (Cambridge: Cambridge University Press), 1996: 329–349.
Na'aman, S., *Lassalle* (Hanover: Verlag für Literatur und Zeitgeschehen), 1970.
Na'aman, S., *Emanzipation und Messianismus. Leben und Werk des Moses Hess* (Frankfurt and New York: Campus Verlag), 1982.
Nation, R.C., *War on War. Lenin, the Zimmerwald Left, and the Origins of Communist Internationalism* (Durham, NC: Duke University Press), 1989.
Nelson, E., *The Greek Tradition in Republican Thought* (Cambridge: Cambridge University Press), 2004.
Nettl, J.P., *Rosa Luxemburg*, 2 vols (Oxford: Oxford University Press), 1966.
Niemeyer, G., 'The Second International: 1889–1914', in Drachkovitch, M.M. (ed.), *The Revolutionary Internationals, 1864–1943* (Stanford, CA: Stanford University Press), 1966: 95–127.
Nimni, E., *Marxism and Nationalism. Theoretical Origins of a Political Crisis* (London: Pluto), 1991.

Nimtz, A.H., *Marx and Engels. Their Contribution to the Democratic Breakthrough* (New York: State University of New York Press), 2000.
Nove, A., *An Economic History of the USSR, 1917–1991. New and Final Edition* (London: Penguin), 1992a.
Nove, A., 'Bukharin as economist', in Kemp-Welch, A. (ed.), *The Ideas of Nikolai Bukharin* (Oxford: Clarendon), 1992b: 25–39.
Noyes, P.H., *Organization and Revolution. Working-Class Associations in the German Revolutions of 1848–1849* (Princeton, NJ), 1966.
O'Boyle, L., 'Theories of socialist imperialism', in *Foreign Affairs*, 1949–1950, vol. 28, nos. 1–4: 290–298.
Offord, D., *The Russian Revolutionary Movement in the 1880s* (Cambridge: Cambridge University Press), 1986.
Oizerman, T.I., 'Marxism and utopianism', in *Russian Studies in Philosophy*, 2001, vol. 39, no. 4: 54–79.
Packull, W.O., *Hutterite Beginnings. Communitarian Experiments during the Reformation* (Baltimore, MD: John Hopkins University Press), 1995.
Palmer, R.R., J. Colton, *A History of the Modern World. Seventh Edition* (New York: McGraw-Hill), 1992.
Panzenböck, E., *Ein deutscher Traum. Die Anschlussidee und Anschlusspolitik bei Karl Renner und Otto Bauer* (Vienna: Europaverlag), 1985.
Pavlov, D.B., *Esery-maksimalisty v pervoi russkoi revoliutsii* (Moscow: Izdatel'stvo Vsesoiuznogo zaochnogo politicheskogo instituta), 1989.
Paxton, J., *Imperial Russia. A Reference Handbook* (Basingstoke: Palgrave Macmillan), 2001.
Pelczynski, Z.A., 'Nation, civil society, state: Hegelian sources of the Marxist non-theory of nationality', in Pelczynski, Z.A. (ed.), *The State and Civil Society. Studies in Hegel's Political Philosophy* (Cambridge: Cambridge University Press), 1984: 262–278.
Pereira, N.G.O., *The Thought and Teachings of N.G. Černyševskij* (The Hague: Mouton), 1975.
Perrie, M., *The Agrarian Policy of the Russian Socialist-Revolutionary Party. From its Origins through the Revolution of 1905–1907* (Cambridge: Cambridge University Press), 1976.
Petegorsky, D.W., *Left-wing Democracy in the English Civil War. Gerrard Winstanley and the Digger Movement* (London: Sandpiper Books), 1999.
Pilbeam, P., *French Socialists Before Marx. Workers, Women and the Social Question in France* (Teddington: Acumen), 2000a.
Pilbeam, P., *The Constitutional Monarchy in France 1814–48* (Harlow: Longman), 2000b.
Pipes, R., 'Narodnichestvo: a semantic inquiry', in *Slavic Review*, 1964, vol. 23, no. 3: 441–458.
Pipes, R., *The Russian Revolution* (New York: Alfred A. Knopf), 1990.
Pipes, R., *Russia under the Bolshevik Regime, 1919–1924* (London: Harvill), 1994.
Pipes, R., *A Concise History of the Russian Revolution* (New York: Vintage), 1996.
Plamenatz, J., *German Marxism and Russian Communism* (London: Longman), 1954.
Plamenatz, J., *Man and Society. Political and Social Theories from Machiavelli to Marx*, vol. 3, *Hegel, Marx and Engels, and the Idea of Progress. New, Revised Edition* (London: Longman), 1992.
Pocock, J.G.A., *The Machiavellian Moment. Florentine Political Thought and the Atlantic Republican Tradition* (Princeton, NJ: Princeton University Press), 1975.

Pocock, J.G.A., 'Machiavelli and Rome: the republic as ideal and as history', in Najemy, J.M. (ed.), *The Cambridge Companion to Machiavelli* (Cambridge: Cambridge University Press), 2010: 144–156.

Pohl, N., 'Utopianism after More. The Renaissance and Enlightenment', in Claeys, G. (ed.), *The Cambridge Companion to Utopian Literature* (Cambridge: Cambridge University Press), 2010: 51–78.

Polinger, E.H., 'Saint-Simon, the utopian precursor of the League of Nations', in *Journal of the History of Ideas*, 1943, vol. 4, no. 4: 475–483.

Polunov, A., *Russia in the Nineteenth Century. Autocracy, Reform, and Social Change, 1814–1914* (New York and London: M.E. Sharpe), 2005.

Pomper, P., *The Russian Revolutionary Intelligentsia* (New York: Thomas Y. Crowell), 1971.

Pomper, P., *Peter Lavrov and the Russian Revolutionary Movement* (Chicago, IL: University of Chicago Press), 1972.

Pomper, P., *Sergei Nechaev* (New Brunswick, NJ: Rutgers University Press), 1979.

Poster, M., *The Utopian Thought of Restif de la Bretonne* (New York: New York University Press), 1971.

Price, R., *An Economic History of Modern France, 1730–1914* (London: Macmillan), 1981.

Priestland, D., *Stalinism and the Politics of Mobilization. Ideas, Power, and Terror in Inter-War Russia* (Oxford: Oxford University Press), 2007.

Priestland, D., *The Red Flag. Communism and the Making of the Modern World* (London: Allen Lane), 2009.

Primoratz, I., 'Patriotism', in Zalta, E.N. (ed.), *The Stanford Encyclopedia of Philosophy* (edition Fall 2013). Available at: http://plato.stanford.edu/archives/fall2013/entries/patriotism/ [retrieved 29 September 2014].

Probert, P., '"Our natural ally". Anglo-German relations and the contradictory agendas of Wilhelmine socialism, 1879–1900', in Eley, G., J. Retallack (eds), *Wilhelminism and Its Legacies. German Modernities, Imperialism and the Meanings of Reform, 1890–1930* (New York and Oxford: Berghahn), 2003: 123–137.

Rabinowitch, A., *The Bolsheviks Come to Power. The Revolution of 1917 in Petrograd* (New York and London: W.W. Norton), 1976.

Radkey, O.H., *The Agrarian Foes of Bolshevism. Promise and Default of the Russian Socialist Revolutionaries February to October 1917* (New York: Columbia University Press), 1958.

Radkey, O.H., *The Sickle under the Hammer. The Russian Socialist Revolutionaries in the Early Months of Soviet Rule* (New York: Columbia University Press), 1963.

Raleigh, D.J., 'The Russian civil war, 1917–1922', in Suny, R.G. (ed.), *The Cambridge History of Russia*, vol. 3, *The Twentieth Century* (Cambridge: Cambridge University Press), 2006: 140–167.

Ramiro Avilés, M.A., J.C. Davis (eds), *Utopian Moments. Reading Utopian Texts* (London and New York: Bloomsbury), 2012.

Ramm, T., *Ferdinand Lassalle als Rechts- und Sozialphilosoph* (Meisenheim and Vienna: Westkulturverlag Anton Hain), 1953.

Ramm, T., 'Die künftige Gesellschaftsordnung nach der Theorie von Marx und Engels', in *Marxismusstudien. Zweite Folge* (Tübingen: J.C.B. Mohr (Paul Siebeck)), 1957: 77–119.

Rapport, M., 'The international repercussions of the French Revolution', in McPhee, P. (ed.), *A Companion to the French Revolution* (Oxford and Cambridge, MA: Wiley-Blackwell), 2013: 381–396.

Rauchensteiner, M., '"Das neue Jahr machte bei uns einen traurigen Einzug". Das Ende des Grossen Krieges', in Konrad, H., W. Maderthaner (eds), *Das Werden der Ersten Republik...der Rest ist Österreich* (Vienna: Carl Gerold's Sohn Verlagsbuchhandlung KG), 2008, vol. 1: 21–44.

Read, C., *Lenin. A Revolutionary Life* (New York: Routledge), 2005.

Read, C., *War and Revolution in Russia, 1914–22* (Basingstoke: Palgrave Macmillan), 2013.

Rihs, C., *Les philosophes utopistes. Le mythe de la cité communautaire en France au XVIIIe siècle* (Paris: Marcel Rivière), 1970.

Rikli, E., *Der Revisionismus. Ein Revisionsversuch der deutschen marxistischen Theorie (1890–1914)* (Zurich: H. Girsberger), 1936.

Roche, D., 'Encyclopedias and the diffusion of knowledge', in Goldie, M., R. Wokler (eds), *The Cambridge History of Eighteenth-Century Political Thought* (Cambridge: Cambridge University Press), 2006: 172–194.

Rojahn, J., 'War die deutsche Sozialdemokratie ein Modell für die Parteien der Zweiten Internationale?', in *Internationale Korrespondenz zur Geschichte der deutschen Arbeiterbewegung*, 1991, vol. 27, no. 3: 291–303.

Rosdolsky, R., *Engels and the 'Nonhistoric' Peoples. The National Question in the Revolution of 1848* (Glasgow: Critique Books), 1986.

Rose, R.B., *Gracchus Babeuf. The First Revolutionary Communist* (Stanford, CA: Stanford University Press), 1978.

Roth, G., *The Social Democrats in Imperial Germany. A Study in Working-Class Isolation and National Integration* (Totowa, NJ: Bedminster Press), 1963.

Rudé, G., *The French Revolution* (London: Phoenix), 1994.

Rudnitskaia, E.L., *Russkii blankizm: Petr Tkachev* (Moscow: Nauka), 1992.

Russell, Conrad, 'England in 1637', in Todd, M. (ed.), *Reformation to Revolution. Politics and Religion in Early Modern England* (London and New York: Routledge), 1995: 116–141.

Ryan, J., *Lenin's Terror. The Ideological Origins of Early Soviet State Violence* (London and New York: Routledge), 2012.

Ryder, A.J., *The German Revolution of 1918. A Study of German Socialism in War and Revolt* (Cambridge: Cambridge University Press), 1967.

Saage, R., 'Die deutsche Frage. Die Erste Republik im Spannungsfeld zwischen österreichischer und deutscher Identität', in Konrad, H., W. Maderthaner (eds), *Das Werden der Ersten Republik...der Rest ist Österreich* (Vienna: Carl Gerold's Sohn Verlagsbuchhandlung KG), 2008, vol. 1: 65–82.

Salvadori, M., *Karl Kautsky and the Socialist Revolution, 1880–1938* (London: NLB), 1979.

Sanchez-Sibony, O., 'Depression Stalinism. The Great Break reconsidered', in *Kritika*, 2014, vol. 15, no. 1: 23–49.

Sarti, R., 'Giuseppe Mazzini and his opponents', in Davis, J.A. (ed.), *Italy in the Nineteenth Century* (Oxford: Oxford University Press), 2000: 74–107.

Savel'ev, P.Iu., S.V. Tiutiukin, 'Iulii Osipovich Martov (1873–1923). The man and the politician', in *Russian Studies in History*, 2006, vol. 45, no. 1: 6–92.

Saxby, T.J., *Pilgrims of a Common Life. Christian Community of Goods through the Centuries* (Scottdale: Herald Press), 1987.

Schaer, R., G. Claeys, L.T. Sargent (eds), *Utopia. The Search for the Ideal Society in the Western World* (New York and Oxford: New York Public Library, Oxford University Press), 2000.

Schama, S., *Citizens. A Chronicle of the French Revolution* (London: Penguin), 1989.
Scharlau, W., *Parvus-Helphand als Theoretiker in der deutschen Sozialdemokratie und seine Rolle in der ersten russischen Revolution (1867–1910)* (PhD dissertation Wilhelms-Universität zu Münster), 1964.
Schieck, H., 'Die Behandlung der Sozialisierungsfrage in den Monaten nach dem Staatsumsturz', in Kolb, E. (ed.), *Vom Kaiserreich zur Weimarer Republik* (Cologne: Kiepenheuer & Witsch), 1972: 138–164.
Schieder, W., *Anfänge der deutschen Arbeiterbewegung. Die Auslandsvereine im Jahrzehnt nach der Julirevolution von 1830* (Stuttgart: Klett), 1963.
Schieder, W., *Karl Marx als Politiker* (Munich and Zurich: Piper), 1991.
Schmidt, J., *August Bebel. Kaiser der Arbeiter. Eine Biographie* (Zurich: Rotpunktverlag), 2013.
Schraepler, E., *Handwerkerbünde und Arbeitervereine, 1830–1853. Die politische Tätigkeit deutscher Sozialisten von Wilhelm Weitling bis Karl Marx* (Berlin and New York: de Gruyter), 1972.
Schröder, H.-C., 'Eduard Bernsteins Stellung zum Imperialismus vor dem Ersten Weltkrieg', in Heimann, H., T. Meyer (eds), *Bernstein und der Demokratische Sozialismus* (Berlin: Dietz Verlag), 1978: 166–212.
Schroeder, P.W., *The Transformation of European Politics, 1763–1848* (Oxford: Clarendon), 1994.
Schuurman, P., 'Fénelon on luxury, war and trade in the Telemachus', in *History of European Ideas*, 2012, vol. 38, no. 2: 179–199.
Schwarz, R., *Die apokalyptische Theologie Thomas Müntzers und der Taboriten* (Tübingen: J.C.B. Mohr (Paul Siebeck)), 1977.
Schwarz, S.M., *The Russian Revolution of 1905. The Workers' Movement and the Formation of Bolshevism and Menshevism* (Chicago, IL: University of Chicago Press), 1967.
Scott, T., *Thomas Müntzer. Theology and Revolution in the German Reformation* (New York: St Martin's Press), 1989.
Seebacher-Brandt, B., *Bebel. Künder und Kärrner im Kaiserreich* (Berlin: Dietz Verlag), 1988.
Seidel-Höppner, W., *Wilhelm Weitling – der erste deutsche Theoretiker und Agitator des Kommunismus* (Berlin: Dietz Verlag), 1961.
Service, R., *Lenin. A Biography* (Cambridge, MA: Harvard University Press), 2000.
Service, R., *Stalin. A Biography* (London: Macmillan), 2004.
Service, R., *Trotsky. A Biography* (Cambridge, MA: Harvard University Press), 2009.
Shanin, T. (ed.), *Late Marx and the Russian Road. Marx and 'The Peripheries of Capitalism'* (London: Routledge & Kegan Paul), 1983.
Sharpe, K., 'Archbishop Laud', in Todd, M. (ed.), *Reformation to Revolution. Politics and Religion in Early Modern England* (London and New York: Routledge), 1995: 71–77.
Shilliam, R., 'Marx's path to *Capital*: the international dimension of an intellectual journey', in *History of Political Thought*, 2006, vol. 27, no. 2: 349–375.
Shulman, G.M., *Radicalism and Reverence. The Political Thought of Gerrard Winstanley* (Berkeley, CA: University of California Press), 1989.
Sigel, R., *Die Lensch-Cunow-Haenisch-Gruppe. Eine Studie zum rechten Flügel der SPD im Ersten Weltkrieg* (Berlin: Duncker & Humblot), 1976.
Silberner, E., *Moses Hess. Geschichte seines Lebens* (Leiden: Brill), 1966.
Skinner, Q., *The Foundations of Modern Political Thought*, vol. 1, *The Renaissance* (Cambridge: Cambridge University Press), 1978.

Slusser, R.M., *Stalin in October. The Man who Missed the Revolution* (Baltimore, MD: John Hopkins University Press), 1987.
Smaldone, W., *Rudolf Hilferding. The Tragedy of a German Social Democrat* (DeKalb, IL: Northern Illinois University Press), 1998.
Smaldone, W., *European Socialism. A Concise History with Documents* (Lanham, MD: Rowman & Littlefield), 2014.
Smirin, M.M., *Die Volksreformation des Thomas Münzer und der Grosse Bauernkrieg* (Berlin: Dietz Verlag), 1922.
Smith, J.M., *Nobility Reimagined. The Patriotic Nation in Eighteenth-Century France* (Ithaca, NY: Cornell University Press), 2005.
Smith, S.B., *Captives of Revolution. The Socialist Revolutionaries and the Bolshevik Dictatorship, 1918–1923* (Pittsburgh, PA: University of Pittsburgh Press), 2011.
Smith, S.A., *The Russian Revolution. A Very Short Introduction* (Oxford: Oxford University Press), 2002.
Soell, H., 'Weltmarkt-Revolution-Staatenwelt. Zum Problem einer Theorie internationaler Beziehungen bei Marx und Engels', in *Archiv für Sozialgeschichte*, 1972, vol. 12: 109–184.
Sonenscher, M., 'Property, community, and citizenship', in Goldie, M., R. Wokler (eds), *The Cambridge History of Eighteenth-Century Political Thought* (Cambridge: Cambridge University Press), 2006: 465–494.
Sperber, J., *The Kaiser's Votes. Electors and Elections in Imperial Germany* (Cambridge: Cambridge University Press), 1997.
Sperber, J., *Karl Marx. A Nineteenth-Century Life* (New York and London: W.W. Norton), 2013.
Spitzer, A.B., *The Revolutionary Theories of Louis Auguste Blanqui* (New York: Columbia University Press), 1957.
Stadler, K.R., *The Birth of the Austrian Republic, 1918–1921* (Leiden: Sijthoff), 1966.
Stayer, J.M., *The German Peasants' War and Anabaptist Community of Goods* (Montreal: McGill-Queen's University Press) 1994.
Stayer, J.M., 'The radical Reformation', in Brady, T.A. et al. (eds), *Handbook of European History, 1400–1600*, vol. 2, *Visions, Programs and Outcomes* (Leiden: Brill), 1995: 249–282.
Stayer, J.M., 'Chiliasmus', in Goertz, H.-J. (ed.), *Mennonitisches Lexikon*, vol. 5, *Revision und Ergänzung* part 2, 2010–14. Available at: www.mennlex.de/doku.php?id=top:chiliasmus [retrieved 22 April 2014].
Steenson, G.P., *Karl Kautsky, 1854–1938. Marxism in the Classical Years* (Pittsburgh, PA: University of Pittsburgh Press), 1978.
Steenson, G.P., *'Not One Man! Not One Penny!' German Social Democracy, 1863–1914* (Pittsburgh, PA: University of Pittsburgh Press), 1981.
Steenson, G.P., *After Marx, Before Lenin. Marxism and Socialist Working-Class Parties in Europe, 1884–1914* (Pittsburgh, PA: University of Pittsburgh Press), 1991.
Steger, M.B., *The Quest for Evolutionary Socialism. Eduard Bernstein and Social Democracy* (Cambridge: Cambridge University Press), 1997.
Steinberg, H.-J., 'Die deutsche Sozialdemokratie nach dem Fall des Sozialistengesetzes. Ideologie und Taktik der sozialistischen Massenpartei im Wilhelminischen Reich', in Mommsen, H. (ed.), *Sozialdemokratie zwischen Klassenbewegung und Volkspartei* (Frankfurt M.: Athenäum), 1974: 52–61.
Steinberg, H.-J., *Sozialismus und deutsche Sozialdemokratie. Zur Ideologie der Partei vor dem 1. Weltkrieg. 5., erweiterte Auflage* (Berlin: Dietz Verlag), 1979.

Stöger, R., 'Der kurze Traum. Strategie und Praxis der Sozialisierung', in Konrad, H., W. Maderthaner (eds), *Das Werden der Ersten Republik...der Rest ist Österreich*, (Vienna: Carl Gerold's Sohn Verlagsbuchhandlung KG), vol. 2, 2008: 123–138.

Ströbel, H., *Die deutsche Revolution. Ihr Unglück und ihre Rettung* (Berlin: Der Firn), 1920.

Suny, R.G. (ed.), *The Cambridge History of Russia*, vol. 3, *The Twentieth Century* (Cambridge: Cambridge University Press), 2006.

Suny, R.G. (ed.), *The Soviet Experiment. Russia, the USSR, and the Successor States. Second Edition* (Oxford: Oxford University Press), 2011.

Sutherland, D., 'Urban crowds, riot, utopia, and massacres, 1789–92', in McPhee, P. (ed.), *A Companion to the French Revolution* (Oxford and Cambridge, MA: Wiley-Blackwell), 2013: 231–245.

Swain, Geoffrey, *The Origins of the Russian Civil War* (London: Longman), 1996.

Swain, Geoffrey, *Trotsky* (London: Longman), 2006.

Sylla, R., G. Toniolo, 'Introduction: patterns of European industrialization during the nineteenth century', in Sylla, R., G. Toniolo (eds), *Patterns of European Industrialization. The Nineteenth Century* (London and New York: Routledge), 1991: 1–26.

Szporluk, R., *Communism and Nationalism. Karl Marx versus Friedrich List* (Oxford: Oxford University Press), 1988.

Taylor, D., 'Gerrard Winstanley at Cobham', in Bradstock, A. (ed.), *Winstanley and the Diggers, 1649–1999* (London: Frank Cass), 2000: 37–41.

Taylor, K., *The Political Ideas of Utopian Socialists* (London: Frank Cass), 1982.

Thatcher, I.D., 'Uneven and combined development', in *Revolutionary Russia*, 1991, vol. 4, no. 2: 235–258.

Thatcher, I.D., *Trotsky* (London and New York: Routledge), 2003.

Tilly, R., 'Germany', in Sylla, R., G. Toniolo (eds), *Patterns of European Industrialization. The Nineteenth Century* (London and New York: Routledge), 1991: 175–196.

Tipton, F.B., 'The regional dimension: economic geography, economic development, and national integration in the nineteenth and twentieth centuries', in Ogilvie, S., R. Overy (eds), *Germany. A New Social and Economic History*, vol. 3, *Since 1800* (London: Arnold), 2003a: 1–34.

Tipton, F.B., 'Government and the economy in the nineteenth century', in Ogilvie, S., R. Overy (eds), *Germany. A New Social and Economic History*, vol. 3, *Since 1800* (London: Arnold), 2003b: 106–151.

Tiutiukin, S.V., *Voina, mir, revoliutsiia. Ideinaia bor'ba v rabochem dvizhenii Rossii 1914–1917gg* (Moscow: Mysl'), 1972.

Tiutiukin, S.V., *G.V. Plekhanov. Sud'ba russkogo marksista* (Moscow: ROSSPEN), 1997.

Todd, M. (ed.), *Reformation to Revolution. Politics and Religion in Early Modern England* (London and New York: Routledge), 1995.

Tomaselli, S., 'The spirit of nations', in Goldie, M., R. Wokler (eds), *The Cambridge History of Eighteenth-Century Political Thought* (Cambridge: Cambridge University Press), 2006: 9–39.

Tucker, R.C., *The Marxian Revolutionary Idea* (London: Allen & Unwin), 1969.

Tucker, R.C., *Stalin as Revolutionary. 1879–1929. A Study in History and Personality* (New York and London: W.W. Norton), 1974.

Tudor, H., J.M. Tudor (eds), *Marxism and Social Democracy. The Revisionist Debate, 1896–1898* (Cambridge: Cambridge University Press), 1988.

Tyacke, N., 'Puritanism, Arminianism and counter-revolution', in Todd, M. (ed.), *Reformation to Revolution. Politics and Religion in Early Modern England* (London and New York: Routledge), 1995: 53–70.
Ulam, A.B., *In the Name of the People. Prophets and Conspirators in Prerevolutionary Russia* (New York: Viking Press), 1977.
van der Linden, M., 'The national integration of European working classes (1871–1914). Exploring the causal configuration', in *International Review of Social History*, 1988, vol. 33, no. 3: 285–311.
van der Linden, W.H., *The International Peace Movement 1815–1874* (Amsterdam: Tilleul Publications), 1987.
van Ree, E., 'Socialism in one country: a reassessment', in *Studies in East European Thought*, 1998, vol. 50, no. 2: 77–117.
van Ree, E., 'Nationalist elements in the work of Marx and Engels. A critical survey', in *MEGA-Studien*, 2000, no. 1: 25–49.
van Ree, E., *The Political Thought of Joseph Stalin. A Study in Twentieth-Century Revolutionary Patriotism* (London and New York: RoutledgeCurzon), 2002.
van Ree, E., 'Lenin's conception of socialism in one country, 1915–17', in *Revolutionary Russia*, 2010, vol. 23, no. 2: 159–181.
van Ree, E., '"Socialism in one country" before Stalin German origins', in *Journal of Political Ideologies*, 2010, vol. 15, no. 2: 143–159.
van Ree, E., 'German Marxism and the decline of the permanent revolution, 1870–1909', in *History of European Ideas*, 2012, vol. 38, no. 4: 570–589.
van Ree, E., 'Georgii Plekhanov and the Communist Manifesto: the proletarian revolution revisited', in *Revolutionary Russia*, 2013, vol. 26, no. 1: 32–51.
van Ree, E., 'Marxism as permanent revolution', in *History of Political Thought*, 2013, vol. 34, no. 3: 540–563.
Venturi, F., *Roots of Revolution. A History of the Populist and Socialist Movements in Nineteenth Century Russia* (London: Weidenfeld & Nicolson), 1960.
von Borcke, A., *Die Ursprünge des Bolschewismus. Die jakobinische Tradition in Russland und die Theorie der revolutionären Diktatur* (Munich: Johannes Berchmans Verlag), 1977.
von Dülmen, R., *Reformation als Revolution. Soziale Bewegung und religiöser Radikalismus in der deutschen Reformation* (Munich: Deutscher Taschenbuch Verlag), 1977.
von Dülmen, R., *Die Utopie einer christlichen Gesellschaft. Johann Valentin Andreae (1586–1654)*, vol. 1 (Stuttgart: Fromann-Holzboog), 1978.
Wade, R.A., *The Russian Revolution, 1917* (Cambridge: Cambridge University Press), 2000.
Wade, R.A., *The Bolshevik Revolution and Russian Civil War* (New York: Greenwood Press), 2001.
Wagner, F.P., *Rudolf Hilferding. Theory and Politics of Democratic Socialism* (Atlantic Highlands, NJ: Humanities Press), 1996.
Wagner, N., *Morelly. Le méconnu des Lumières* (Paris: Librarie Klincksieck), 1978.
Waldman, E., *The Spartacist Uprising of 1919 and the Crisis of the German Socialist Movement. A Study of the Relation of Political Theory and Party Practice* (Milwaukee, WI: Marquette University Press), 1958.
Walicki, A., *The Controversy over Capitalism. Studies in the Social Philosophy of the Russian Populists* (Oxford: Clarendon), 1969.
Walicki, A., *A History of Russian Thought. From the Enlightenment to Marxism* (Stanford, CA: Stanford University Press), 1979.

Walicki, A., *Marxism and the Leap to the Kingdom of Freedom. The Rise and Fall of the Communist Utopia* (Stanford, CA: Stanford University Press), 1995.

Wallace, P.G., *The Long European Reformation. Religion, Political Conflict, and the Search for Conformity, 1350–1750* (Basingstoke and New York: Palgrave Macmillan), 2004.

Walzer, M., *The Revolution of the Saints. A Study in the Origins of Radical Politics* (Cambridge, MA: Harvard University Press), 1965.

Weeks, A.L., *The First Bolshevik. A Political Biography of Peter Tkachev* (New York: New York University Press), 1968.

Wehler, H.-U., *Deutsche Gesellschaftsgeschichte*, vol. 3, *Von der 'Deutschen Doppelrevolution' bis zum Beginn des Ersten Weltkrieges, 1849–1914* (Munich: C.H. Beck), 1995.

Werner, E., 'Popular ideologies in late medieval Europe: Taborite chiliasm and its antecedents', in *Comparative Studies in Society and History*, 1960, vol. 2, no. 3: 344–363.

Wette, W., *Kriegstheorien deutscher Sozialisten. Marx, Engels, Lassalle, Bernstein, Kautsky, Luxemburg. Ein Beitrag zur Friedensforschung* (Stuttgart: Verlag W. Kohlhammer), 1971.

Wheeler, R.F., *USPD und Internationale. Sozialistischer Internationalismus in der Zeit der Revolution* (Frankfurt M. and Vienna: Ullstein), 1975.

Wheen, F., *Karl Marx. A Life* (New York and London: W.W. Norton), 2001.

White, J.D., *Karl Marx and the Intellectual Origins of Dialectical Materialism* (Basingstoke: Macmillan), 1996.

White, J.D., *Lenin. The Practice and Theory of Revolution* (Basingstoke: Palgrave Macmillan), 2001.

White, J.D., 'Alexander Bogdanov's conception of proletarian culture', in *Revolutionary Russia*, 2013, vol. 26, no. 1: 52–70.

White, P., 'The *via media* in the early Stuart church', in Todd, M. (ed.), *Reformation to Revolution. Politics and Religion in Early Modern England* (London and New York: Routledge), 1995: 78–94.

Willms, J., *Nationalismus ohne Nation. Deutsche Geschichte von 1789 bis 1914* (Düsseldorf: Claassen), 1983.

Winkler, H.A., *Von der Revolution zur Stabilisierung. Arbeiter und Arbeiterbewegung in der Weimarer Republik 1918 bis 1924* (Berlin: Dietz Verlag), 1984.

Wirtschafter, E.K., 'The groups between: *raznochintsy*, intelligentsia, professionals', in Lieven, D. (ed.), *The Cambridge History of Russia*, vol. 2, *Imperial Russia, 1689–1917* (Cambridge: Cambridge University Press), 2006: 245–263.

Wisner, D.A., *The Cult of the Legislator in France 1750–1830. A Study in the Political Theology of the French Enlightenment* (Oxford: Voltaire Foundation), 1997.

Woehrlin, W.F., *Chernyshevskii. The Man and the Journalist* (Cambridge, MA: Harvard University Press), 1971.

Wokler, R., *Rousseau. A Very Short Introduction* (Oxford: Oxford University Press), 2001.

Woloch, I., 'A revolution in political culture', in McPhee, P. (ed.), *A Companion to the French Revolution* (Oxford and Cambridge, MA: Wiley-Blackwell), 2013: 437–453.

Woodruff, D.M., 'The Politburo on gold, industrialization, and the international economy, 1925–1926', in Gregory, P.R., N. Naimark (eds), *The Lost Politburo Transcripts. From Collective Rule to Stalin's Dictatorship* (New Haven, CT: Yale University Press), 2008: 199–223.

Wright, J.K., *A Classical Republican in Eighteenth-Century France. The Political Thought of Mably* (Stanford, CA: Stanford University Press), 1997.
Yassour, A., 'The later Marx and the fate of the Russian *obščina*', in *Studies in Soviet Thought*, 1987, vol. 33, no. 1: 3–17.
Zamoyski, A., *Holy Madness. Romantics, Patriots and Revolutionaries 1776–1871* (London: Phoenix Press), 1999.
Zeman, Z.A.B., W.B. Scharlau, *The Merchant of Revolution. The Life of Alexander Israel Helphand (Parvus), 1867–1924* (Oxford and New York: Oxford University Press), 1965.
Zwick, P., *National Communism* (Boulder, CO: Westview), 1983.

Index

Adler, Max (1873–1937): 157
Adler, Victor (1852–1918): 157–8
Aksel'rod, Pavel Borisovich (1850–1928): 105, 135, 189
d'Alembert, Jean le Rond (1717–83): 38
Aleksandr II Nikolaevich, tsar of Russia (ruled 1855–81): 91, 93, 96, 107
Aleksandr III Aleksandrovich, tsar of Russia (ruled 1881–94): 108
Alter, Peter: 79
Archytas (428–347 BC): 18

Babeuf, François-Noël (Gracchus) (1760–97): 40–4, 106
Bakunin, Mikhail Aleksandrovich (1814–76): 94, 96
Balodis, Kārlis (Carl Ballod) (1864–1931): 127, 155, 189
Bauer, Otto (1881–1938): 157–60, 167, 189, 193
Bebel, Ferdinand August (1840–1913): 6, 85–9, 127, 129, 191
Berghahn, V.R.: 118
Bernstein, Eduard (1850–1932): 6, 86, 104, 116, 126–7, 130, 156, 189
Beukelszoon (van Leiden), Jan (1509–36): 24–5, 41
Bismarck-Schönhausen, Otto Eduard Leopold von (1815–98): 104, 107, 117–18, 123
Blanc, Louis Jean Joseph Charles (1811–82): 69
Blanqui, Louis Auguste (1805–81): 43–4
Bloch, Joseph (1871–1936): 126
Brissot, Jacques Pierre (1754–93): 40
Bruni, Leonardo (ca. 1370–1444): 28
Bukharin, Nikolai Ivanovich (1888–1938): 2–3, 136, 143, 167, 170–1, 176–81, 184, 189–90

Buonarotti, Filippo Giuseppe Maria Ludovico (1761–1837): 43–4

Cabet, Étienne (1788–1856): 10
Callahan, K.J.: 7
Calvin, Jean (1509–64): 32
Calwer, Richard (1868–1927): 126, 128, 189
Campanella, Tommaso (1568–1639): 30–1, 39, 75, 193
Carr, E.H.: 184
Charles I, king of England (ruled 1625–49): 32
Charles II, king of England (ruled 1660–85): 32
Charles X, king of France (ruled 1824–30): 43
Cherniavskii, G.: 172
Chernov, Viktor Mikhailovich (1873–1952): 110
Chernyshevskii, Nikolai Gavrilovich (1828–89): 93–4
Cohen, S.F.: 3, 177
construction of a socialist economy: in industrially backward countries: 62–3, 92–101, 109–11, 134, 140–2, 144, 163–5, 167–71, 177–81, 189, 194–6; in industrially developed countries: 117, 129–30, 138–40, 154–6, 158–9
Conze, W.: 6
Cromwell, Oliver (1599–1658): 32–4
Cunow, Heinrich (1862–1936): 129–30, 155

Däumig, Ernst (1868–1922): 155–6
Danton, Georges (1759–94): 41–2
Day, R.B.: 3, 171, 181
Deschamps, Léger Marie (Dom) (1716–74): 39

Dézamy, Alexandre Théodore (1808–50): 10, 44, 106, 193
Diderot, Denis (1713–84): 38
Diodorus Siculus (first century BC): 17
Draper, H.: 56
Dühring, Eugen Karl (1833–1921): 86–8, 188, 191, 193

Ebert, Friedrich (1871–1925): 129–30, 154–5
egalitarianism: 37–8, 40–1, 44, 63
Engel'gardt, Mikhail Aleksandrovich (1861–1915): 111, 189
Engels, Friedrich (1820–95): 2–4, 6–9, 23, 53–8, 62–9, 75, 77–9, 85–6, 88, 95–6, 98–100, 105–7, 109–10, 115–17, 120, 124, 126, 128, 134–5, 141, 153, 177–8, 184, 188–9, 191–6

Fel'shtinskii, I.: 172
Fénelon, François (1651–1715): 38
Fichte, Johann Gottlieb (1762–1814): 125
Fletcher, R.: 126
Fourier, Charles (1772–1837): 63

Groh, D.: 6

Haase, Hugo (1863–1919): 129, 154
Haenisch, Konrad (1876–1925): 129, 189
Headly, J.M.: 30
Hegel, Georg Wilhelm Friedrich (1770–1831): 76, 78
Heine, Christian Johann Heinrich (1797–1856): 45
Henry VII, king of England (ruled 1485–1509): 28
Henry VIII, king of England (ruled 1509–47): 29, 32
Herzen, Alexander (Gertsen, Aleksandr Ivanovich) (1812–70): 92–6
Hess, Moses (1812–75): 54–5, 58, 188
Hildebrand, Gerhard (1877–?): 126
Hilferding, Rudolf (1877–1941): 117, 154–7, 160, 167, 189, 193
Hill, C.: 3
historical and history-less nations: 77–8
Hobsbawm, E.J.: 65, 115
Höchberg, Karl (1853–85): 88
Hoffman, Melchior (ca. 1495–1543): 23–4
Hus, Jan (1369–1415): 21
Húska, Martin (?—1421): 22
Hutter, Jakob (ca. 1500–36): 23

industrialisation:
 the industrial revolution: 56, 63; the industrialisation of Germany and France: 63–4, 67–70, 99, 107, 115–17; The industrialisation of Russia: 91, 98–9, 107
initiator-state: 9, 21, 42, 56, 94, 106, 111, 128, 142–3, 157, 182, 193
international revolution:
 contagious revolution: 8, 56, 89, 124–5, 156, 188; European revolution: 124, 135–6, 138, 159, 189; universal revolution: 53, 55–6; world revolution: 1, 9–10, 137, 163, 165–6, 191
international workers' solidarity: 166–7, 171

Jansen, R.: 88

Kamenev (Rozenfel'd), Lev Borisovich (1883–1936): 15, 176–82, 184, 190
Kaminsky, H.: 21–2
Kamkov (Kats), Boris Davidovich (1885–1938): 169
Kautsky, Karl (1854–1938): 3, 6, 9, 58, 86, 104, 116–17, 119–20, 124–7, 130–1, 135, 153, 155, 157, 160, 167, 184, 189–91, 193–4
Kluge, U.: 153
Kun, Béla (1886–1939): 1

Lafargue-Marx, Jenny Laura (1845–1911): 58
Lafargue, Paul (1842–1911): 53
Lahautière, Richard (1813–82): 44
Lambert, M..: 20
Laponneraye, Albert (1808–49): 44
Lassalle, Ferdinand (1825–64): 85–8, 123, 188, 193
Laud, William (1573–1645): 32
Lavrov, Petr Lavrovich (1823–1900): 92, 95–8, 104, 106, 191
Lenin (Ul'ianov), Vladimir Il'ich (1870–1924): 1, 3, 9, 11, 108, 120, 135–44, 163–72, 176–80, 182, 184, 190–3
Lensch, Paul (1873–1926): 129, 189
Liebknecht, Karl (1871–1919): 1, 129, 155–6, 160, 190
Liebknecht, Wilhelm (1826–1900): 85–6
Lih, L.T.: 120
List, Georg Friedrich (1789–1846): 76
Loades, D.: 28

Louis XIV, king of France (ruled 1643–1715): 37
Louis XVI, king of France (ruled 1774–92): 40
Louis Philippe, king of the French (ruled 1830–48): 43
Logan, G.M.: 29
Luther, Martin (1483–1546): 23
Luxemburg, Rosa (1870–1919): 1, 129, 137, 139, 155–6, 160, 190
Lycurgus (ca. 820–730 BC?): 43

Mably, Gabriel Bonnot de (1709–85): 39–41, 43, 193
Machiavelli, Nicoló (1469–1527): 28
Manuel, F.E.: 62
Maréchal, Pierre Sylvain (1750–1803): 42
Martov (Tsederbaum), Iulii Osipovich (1873–1923): 108, 135
Marx, Karl (1818–83): 2, 4, 6–11, 17, 53–8, 62–70, 75–9, 85–8, 96, 98–101, 105–6, 109–11, 115–16, 119–20, 124, 126, 128, 134–5, 141, 153, 170, 177–8, 184, 188–9, 191–6
Matthijs, Jan (ca. 1500–34): 24
Mazzini, Giuseppe (1805–72): 9, 79
Mikhailov, Mikhail Larionovich (1829–65): 94, 189
Mikhailovskii, Nikolai Konstantinovich (1842–1904): 100
millennialism: 20, 22, 24–5, 30–1
Miller, S.: 130
Milton, John (1608–74): 33
Montesquieu, Charles de (1689–1755): 37
More, Thomas (1478–1535): 7–9, 28–32, 43, 192–3
Morelly, Étienne-Gabriel (eighteenth century): 39, 41
Müntzer, Thomas (ca. 1489–1525): 23, 69
Mumford, L.: 18

Napoleon Bonaparte (1769–1821): 43
Nation, R.C.: 164
Nechaev, Sergei Gennadievich (1847–82): 94–6, 189
Nikolai II Aleksandrovich, tsar of Russia (ruled 1894–1917): 108, 140
Nikolai I Pavlovich, tsar of Russia (ruled 1825–55): 92

Ordzhonikide, Grigorii Konstantinovich (Sergo) (1886–1937): 184

Osinskii, N. (Valerian Valerianovich Obolenskii) (1887–1938): 167
Ovid (Publius Ovidius Naso) (43 BC–17/18 AD): 17

Parvus, Aleksandr L'vovich (Izrail' Lazarevich Gel'fand) (1867–1924): 108, 117, 129
peaceful coexistence: 29–30, 97, 166–7
permanent/uninterrupted revolution: 63–5, 105–6, 109–10, 120, 141, 177–8, 195–6
Pilbeam, P.: 43
Pillot, Jean-Jacques (1808–77): 10, 44, 106
Plato (ca. 424–ca. 347BC): 7, 17–19, 29, 43, 188
Plekhanov, Georgii Valentinovich (1856–1918): 104–10, 116, 118, 120, 134–5, 141–3, 193–4
Preobrazhenskii, Evgenii Alekseevich (1886–1937): 143, 170–1, 177
Primoratz, I.: 5
proletarian internationalism: 4–5, 7, 124
proletarian revolution:
in industrially backward countries: 62–70, 92–101, 105–11, 115–20, 138, 141; in industrially developed countries: 64, 117–19
Pythagoras (ca. 570–ca. 500 BC): 18

Radek, Karl Berngardovich (1885–1939): 139
Ramm, T.: 58
Renner, Karl (1870–1950): 157–9
Reitern, Mikhail Khristoforovich (1820–90): 98
Restif de la Bretonne, Nicolas-Edme (1734–1806): 42, 75
revolution by example: 25, 34, 41–3, 130–1, 157, 159, 167, 189, 192
revolutionary war: 1, 21–2, 24–5, 29–31, 38, 41–3, 45, 57–8, 97, 127–8, 136–40, 144, 164–7, 190, 192
Robespierre, Maximilien-Marie-Isidore de (1758–94): 40, 44
Rodbertus-Jagetzov, Karl (1805–75): 86, 87
Rother, Erich (?–?): 127–8, 189
Rousseau, Jean-Jacques (1712–78): 17, 37, 41
Rose, R.B.: 41
Roux, Jacques (1752–94): 40
Rudé, G.: 40

Ruge, Arnold (1802–80): 54, 75
Ryan, J.: 139
Rykov, Aleksei Ivanovich (1881–1938): 141–2

Saint-Just, Louis Antoine (1767–94): 40
Saint-Simon, Claude Henri de (1760–1825): 55, 58
Salvadori, M.: 124
Schäffle, Albert Eberhard Friedrich (1831–1903): 86–7
Schapper, Karl (1812–70): 44–5
Scheidemann, Philipp (1865–1939): 130
Schippel, Max (1859–1928): 126
Seneca, Lucius Annaeus (ca. 4 BC–65 AD): 17
Shelgunov, Nikolai Vasil'evich (1824–91): 94, 189
Shulman, G.M.: 33
Sigel, R.: 129
Sigismund of Luxemburg, Holy Roman Emperor (ruled 1433–7): 21
Skinner, Q.: 28–9
Smaldone, W.: 154
socialism and communism:
  communal and peasant socialism: 92–101, 107; communism as elite lifestyle: 17–19; communitarianism: 8–9, 30, 123, 192; community of goods: 8–10, 17, 19, 21–4, 28–9, 31–3, 37, 39, 42–3, 53–4, 62, 153; socialism as armed fortress and embattled community: 2, 8, 22, 24–5, 29–31, 38–40, 42–5, 58, 124, 127, 155–6, 159–60, 164, 168, 170–1, 179, 181–3, 189–90, 192; the future of nations under communism: 58, 78–9; the terms communism and socialism: 10–11; two stages of communism: 11, 97–8
socialism and communism in one country:
  as autarkic state: 3, 38–9, 41, 43–5, 56, 123–8, 139, 153, 169, 171–2, 181–2, 189, 192–3; as colonial empire: 123, 125–8; as economically superior nation: 3, 31, 33, 42, 57–8, 75, 86–9, 111, 123, 139, 164–5, 188, 192–3; as strong nation-state: 29, 32, 34, 38–9, 43, 153, 155–60; as superior military power: 3, 18, 23–5, 31, 33–4, 38–45, 54, 57–8, 75, 88, 97, 111, 127, 137–9, 144, 156, 164–5, 167, 190, 192–3; as vast state: 44, 93, 96–8, 124–5, 170, 172, 179, 188; in one city: 7, 18–19, 21–2, 24–5, 30–1, 39, 111, 153; in one region or in a small state: 23–4, 42–3, 45, 95, 124; intra-socialist debates about socialism in one country: 87–9, 138–9, 176–84, 191; on an island: 7–9, 28–31, 59, 192; one country pioneering socialism: 2, 7, 9, 33–4, 42, 63, 76–7, 86, 92–6, 111, 127–9, 138, 140, 142–3, 159, 189, 193; the doctrine of socialism in one country: 1–4, 7–10, 53–7, 68, 87–9, 95–8, 109–10, 124–6, 130–1, 134–40, 143–4, 153, 155–60, 164–72, 176–84, 188–90
socialism as confederacy:
  Central Europe: 128, 189; Triple Alliance: 8, 53–4, 57–9, 62, 89, 124; United States of Europe: 89, 124, 136, 138, 157
socialist patriotism and anti-patriotism: 5–7, 9–10, 31, 33, 58, 63–4, 75–8, 92–6, 98, 106, 111, 129, 135–7, 144, 166, 189, 193
Stalin (Dzhugashvili), Iosif Vissarionovich (1878–1953): 2–3, 5, 7, 9–10, 138, 143, 170, 176–84, 190–2, 194
state capitalism: 117, 129–30, 142, 163, 168, 171, 189
Stayer, J.M.: 23–4
Stolypin, Petr Arkad'evich (1862–1911): 107

Tkachev, Petr Nikitich (1844–86): 94–6, 99, 189
Trotsky (Trotskii/Bronshtein), Leon (Lev) Davidovich (1879–1940): 3, 5, 8, 108–10, 120, 134–6, 138, 143, 163, 165, 171–2, 176–84, 189–92, 195
Trutovskii, Vladimir Evgen'evich (1889–1937): 169
Tucker, R.C.: 143
Turski, Kasper Michal (1847–1926): 95

Ul'ianov, Aleksandr Il'ich (1866–87): 108
Utopia: 28–31, 193

Vairasse, Denis (ca. 1630–ca. 1696): 39
Virgil (Publius Virgilius Maro) (70–19 BC): 17
virtue: 18, 28–30, 33, 37–9, 44
Voltaire (François-Marie Arouet) (1694–1778): 37
von Borcke, Astrid: 94

von Bülow, Bernhard Heinrich Karl Martin (1849–1929): 118
von Vollmar, Georg (1850–1922): 3, 8–9, 87–9, 123, 184, 188, 191, 193
Vrangel', Petr Nikolaevich (1878–1928): 163

Weitling, Wilhelm (1808–71): 44–5, 53–4, 75
Wilhelm II, emperor of Germany (ruled 1888–1918): 118
Winstanley, Gerrard (1609–76): 7, 10, 31–4, 39, 41, 75, 86, 131, 167, 193
Witte (Vitte), Sergei Iul'evich (1849–1915): 107
Wright, J.K.: 39

Zaichnevskii, Petr Grigor'evich (1842–96): 94, 189
Zamoyski, A.: 115
Zasulich, Vera Ivanovna (1849–1919): 100, 105
Zinov'ev [Radomysl'skii Apfel'baum], Grigorii Evseevich (1883–1936): 139, 143, 176–82, 184, 190
Žižka, Jan (ca. 1360–1424): 21